Language, sexuality, narrative:
the *Oresteia*

Learner

Language, sexuality, narrative: the *Oresteia*

SIMON GOLDHILL

Fellow of King's College, Cambridge

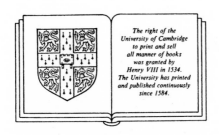

The right of the
University of Cambridge
to print and sell
all manner of books
was granted by
Henry VIII in 1534.
The University has printed
and published continuously
since 1584.

CAMBRIDGE UNIVERSITY PRESS

CAMBRIDGE

LONDON   NEW YORK   NEW ROCHELLE

MELBOURNE   SYDNEY

PUBLISHED BY THE PRESS SYNDICATE OF THE UNIVERSITY OF CAMBRIDGE
The Pitt Building, Trumpington Street, Cambridge, United Kingdom

CAMBRIDGE UNIVERSITY PRESS
The Edinburgh Building, Cambridge CB2 2RU, UK
40 West 20th Street, New York NY 10011–4211, USA
477 Williamstown Road, Port Melbourne, VIC 3207, Australia
Ruiz de Alarcón 13, 28014 Madrid, Spain
Dock House, The Waterfront, Cape Town 8001, South Africa

http://www.cambridge.org

First published 1984
First paperback edition 2004

A catalogue record for this book is available from the British Library

Library of Congress catalogue card number: 84-7082

ISBN 0 521 26535 5 hardback
ISBN 0 521 60430 3 paperback

*For my parents
with love and thanks*

Contents

Acknowledgements

I have received much help in the preparation of this, my first book. Among my readers, I must thank in particular Pierre Vidal-Naquet and Charles Segal for their astute comments and great encouragement of the enterprise. Professor Froma Zeitlin was one of the first to see my work and has on innumerable occasions since offered me a friend's advice, close reading, and enthusiasm for the exchange of ideas on both sides of – and across – the Atlantic. Pat Easterling, who directed my Ph.D. research, not only read my work in all its forms with a patience, carefulness and critical eye far beyond the call of duty, but also provided me with a model of scholarship and sense in approaching Greek Tragedy. Above all, the classical Fellows at King's College created the sort of atmosphere and surroundings from which writing and research naturally arose. In particular, this book could not have come into being without Professor Geoffrey Lloyd, who constantly furnished stimulation to read beyond the confines of the discipline of classics, to question and think about Greek literature and society, and Dr John Henderson, whose knowledge, probing intelligence and insight were never separate from intellectual and emotional support.

The officers of the Press, Pauline Hire and Susan Moore, have been patient and diligent with an extremely difficult manuscript. And my family, especially Sho, my wife, was always there, to help see it through to the end.

Cambridge 1984   S.D.G.

A light from the editor of *The Times'* crossword: 'To be or not be, that is the...' (11). Answer: aposiopesis.

ὁ ἄναξ οὗ τὸ μαντεῖόν ἐστι τὸ ἐν Δελφοῖς οὔτε λέγει οὔτε κρύπτει ἀλλὰ σημαίνει.

(The lord whose oracle is in Delphi neither speaks nor hides, but uses signs.)
Heraclitus

I am become a name

For always roaming...
Tennyson

Introduction

In the face of the accumulated weight of Aeschylean scholarship, this study marks something of a departure. In this introduction, which is precisely a leading in[1] to the departure, I intend to consider briefly the nature of what is to follow; to consider in what sense it is a 'departure'.

What is to follow is a reading of the *Oresteia*; it is a discussion of the term 'reading' which will constitute the remainder of this introduction and will be a continuing concern, for reasons which will become clearer. Perhaps one should first distinguish this reading from the extensive tradition of *editiones cum notis variorum*, at the apex of which stands Fraenkel's edition of the *Agamemnon*: yet this distinction, although there will be few discussions of 'text' in these problematic texts, is to be rendered less rigid (and more precise) through the term 'text': for my work at first sight appears to follow a format culled from the many editions (as indeed it refers to them again and again), a procedure of line-by-line analysis, a network of references developing and outlining meanings within the text and intertextually with other texts – towards what we might call the text's 'textuality'.[2] This also helps to distinguish this work from the equally long and varied tradition of 'literary studies' in/on the *Oresteia*. For these, all too often contained in books on Greek

---

[1] That is, not a preface to outline in précis what will be said. I am writing with the following texts in mind: Hegel's preface on prefaces ('Preface to *The Phenomenology of Mind*'); Derrida's analysis of Hegel and the logic of prefaces (*Dissemination*, pp. 1ff.). Cf. also Spivak's preface on Derrida on Hegel ('Preface to *Of Grammatology*' pp. ix ff.). Hegel writes 'For the real subject matter is not exhausted in its purpose, but in working the matter out; nor is the mere result attained the concrete whole itself, but the result along with the process of arriving at it' (p. 96). It will become apparent during my reading of the *Oresteia* in what way these hints towards the problem of 'beginnings', 'origin', 'saying ahead', are not merely gestures of tribute towards a discussion which has recently had much attention in literary and philosophical writings (cf. e.g. Said 1975); they are indeed (as my departure) also part of the 'process of arriving', part of 'working the matter [reading the *Oresteia*] out'.

[2] By 'textuality' I mean the qualities constituting the text *as* text: it will, I hope, become clearer in the process of the book what further is meant by this term. There is an extraordinary range of material specifically dealing with the terms 'text' and 'textuality'. Cf. as an introduction the collections of essays edited by Young 1981 (particularly Barthes, pp. 31–47) and by Harari 1979a. Also Barthes 1975a, 1979; de Man 1971, 1979c; Derrida 1967a, 1974, 1976a; Donato 1976; Felman 1977; Hartman 1970, 1980, 1981; Kristeva 1969, 1980; Miller 1980, 1980–1; Tanner, 1980.

Tragedy in general (or even 'as a whole') or as introductions to translations, have tended to favour the attempt to contain the *Oresteia* in some twenty or thirty pages of generalisations interspersed with choice quotations – although length alone does not determine this containment. It is the complexity and difficulty of reading the *Oresteia* which I will be discussing at some – this – length, and which will be placed in opposition to the violence of such limiting and limited generalisations. An example from a book-length study: Lebeck (1971) analyses the *Choephoroi* from 480 until the end thus: 'The rest is action'!

There have also been numerous articles on specific themes of the trilogy, on specific series of images, or problems of theological implication. Many of these will be referred to in the course of my reading. Some of these contain excellent analyses of detail and indeed try to relate the passages they deal with to some notion of the 'whole' – but what is lacking is a sense of the interrelationships of the text which constitute the narrative, a sense of the difficulty of abstracting, extracting 'ideas': all too often the text is divided into conveniently packaged 'themes' without regard for the constituting act of division. Lebeck, for example, concentrates on the choral lyrics with little or no reference to the iambic passages with which they are in counterpoint, as if the 'meaning' or even the 'structure' of the choral lyrics could be determined as separate from the play. Yet despite the format, scope, and 'literary' focus, this piece is not simply an *explication de texte*:

> Since narrative is both merchandise and the relation of the contract of which it is the object, there can no longer be any question of setting up a rhetorical hierarchy between two points of the tale, as is common practice...two parts of the text are not detached from one another according to the so-called principle of 'nested narratives' (a narrative within a narrative). The nesting of blocks of narrative is not (merely) ludic but (also) economic...Narrative is determined not by a desire to narrate but by a desire to exchange: it is a *medium of exchange*, an agent, a currency, a gold-standard. What accounts for this central equivalence is not the 'plan'...but its structure. The structure is not the plot or the plan. Therefore, this is not an 'explication de texte'.[3]

This abrupt and certainly rhetorical use of a quotation from Barthes with its constellation of technical terms from linguistics and narratology serves to mark further the distinction of this work from earlier Aeschylean criticism in terms of methodological approach to what we might have called 'literary reading', 'literary criticism'. For

---

[3] Barthes 1975a, p. 90.

it is concerned with how the text means: not only the meaning of words but also the structuring of narrative – which is not simply an extension of textual criticism on the one hand and literary criticism on the other. For when I say 'how the text means', I have already implied a series of positive and negative presuppositions about semantics, about the semantics of reading. I have implied, for example, in 'how' that meaning is a process, not an immanence (which negates the possibility of a simple distinction between meaning of words and narrative). Consider, for example, *Cho.* 663–4:

ἐξελθέτω τις δωμάτων τελεσφόρος
γυνή τόπαρχος ἄνδρα δ᾽ εὐπρεπέστερον

τελεσφόρος is translated by L.-S.-J., Verrall, Tucker, Sidgwick, and Lloyd-Jones as 'bearing authority', from τέλος in the sense of 'authority', 'magistracy'. But in terms of the narrative at this point the 'woman' who 'is to come out' also constitutes the aim of Orestes' actions, she brings (φέρειν) the *telos*. Furthermore the killing of his mother (his forcible rejection of her) has been seen in terms of a generalised pattern of initiation rites for Orestes: τελεσφόρος 'bringing the initiation' (τέλος). Cassandra and Clytemnestra depicted the killing of Agamemnon as a sacrifice; the *parodos* of the *Agamemnon* also talked of 'another sacrifice' – τελεσφόρος 'bringing the sacrificial rite' (τέλος). The opening lines of the trilogy prayed for release, for an end; Clytemnestra's murder is depicted by Orestes as the 'final act': τελεσφόρος, 'bringing completion, consummation'. Clytemnestra is to die; Orestes prays to die having killed her (and indeed the reciprocity of action suggests he may): τελεσφόρος, 'bringing death' (τέλος). Within the economic imagery, τέλος may imply 'tax', 'that which is paid' – the penalty of action; so Clytemnestra is to come out τελεσφόρος. As we will see, all these senses of τέλος are inscribed in the narrative of the *Oresteia*: the term τελεσφόρος is sited within this system of differences: it resists the simple reading offered by the lexica *et al.* by being in a series, each occurrence of which is set in the further series of the sentence(s) of which it is a constituent part, of the interrelations of sentences which make up the narrative – and the same procedure could be adopted for each of the terms of this sentence.[4] Where is the limit to reading this sentence, where can we bring the end? Are we faced with 'an uncontrollable echoing: a mad round of verbal associations or signifier–signifying signifiers'?[5] The anxiety raised by language as language is that 'this echoing movement cannot be economised, that

---

[4] For further implications of τελεσφόρος, see Goldhill 1984.
[5] Hartman 1981, p. 111.

it is a fluid case...'[6] Barthes concludes that '...reading is absorbed in a kind of metonymic skid, each synonym adding to its neighbour some new trait, some new departure...Only an infinite thematics, open to endless nomination, can respect the enduring character of language, the production of reading, and no longer its products.'[7] This book is not, of course, an 'infinite thematics', nor can any reading hope so to be – nor is that disclaimer a disingenuous veiling of the violence inherent in all interpretations. This is a partial (in all its senses) reading. It attempts in its violence not to offer some exhaustive meaning(s) or to catalogue multivalencies or ambiguities, but to recognise the 'metonymic production of language' (hence 'how it means'), dis-covering the text's plurality, its openness to the production of meaning, its 'textuality'. I shall be analysing, then, the difficulty of restricting the echoing play of meaning with the 'inevitability of a dice-throw, which can arrest and fix the skid of names'.[8] I shall be analysing the difficulties of placing defined limits to the text's meaning. I shall be analysing (reaching towards rigour) how the (rigorous) search for meaning (δεσπόσω λόγου) is outplayed (eluded) by the play's own working – πέφευγε τοὔπος. Hence both my questioning of the textual critics in their prescriptive readings, their assumption of the corrupt and to-be-corrected text, and also my questioning of the literary critics who 'slipping the universal passkey into all lacunae of signification',[9] find 'a critical level is established, the work is closed, the language by which the semantic transformation is ended becomes nature, truth, the work's secret'.[10] Hence the resistance to breaking the work of my reading into conveniently packaged thematic units, to adopting the 'critical level'; hence the resistance to the way in which Classical Studies (to reunite the traditions separated far too neatly above) has formulated its attitude to texts, its approach to reading the Classics. It is to be hoped thereby that this study, in its challenge to the rigidity of boundaries between 'textual criticism' and 'literary criticism', will be of interest to Classicists of whatever credo.

Although I have certainly made no attempt to fit the *Oresteia* into any prescribed or prescribing framework of dogma – this is not a Structuralist/Freudian/Marxist Reading – it may none the less be regarded as useful for me to cite here some of the influences on my writing: in the main body of the text, these critics will be occasionally quoted to offer some links between my reading and contemporary

---

[6] Hartman 1981, p. 111.   [7] Barthes 1975a, pp. 92–3.
[8] Barthes 1975a, p. 93.
[9] Derrida 1974b, p. 36b, quoted in Hartman 1981, p. 103.
[10] Barthes 1975a, p. 93.

critical concerns. I cannot hope to develop or précis – especially in such an introduction – a theory of language, literature, meaning, but I can point here towards the extensively discussed material that I draw on. In my questioning I have been influenced in particular by a debate involving numerous philosophers of language and critics and arising notably in reaction to the work of Derrida and Barthes. In particular, it is through their different insights into language and writing that I hope to have opened some new vistas on the *Oresteia* and how we read it. It is through the viewing of language as language, rather than as a transparent veil through which we pass to 'meaning', that this study is marked as a 'departure'. It is in the recognition (stemming from de Saussure) of the production of meaning in difference – and followed through with Derrida's 'logique de la différance'.[11] It is the recognition (stemming from numerous texts, among which one would include Marx, Freud, Lévi-Strauss, Foucault, Barthes, Derrida) that there can be no 'innocent reading'; there can (because of the production of meaning in reading) be no reading separated from the interplay between discourse of the text and discourse of the reader. The belief in an innocent or natural reading, a 'simple appreciation', is itself a methodological statement about the nature of meaning and narrative the presuppositions of which are open to questioning as much as the explicit methodological statement. Such a belief in a 'natural' way of reading, a belief in 'what we all know' to be 'likely', 'probable', 'suitable', 'of course', 'standard', 'appropriate', 'traditional' defends itself by negative categorisations of 'jargon', 'unlikely', 'inappropriate' etc. (as if the categories of 'natural' etc. and 'jargon' etc. were not mutually constitutive).

Furthermore, by this hierarchical categorisation such a belief regards it as unnecessary ('inappropriate', 'unsuitable', 'pretentious') to consider its own discourse, rather protecting and authorising its dynamics of institutionalisation with what Adorno nicely calls the 'jargon of authenticity'. We all have our jargon of criticism,[12] and

---

[11] *Différance* is a neologism of Derrida's which combined the senses of 'differing' and 'deferring'. It is notably difficult to define Derrida's terminology. B. Johnson writes: 'The very fact that a word is divided into a phonic *signifier* and a mental *signified*, and that, as Saussure pointed out, language is a system of differences rather than a collection of independently meaningful units, indicates that language as such is already constituted by the very distances and differences it seeks to overcome. To mean, in other words, is automatically *not* to be. As soon as there is meaning, there is difference. Derrida's word for this lag inherent in any signifying act is *différance*...The illusion of self-presence of meaning...is thus produced by the repression of the differential structures from which they spring' (Introduction to Derrida 1981, p. ix). See in particular Derrida 1968, translated in Derrida 1973.

[12] This is not to say there is not material here which will seem to some Classicists a departure from their traditional scholarship: that is part of the 'dynamics of institu-

much of my questioning of past scholarship will be focusing on the
veilings of critical language and rhetoric. I will be trying to tease out
the paradoxes, obscurities, contradictions and difficulties in reading
even the proclamations of the virtues of clarity, ease, simplicity.[13] For
this book's departure is marked in the recognition of the difficulty
not only of reading Aeschylus – a difficulty admitted by textual critics
and literary critics alike – but also of reading (and) writing about
Aeschylus. And in the unwillingness to translate these difficulties into
the violence of simplification.

But more than this: for this concern with the hermeneutics of
reading and the nature of meaning does not develop merely from
studies in literary theory. For who can read, for example, the
recognition scene of the *Choephoroi*, who can read that process
whereby Electra produces a relation between her brother, a footprint
and a lock of hair, without registering the shock, the violence which
breaks through our preconceptions of logic, truth, categorisation.
Who can read the beacon-speeches scene, with its explicit discussion
of what – how – a signal means, without feeling some of the confusion
registered by those critics who fall back on Aeschylus' postulated
'passion for geography'.[14] In both cases, an argument is based
explicitly on the relationship between signifier and signified, in both
cases we see the marked challenge to produce meaning, to interpret.
What of the Cassandra scene, which revolves around the dramatic
situation of a woman speaking the truth which no-one believes or
understands? Consider the deceit of Orestes which beguiles the
beguiler Clytemnestra, or the persuasive power of Athene at the end
of the *Eumenides*, the resolution of oppositions by the force of
language, the redefinition of the Erinues as Eumenides. In all these
important scenes, and, as I will also show with such recurrent features
as etymologies, questions about what language to use, the expressed
need for interpreters etc., throughout the trilogy, language, communication, hermeneutics, the exchange and interpretation of signs,
are brought to the fore. This has often been noted by Classical
scholars,[15] but not treated in depth. Thus working on this play is
further complicated by the interrelations of one discourse of hermeneutics considering, in play with, another discourse of hermen-

---

tionalisation' of Classical Studies. I have tried to indicate more precisely, particularly
in the notes, some of the influences on my writing. In a work, however, which considers
at length the difficulties of defining boundaries of meaning, a glossary of definitions
(or some such preface) would seem a somewhat ironical procedure.

13 Cf. e.g. Fraenkel (pp. 69–70); Dawe (pp. 70–2); Gould (pp. 73–4); Gagarin (pp.
257–8); Easterling (p. 72); Taplin (p. 204).   14 R. D. Dawe's phrase.

15 Cf. e.g. Ramnoux 1955, pp. 90ff.; Peradotto 1969b; Jouan 1978; Vicaire 1963; Segal
1981, pp. 52–9.

eutics. Thus the argument of this introduction could be reversed to begin with the well-known emphasis in the *Oresteia* on communication, the exchange of words, or interpretation of signifiers (perhaps underlining its significance for Greek Drama in general – indeed, Greek culture's 'intense interest in the possibilities and limitations of language'[16] – linking it to the nascent Sophistic movement, its emphasis on logos, and the particular influence of Heraclitus, Gorgias, Protagoras)[17] out of which would be seen to develop the theoretical material; the recognised emphasis on hermeneutics in the *Oresteia* leading to the wider discussion of hermeneutics in the light of modern hermeneutic research. The sense of 'development' would be misleading, however. For the theoretical studies and the concerns of the *Oresteia* are mutually implicative; the object of study and methodology are not simply to be delineated and separated. A methodology is not a supplement to reading but constitutive of it. The work of interpretation in this reading takes place in the interplay between two discourses of hermeneutics: hence what may appear as complex passages of argumentation, the questioning of one's own reading, the further questioning of the possibility of the haven of a 'simple', 'natural' reading.

So this opening to a departure returns back on itself. So too with the reading of the *Oresteia*: despite its line-by-line format of analysis, it constantly refers back and forward in the structuration of the narrative developing a network of meanings in a system of differences, questioning itself and other critics, involved in the complex activity of reading.

Is this introduction, then, an apologia for the book's 'style' and 'content' (the irony of which terms should be apparent, if not now, by the end of the book)? It is more a reminder of the complex hermeneutic process of reading, a statement of reluctance to efface that process in either a series of shorter thematic chapters, or a procedure tied less closely to the text. Nor is this introduction a full (what could be?) methodological statement. Rather it is something of a departure. A series of fragments in constant regression to the author-ity of those who would question the process of authorisation. Let us turn, therefore, to the work of (the) reading (itself).

[16] Guthrie's phrase. Cf. e.g. Kahn 1978; Ramnoux 1955; Zeitlin 1983; Detienne 1967, for further recent studies on this interest in language.

[17] Cf. e.g. Rosenmeyer 1955; Gladigow 1974; Segal 1962a. Discussions of responsibility, causality, empiricism, the definition and correct use of language, for example, occur often in later and earlier writings. Cf. e.g. Kerferd 1981, pp. 68ff.

1

Heuristics and hermeneutics: communication and exchange in the *Agamemnon*

φάτις αὐτοῖσι μαρτυρεῖ παρεόντας ἀπεῖναι

Heraclitus

Saying and showing: the watchman speaks

The play opens with a desire, a prayer, for closure, a prefigurement of the end – ἀπαλλαγὴν πόνων, which will, is to, come from the gods, θεοὺς μὲν αἰτῶ. The phrase ἀπαλλαγὴν πόνων seems[1] to allude to the ritual language of the mysteries, which invests πόνων with a connotation more general than the immediate context of the guard's watch and which, with θεούς...αἰτῶ, suggests that the solution of the πόνων will be connected with some form of divine epiphany. The sense in which these πόνων are conceived in a more general way is developed in the prologue.

The watchman states that he has been watching the stars for a whole year and that he knows them well, 'through and through', κάτοιδα (4). The stars bring winter and summer for mortals: χεῖμα καὶ θέρος is an extension of ἐτείας μῆκος (2), the pattern of the year in nature. φέροντας expresses a sense of direction and control, however, which is picked up in λαμπροὺς δυνάστας, 'masters', and λαμπρούς itself, 'clear', 'shining', 'distinct' is developed in ἐμπρέποντας αἰθέρι, 'to be distinctly visible, bright, in the sky'. These terms are important and will be recalled many times throughout the trilogy: for the stars are the first of what we will see to be a series of visible signs (cf. the beacons, the tokens of recognition), and they will be referred back to on several occasions. What sort of signs are they? As with Hesiod in the *Works and Days*, they are clear and absolute controllers of a pattern in time, a narrative; they are understood through the act of seeing them, through the modality of the visible. 'Whenever they rise or set' (7), they are clear, visible signs of what is to happen, is happening.

καὶ νῦν (8) is a connective introducing a particular example of a general state already expressed:

...φυλάσσω λαμπάδος τὸ σύμβολον (8)

---

[1] Cf. Thomson 1935. Tierney 1937.

This is indeed a γρῖφος, 'riddle', not properly understood until its substantiation (22–30) and Clytemnestra's explanation (281–351), but it is immediately noticeable that the relationship between this light and the process of signification is quite different from the general case of the stars that it is syntactically implied to particularise. The λαμπάς 'brings' – φέρουσαν (9) picks up φέροντας (5) and emphasises the parallelism – φάτιν...βάξιν, 'speech', 'a spoken message'.[2] The beacon is a symbol for a communication which itself needs interpreting. It no longer *shows* (the visible mode), directs, but works through another medium, that of language. There is no longer a direct, unbroken, relationship between the visible sign and its signification but by the very nature of σύμβολον one sign stands for another: there is a heuristic gap between the signifier and signified. Indeed, rather than an 'application of the general idea to the circumstances of the moment' (Fraenkel), καὶ νῦν φυλάσσω λαμπάδος τὸ σύμβολον κτλ. sets in opposition two different modes of communication, showing and speaking.

The connective γάρ (10) implies that lines 10–11 explain the previous sentence. As Fraenkel notes, κρατεῖ is a rather general expression: 'for such is the nature of the power of...' The delaying of the subject constitutes the sentence with a strong force on the predicates. Each, as we will see, is important throughout the play: we are dealing with, in syntagmatic order, power, a woman juxtaposed to man and counselling as – or against – a man (woman opposed to man in terms of power), expectation/desire, and 'heart'. The juxtaposition of γυναικός and ἀνδρο – is pointed, and the rare adjective ἀνδρόβουλον draws attention to the peculiarity of the situation, as indeed does the uncommon construction of ἐλπίζω without an object: a generalised force of expectation/desire which leaves its object noticeably unspoken. In the place of this unspoken, stands the sleeplessness of fear:

$$...φόβος γὰρ ἀνθ' ὕπνου παραστατεῖ \qquad (14)$$

So, ὧδε γὰρ κτλ. is not so much an explanation, as a general statement of affairs where the central terms remain enigmatic or unspoken, and replaced by fear. It is a similar construction to that which Barthes calls the Hermeneutic sentence:[3]

---

[2] The adjective predicated of βάξιν, ἁλώσιμον, is translated normally 'of an (easy) capturing'. After Aeschylus it seems to have a primarily passive sense, 'easily captured' (cf. Her. 3.153; Eur. *Hel.* 1662; Thuc. 4.9.), indeed, it is used at Soph. *Phil.* 863 apparently to mean 'easily understood', 'grasped', which sense is equally predicable of βάξιν. Such an ambiguity would further mark the difference between the communication of light and of language.

[3] Barthes 1975a, pp. 84–5.

ὧδε γὰρ κρατεῖ: promise of answer to enigma.

γυναικός: 'of a woman' – suspended answer (the use of the genitive in particular suspends the sentence; the noun itself offers a partial answer).

ἀνδρόβουλον: ambiguity: in some way what it is of-a-woman has also some connection with masculinity of mind.

ἐλπίζον: 'expecting/hoping' but with no object, a re-formulation of the enigma of waiting, the answer 'jammed'.

In the formulation of this sentence, then, are constituted some of the basic terms of the discourse and, as with the opening prayer, in such a way that the 'hermeneutic terms structure the enigma according to the expectation and desire for its solution'.[4] We are being led towards a conclusion of truth. 'To delay truth is to constitute it.'[5] We are being led towards a conclusion which will be constituted in these enigmatic terms of sexual opposition, κράτος, and expectancy.

Fear turns to misery: κλαίω (18), 'I weep', and again the object of his bewailing is proposed in a general way: συμφοράν is a word indicating good or bad luck – the use in 24 to indicate presumably the opposite of its sense here is marked[6] – and this ambiguity helps to constitute the dependent genitive phrase as a referent for the discourse. The terms of this phrase, too, will become increasingly important:[7]

<u>οἴκου</u>...
οὐχ ὡς τὰ πρόσθ' ἄριστα διαπονουμένου   (18–19)

The general βροτοῖς (5) is limited, focused, to οἶκος, the household, the family. Once, the house 'was being worked diligently in the best way'. The root of the participle is πόνος as in ἀπαλλαγὴ πόνων. It would seem that the prayer for release from πόνων is being redefined in a less absolute, definite sense through this play of active and passive moods, and through the qualification of πον- by ἄριστα. Indeed, the immediate rounding off of the first period with a return to the prayer for ἀπαλλαγὴ(ν) πόνων seems to point this sense of qualification: the indicative of 1 becomes the less definite optative, the source of the solution is unstated, and ἀπαλλαγήν is qualified by εὐτυχής, 'fortunate', which implies its opposite, as ἄριστα διαπονουμένου undercuts the simplicity of πόνων. The absolute first prayer needs modification. This movement from assurance (in

---

[4] Ibid. p. 75.   [5] Ibid. p. 262.
[6] See also 325 and *Cho.* 931 for this play worked out further, συμφορᾶς διπλῆς.
[7] Cf. Jones 1962, pp. 82–111 on the importance of the *oikos*.

language, desire, control) to misgiving, uncertainty, doubt, will be seen many times in the play.

The genitive absolute phrase that concludes the first period marks the tensions of the discourse: εὐαγγέλου is juxtaposed to φανέντος, language (the prefix εὐ- again indicating the possibility of alternative predication) to showing, the visible mode. (Note, too, the root φαίνω is connected with φῶς, i.e. 'come to light', 'be visible in/as light'.) ὀρφναίου πυρός, 'dark fire', is an oxymoron of the boldest form. The 'appearance of speaking dark fire' is the condition of possibility of successful ἀπαλλαγὴ πόνων, that is, the solution of the πόνων is constituted in the opposition of these terms – language/showing: dark/light.

The light appears. Fraenkel notes the critical debate concerning the placing of a comma after νυκτός. The imposition of the critic's boundary of punctuation here particularly seeks to repress the ambiguity of the *apo koinou* construction of juxtaposition. For the natural syntagmatic force of the sentence leads us to read λαμπτὴρ νυκτός, 'the light-giver of night', a phrase parallel to though not as forcefully constructed as ὀρφναίου πυρός; but the juxtaposition νυκτὸς ἡμερήσιον φάος is also strongly marked: showing 'the light of day out of /from/ instead of night'. There is a shift, a conflation, between the oxymoron of 'dark fire' and the sense of light as 'salvation'.[8] In the sense in which light and communication have been linked, this ambiguity points to the ambiguity of speech itself: for the torch is πιφαύσκων (again the root *φάω), 'showing', 'making plain' (the watchman says), but what it shows is (etymologically at least) a tautology. It shows 'light', φάος. It is clear only as a signifier: indeed, as the watchman attempts to explain the message (i.e. treating the beacon as a sign) his initial assertion of complete clarity and understanding σημαίνω τορῶς slips into the conditional: εἴπερ Ἰλίου πόλις | ἑάλωκεν (29–30), 'If indeed the city of Troy has been taken.' And then into the optative (34–5), a refusal to speak and explain (37–8), and finally complete silence. The problem lies precisely in the nature of the communication, that is, in the difference between speaking and showing, and in the gap between signifier and signified in language exchange that constitutes that difference. This difference is emphasised in the juxtaposition ἀγγέλλων πρέπει (30) – ὡς ὁ φρυκτὸς ἀγγέλλων πρέπει, 'as the beacon announcing is clear / shows': what the beacon 'shows' is light (φάος πιφαύσκων), what the beacon 'announces' is a message in language, φέρουσαν...φάτιν (9), which is open to uncertainties and ambiguities (the conflation of dark–light, light as

---

[8] As noted by Ahrens, quoted in Fraenkel, p. 17.

salvation etc.), hence the slip from certainty to the conditional (and with his fear, into silence). πρέπει here also picks up ἐμπρέποντας αἰθέρι (6), indicating the parallelisation and difference (again) between the stars in the sky and the beacon as modes of communication.

This gap between the signifier and signified in communication is widened to the heuristic gap between subject and object, between addresser and addressee: the watchman concludes:

> ὡς ἑκὼν ἐγὼ
> μαθοῦσιν αὐδῶ κοὐ μαθοῦσι λήθομαι   (38–9)

'willingly I tell those that know, and for those that don't know, I forget'. This phrasing (reminiscent of the vow of silence for initiands to the mysteries, as is βοῦς ἐπὶ γλώσσῃ μέγας βέβηκεν, cf. n. 1) highlights the problem. Speech is used (αὐδῶ) only to those who already know what it says. The system of language becomes tautologous, negated, unusable as a system of communication.

> οἶκος δ' αὐτός, εἰ φθογγὴν λάβοι
> σαφέστατ' ἂν λέξειεν   (37–8)

'The house would speak most clearly if it were to have a voice.' Following the confusion of dark–light / day–light and the shift from τορῶς to εἴπερ, we see that the desire for clarity in communication is becoming paramount, the need for a true form of speech which reduces the gap between signifier/signified, addresser/addressee to the assumed clarity of showing. The centrality of the *oikos* is already noticeable, not only in the sheer physical presence (he's lying στέγαις 'Ατρειδῶν) but also in that it is a recurring element of the discourse: it is, as noted above, for the συμφορὰν οἴκου that he weeps; the king is to be greeted as ἄνακτος οἴκων (35) – in his role in the house, not the country or the expedition etc. – and here the house is raised to a position of knowledge beyond humans, a possible transcendent, lacking only a voice.

So the prologue opens with a desire for solution, and although the πόνοι are in the watchman's fear and reticence not clearly defined or explained they are constituted within various polarities and referents: showing/saying (centred on clarity and the gap between signifier and signified); male/female (centred on power and the house); light/dark. As I hope to show, all these will become important.

Past, present, future: control and indeterminacy

From the silence of the watchman the chorus begin with the great *parodos*, which, as Kitto expressed it,[9] bears the weight of the trilogy. It is in some respects a more extended explication of the general circumstances leading up to and consisting of the πόνοι of the *oikos* and the watchman, but the tensions of the prologue are developed in greater depth. Through descriptions of the past, hopes and fears for the future, and statements of the present (which together constitute the narrative) this song develops a series of tensions between control and indeterminacy (in narrative and language). It is a highly complex piece of lyric verse and bears close analysis.

The *parodos* opens with the narrative of events leading towards the Trojan expedition. ἀντίδικος (41), 'adversary in law', as an opening description of Menelaus, is important not only for the legal overtones which reach fulfilment in the court scene of the *Eumenides*, but also for the force of ἀντι-, 'over', 'opposite', 'against'. This sense of opposition, the essence of reciprocity, is developed at the very core of the narrative action, where events, people, images are constantly being forced into a position of opposition. This, too, has been hinted at in the prologue – for example, in the phrase ὕπνου... ἀντίμολπον...ἄκος (17) where as Fraenkel notes, L.-S.-J.'s 'song, sleep's substitute' is an insufficient rendering because it reduces the sense of opposition, 'contra somnum'. ἀντί also implies, however, a mutual exclusivity as well as opposition: fear *replaces* sleep. Opposition/ exclusion will also be seen to be an important coupling in the play, particularly in its narrative of revenge.

The conjunction of Menelaus and Agamemnon in one household, and here the depiction of them as 'twinned in power' and position, maintains the focus on a single household. Especially when compared with the Homeric narrative, where it is quite plain that the two brothers live in different places, it becomes most pointed that the relation of opposition between Paris and the house of Atreus is to be viewed as binary, between a single household and a ξένος. This is brought out strongly by the repeated emphasis on Zeus Xenios as moving force behind the Trojan expedition (in fact, Kitto says this chorus presents the expedition in a 'theological aspect').[10] Here (43) it is to be noted that the power and authority of the brothers is from Zeus, Διόθεν. And as vultures they go, the agents of Zeus, shouting the name of the War God. πτερύγων ἐρετμοῖσιν ἐρεσσόμενοι (52), 'rowing with oars of wings', is an oddly inserted phrase within the

---

[9] 'It lays down the intellectual foundations of the whole trilogy' (1961 (1939), p. 65).
[10] 1956, p. 1. Though see Winnington-Ingram 1974, pp. 3ff.

vulture simile; a metaphor drawn precisely from the tenor (to use Silk's and Richards' terminology) of the simile, that is, from στόλον... χιλιοναύτην... ἦραν... κλάζοντες, 'shouting, they set in motion an expedition of a thousand ships'. There is a slide between subject and object as the structure of the simile (*x* is like *y*) becomes self-referential (*x* is like *y* in that *y* is like *x*) – and thus subverted away from the function of generating new meaning.[11] The lyric language here is parallel to the watchman's last remark.

The male gods Apollo, Pan, Zeus hear, and send against the transgressors ὑστερόποινον... Ἐρινύν. (Note Zeus now sends not eagles but avengers of the eagles.) The punishment may come late but it will be in a form fitted exactly to the crime: ποινή implies 'were-gild', money (and the economic imagery is important) that is an exchange of equal value: opposition and reciprocity.

οὕτω δ' promises the 'cashing out' of the simile and again the focus is clear. The παῖδας of Atreus linked together stand for the whole expedition; the moving force (πέμπει) is Zeus Xenios, Zeus the god of social relationships, particularly between *oikoi* and strangers, between the household and the outsider. And the cause of the struggle is γυναικός, 'woman', which comes rather barely at the end of the line. Helen has not yet been named, nor will she be until the chorus expressly deals with the process of naming her (681–7). When she places herself outside society by her action of adultery, it is as if she loses her name in and for society, she loses that by which society individuates, that on which social identity depends.[12] It is simply as 'woman' that she stands here, and, as at 11, the word is juxtaposed to a compound adjective with the root ἀνδρ- to draw greater attention to the male–female juxtaposition. As with ἀνδρόβουλον, πολυάνορος is a word expressing a position of anti-sociability,[13] a woman in a role opposed to that defined for her by society. The results of her action are for society disruptive, 'a prolonged period of carnage and turmoil on a scale that is virtually cosmic'.[14]

> πολλὰ παλαίσματα καὶ γυιοβαρῆ
> γόνατος κονίαισιν ἐρειδομένου
> διακναιομένης τ' ἐν προτελείοις

---

[11] Although παιδῶν ἄλγεσι... πόνον ὀρταλίχων, a referent for the simile 'the loss of their *children*' marks a difference from the Atreids, who have lost a woman, a wife. But the wife, in Lévi-Straussian terms, is the woman exchanged, that is, the daughter of the giver of the bride in exchange: therefore both παῖς and not παῖς.

[12] See Tanner 1980, *passim*, and in particular pp. 127, 129, 141, 301–7.

[13] Tanner, whose book deals in part with the implications of the unsociability of being πολυάνορος, quotes Middleton as an epigraph: '...for if a woman/ Fly from one point, from which she makes a husband/ She spreads and mounts then like arithmetic/ One, ten, a hundred, a thousand, ten thousand.'   [14] Tanner 1980, p. 27.

κάμακος, θήσων Δαναοῖσιν
Τρωσί θ' ὁμοίως   (63–7)

προτελείοις is a word of ritual indicating 'preliminary sacrifices', particularly those connected with marriage. Here it is used ironically of the shattered spear as a first sacrifice before the completed rite (death/destruction of Troy) and also points out the corruption of the adulterous alliance, which in transgressing the rules of society lacked precisely προτέλεια. The corrupt exchange affects both sides, Δαναοῖσιν Τρωσί θ' ὁμοίως.

The workings of the 'corrupted sacrifice' have been analysed by Zeitlin (1965). She notes here 'the punishment of Agamemnon, the major dramatic event of the play...will also be imaged in the language of sacrifice. This coming death of Agamemnon is darkly riddled in τελεῖται δ' ἐς τὸ πεπρωμένον. *teleitai*, that word of many meanings, primarily connotes fulfilment or end. However, in its punning word play with *proteleia* it assumes the colour of its kindred definition the performance of a holy rite'.[15] She is quite correct on the ambiguity of *teleitai* (which will be further seen, cf. p. 93). But it is more than 'darkly riddled'. The full sentence is ἔστι δ' ὅπη νῦν ἔστι, τελεῖται δ' ἐς τὸ πεπρωμένον. 'It is where now it is...' Here the language is again tautologous,[16] a summation of the present which merely asserts its existence in terms of itself, juxtaposed to an expression of the future which joins a sense of 'end' (not forgetting the religious overtones of *teleitai*) to its own fated moment, that is, which simply asserts the teleology of *teleitai*! There is a sense in which narrative itself, by this juxtaposition of, and consequent lack of transition between, ἀρχή (νῦν) and τέλος, is reduced from a pattern (of cause and effect) as expected of and promised by the chorus to a tautologism equal to that of the language; and in the same way that the tautology of language leads to an occlusion, an erasure, of meaning, so this expression of narrative is incapable of generating what may be termed 'narrative meaning'. The relationship, however, between description of the present and prediction of the future, and a narrative towards a *telos* becomes a major concern. The desire that we have already seen for clarity and accuracy in language will be expressed again and again with regard to the desired efficacy both of prediction and description of narrative events.

As Zeitlin points out, it is noticeable that the continuation of the narrative here (69) is through the imagery of sacrifice and its failure to control wrath – an ominous presaging. This will prove an ironic

---

[15] Zeitlin 1965, p. 465. See also Lebeck 1971, pp. 68–73.
[16] 'When language starts to define itself in terms of itself then we reach a state of affairs that may be called total tautology or solipsism' (Tanner 1980, p. 330).

contrast with Clytemnestra's sacrifices of thanksgiving (87ff.) which the chorus hope will reduce their forebodings.

ἡμεῖς δέ (72) marks a strong break and change of subject. The chorus talk of themselves: they are old men, σαρκὶ παλαιᾷ (72), who possess strength equal to children, ἰσχὺν ἰσόπαιδα (74–5). The oxymoron (ἰσχύς being used normally of, in particular, male military and bodily strength and essentially not predicable of children) emphasises the trigenerational span (old men, men, and children), as indeed ἐπὶ σκήπτροις and τρίποδας μὲν ὁδούς seem to point to the famous riddle of the sphinx in the Oedipus story, the basis for which is the trigenerational structure of human life. Here we are presented with the old men first in contrast with the virile man, for whom war is his proper sphere,[17] Ἄρης δ᾿ οὐκ ἐνὶ χώρᾳ, and secondly as similar to the young to whom they are equal in strength (i.e. weak) παιδὸς δ᾿ οὐδὲν ἀρείων. The trigenerational structure is important throughout the trilogy,[18] as it is this, a structure at the basis of society, which is threatened by the actions of Clytemnestra, and by the incest and cannibalism which is at the root of the familial conflict of the house of the Atreids (cf. 1214ff., 1583ff.), and even by the adultery of Aegisthus and that of Paris.

All these acts add up to a sort of compendium of the dreaded (and thus tabooed) deeds that threaten the very possibility of civilization itself, since, quite apart from the horror attendant on the deeds, cannibalism of one's own children negates generational continuity, incest not only involves a chaotic confusion of generations by sexuality, bringing together precisely the two figures who should be kept apart when it comes to sexuality and mating, it also effectively refutes and nihilates that transaction, or interfamilial exchange of the daughter in marriage, on which society depends. It is the ultimate travesty of endogamy from which no healthy future can come.[19]

This perhaps helps to explain the allusion to the riddle of the sphinx and the Oedipus story here in juxtaposition to the story of adultery: the construction of the trigenerational system contains an allusion to its, and hence society's, collapse through the collapse of distinctions, inherent in the allusion to the Oedipus story, and explicit in the action of Paris.

Significantly, we move immediately to a direct address to Clytemnestra;[20] Clytemnestra addressed as 'daughter of Tyndareus'

---

[17] See Vernant 1980 (1974), Ch. 2.

[18] And indeed throughout Greek society in general: see, for example, Roussel 1951.

[19] Tanner 1980, pp. 28–9.

[20] Cf. Fraenkel's note (ad loc.) which, after cataloguing other misguided attempts at pontificating the 'correct' stage direction, adds his own: 'For it never happens that

and as 'queen'. It is precisely as 'daughter of Tyndareus' that she became 'queen', i.e. was married to Agamemnon, entered the system of alliances as an object of exchange.[21] The juxtaposition of 'Clytemnestra' to the beginnings of the story of her sister, and the trigenerational structure of society, is pregnant. Clytemnestra, too, in her adultery and the killing of her husband and threat to kill her son, breaks the basic bonds of the ordering of culture. The connective particle δέ (83) in the ambiguity of 'and'/'but' marks both the apparent change *and* the continuity of subject.

ἀγγελίας πειθοῖ (86–7) introduces a new concept which will become central, that of πειθώ: between the subject and the object (speech) we have seen the problem of interpretation and the corresponding desire for clarity, precision. πειθώ is sited in a position between speaker and listener, a quality of language (though not solely language, cf. Buxton 1976) pertaining to the utterance of speech and, as we will see, to the speaker, leading to the acceptance or understanding on the part of the listener: πειθώ is a means of bridging the gap between subject/object, signifier/signified: so it is important that it occurs here concerning the interpretation of the beacons.

Clytemnestra is sacrificing and we return to the imagery of light: βωμοὶ...φλέγονται...οὐρανομήκης λαμπάς ἀνίσχει. This links the torch, the flame, back both to the beacon and the stars of the watchman's speech. λαμπάς is the word used of the beacon light itself, and οὐρανομήκης, 'sky-measuring', links the torchlight to the position of the stars. 'Light' is furthermore connected with the differing process of communication, as it was with the stars and the beacons. The flame is 'drugged by the *soft, guileless exhortations* of holy oil' (94–5). Again speech predicated of an inanimate object (as it was of λαμπάς originally, 9–11) is described in terms which, while implying purity, are profoundly ambiguous: *malakos* is used in Homer of words to express flattering, guile, untransparent language.

a leading character enters the scene for the first time and then leaves it again without having uttered a word.' Beyond the transcendental originary metaphor of performance to restrict meaning(s) (cf. pp. 203–4), his use of the term 'never' is indicative of a particular, questionable, form of criticism: to draw up two lists of phenomena, only to discount one list as wrong, mistaken, or non-existent, is a process which under an appearance of scientificity (it is a technique often used by textual critics) cloaks merely an assertion of categorisation of a prior-made system and an attempt to force examples into it. It is difficult to prove or disprove Clytemnestra's presence or absence here by an appeal to 'it never happens', as that 'never' contains the answer to the question before the question was set! It is not analysis but assertion, which logically could 'disprove' any unique occurrence, word or construction in our limited corpus. This scene has continued to be discussed by critics in terms of 'stagecraft'. See Taplin 1977, pp. 280–5.   [21] See Lévi-Strauss 1969 (1949), *passim*.

It is the adjective used by Athene[22] to describe the speech of Calypso trying to seduce Odysseus from his *nostos*; Paris describes[23] Helen's persuasions for him to take the field as μαλακοί; Hephaestus suggests[24] Hera use such words to get round Zeus. *Malakos*, indeed, becomes linked to 'womanish', 'weak' and such meanings in later writing. In fact, it could almost be described as the opposite of ἄδολος. παρηγορία, a rare word, 'persuasion', language invested with rhetorical force, is language which is not necessarily transparent. φαρμασσομένη, the present passive participle of φαρμάσσειν, 'to use a *pharmakon*', itself implies 'adulterate', 'poison', 'enchant' as well as[25] 'heal by medicine'. This confusion or ambiguity in terms of speech applied to a message of light stands as a prelude to the beacon-speeches scene (where such questions are reiterated by the chorus 268ff.) and leads here to the worry of their prayer (again a slip from a statement into a wish): παιών τε γενοῦ τῆσδε μερίμνας. The metaphors of sickness have been catalogued by Dumortier and developed in their implications by Zeitlin[26] and need little further explication here – a transformation of the opening prayer for a solution, a release, into the structure (equally teleological) of sickness and health. The μέριμνα is broken down, however, into an opposition between κακόφρων – 'malicious' (the development of μαλακός and the possibility of deceit implied in ἀδόλοισι) – and ἐλπίς which 'wards off, defends the mind from...' and the text is obelised by Page at that point. The sense of opposition is strongly marked by the syntax νῦν τότε μέν...τότε δέ. The sense of foreboding is paralleled to the sense of hope/expectation: between the present and the future, similar to the optative (its modal form) stands prediction in the form of ἐλπίς on the one hand, φόβος on the other. The tone of this chorus, through the repeated refrain αἴλινον αἴλινον εἰπέ, τὸ δ' εὖ νικάτω is constituted in this form of hope, fear and prayer for the future.

With the change of metre (104), the chorus return to the story broken off at 65. The authority for the narrative is proclaimed in terminology with 'a legal ring' (Fraenkel). κύριός εἰμι θροεῖν 'I have the authority...' The story that follows is marked as the story of the work of men, ἀνδρῶν, men with *kratos*. The reason offered for their authority, although the precise wording of the parenthesis is lost, seems to be the force of *peitho* which comes from the gods. The song's power is the authority of the old men, as the ὅδιον κράτος is that of the men of military age.[27] Lines 109–11 in their stressing of the

---

[22] *Od.* 1.56.   [23] *Il.* 6.337.   [24] *Il.* 1.582.

[25] See Derrida's analysis of Plato's double use of *pharmakon* in the *Phaedrus* (1981, pp. 63–171). Also, the earlier work of Artelt.   [26] 1965, particularly pp. 501–2.

[27] As one might expect, cf. Vernant 1980 (1974); Roussel 1951. The power of language will be often discussed below.

δίθρονον κράτος are reminiscent of the beginning of the *parodos* (43). Indeed, the constitution of the sentence with delayed subject, closely parallel in form to 62 with πέμπει repeated here, may lead us to expect a phrase similar to 'Zeus Xenios' as subject. In fact, we have the famous omen of the eagles devouring the hare. On the one hand, this seems to link the birds of Zeus back to Zeus Xenios, linking more closely Agamemnon and Menelaus, who have already been depicted as birds of prey, with the motive force of the king of the gods. On the other hand, the surprise of the expression and its riddling nature (γρῖφος) constitute the omen as a sign of a particular sort, a sign which needs analysis in the present but which indicates the nature of the future, its narrative. The omen stands, that is, as an unclear, untransparent communication[28] which may have a direct relation with the future. The signifier in language has a second-level referent or rather the sign (the depiction of the eagles) becomes a signifier (of the future action). Here, then, the gap between signifier and signified, and the gap between the present (its analysis) and the future (its prediction) are interconnected, again linking narrative and language in the desire for clarity and control. Immediately, the chorus turn to prayer, which we have seen with ἐλπίς as a means of bridging the gap between present and future, now expressed also in terms of speech: αἴλινον αἴλινον εἰπέ, τὸ δ' εὖ νικάτω, '*Speak* now, *say* ailinon, the song of woe, but let the good prevail.' The contrast between the particularised aorist imperative 'Speak!' and the generalised wish of the present imperative (νικάτω) adds to the 'strong contrast' noted by Fraenkel between αἴλινον and τὸ εὖ.

The antistrophe limits, to a degree, the openness[29] of the image of the eagles through the interpretation of the μάντις, Calchas: the role of the *mantis* is important because his art, τέχνη, is an attempt to close the gap between the interpretation of the present and the prediction of the future – a formalisation of the emotional ἐλπίς or optative mood: it has significantly its own tense, the prophetic present ἀγρεῖ (126), whereby the depiction of the future is contracted to a statement, analysis, description of the present sign syntactically, as indeed the general procedure of the mantic *techne* is an attempt to conflate the present and the future, to depict the future in the present, to remove, erase the gap. τεράζων at the end of the line (125) and marking the beginning of the direct speech of Calchas could well be a coinage of

---

[28] Note the eagles 'appear' φανέντες. *φαω again points back to the distinction between showing/saying in communication. The eagles 'appear' (like the stars) but they communicate a message (like the beacons).

[29] This openness has been often noted: Kitto 1961 (1939), pp. 65–6, Whallon 1961, Peradotto 1969, West 1979.

Aeschylus. Certainly, it is a very rare word in an emphatic position, which draws attention to the mantic nature of the speech to follow.

Calchas begins by stating that the *telos* of the expedition will be achieved. But immediately this is countered by οἷον μή – the future is depicted still in terms of opposition. The opposition here is ἄγα θεόθεν: as the expedition is sent by Zeus Xenios, so there is a force of envy, malice, wonder in opposition at the level of the divine – an extremely open-ended expression – a force which may κνεφάση... στόμιον...Τροίας. κνεφάση continues the imagery of light, 'cloud', 'obscure', and it is boldly conjoined with στόμιον, 'cloud the curb-chain'. I will have more to say about this below.

The openness of ἄγα θεόθεν is explained, defined, by the naming of Artemis: it is she who stands in opposition to the expedition. She is ἐπίφθονος and the cause of her φθόνος is depicted first as a *griphos* – πτανοῖσιν κυσὶ πατρός (135): 'The winged dogs of her father'. It is noticeable, however, that the position of opposition to Zeus is emphasised first by the reference 'her father' (as her opposition will require the transgression of Agamemnon's paternal relation to his daughter), and secondly by the emerging fact that it is anger at the birds themselves who, as we have seen, are linked[30] both to Zeus and to Agamemnon and Menelaus as those sending the expedition: it is the whole motive force of Zeus Xenios and his agents that she opposes through her opposition to the birds' feast:

> στυγεῖ δὲ δεῖπνον ἀετῶν   (137)

This phrase, as with the naming of Artemis (134) 'solves', determines through designation the openness of the *griphos*.[31] However, although it may explicate and define the riddling, metaphoric structure that preceded it, it is still read[32] as having an excess of semantic content: it remains metaphoric in the sense that it is a sign standing for, designating another sign or series of signs.[33] Although we see an apparent limiting of the denotative sense of the phrase 'winged dogs of the father' (as 'eagles'), the expression στυγεῖ δὲ δεῖπνον ἀετῶν scarcely limits the connotative signification of the text (cf. n. 32). The boldness – and difficulty – of Aeschylean metaphor (such as κνεφάση...στόμιον...Τροίας) is linked to this use of *griphos* and solution, and the reading of such dense metaphoric poetry is one of

---

[30] An 'intolerable confusion between the world of the portent and the world of reality it happens to symbolize' Lloyd-Jones 1962, p. 189. Cf. Lebeck 1971, p. 2.

[31] 'Movement from enigmatic utterance to clear statement, from riddle to solution dominate the structure of the *Oresteia*' (Lebeck 1971, p. 2).

[32] As the critics' discussions of the topic show; see no. 29.

[33] One sign standing for another, or one series of signs standing for another series of signs is a traditional definition of metaphor since Aristotle. See Derrida 1974a, p. 13.

the recurring problems of Aeschylean criticism. Modern critics[34] have written a great deal on the analysis of metaphor particularly with regard to theories of meaning and reading. A brief discussion of some of this writing will help, I hope, to recognise and analyse the difficulties of this much-debated and important topic. For there is an interesting relation between the metaphors, riddles, and mantic prophecy, which inform the narrative here.

In an influential and lengthy study, Ricoeur, who is concerned to place the *role of the reader* in the recognition and construction of metaphor, moves towards what he calls a *hermeneutics of metaphor* (which he sets in opposition to, though not replacing, both the rhetorical tradition developing from Aristotle, and the semanticists of metaphor with whom he classes amongst others I. A. Richards). Of the semantic productivity of metaphor, he writes 'metaphorical meaning...is not the enigma itself, the semantic clash pure and simple, but the solution of the enigma, the inauguration of the new semantic pertinence' (1978, p. 214). The use of metaphor, then, and as formalised and pointed by the use of *griphos*, is, for Ricoeur, apparently towards the production of such a (new) meaning.

But at the same time, in the process of such production, the apparent solving cannot fully repress or totally solve the enigma;[35] indeed, in the very process of production, Ricoeur's notion of 'the inauguration of the new semantic pertinence' would seem to open itself to the possibility of excessive, unbounded metaphoricity. Derrida expresses this potentiality of metaphor in characteristic style: 'metaphor is the moment of possible sense as a possibility of non-truth' (1974a, p. 42). This is not, however, just a notion of the open-endedness of a poetic figure of speech: the argument invades the notion of metaphor, metaphoricity itself. Ricoeur translates part of Derrida's reasoning towards the *uncontrollability of metaphor* thus:

The paradox is this: there is no discourse on metaphor that is not stated within a metaphorically engendered conceptual network. There is no non-metaphorical standpoint from which to perceive the order and the demarcation of the metaphorical field. Metaphor is metaphorically stated. The word *metaphor* and the word *figure* alike attest to this recurrence of

---

[34] Not, of course, only modern critics (see n. 36). Ricoeur has a useful bibliography. A more extensive bibliography may be found in Warren A. Shibles, *Metaphor: an annotated bibliography and history*, Wisconsin 1971. Since 1971, as well as several books, two important collections of articles have appeared, namely, *New Literary History* 6 (1974), and *Critical Inquiry* 5: i (1978). See also the tropological criticism of de Man, or a work such as Genette's *Figures* for different implications of such study. For an interesting further series of studies and approaches, see Ortony 1979a, b and c.

[35] As we see, in the simplest form, with commentators' contradictory interpretations of Calchas' interpretation of the omen, cf. n. 32.

metaphor. The theory of metaphor returns in a circular manner to the metaphor of theory which determines the truth of being as presence.[36] If this is so, there can be no principle for delimiting metaphor, no definition in which the defining does not contain the defined; metaphoricity is absolutely uncontrollable...Were one successfully to establish order amid figures, still one metaphor at least would escape: the metaphor of metaphor.[37]

Thus, concludes Derrida, 'The field is never saturated' (p. 18). We shall be looking at this decentring of the (metaphoric) text in Aeschylus again in several places,[38] particularly at moments in and

[36] There are three points in Ricoeur's exposition which may benefit from still further clarification. First: Derrida's critique of Western metaphysics as determining Being as Presence is a recurring argument in Derrida's writing. He writes (for example) 'Its [the history of Western metaphysics] matrix – if you will pardon me for demonstrating so little and for being so elliptical... – is the determination of Being as *presence* in all the senses of this word. It could be shown that all the names related to fundamentals, to principles or to the centre have always designated an invariable presence – eidos, arche, telos, energeia, ousia (essence, existence, substance, subject) aletheia, transcendentality, unconscious, God, man, and so forth.' Much of his work is concerned with the analysis and implications of that statement. These ideas, which draw extensively on a continental tradition of Hegel, Husserl, Heidegger, have been often expressed in general outline (see, for example, his translators: Bass 1978, pp. xiff.; Johnson 1981, pp. viiiff.; Spivak 1976, pp. xiiiff. See also Norris 1982, pp. 68ff., Culler 1974, 1979) but are too complex in detail to be gone into here. Secondly (and of greater relevance here): an essential part of the argument in question is to emphasise that a notion of metaphor is always already part of a philosophical system: 'the metaphor remains in all its essential features a classical element of philosophy, a metaphysical concept...it is the product of a network of elements of philosophy, which themselves correspond to tropes and figures and are coeval with them or systematically bound to them' (p. 18). As Heidegger succinctly puts it 'The metaphorical exists only within the metaphysical.' These first two points are seen in Derrida's analysis of Aristotle on metaphor (particularly pp. 30ff.), e.g. 'The whole theory of names which governs the theory of metaphor, the whole Aristotelian doctrine of simple names (*Poetics* 1457a, 10ff.) is constructed to guarantee the havens of truth and of that which is proper. Like mimesis, metaphor *comes back* to physis, to its truth and its presence' (p. 45). The third point is a common comment in the face of Derridean texts, that is, the difficulty (in principle as well as application) of reducing his argumentation: Ricoeur's précis, for example, is of only the beginning of Derrida's second section entitled 'More and no more metaphor', on what Derrida calls ('For convenience') 'metaphorical supplementation'. Ricoeur does not follow through the extent of Derrida's piece. My purpose here is not to offer a critique of Ricoeur's reduction, or of Derrida's arguments, still less a summary of their views: but by invoking and evoking their intertwined arguments to lead towards a recognition of the double way the concept of metaphor *both opens and veils* the work of interpretation; and to develop through this shifting, decentring 'metaphoricity' of the text the recognition of what I have called the textuality of the text, its plurality.

Nor is it to be forgotten with this lengthy note that it is appended to a passage of mantic prophecy: it is the connections between mantic prophecy (sign-reading) and metaphor (sign standing for sign) that I am trying to follow through in this my reading of the textual signs.

[37] Thus Derrida places his intention not to attempt such a delimitation but to consider the conditions of its impossibility.

[38] Cf. pp. 68–9, 133–7.

around the recognition scene, that inauguration and delimitation of a proper identity. Derrida's analysis of the boundaries between metaphor and a notion of 'sens (nom, qualité) propre' (which undercuts both notions)[39] challenges not only some Classicists' attempts at cataloguing metaphors by categorisations either of the vehicle (cf. e.g. Lilja) or of the tenor (cf. e.g. Sansone) (there are many more traditional attacks on such approaches) but also the subtler demarcations of Silk, which are based on definitions of 'usage', 'dead metaphor', 'literal meaning'.[40] Furthermore, it questions the very rigour of the terms by which I introduced this discussion, such as 'the boldness of Aeschylean metaphor' (where even the metaphor 'boldness' seems to trace the difficulties of talking about metaphor without metaphor, of separating out for analysis metaphor(icity) from a literal or scientific language). It articulates a challenge to the possibility of and reasons for drawing an untransgressed boundary between literal, proper discourse and its other, figural language.

This challenge to *vraisemblance* by the metaphoric text and *griphos*, and the apparent production of new meaning(s) is dramatised in this chorus by Calchas' interpretation of the omen and our interpretation of Calchas. Attention is drawn, thus, to the process of signification based on signifier and signified, or rather, on one sign designating another, and thus to the possible gaps in the process of communication in language in which we have seen the major tensions of this text and our reading of it constituted.[41] Moreover, here the mantic utterance of Calchas is the attempt to read on the level of narrative one sign as designating another ('the appearance of the eagles means such and

[39] Culler (1974, p. 229) suggests 'the notion of metaphor should be scrapped'. This seems to take the sword to Derrida's more subtle analysis which seems to place metaphor 'sous rature' (as Spivak 1976, p. xxiv notes).

[40] Silk (1974): 'The contrast between normal and abnormal usage remains black and white.' Ricoeur, too, while recognising the force of Derrida's arguments, particularly questions the erosion of the boundary between literal and figurative, claiming with Le Guern that the 'lexicalisation of metaphor' means that dead metaphors 'are no longer metaphors, but instead are associated with literal meaning extending its polysemy' (1974, p. 290). This presupposes a separation between literal and proper sense: 'Literal does not mean proper in the sense of originary, but simply current, "usual".' He quotes as support Aristotle, *Poetics* 1457b, where he says κύριον means 'current', and not 'literal' as 'proper', which seems a difficult reduction of the normative sense of κύριος. He also writes, however, 'It is use in discourse that specifies the difference between literal and metaphorical.' Apart from the difficulties of taking 'use' and 'discourse' as fixed criteria in *textual* studies (cf. Derrida) it is precisely the difficulty of specification of these terms *in* the discourse of the *Oresteia* (in Greek Tragedy, Greek) that we shall be investigating. Cf. p. 68.

[41] Another way of putting this question may be 'What are the differences between (a) Calchas saying "the eagles mean Troy will fall", that is between saying one sign "actually means" another sign; and (b), Clytemnestra's lying and hypocrisy, that is, where what she says "actually signifies" something different; and (c), our interpretation, "in other words..."'

such will happen'). It acts as a similar stimulus to deconstruction at the level of the narrative, the process of cause and effect.[42]

So, then, mantic prophecy, metaphor and the *griphos* function in similar and interrelated ways, drawing attention to the process whereby language and narrative sense are produced, and are at risk. In the very attempt for control (over language, narrative) that mantic prophecy, sign reading, instigate, there is also set in play the sliding indeterminacy of signification – the chain (marked by its gaps) of sign for sign...

Further reason for the anger of Artemis follows (140–3), which continues the explanation of στυγεῖ δὲ δεῖπνον in positive terms: τόσον περ...τερπνά κτλ. Despite her opposition, she accepts (αἰτεῖ and αἰνεῖ both offer positive senses) the ratification of the signs. But as they are accepted, so immediately they are broken down to polar opposites again:

δεξιὰ μὲν κατάμομφα δὲ φάσματα   (145)

This pattern of opposition leading to a moment of ratification, decision, determination, which itself leads to further opposition will be seen to be a structuring movement of the trilogy.

This pattern, too, calls out for healing – Calchas calls on Apollo the Healer to stop, prevent the opposition. As Fraenkel notes, 'the baneful element...κατάμομφα δέ...comes to the fore with greater intensity and in greater detail', as the opposition rather than the point of ratification is emphasised. ἀντιπνόους (147) – the ἀντί we recognise from ἀντίδικος/ἀνθ' ὕπνου; and ἐχενῇδας ἀπλοίας τεύξει (148) negates the essential terms of στόλον...χιλιοναύτην...ἦραν (45ff.), πέμπει ξὺν δορί (111). Her desire is for a 'second sacrifice', θυσίαν ἑτέραν (150). This refers back to the omen of the eagles devouring the hares, 'as sacrificers', θυομένοισι. This second sacrifice is to be ἄνομον, ἄδαιτον 'without law' and 'without feast' – its negativity stemming from the fact that rather than being 'a deliberate act...absorbing all the internal tensions, feuds and rivalries pent up within the community'[43] it will be νεικέων τέκτονα. Instead of being an act to stem dissension, the action 'naturally' and 'inherently' σύμφυτον (151) (*pace* Fraenkel) leads to opposition, an opposition which is οὐ δεισήνορα, 'not afraid of man': that is, constituted in the conflict between the sexes. Calchas' final words are equally menacing and sinister – and will be echoed throughout the trilogy. μίμνει γάρ is in emphatic first position: 'it remains' – whatever you

---

42 Blomfield, quoted in Fraenkel, 'hoc portentum non tam *caussa* quam *signum*.'! As Lebeck puts it, it is 'rather a symbol of the cause, for the language of prophecy knows no sharp division between symbol and thing symbolised, between cause and effect' (1971, p. 33).   43 Girard 1977 (1972), p. 7.

may do to prevent it. This is picked up in παλίνορτος and μνάμων (154–5); and τεκνόποινος, both 'child-avenging' and 'avenged by a child', is also reminiscent perhaps of ὑστερόποινος (58) as well as being prophetic of both Clytemnestra's justification of the regicide and the action of the *Choephoroi*. It is 'fearful', 'unclear/deceitful', and 'wrath' – φοβερά, δολία, μῆνις. It is in control of, ordering the house, οἰκονόμος. The confusion of what precisely is the subject of the sentence, what is in apposition, indeed, even the adjectival or nominal status[44] of the words adds to the inchoate emotional feeling of fear and worry. As Diskin Clay says[45] 'the present can only hope darkly with no reason to hope and every reason to fear naming its fear'. The similarity to the watchman's φόβος/πόνοι needs no further explication.

A final point on this epode: τοιάδε...ἀπέκλαγξεν...οἴκοις βασιλείοις (156–7). Precisely when one would expect the kings to be depicted in terms of their military, 'international', status, the seer's speech is directed not to the army, the council etc. but to the household, οἴκοις. The focus is again on the *oikos* and the expedition is subsumed as an event (a vastly important event, of course) in the history of the Atreid house.

The hymn to Zeus is a strong break in the narrative, a change in metre and subject. First let us note that it is not a prayer or a hymn in the normal sense of the words in the Greek world. It nowhere addresses Zeus in the second person,[46] and despite certain details of expression which are reminiscent of religious formulas, structurally the passage (160–83) is so far different from the expected form that some commentators have postulated a special Zeus-Religion.[47] This passage is not a prayer; it is only a hymn in the loosest sense of the term (certainly it is quite different from, say, the Homeric hymns, and even kletic hymns) and one only continues to call it such for the convenience of maintaining a terminological tradition. The juxtaposition of Zeus and his attributes to the stanzas singing of Artemis, her qualities and her opposition to Zeus, places the opposition of Zeus and Artemis on a wider plane, not merely as supporter and opposer of the Trojan expedition, but as motive forces behind the play's action in general, behind the structuring of the text. The marked asyndeton emphasises the juxtaposition as such. We will see more of the substance of this opposition when I consider the hymn's language in detail. Before, we must note also that the juxtaposition of Artemis and Zeus at this point in the narrative seems to constitute the ἀμηχανία

---

[44] Fraenkel, for example, disagrees with Sidgwick and Headlam.
[45] Clay 1969, p. 3.   [46] As normally: cf. Norden 1956, pp. 163–6.
[47] On this, see Lloyd-Jones 1956, Golden 1961, Grube 1970, Smith 1980.

of Agamemnon as a decision to follow one or other of these motive forces and his sacrifice is to be seen as an action within that choice. (Choice here is not meant to imply a concept of 'will', nor do I wish to become involved here in the 'freedom of action in Aeschylus' debate; 'choice' is to imply that a course of action is undertaken which excludes a different course of action, which may stand in opposition to it.) Agamemnon's choice that follows is juxtaposed to and intertwined with a theological narrative in such a way that his course of action seems to side him with Zeus, indeed, seems to place him within the theological imperative as an agent of Zeus. It is not because of an (unmentioned) sin of Agamemnon that Artemis holds back the winds but within the structuring of her opposition to Zeus and his agents.

Zeus is set up in opposition to Artemis in that it is he who can remove doubt from the mind (the doubt which crept in to dominate Calchas' speech and the watchman's soliloquy). Zeus can control such indeterminacy completely:

εἰ τὸ μάταν ἀπὸ φροντίδος ἄχθος
χρὴ βαλεῖν ἐτητύμως   (165–6)

The contrast between μάταν and ἐτητύμως[48] is marked by the emphatic position of ἐτητύμως: it is not merely releasing φροντίς from toil, but doing so with complete clarity, accuracy, hitting the mark precisely that is the quality of the god. The basis of this assertion of Zeus' *absolute* nature, the condition for the conditional clause to be true, is interesting. It shows a link between language, metaphysics and theology within the structures of language that we have been considering. For Zeus, however he is named (ὅστις ποτ' ἐστίν), remains the same: the naming (signifier) depends on his own desire εἰ τῷδ' αὐτῷ φίλον κεκλημένῳ. Unlike the chain of signs we have seen already in the chorus, whereby one sign may through metaphor, riddle, prophecy slide into another, become a signifier, a producer of new knowledge, Zeus is precisely unmetaphorisable:

οὐκ ἔχω προσεικάσαι
. . .
πλὴν Διός   (163–5)

He can be likened only to himself. His transcendence is his unitary stableness of being above and beyond comparison or likeness. This constitution of the divinity of Zeus finds interesting echoes in what Derrida calls in his view of the history of Western metaphysics a 'transcendental signified' – that 'which supposedly does not in itself, in its essence, refer back to any signifier but goes beyond the

---

[48] 'ἐτητύμως is the exact opposite of μάταν' (Fraenkel, p. 103).

chain of signs and itself no longer functions as a signifier'.[49] The
theological position of Zeus, his postulated ability (note it remains
nevertheless within a conditional clause) to remove doubt ἐτητύμως,
depends upon his position in language.

ὅστις πάροιθεν ἦν (168) is parallel to ὅστις ποτ' ἐστίν (160) as
οὐδὲ λέξεται πρὶν ὤν (170) is to τοῦτό νιν προσεννέπω (162). For
the deposed there is no name in language, a contrast to Zeus' control
and choice of all his names. The transcendental signified transcends
precisely the naming function of society (categorising, defining) in
that it is postulated as a present constant not dependent on definition
in language, as opposed to the loss or change of status (in language,
society) which normally comes with loss or change of name (as for
example here Cronos, Uranos, Helen). Also the second generation is
mentioned (without name) ὅς δ' ἔπειτ' ἔφυ (171). The noun τριακτῆρος
(171) draws further attention to the trigenerational form. Zeus
achieved his position by the rejection (binding) of his father, who
had castrated his father: not only a trigenerational structure, but
intergenerational conflict. Ζῆνα...ἐπινίκια κλάζων continues
through the language of the wrestling-school the sense of conflict. As
opposed to the unnamed vanquished, only the victor has his *name*
proclaimed before the assembled people by the herald: Ζῆνα
(174) – after Ζεύς (160) and Διός (165), the third name for the
thrice-victorious god 'Zeus'.

To cheer earnestly, προφρόνως (174), for Zeus is to get understanding, φρενῶν (175); Zeus sets straight the path for mortals to get
understanding, φρονεῖν. Great emphasis is on the root *φρην with
this threefold repetition (looking back to φροντίδος (165)). For the
moment, I wish just to say that φρονεῖν, which is connected with the
processes of thought in many ways but particularly with the power
of rational, logical, symbolic thought, the process of argumentation,
is regarded as the quality which is reached by siding with Zeus.[50]
Knowledge is intimately connected with experience, or 'suffering',

[49] Derrida 1972, p. 23. I make use of Derrida's term here because I want to mark that
the notion of a transcendence which is postulated to be beyond language, unchanged
and unchanging, is not always limited to the divine but is an important and various
notion in linguistics, metaphysics – and is a notion much in debate in recent years,
particularly under the influence of Derrida's questioning. (His own most general
statement may be found in Derrida 1972, pp. 67–8.) The implications of the
transcendence of god in this theological narrative are not limited to 'religious dogma'
nor to be subsumed under some examination-like rubric as 'Aeschylus' view of the
divine', 'gods in the *Oresteia*', but rather are implicated throughout the play's
language and narrative. The term 'transcendent signified' is here deployed to offer
a certain entrance to a wider sense of a 'theological narrative'.
    We shall return to the transcendence of Zeus, especially pp. 147, 157–8, 249ff.
[50] See below p. 37.

as it is often translated. This statement, a conclusion of their search for clarity in narrative in a generalisation, a pattern, a model for narrative, 'has authority', κυρίως ἔχειν; Zeus has 'laid it down', θέντα. As they were authorised to sing their story (κύριος...θροεῖν, 104) and their power was from the gods (θεόθεν, 105), so their song returns to the authorisation of god for its patterning. But (following on from πάθει), instead of respite, there is μνησιπήμων πόνος (180). This refers back to μίμνει...μνάμων (155) and to the *ponoi* of the prologue. Not only is there toil, but toil that is reminiscent of, remembering, pain: there is a narrative of suffering. But even the unwilling learn σωφρονεῖν (180–1). This shows the same root *φρην but, as the etymology of the word shows (σάος φρενάς), a different sense. The unwilling learn to 'show self-control', 'be prudent'; they learn to restrain what might be in opposition to φρονεῖν, good sense. 'For the grace of the gods comes by force' – there is a grim irony in the use of που and the oxymoron χάρις βίαιος ('grace' / 'physical violence'). As many commentators have noticed in their different ways, this passage is to some degree programmatic for the divine–human interaction of the trilogy.[51]

The apparent example of this general passage (καὶ τόθ᾽...)[52] is the return to the Aulis narrative. But how is it an example? How precisely is the hymn applicable to the circumstances at Aulis? Is it through the association of Agamemnon and the Zeus supporter? Or the unwilling? The 'forced grace'? As often with Aeschylus (we noted it first on p. 8), it is the gap between the general statement and its apparent particular example that constitutes the possibilities (and problems) of interpretation. For the dialectical movement between general statement and example to which the choric/episodic structuring of Greek tragedy seems particularly suited, introduces a play of difference which requires especially careful analysis. The strategy of treating the choric passages simply as 'commentary', 'authorial comment', 'the profound truth of the episodes' seeks to repress that particular dialectic and, as in the passage under discussion, points to the danger of drawing a boundary between general statements and examples that seeks to hypostatise the former as a repository of (true) meaning, as if their meaning should/could be read as separate (the boundary) from their context, without the play of difference (cf. also pp. 64–6).

The narrative is, then, marked by the gap. The formulation of the delay at Aulis has been left out (it is presented as a *fait accompli* ἐπεί...); or rather it has been depicted in the opposition of Zeus and

---

[51] See below pp. 157–8.   [52] See Fraenkel for this connection.

Artemis: we left the story with Calchas predicting a possible delay and sacrifice: we rejoin it with the delay taking place:

> ...ἀπλοίᾳ κεναγγεῖ βαρύ-
> νοντ' Ἀχαιϊκὸς λεώς   (188–9)

And we move quickly to the condition of the solution of the impasse, though it is expressed in veiled terms:

> ἐπεὶ δὲ καὶ πικροῦ
> χείματος ἄλλο μῆχαρ
> βριθύτερον   (198–200)

although the source of the opposition is, again, made clear:

> ...προφέρων
> Ἄρτεμιν   (201–2)

The speech of Agamemnon (206ff.) has received much critical attention in the last twenty years and I do not wish to repeat the arguments here.[53] There is, however, a general tendency with which I agree, moving away from apportioning 'guilt' to Agamemnon, stressing not the elements of choice and will (as did some earlier critics in particular)[54] but that, as Rivier notes of Orestes in the *Choephoroi*, 'La...question qui se pose et qu'il pose est: aura-t-il la force et la courage de faire ce qu'il a décidé de faire?'.[55] Certainly, here it is disobedience to Zeus that is described in negative terms, while the sacrifice is expressed positively (206–7). It is the impossibility of disobedience that is followed up with the stark question πῶς λιπόναυς γένωμαι ξυμμαχίας ἁμαρτών; (212–13) of which Fraenkel says 'The answer implied in this "rhetorical" question can only be "impossible".'[56] The explanation (γάρ) of this clearly taken decision leaves little doubt as to his reaction: ὀργᾷ περιόργως ἐπιθυμεῖν θέμις (216–17)[57] – 'It is right to desire this with a passion that is extremely impassioned.' I wish here, however, to note how the focus on the household is developing. Agamemnon's daughter, in the context of the Trojan expedition, is still δόμων ἄγαλμα. ἄγαλμα is a word used particularly in the *Odyssey* of votive gifts of the gods: she is a 'glory of the household'. Iphigeneia, by her sacrifice is to become, however, a 'votive gift' of the expedition, of the state, of the ξυμμαχία.

---

[53] E.g. Lloyd-Jones 1962; Rivier 1968; Lesky 1966; Hammond 1965; Vernant and Vidal-Naquet 1972, pp. 41ff. Cf. n. 37.   [54] E.g. Lesky 1966.

[55] Rivier 1968, p. 32. The most extreme position, perhaps. Cf. Vernant and Vidal-Naquet 1972, pp. 41ff.

[56] See, however, Winnington-Ingram 1974, pp. 3ff.

[57] Fraenkel's text; which Winnington-Ingram, most recently, has attacked in favour of Bamberger's emendation (1983, p.85; 1974, pp. 7–8). His analysis of the problems with γάρ is cogent. The ambiguity of the referent for σφε is unsolvable and the emendation certainly offers no solution to the difficulty of reading this passage. The doubts on causality, motivation, divine influence will recur throughout.

There is also a strongly marked juxtaposition between πατρῷος and τέκνον/πάρθενον/παρθενοσφάγοισιν which will be continued throughout the chorus (see below on 225/228/229/231). Within the house, the sacrifice is father killing daughter, παρθένου αἵματος, within the expedition it is παυσανέμου θυσίας, a (nameless) sacrifice to stop the wind. The juxtaposition of these phrases (214) is both the explanation of the validity of the action for Agamemnon and also the tension within it.

The temporal sequence of the next sentence (218–21) is strongly marked: ἐπεί...τόθεν 'it was when...then he...' The present participle is an open form expressing a contemporaneity of condition, 'breathing' (πνέων). In other words, it was *when* Agamemnon followed the course of necessity, *with* his mind having a δυσσεβῆ τροπαίαν ἄναγνον ἀνίερον, *then* he reversed his thinking to utter recklessness. The emphasis is not so much on necessity as on the temporal sequence and the change into 'utter recklessness', which will be seen to be an important phrase. φρονεῖν refers back to the hymn to Zeus (164, 174, 175, 176), but here the qualification παντότολμον is relevant. For there is also an emphasis on the excessive nature, the overvaluing, of his power of φρονεῖν which allows him to perform the unholy, impure, act. It is a παρακοπά (223), a 'false-coining' – the sense of false value and false signification is inherent – that is the first cause of the trouble, πρωτοπήμων (223) 'and it emboldens men to base plans'. So then, it is a false valuing, a false definition, an excess that leads to the moral ambiguity of the necessity[58] of Iphigeneia's sacrifice.

She, however, has not yet been named (nor will be): for it is still the relationship between her and Agamemnon that is stressed in the alliterative θυτὴρ γένεσθαι θυγατρός (224–5), and γυναικοποίνων draws attention to the aspect of sexual difference once more. As with τεκνόποινος (155), there is a play on the active and passive senses of this last adjective. It implies on the one hand 'to punish a woman' (Helen); on the other, it implies 'to be punished by a woman' (i.e. Clytemnestra). The narrative maintains a strong tension between the sexes, as it does between the generations, in the reversals of revenge. The tension between the generations is further stressed as fatherhood becomes a central motif in the lead up to the moment of sacrifice. πατρῷους, contrasted with παρθένειον, (as above 209–10), the repetition of πάτηρ, πατρός, πατρός (231, 244, 245), and the concentration on the pathos of the earlier life in the house, all

---

[58] Lloyd-Jones places Agamemnon's tragedy precisely in the tension between the necessity of sacrifice and the παρακοπά which follows (1962, 196ff.).

emphasise the relationship between father and daughter in the house (οἴκοις, 237), which stands in contrast to the military expedition, πολέμων ἀρωγάν καὶ προτέλεια ναῶν (226–7). As Froma Zeitlin has commented,[59] the memory of the sacrifice pervades the play, not only as a significant point of action, a cause of future narrative developments, but also as a model, the 'prototype'[60] of the other murders. The corrupt nature of the sacrifice is particularly noticeable both in the understated horror of δίκαν χιμαίρας (232) – it is, of course, precisely the manner in which she is not like a goat that is important – and also in the *force* of the action, βιᾳ χαλινῶν τ' ἀναύδῳ μένει (238), which is in such pathetic contrast with her father's previously joyful τριτόσπονδον...παιῶνα. The libation to Zeus Soter will be parodied in a corrupted form by Clytemnestra over the body of her husband. The significance of the third libation will be discussed there.

ἀταύρωτος (245) is an interesting choice of word for the maiden – a metaphor presumably from farming, 'not taken to the bull', i.e. 'virgin'. This draws attention not only to the corrupted sacrifice – she is being treated literally as a cow for sacrifice – but also to the corrupted nature of her relationship with her father, who, instead of giving his daughter in marriage exchange ('to the bull'), has given her in sacrifice (like a bull?) for the expedition.

The moment of sacrifice, however, towards which the narrative has been progressing, is avoided:

$$\text{τὰ δ' ἔνθεν οὔτ' εἶδον οὔτ' ἐννέπω} \tag{248}$$

As with the watchman's βοῦς ἐπὶ γλώσσῃ, the moment of fear, the naming of fear is passed over in silence, by a refusal to speak. The *telos* of the sacrificial narrative is hinted at, however, in a deliberately mysterious and horrific way:

$$\text{τέχναι δὲ Κάλχαντος οὐκ ἄκραντοι} \tag{249}$$

The double negative seems to distance the language even further from a direct statement of the event. Indeed, the obscure passage of general conclusion which the chorus draw from this narrative is also to do with the nature of events in general: it is a statement drawn from and about narration as well as the narrative: 'It is for[61] those who have experienced to know.' We should not necessarily introduce a notion

---

[59] 1965, p. 466.

[60] Ibid. p. 489. But this is not to say that it is a prescriptive, controlling, model: there is no paradigm without syntagm – the play of differences cannot be reduced by an appeal to 'model'.

[61] Note that δίκα 'tilts', ἐπιρρέπει, as opposed to the 'balance' one normally associates with Justice. There is from the force of ἐπι- a sense of conflict even in this general statement, which picks up the language of the hymn to Zeus, suggesting perhaps the bias of the process of παθοῦσιν μαθεῖν.

of 'suffering leading to wisdom'. The Greek words are barer and are more closely linked to τὰ δ' ἔνθεν οὔτ' εἶδον οὔτ' ἐννέπω and are connected to the idea of a μάρτυς, one who sees with his own eyes or hears with his own ears, as being the only reliable source of evidence.[62]

From this statement about knowledge of experienced events, the chorus move to a consideration of the possible knowledge of events in narrative, the passage towards the future, which recalls the foretelling of Calchas:

τὸ μέλλον δ'
ἐπεὶ γένοιτ' ἂν κλύοις   (251–2)

'But what is going/likely to be, when it has happened, you may hear.' An obscure sentence; the vagueness is marked by the shift into a non-indicative form, expressing the doubt we have seen throughout the chorus and the prologue; a doubt which again slips to fear, foreboding, grief when considering the passage from present to future:

προχαιρέτω
ἴσον δὲ τῷ προστένειν   (252–3)

Before the event, 'greeting' is equal to 'grieving'. This is because (γάρ, 254) 'the future is always revealed by the morrow'.[63] Is prediction, then, doomed to complete vagueness, as expressed in the interchangeability of opposites χαιρέτω/στένειν? Here the narrative is expressed in the imagery of light (see also Clytemnestra's opening words below) linking narrative and the process of communication together in their parallel desire for clarity as imaged in the move from darkness to light. And the chorus conclude their extraordinary and complex *parodos* with another prayer, the optative mood, a general expression:

πέλοιτο δ' οὖν τἀπὶ τούτοισιν εὖ πρᾶξις...   (255)

The chorus' struggle to link past, present, and future in a coherent narrative (of cause and effect) constructs, then, a complex dialectic of control and indeterminacy. The control offered by mantic prediction, sign reading, the prophetic present, slides in tension with the uncertain openness of language, particularly the language of the seer himself, where the exchange of sign for sign (in the chain of language)

---

[62] For the connection between eye-witness/first-hand knowledge and Greek epistemological vocabulary, particularly as forming modern critical vocabulary, see Rorty 1980, *passim*. I shall be considering this primacy of empiricism in greater depth in Ch. 2.

[63] Méautis, quoted by Fraenkel, p. 144: an apparent tautology, or at least denial of the possibility of prediction, which picks up 251–2, where the possibility of hearing only after the event would seem to place 'prediction' at risk, certainly to throw doubt on its possibility of success.

is not the simple economic exchange that 'cashing a metaphor' metaphorically may suggest.[64] Finally, the very possibility of pre- diction seems subsumed in the statement that the future is knowable only when past/passed, as, indeed, the chorus earlier had drifted into the reductiveness of what I termed a 'narrative tautology'. The search for the control offered by clarity of communication slides in tension with the gaps and repressions of the unsaid, the riddling, the blocked answers. Even the postulation of the control of the divine above the slidings and uncertainties is also part of the over- determining and over-determined structuring of divine motivation of events, particularly in the uncertain relation between the motivating forces of Zeus, Artemis. So apparent assurance of statement drifts towards the uncertainties of the optative mood, into vagueness, hopes and fear as expressions of the linking of past, present and future. Now the chorus at the end of the great *parodos*, faced still with the gap between present and future, the uncertain meaning of the past, can resort once again only to a simple and general prayer that all may be well. A prayer that marks indeterminacy in its desire for control. The *parodos* ends, then, in a tone of φόβος, ἐλπίς, ἀπορία, similar to the end of the prologue, a tone made up of tensions in language (constituted in oppositions) and the desire for their solution.

Vive la différence!

The continuation of the chorus in iambics and the short scene that follows ('the beacon-speeches scene') further investigates what I have outlined as the problematic of language in the prologue and the *parodos*, particularly in terms of the tension between showing and saying and the oppositions of male, female; light, dark. First, as Clytemnestra prepares to speak, we see the debate set up within the terms of sexual difference, as indeed the scene will end with a reference (351) to this opposition of male and female, framing the speeches of Clytemnestra. κράτος (258) refers back to the watchman's ὧδε γὰρ κρατεῖ: 'power' is an odd word to use of a woman (it is the focus of the sexual tension) and it is immediately explained (259–60). The hermeneutic sentence:

δίκη γάρ ἐστι: the answer promised.

φωτὸς ἀρχηγοῦ: partial answer and 'jammed' answer; the genitive case.

τίειν γυναῖκ': reformulation of the 'riddle' ἥκω σεβίζων σόν κτλ., specifying the sexual tension.

[64] I am grateful to John Henderson for helping me to formulate this point.

ἐρημωθέντος ἄρσενος θρόνου: reason for the answer given in the form of a lack.

The juxtaposition of γυναῖκ', delayed to start the verse line, with ἄρσενος, the term used in medicine, grammar, and philosophy for the male principle,[65] constitutes the implicit oddness of the juxtaposition σόν, Κλυταιμήστρα, κράτος explicitly in terms of sexual roles. Her power is because of the lack not just of the ruler but of the 'male'. The subtext constructs the diagram φωτός – $\frac{γυναῖκ'}{ἄρσενος}$.

The chorus seek for news. The phrase they use to describe Clytemnestra's reason for sacrificing is markedly odd: εὐαγγέλοισιν ἐλπίσιν. εὐάγγελος refers back to εὐαγγέλου φανέντος ὀρφναίου πυρός (21), but is here very oddly predicated of ἐλπίσιν. It seems to point to a link, between on the one hand the problematic of showing/saying, the difficulty of finding clarity in language (εὐάγγελος, as in 21, implying the possibility of its opposite) and on the other hand the difficulty of the transition from present to future, the problematic of clarity in narrative, which is the locus of ἐλπίς. This link between narrative and language revolves around the power of language to predict (curse, define) and hence, if accurate and absolute, to give accurate and absolute knowledge of events to come, to repress that doubt and lack of control felt by the chorus. The theatre of narrative is 'the theatre of language'.[66]

Scholars have interpreted this phrase differently. For example, Schütz: 'εὐαγγέλοισιν ἐλπίσιν pro ἐλπίδι εὐαγγελίας.' Faced with the difficulty of the expression, a break in the apparently transparent flow of sense, a juxtaposition of normally unjuxtaposable terms, this critic merely translates the words into a readily assimilable expression, he normalises. So too Paley: 'The more correct and logical enunciation would have been εἴτε κεδνόν τι πεπυσμένη εὐαγγέλια θύεις, εἴτε μή τι πεπυσμένη ὑπὸ ἐλπίδος ἐπαίρει εἰς θυσίαν.' The words 'more correct' show the attempt in his reading to normalise the language of Aeschylus to a preconceived structure, to limit the play of language to his view of 'logical enunciation'. Schütz is followed by Fraenkel and Denniston–Page and many others translate similarly.[67]

Clytemnestra picks up the chorus' use of εὐαγγέλοισιν and ἐλπίς and puns on their use of εὔφρων:

εὐάγγελος μέν, ὥσπερ ἡ παροιμία,
ἕως γένοιτο μητρὸς εὐφρόνης πάρα   (264–5)

[65] See Lloyd 1966, *passim*.
[66] M. Lynn-George's phrase, privately communicated.
[67] Headlam's translation is an exception. See also the gloss of Winnington-Ingram 1983, pp. 103–4, who notes the echoes of the watchman's speech here.

Her language also links the imagery of light and language again, and refers back to the chorus' hope for clarity (254), and their wish that 'all may be well', and also to the watchman's speech (e.g. 21, 30). Her pun εὔφρων/εὐφρόνης is important because 'in a play on words...the word is...only a sound image, to which one meaning or another is attached'.[68] That is, the word is treated as a signifier,[69] and a signifier which joins in play 'normally' separated meanings (signifieds). In marking the shifting relation between signifier and signified, it functions as a stimulus to the deconstruction of the signifier–signified relation in the sign. Furthermore, in her deliberate recognition of the play in the construction of language, she indicates an attempt to be the master of words, to exert some control over the *glissement* of meaning by the deliberate act of recognition and deliberate use of ambiguity.[70] This is paralleled by her two long speeches that follow (281–316), (320–50), the expression of her power which organised the controlled sending of a message across the world through the use of the beacons, the signifiers.

The chorus retort, however:

πῶς φῄς; πέφευγε τοὔπος ἐξ ἀπιστίας   (268)

'The "word" escapes, and has escaped, because of lack of πίστις.' This points precisely to the heuristic gap between speaker and listener, as developed in the prologue and *parodos*: the word, the utterance, once spoken escapes the listener. The reason is ἀπιστία. πίστις is related etymologically to πειθώ and is a closely related concept: if ἔπος or the speaker of ἔπος has πειθώ, in the listener is engendered πίστις: it is the result in the listener of the bridging of the gap between speaker and listener: πίστις is that which indicates assurance, confidence, surety.

Clytemnestra restates that Troy is in the hands of the Greeks, and adds ἤ τορῶς λέγω; (269). τορός, similar to ἐτητύμως, is as we saw at 26, a key term: to speak 'precisely', 'clearly', 'piercingly'. It will recur in three further significant places in the play: 616, 1062, 1162. In the first two examples, it is in the adjectival form predicated of the word ἑρμήνευς – that is, precisely the figure whose locus is the

---

[68] S. Freud, Vol. VIII, Standard Edition, *Jokes and their Relation to the Unconscious*, p. 46.

[69] Saussure defines signifier as 'sound-image' (1959 (1916), p. 67).

[70] This is a common trait in, for example, Shakespearean 'villains', whose violence is as much verbal as physical – e.g. Richard III with Ann, Iago with Othello. It is in societies' interest (it even constitutes society, some might say) to attempt to maintain rigid distinctions in naming, the use of language. It is not surprising to see the 'villain' who stands apart from society, as having a special relationship to language, particularly as the powerful distorter, manipulator. This, perhaps, adds to the paradoxical attraction of these characters (including Clytemnestra?). Freud was well aware of the pleasure of licensed transgression of law/language.

gap between utterance and receiver of utterance, the 'interpreter':
significantly, on both occasions it is used with reference to a third
party understanding, interpreting the speech of Clytemnestra. In the
third case, it is used for the chorus' own sudden insight into the
meaning of Cassandra's words: τί τόδε τορὸν ἄγαν ἔπος ἐφημίσω
(1162). In each of these cases it is sited within the function of
communication as the quality of precision of language necessary for
complete understanding, capable of stopping the *glissement*, sliding
of signs, capable of producing a single meaning. Here (269) it is used
precisely to stop the escaping of the word, to pierce it through.

The chorus begin to cry for joy and Clytemnestra comments:

εὖ γὰρ φρονοῦντος ὄμμα σοῦ κατηγορεῖ   (271)

κατηγορεῖ is a strong word to use; it means to 'speak against',
'accuse' (this is its most common usage): later, it comes to mean
in logic 'to say positively', 'predicate'. Here, as at *Sept.* 439,
following Schadewaldt,[71] Fraenkel translates 'gives evidence' and in
the notes of his edition 'indicates'. The chorus' eyes 'show' that the
chorus is 'well-minded', εὖ φρονεῖν – this picks up in particular the
repetition of φρεν-/φρον- (174–6) – but even so the 'showing' is
expressed through a word of *speech* (cf. ἀγορεύω). The use of a word
of speaking to express the relation between the eye (i.e. tears) and
thought (i.e. the reason for the tears) once again puts into question
the nature of the signifier–signified relation in language. Indeed, in
Clytemnestra's description of the passage of the beacon fires, we see
a similar use of words of speaking (particularly ἀγγέλλω) to express
the transmission of light from one beacon to another: οἱ δ' ἀντέλαμψαν
καὶ παρήγγειλαν (294), παρῆκεν ἀγγέλου μέρος (291), φάος...οὐκ
ἠναίνετο φρουρά (300–1), σέλας παραγγείλασα (289). This juxtaposition of terms of light and speech serves to heighten the opposition
between direct, visible communication, and language.

Significantly, the chorus respond:

ἦ γάρ τι πιστόν ἐστι τῶνδέ σοι τέκμαρ[72]   (272)

πιστόν refers back to ἀπιστίας (268) and τέκμαρ, which continues
the legal-logical vocabulary of κατηγορεῖ, juxtaposed to Clytemnestra's previous remark, questions the nature of the process of signification that she has asserted. This notion of 'proof', τέκμαρ,
will become increasingly important in the dialogue that follows
(273–7) and indeed throughout the trilogy.

The chorus suggest first that the basis of her proof is the appearance
(φάσματα, root *φάω/φαίνω) of dreams, that which is seen. εὐπιθῆ

---

[71] *Hermes* 81 (1936) p. 42. See also Headlam ad loc.
[72] Fraenkel's text – it makes little difference to what I want to say here to read as Page.

continues the connection between proof and πειθώ. There is a certain patronising quality in the prefix εὐ-, 'easily persuading', particularly with the strong term σέβεις, 'revere', which Clytemnestra dismisses brusquely:

οὐ δόξαν ἂν λάβοιμι βριζούσης φρενός (275)

δόξαν can mean a 'vision' (see 421) as well as 'estimation', 'opinion', 'expectation', its more common usages. This ambiguity is significant here. For it appears first that δόξαν picks up φάσματ' and means simply 'I wouldn't take up, use, a vision...', but the dependent genitive phrase βριζούσης φρενός implies the senses of δόξαν more of 'estimation', 'opinion', 'expectation': 'I wouldn't use the expectation of a sleeping mind.' Clytemnestra at first appears to agree with the terminology of the chorus, but then qualifies it radically.

The chorus suggest a rumour, φάτις (cf. 9),[73] has 'fattened' Clytemnestra. She is equally dismissive.

παιδὸς νέας ὡς κάρτ' ἐμωμήσω φρένας (277)

φρένας at the end of the line is in the same metrical position as φρενός and φάτις in the previous two lines, and, marked by this repetition and alliteration, it has a strong emphasis and refers us back to 174–6 and the hymn to Zeus. The opposition between judging from appearances (φάσμα – itself often opposed to reality as 'illusion'), which the chorus impute to Clytemnestra, and judging by φρονεῖν, by which Clytemnestra rebukes the chorus, as the basis for acceptable proof, becomes important particularly because of its significance in the debate about paternity. For the role of the mother in procreation is the perceived, visible function (hence the obvious relation between mother and child, which is precisely what Apollo attacks in the *Eumenides* 657ff.) whereas 'fathers are not self-evident as mothers are. "Genitor" is a social status.'[74] The role of the father in procreation is a culturally assumed and culturally defined status, that which is *conceived* rather than *perceived*. φρονεῖν, then, the power of conceiving in thought, is that by which paternity, the non-visible given, essential to the continuation of patriarchal society, obtains, and, as such, it is the function of Zeus, the patriarchal divinity, τὸν φρονεῖν βροτοὺς ὁδώσαντα (176–7) 'to straighten the path for mortals to φρονεῖν'. The function of proof by mere vision is what the chorus impute to Clytemnestra, as a female, and what she rejects by her repetition of φρενός/φρένας, the male principle of proof. The jurors

---

[73] Here, φάτις seems to imply speech which may be true but probably is not, speech without a basis of proof, 'women's speech'.

[74] Barnes 1973, p. 68.

of the *Eumenides* will be asked to decide on (in all its senses) female conception.

The chorus ask:

καὶ τίς τόδ' ἐξίκοιτ' ἄν ἀγγέλων τάχος;   (280)

Clytemnestra's long speech in reply starts by continuing the per-sonalisation implied by the use of the word of speaking (ἀγγέλων) and the pronoun τίς, in the name of Ἥφαιστος (281), the first word of her speech, but it becomes quickly apparent that what is sent is not a message in speech[75] – we must wait until the next scene for the true ἄγγελος – but light: ἐκπέμπων σέλας (281). As Clytemnestra's narration continues and the light is passed from place to place, despite (or perhaps because of) the conflation of words of speaking and words of showing (as mentioned above) and the personalisation in such phrases as παρῆκεν ἀγγέλου μέρος,[76] it appears that the basis for her proof is the passage of the signals from place to place, the chain itself. Although an expression of the great power of Clytemnestra, it is firmly fixed in the visual mode, the mode of showing: it is merely the *appearance* of the fire that she demonstrates.

πλέον καίουσα τῶν εἰρημένων   (301)

'Burning more than the things that had been said.' Fraenkel translates with Weil, 'Custodes dicuntur flammam accendisse etiam maiorem quam iussi erant.' But notice how the juxtaposition of καίουσα and τῶν εἰρημένων points to the different systems of communication. Indeed, the concluding lines of the speech express this in a most marked way:

τέκμαρ τοιοῦτον σύμβολόν τε σοὶ λέγω
ἀνδρὸς παραγγείλαντος ἐκ Τροίας ἐμοί   (315–16)

The conjunction of τέκμαρ (which implies that she has given the answer to the question of 272) and σύμβολον, which recalls the prologue's tensions, links the opposition of perception and conception to the opposition of showing and saying. Her speech is a proof and a sign of ἀνδρὸς παραγγείλαντος ἐκ Τροίας. The lack of an object for παραγγείλαντος is noticeable. As well as its most common usage 'encourage by words', 'exhort', παραγγέλλω can mean in a more technical sense 'pass the watchword'. This sense of passing a desemanticised term along a line is good for the system of beacons. As with a password, the message itself is incapable of generating meaning; its signification comes from contextualisation, a code. It must be known before. The beacon, then, indicates only the fact that

---

[75] As the watchman had suggested φέρουσαν φάτιν (9).
[76] The light is expressly in 'the place of a messenger': the contrast depends simply on the possession of speech.

the watchword has been passed: the lack of an object for παραγγείλαντος indicates this lack of a message in language. Clytemnestra's narration relates merely the visible connection between Troy and the palace, because there is no message in language to relate. Clytemnestra can only say how the message shows.

The chorus, commenting on this speech, express their astonishment and desire to hear the story again. They call Clytemnestra here (317) ὦ γύναι, 'woman'. Previously, they have addressed her only as βασίλεια or by her name. After the next speech, however, where we read, prefixed by the term οἶμαι, an imagined narrative of what the beacon might mean in a referential sense, that is, a description of the sack of the city, a 'cashing out' of the significance of the light in language, the chorus say:

> γύναι, κατ' ἄνδρα σώφρον' εὐφρόνως λέγεις
> ἐγὼ δ' ἀκούσας πιστά σου τεκμήρια   (351–2)

After the first speech, they are unwilling to accept the visible proof – the address ὦ γύναι points to the connection between the visible mode of proof and the female which was implied in 272–7. After the second speech, where the light is regarded as a full message in language, where the connotation of the beacon is apparently decoded, the chorus call her 'woman' again, γύναι, only to qualify it by κατ' ἄνδρα σώφρον' εὐφρόνως λέγεις. Now Clytemnestra speaks *like a man*, she is in possession of φρένες, εὐφρόνως. *This* is sufficient proof for the chorus, πιστὰ τεκμήρια.

As the first of Clytemnestra's speeches, then, says how the message shows and traces the passage of the signifier, so the second of her lengthy addresses tells what such a message might be thought to contain. The fact that she could not ('in fact') know what she is describing (a fact which has worried critics) serves to mark all the more vividly the separation of the signifier (the beacon signal) and the signified (the beacon message) in her two speeches. Or rather it serves to mark the arbitrary connection between signifier and signified in Clytemnestra's manipulation of signs (language and beacons).

So the stichomythia and the two long speeches of Clytemnestra which make up this episode juxtapose two modes of proof, of finding πίστις, of τορῶς λέγειν, the one connected with the female and based on the visible mode, showing; the other connected with the male, referring back to Zeus Xenios, and based on the noetic mode, on φρονεῖν, the power of conceptualisation in language. The chorus return explicitly to this interplay of male and female with regard to the beacons' message at 475–87, after they have considered some of the further implications of what they have been told:

πυρὸς δ' ὑπ' εὐαγγέλου
πόλιν διήκει θοὰ
βάξις. εἰ δ' ἐτήτυμος,
τίς οἶδεν, ἤ τι θεῖόν ἐστί πη ψύθος;
τίς ὧδε παιδνὸς ἤ φρενῶν κεκομμένος,
φλογὸς παραγγέλμασιν
νέοις πυρωθέντα καρδίαν, ἔπειτ'
    ἀλλαγᾷ λόγου καμεῖν;
γυναικὸς αἰχμᾷ πρέπει
πρὸ τοῦ φανέντος χάριν ξυναινέσαι.
πιθανὸς ἄγαν ὁ θῆλυς ὅρος ἐπινέμεται
ταχύπορος. ἀλλὰ ταχύμορον
γυναικογήρυτον ὄλλυται κλέος   (475–87)

First we note that although they describe the fire as εὐαγγέλου, they still remain uncertain as to its import: εἰ δ' ἐτήτυμος – this refers back to the construction in the prologue σημαίνω τορῶς...εἰ (26ff.) and to the desire in the hymn to Zeus εἰ...ἐτητύμως κτλ. (166ff.). The doubt remains implicit in the possibility of predication contrary to εὐ-αγγέλου. The juxtaposition of φρενῶν κεκομμένος and φλογὸς παραγγέλμασιν...πυρωθέντα marks the distinction we are tracing: to follow the 'exhortation' or 'password' of fire, you must have lost, precisely, φρενῶν. ἔπειτ' ἀλλαγᾷ λόγου καμεῖν by its assertion of the future (ex-)change of language points to the lack of language of the beacon lights, or the story Clytemnestra imagines the light to have brought, and it also presages the real messenger speech – λόγος, 'speech', 'language' is opposed to the 'password', παράγγελμα, of the beacons. This opposition is then sited in terms of sexual difference: πρέπει, 'it is fitting', followed by πρὸ τοῦ φανέντος, refers back also to the process of 'showing' and the stars in the sky (cf. 6, 30), and after the repeated question τίς; τίς; γυναικός as first word has a strong emphasis as at least the partial answer to the question – as if 'woman' were the one so 'childlike' or so lacking in φρενῶν to get excited too early because of a 'password of fire' rather than the 'exchange of logos'. γυναικός is further picked up in γυναικογήρυτον, 'woman-spoken'. 485, however, is as Page notes laconically in his apparatus 'obscurus'. It would appear that the chorus is rejecting Clytemnestra's attitude because of some (female) quality of her approach to the message – a connection between the exchange of signs and female (as opposed to male) qualities. Some readers will no doubt find the problem of ὅρος finally insurmountable (as do Denniston–Page). I hope, however, to offer a more detailed analysis that at least attempts to read the text as it stands within the context of the narrative. ὅρος can mean 'definition', 'limit', 'rule'. The phrase seems to imply 'a female's laying down, saying that such a thing is such and such', a reading that Denniston–Page reject as 'so odd, crabbed and obscure', and Fraenkel dismisses as unparalleled.[77] It is, however, as I hope to show, a summing up in the discourse we have been considering. Female determination as evinced by Clytemnestra's description of the passage of the beacons, which in some ways reduced language as a means of communication to the visible passage of light, can be called πιθανός, 'likely to persuade', precisely because it bridges (as we have seen *peitho* is intended to do) the heuristic gap between addresser and addressee; indeed, it removes, erases that gap. But it is ἄγαν πιθανός because by this unification, this reduction to a single signifier (the beacon) of the difference in which meaning is constituted, we have not the intended single meaning, the limitation implied by ὅρος, but rather, as the second speech of explanation of Clytemnestra showed, we have a complete open-endedness of meanings – ἐπινέμεται, 'it spreads over'.[78] This reading is to indicate that Schütz's interpretation of ὁ θῆλυς ὅρος can lead to a recognition that the generalisation offers more than 'very acrimonious...thinly veiled language' (Fraenkel) to be applied to Clytemnestra as a woman in government, but rather is also a comment more specifically applicable to the scene which has just passed; it also leads into the opening of the next scene, where we see the questions asked again: What sort of message was it? How is the messenger's message different?. Furthermore it hints towards the ἄγαν πιθανός woman's talk of the carpet scene. For there, as with

[77] Denniston–Page agree at least provisionally with Fraenkel's analysis of the syntax, but dismiss his translation of ὅρος and find the problem of ὅρος finally insurmountable. Fraenkel glosses ὁ θῆλυς ὅρος with τὸ ὑπὸ γυναικὸς ὡρισμένον, but demands then the translation 'rule of conduct', despite recognising the use of ὁρίζειν as 'decree', 'lay down' (cf. Wilamowitz on Eur. *Ion* 1222) even in the *Oresteia* itself (*Cho.* 927). Fraenkel's own gloss would seem to argue against the certainty with which he rejects the less specific 'ruling', 'determination', in favour of his own precise 'rule of conduct', referring to the sacrifices of thanksgiving. The oxymoronic conjunction of ὅρος 'boundary-(stone)' and ἐπινέμεται, 'transgress', 'graze over', 'spread', with its suggestive range of possible metaphorisation seems a peculiarly Aeschylean conjunction to me.

[78] The normal interpretation translates 'spreads abroad', referring to the spread of rumour over the city, cf. 476–7. There is, however, a considerable difference between ὅρος and κλέος, which should not be conflated to harmonise the expression into a simple commonplace about women's gossip: κλέος is an added slur to colour ὅρος, drawing its force from but not simply repeating the 'sexist' commonplace. Or one could say rather that the use of the odd word ὅρος extends the possible reference to the previous scene, where a woman's determination was so important.

Headlam notes that ἐπινέμεσθαι was 'so commonly applied' to fire 'that the original metaphor was forgotten'. If this is the case, the overlaid associations between 'fire' (i.e. the beacons) and 'a woman's determination' here make this usage very much a 'live metaphor' with reference to the beacon-speeches.

the beacon-speeches scene, we will see Clytemnestra's power through the manipulation of signification.

I will shortly show how this conclusion is approached in the lyrics of the chorus – but first there are three remaining points I wish to make about Clytemnestra's speech (320–50), which echoes in its tale of capture the language of the *parodos*, the tale of the expedition's constitution and departure. First there is an emphasis on the reciprocal nature of the action which I mentioned with regard to the active/ passive senses of τεκνόποινος, γυναικόποινον, and which will return in the first stasimon. This is seen particularly in the phrase οὔ τἄν ἑλόντες αὖθις ἀνθαλοῖεν ἄν. This use of ἀντι- with regard to the opposition and exclusion of revenge has been commented on above (p. 13). There is also a subtext of reversal, things twisting back on themselves and repeating themselves in opposite forms: κάμψαι διαύλου (344), ἀναμπλάκητος (345). This, too, is seen again in the lyrics that follow. Secondly, the course of praying that something will not happen which promptly is seen to occur, is a process similar to that seen with Calchas' οἷον μή τις κτλ. (131ff.). Praying for that which does not occur, praying against that which does happen: such attempts at ordering, directing the future point to the desire for narrative control – but a desire which is blocked. Thirdly, there are images of mixing, particularly of confused sound, 'shouting', 'groaning'. The physical violence of the sack finds a parallel in the violence of its vocal utterances – sounds which have no meaning (although expressive of violent emotions).

Clytemnestra's first exchange with the chorus, then, in its discussion of the beacon-signal is not merely the rhetorical colouring of 'the powerful and disturbing character of the queen'. For Clytemnestra's manipulation of language and her manipulation of the beacon-chain and the signification of the beacon-chain (her manipulation of signs) continue and develop the oppositions and terms of the prologue and *parodos*, as, indeed, do the specific determinations of the difference between Clytemnestra's two long speeches (and the difference between conditions of proof) in terms also of the difference between the sexes (in the use and exchange of signs). The play of difference between male/female, saying/showing, signifier/signified in the exchanges of this scene not only recalls the prologue and the *parodos*, then, but also looks forward importantly, as we shall see, to the exchanges between Clytemnestra and the messenger, and the carpet-scene itself.

The explanatory end?

The long first stasimon which follows the beacon-speeches scene, further retells a narrative of the events surrounding the Trojan War in the light of the information that the queen has forwarded, as the chorus attempt again to order a pattern of events. Does the fall of Troy really constitute an end? Is it an end through which a certain structuring can be perceived?

The desire for narrative control, knowledge of the course of events in a readable sequence, cause and effect, is the point which the chorus begin to develop in the stasimon. First in the anapaestic prelude, they state boldly that Zeus the king and Night have thrown a net around Troy. The net will return again as an image to describe the woven material thrown around Agamemnon. The chorus recognise and state the success of the motive force they outlined in the *parodos*:

> Δία τοι ξένιον μέγαν αἰδοῦμαι
> τὸν τάδε πράξαντ᾽, ἐπ᾽ Ἀλεξάνδρῳ
> τείνοντα πάλαι τόξον   (362–4)

But as the stasimon begins, while they recognise that the general force of Zeus is what the combatants may recognise, there is a slip into a less confident form of expression:

> Διὸς πλαγὰν ἔχουσιν εἰπεῖν,
> πάρεστιν τοῦτό γ᾽ ἐξιχνεῦσαι   (367–8)

τοῦτό γε: 'this at least' implies that there are other things that they cannot trace ('track' also implies that one is judging only from signs, marks). As Fraenkel puts it, 'many of his paths run in darkness undiscoverable'. ἔπραξεν ὡς ἔκρανεν (369) is a strange phrase. The editions either pass over it in silence or try to make the phrase mean 'he did as he ordained'. As Fraenkel says, before translating it 'he achieved it as he decreed', κραίνειν needs more detailed discussion. For the word used absolutely seems usually to mean *perficio* – Dindorf includes all examples of the word in Aeschylus under this heading. It sometimes means 'to fulfil what has been said', 'to make to happen' (Benveniste connects the word etymologically with *kara*, 'head', 'nodding' as symbol of divine assent and authority). This sense seems close to '*perficio*', but it is usually used with a word such as ἐφετμάς (*Il.* 5.508) or ἐέλδωρ (*Il.* 1.41.). It can also mean 'to hold sway over', again usually with an object (in the genitive, cf. Soph. *Aj.* 1050, Soph. *O.C.* 862). These three headings contain almost every example listed by Fraenkel and L.-S.-J. The two most interesting passages are both in Euripides, *Suppl.* 139 and *El.* 1248. At *Suppl.* 139 (τί δ᾽ εἶπ᾽ Ἀπόλλων, παρθένοις κραίνων γάμους), it makes excellent sense simply as *perficio*, 'to make to happen', and the specific sense of divine *ordinance* seems to have entered from the context and its juxtaposition to the name of Apollo. Similarly, at *El.* 1248 (τἀντεῦθεν δὲ χρὴ | πράσσειν ἃ Μοῖρα Ζεύς τ' ἔκρανε σοῦ πέρι) there is considerable qualification by the presence of Ζεύς, Μοῖρα, σοῦ πέρι (as well as the general context of the speech) which allows a general sense of 'have accomplished', 'made happen' without the specific idea of 'divine ordinance'. The phrase ἔπραξεν ὡς ἔκρανεν would seem to mean, then, something like 'he did as he made to happen'. As with τελεῖται δ' ἐς τὸ πεπρωμένον, there is a strong sense of narrative tautology, which expresses the chorus' inability to see the whole pattern of events, their doubts, as evinced by τοῦτό γε. Fraenkel's is the easier and more comfortable reading, an accustomed sense which gives precisely the pattern of cause (divine) and effect that the chorus seek for. It remains undercut, however, by the limitative γε and the possibility of tautology as the 'answer' to the question of cause and effect, narrative progression. Once more, the unsaid, the unexplained circumscribes and undercuts the postulation of a certainty.

The chorus go on to maintain the connection between divine and human action (369–75) in the form of divine punishment for transgression; transgression which may be in the form of excessive wealth (while the emphasis is on excess and transgression, the economic imagery should not be ignored.) The transgression of Paris who (398) will be seen to be the example of this generalisation, is against the laws of society laid down by divine force (of Zeus), and so he is seen to be punished by Zeus. The conjunction of βιᾶται and πειθώ is interesting: for normally[79] πειθώ is set in opposition to βία both in political and sexual contexts. As with πιθανὸς ἄγαν (whatever the sentence (485) may mean) there is a sense here of corrupted πειθώ, which may be seen as that which uses force (as Aegisthus later, and Paris here), that which falsifies the relationship between speaker and listener (πειθώ δόλια – as Clytemnestra addressing Agamemnon), or that which fails to bridge the gap between speaker and listener (ἔπειθον οὐδέν' οὐδέν (1212) – Cassandra). These lead up towards the πειθώ of Athene, as we shall see.

> λιτᾶν δ' ἀκούει μὲν οὔτις θεῶν   (396)

With the man who is οὐκ εὐσέβης no god listens: as we have seen, the function of the prayer and its fulfilment or denial expresses, like prediction, the desire for control of narrative events to come (not least in its assumption of a divine controlling force). Hence the relation

---

[79] See Buxton 1982, *passim*.

between the wish and the lack of assurance of the optative mood? Control *and* indeterminacy...

The long general passage is particularised:

οἷος καὶ Πάρις ἐλθὼν
ἐς δόμον τὸν Ἀτρειδᾶν
ᾔσχυνε ξενίαν τράπε-
ζαν κλοπαῖσι γυναικός   (399–402)

The emphasis remains still on the individual house and the shaming, corrupting, of the ξενίαν τράπεζαν. This refers us back to Zeus Xenios and points once more to the anti-social behaviour of Paris. The word γυναικός, as the last word of the sentence and antistrophe, has a considerable emphasis. Helen is once more not named: it is as her role as a woman in society, not as an individual, that she is depicted.

It is the woman on whom the chorus now concentrate: λιποῦσα... ἄγουσα...βέβακει. The subject is still unnamed and inherent only in the feminine form of the participles. ἀντίφερνον...φθοράν (406) indicates the corruption of their alliance: instead of (ἀντί again) the gift of the dowry which indicates the reciprocity of the alliance of marriage between groups, she brings 'destruction': as the marriage lacked προτέλεια as an indication of its socially acceptable and defined status, so too it lacks a dowry. The sense of willingly going beyond the rules of society is expressed neatly with ἄτλητα τλῆσα (408) 'she dared' – it is not merely the action that counts but the desire for it which must be stringently controlled by society:

The emergence of symbolic thought must have required that women, like words, should be things that were exchanged. In this new case, indeed, this was the only means of overcoming the contradiction by which the same woman was seen under two incompatible aspects: on the one hand as the object of personal desire...on the other as the subject of desire of others, and seen as such i.e. as the means of binding others through alliance with them.

To this very day mankind has always dreamed of seizing and fixing that fleeting moment when it was permissible to believe that the law of exchange could be evaded, that one could gain without losing, enjoy without sharing...a world in which one might *keep to oneself.*

The magic of this dream, its power to mould men's thoughts unbeknown to them arises precisely...because culture has opposed [it] at all times and at all places.[80]

---

[80] These three quotations which I have set in juxtaposition with the story of Helen and Paris, are from Lévi-Strauss' influential work on kinship (1969 (1949), pp. 496, 497, 491), a work which develops reciprocity and exchange as a basis for societies' orderings. The universality of his theories has been challenged particularly by certain

'Daring the not-to-be-dared' marks both the contract and the transgression of the orderings of sexual alliances, which are founded – and founder – on the reciprocities of exchange. Lévi-Strauss also says when considering certain New Caledonian and Malay Peninsula prohibitions, which all lead to disaster if transgressed:

These prohibitions are all thus reduced to a single common denominator: they all constitute a *misuse of language* and on this ground they are grouped together with the incest prohibition or with acts evocative of incest. What does this mean except that women themselves are treated as signs, which are *misused* when not put to the use reserved to signs, which is to be communicated?[81]

Helen and Clytemnestra, her sister, by their acts of adultery subvert the system of exchange by following their own private passions: which is seen in Clytemnestra's subversion of the exchange of language, both in the non-communication of language of the beacons' light, and in her deceitful *peitho*, which by her misrepresentations separates words from a referential function. Her actions *and* words are a misuse of the process of communication: as they say in New Caledonia: 'The evil *word* is adultery.'[82]

The significance of Helen's action is for the house:

ἰὼ ἰὼ δῶμα δῶμα   (410)

This speech is put in the mouths of the δόμων προφῆται, those who predict the future for the house. By the desire of/for (both objective and subjective genitive with πόθῳ, 'desire') her across the sea, it is the leadership of the house that is threatened, δόμων ἀνάσσειν (415). The evils are summed up as τὰ μὲν κατ᾽ οἴκους ἐφ᾽ ἑστίας ἄχη (427) and the general suffering that arises from the expedition is regarded as a suffering δόμῳ 'ν ἑκάστου (431). The army is depicted as a collection of individuals, each from an *oikos*; each death is seen as returning to a household εἰς ἑκάστου δόμους (435–6). Even the punishment of Zeus against sinners is aimed at households, βάλλεται γὰρ οἴκοις Διόθεν κεραυνός (469–70). We are not to consider, in other words, the actions of Paris, Helen, Clytemnestra, Agamemnon, Orestes, etc. as the actions simply of 'individuals'. Each person is conceived of within the *oikos* and the relationships therein defined.

ὀνειρόφαντοι...δόξαι (420–1) refers back to the ὀνείρων φάσματα...δόξαν (274–5). Here we find explicitly mentioned what

feminist critics (cf. e.g. Leacock 1981, esp. pp. 209ff.). I am more interested in the insights he can offer into the *Oresteia*. For reservations on the use of certain anthropological ideas in the reading of literature, see below pp. 184–5. See also Tanner 1980, 79–87, whose use of and doubts on Lévi-Strauss are admirable.
[81] 1969 (1949), p. 496.   [82] 1969 (1949), pp. 495–6.

was implicit there: φέρουσαι χάριν ματαίαν (421–2) The reason for the 'vain joy' is that vision, ὄψις, disappears, goes away, changes, παραλλάξασα διὰ χερῶν (424–5). On the one hand, this refers to the imagery common in classical poetry, since Odysseus in the underworld, of reaching out for a ghost or dream, only to have it slip through the grasp. παραλλάσσω, on the other hand, can mean 'interchange', 'overlap', or simply 'alter', and ὄψις is the normal, general term for 'sight', 'vision', the 'appearance' of someone/ something. In both senses it bears on the nature of the proof of the meaning of the beacons as suggested by the chorus and as evinced by the speech of Clytemnestra (282–315). The expression is applicable to the desires of dreams, a paradigmatic example of the insubstantiality of vision, *and* to the modality of the visible in general. The modality of the visible is likened to the insubstantiality of dreams, and thus again implies the doubts of the chorus concerning the nature of the message and its proof offered by Clytemnestra. This also prepares us for the epode's conclusion.

The chorus continue (433–55) to consider the effects of the war on the houses and people left behind, the disastrous outcome of Helen's actions. The imagery of exchange, pointing both to the reciprocal nature of the action that we have noted before, and to the corrupt nature of the alliance of Helen and Paris, is very strongly drawn here: ἀντὶ δὲ φωτῶν τεύχη (434–5), ὁ χρυσαμοιβὸς Ἄρης (438, a marvellous phrase, picking up the economic imagery, and the sense of 'scales', 'weighing': cf. 815), ἀντήνορος σποδοῦ (442–3). And the cause is again stated forcefully διαὶ γυναικός (448–9). As we might expect by now, Helen is not named but called 'woman'. This leads to the murmurings at home and the feeling of misgivings we have seen in the prologue and earlier choric lyrics:

> μένει δ' ἀκοῦσαί τί μου
> μέριμνα νυκτηρεφές　　　　　　　　　　　　　　　　(459–60)

νυκτηρεφές continues the imagery of light and dark and μένει recalls μίμνει γάρ... (154–5); and the οὐκ ἄσκοποι θεοί (462) and κελαιναί...Ἐρινύες (462–3) refer back to the suggested pattern of divine reaction of 367–97, and the by now overwhelming sense that someone is to be punished for a wrong. It is, however, an open-ended equation: we have seen the punishment of Paris, but now we wait (hence the misgiving) to complete the open-ended question of the punishment and sin of Agamemnon and the army.

The antistrophe ends with a prayer (by now, the accustomed mode of concluding a passage of doubt and misgiving), a prayer for the 'middle road', to avoid the success (excess) that leads to φθόνος.

We have seen, then, a discussion of the sin of Paris and his punishment, the disastrous war following on the act of adultery of Helen (striking at the very roots of society). We have read the expressions of the misery of those at home during the war, the ranks of dead left behind in Troy, the worry of impending disaster. We have read a conspicuous lack of praise or thanks for the victory that Clytemnestra has proclaimed, bar the sobering recognition of the hand of god – at least in the destruction. And we have discussed the continuing mistrust of the proof of visibility that has been offered at least in part for the celebration. What interpretative moves are required, then, to follow the commentators' claim that the epode is a 'reversal of tone' and attitude on the part of the chorus? One need not resort to 'psychological speculations'[83] to explain these final remarks of the chorus, but merely note how similar oppositions of language obtain in the epode to those in the scene and chorus preceding it, and to remember that the slide from surety and certitude to misgiving and doubt has been a recurring movement in the play, defining much of its 'dark tone'. The end of the first stasimon, then, traces the uncertainty surrounding the fall of Troy, and an uncertainty as to its status as an end-point in the narrative of cause and effect.

The truth, the whole truth, and nothing but the truth?

After the first scene, which revolved around the arrival and nature of the beacons' message in light, the second scene is a 'messenger scene', with the arrival of a herald from the scattered fleet of the Argives to announce, as the beacon had for Clytemnestra, the capture of Troy. The juxtaposition of these two scenes of messages significantly precedes the carpet scene, where a further drama of language is played in Clytemnestra's victory in *peitho*. For, as we will see, this messenger scene is not the staging of a simple, transparent exchange of language – the messenger is often regarded by critics as bringing a clear and direct, if heightened, representation of events – but rather it points the gaps, confusions, and doubts that we have seen surrounding the use of language in the *Oresteia*.

The scene opens with a speech which marks the juxtaposition (as messages) of the herald with language and the beacon-signal. After the closing lines of the first stasimon, which drew the opposition between male and female in terms of their use and exchange of signs,

---

[83] Denniston–Page's phrase here. See Kranz for an example of such speculation; or Winnington-Ingram 1983, pp. 209–16 for a more interesting characterisation of the chorus.

these opening sentences also recall the chorus' imputation to Clytemnestra of judging by dreams (like a woman?), as the rejection of dreams as set against a true basis of proof is made explicit:

τάχ᾿ εἰσόμεσθα λαμπάδων φαεσφόρων
φρυκτωριῶν τε καὶ πυρὸς παραλλαγάς,
εἴτ᾿ οὖν ἀληθεῖς εἴτ᾿ ὀνειράτων δίκην
τερπνὸν τόδ᾿ ἐλθὸν φῶς ἐφήλωσεν φρένας   (489–92)

The beacons are 'light-bearing', φαεσφόρων, (i.e. not speech-bringing, φάτιν φέρουσαν) and παραλλαγάς, which picks up παραλλάξασα (424), where it referred to the 'escaping', 'changing' of ὄψις, is used to describe the fire, rather than παράγγελμα, παραγγέλλω, which was used by Clytemnestra to describe the beacons. The similarity in sound between παραγγελ/παραλλαγ emphasises the difference – the change – in sense between the 'watchword' (or is it an 'announcement' of a sort?) and the 'transmission' (or is it 'variation', 'change'?) of fire. ὀνειράτων δίκην refers to 420 (the shifting world of dream vision) and to 274, where the chorus imputed a belief in dreams to Clytemnestra. And the indirect question sums up finally the question arising from these tensions in language: φῶς ἐφήλωσεν φρένας 'Has light' – both the fire and the whole mode of the visible – 'deceived φρένας'. Such was the implication of 274ff., refuted apparently by the second beacon-speech as proof. κῆρυκ᾿ (493) now provides the difference: the man with λόγος. The following lines (494–7), which have been amusingly parodied by Housman,[84] are not merely a high-flown tragic periphrasis. They point to the process of signification and proof we have been considering: μαρτυρεῖ δέ μοι, 'it bears witness' (the legal vocabulary again), 'it proves by signification'. κάσις πηλοῦ ξύνουρος (494–5) is a *griphos* which is instantly cashed out: διψία κόνις. The *griphos*, as we saw above, functions as a stimulus to deconstruction of the process of signification as indeed does the tenor of the sentence as a whole:

μαρτυρεῖ δέ μοι κάσις
πηλοῦ ξύνουρος διψία κόνις τάδε
ὡς οὔτ᾿ ἄναυδος οὗτος[85] οὐ δαίων φλόγα
ὕλης ὀρείας σημανεῖ καπνῷ πυρός   (494–7)

'Dust bears witness to these things', dust 'signifies': again we are pointed towards the process of one sign standing for another. This fellow is 'not without a voice' – as was the beacon message – and 'not kindling the flame of mountain wood with the smoke of fire' (as did the beacon). The opposition is drawn precisely between the signification of the light of the beacon and the speech of the

---

[84] E.g. 'Mud's sister, not herself, adorns my shoes.'   [85] Fraenkel's text

messenger. σημανεῖ, 'he will signify', 'use signs', but it will be in language, ἐκβάξει λέγων: 'he will speak out, saying'.

The κῆρυξ has a long speech of greeting and joy: it is, however, undercut at several points by ironies which enforce the foreboding and misgiving that we saw in the stasimon above: 505 πολλῶν ῥαγεισῶν ἐλπίδων could be read as referring also to the many hopes and expectations we have seen floated in the play so far (and the hopes and expectations to come): another example of the characters' desire for and lack of control over the events of narrative. βωμοὶ δ' ἄιστοι καὶ θεῶν ἱδρύματα[86] is the recognition (for the reader) of the fulfilment of Clytemnestra's apparently holy prayer (338ff.) which in the context of reciprocal sin and punishment increases the ominous impressions of impending doom. This reciprocity returns in the legal expressions of punishment in 534–5, and in the general statement of the outcome of the war, which recalls the *parodos*' expressions of its inception: Πάρις οὔτε πόλις ἐξεύχεται τὸ δρᾶμα τοῦ πάθους πλέον, 'neither Paris nor his city boasts out loud that their doing was more than their suffering'. And this sense of the reciprocity of punishment reverberates particularly in the term δικηφόρου (525: picked up in δίκην, 534), which seems to be a new coinage, and on which Kitto bases much of his interpretation.

He prays to and greets exclusively the male gods, taking pains to rehabilitate Apollo:

> νῦν δ' αὖτε σωτὴρ ἴσθι καὶ παιώνιος
> ἄναξ Ἀπολλον   (512–13)

Zeus is recognised as the force behind their expedition: Διὸς μακέλλῃ (526). The messenger's long greeting works up to the 'name-cap'[87] first of the returning army and secondly of the king, as leader of the army:

> εἴ που πάλαι, φαιδροῖσι τοισίδ' ὄμμασιν
> δέξασθε κόσμῳ βασιλέα πολλῷ χρόνῳ
> ἥκει γὰρ ὑμῖν φῶς ἐν εὐφρόνῃ φέρων
> καὶ τοῖσδ' ἅπασι κοινὸν Ἀγαμέμνων ἄναξ   (520–3)

The name of the king resounding at the end of the line and sentence leads into an account of his triumphs. The description of Agamemnon as φῶς ἐν εὐφρόνῃ φέρων is interesting: Clytemnestra in her opening lines punningly referred to light being born *from* dark (its mother) παρὰ εὐφρόνης. Here, with Agamemnon, light is *brought into*, carried in, darkness: the imagery is for the female birth, but for the male penetration. And further sexual connotations of light/fire will

---

[86] Fraenkel, for, as Deniston–Page show, unconvincing reasons, deletes this line.
[87] Bundy's term; see Bundy 1962.

return in Clytemnestra's descriptions of her relationship both to Agamemnon and to Aegisthus (cf. 968–9, 1435–6, p. 91).

The chorus and the herald exchange greetings, and the herald begins to cry, an act parallel to the chorus' own tears at 270 (χαρά, 270; χαρᾶς, 541). Similarly to that previous passage of stichomythia, the conversation breaks down to a discussion about language: the chorus offer an obscure comment on his tears, a riddle:

τερπνῆς ἄρ' ἦτε τῆσδ' ἐπήβολοι νόσου   (542)

This is beyond the messenger, who replies:

πῶς δή; διδαχθεὶς τοῦδε δεσπόσω λόγου   (543)

He desires to be taught, so that he can 'master the word': as with πῶς φῄς; πέφευγε τοὖπος (268), we see in the dialogue a recognition of the (heuristic) gap between speaker and listener in the exchange of logos, which the characters desire to master, to control. The reference to 'mastery'[88] may refer us back to the λαμπροὺς δυνάστας of the prologue (6), and is particularly important here after the first messenger speech. The messenger is always accepted as telling the truth, of narrating events clearly. In this dialogue, however, the messenger's own disavowal of the transparency of language shows a recognition of the possibility of the non-transparency of language (including his own). This hint of incertitude we will see developed through the rest of this scene.

Even after the chorus' brief explanation of their comment, the messenger asks another clarifying question:

ποθεῖν ποθοῦντα τήνδε γῆν στρατὸν λέγεις;   (545)

λέγεις, last word, points to the function, that of language, that we are observing. The chorus reply:

ὡς πόλλ' ἀμαυρᾶς ἐκ φρενός ⟨μ'⟩ ἀναστένειν   (546)

ἀναστένειν is the note of grief we have mentioned, which recalls, for example, the prologue's reaction to the house under Clytemnestra's rule. ἀμαυρᾶς ἐκ φρενός is a strong image (it is repeated at *Cho.* 158). ἀμαυρᾶς indicates both 'dark' and 'blind': that is, it stands both within the structure of light and dark imagery and within the problematic of the visible (two constellations of ideas difficult to separate). Thus it qualifies φρενός in an important way. Under the power of Clytemnestra (548–50 make it clear that it is repression from the authorities), φρενός is both 'darkened' and 'blind'. This leads

---

[88] 'Mastery', connected to terms like 'narrative control', 'predictive certainty', etc. will be a recurring topic of discussion in this text. On the mastery of language, Gorgias is an interesting text to read in conjunction with the *Oresteia*, particularly in his claim that λόγος is the δυνάστης! On Gorgias and Aeschylus, see Rosenmeyer 1955.

to silence, the denial of logos – that we have seen from the watchman and chorus earlier:

πάλαι τὸ σιγᾶν φάρμακον βλάβης ἔχω   (548)

'Silence' is the remedy of hurt. As with the watchman's speech, there is 'every reason to fear naming its fear'.[89] Indeed, the chorus end the stichomythia with a statement of deep misgiving that picks up explicitly the messenger's exaggerated expression of joy, turning it to ominous dread:

ὡς νῦν, τὸ σὸν δή, καὶ θανεῖν πολλὴ χάρις   (550)

This complete change of connotation in the same expression points once more to the non-transparent nature of the herald's words, the heuristic gap between addresser and addressee. Indeed, the messenger misunderstands the tone of the chorus and replies briefly:

εὖ γὰρ πέπρακται   (551)

'Yes, for it has been well done': he dismisses the interchange to begin his story. The disruption between the chorus' remark and the herald's reply is a significant prelude to the second long speech of the messenger, and colours the whole reading of it, up to πάντ' ἔχεις λόγον, the concluding remark, which, while implying merely 'you've heard all I'm going to say', points also to the messenger's belief that what he utters will be fully received: πάντ' ἔχεις, 'you *have*, possess, in your power, *it all*'; no diminution, change, in the process of communication. The chorus reply, however, νικώμενος λόγοισιν οὐκ ἀναίνομαι, 'conquered by words...' The chorus do not 'have' the words, but 'are defeated' by λόγος δυνάστης. The interchange marks the recognition of the heuristic gap in the process of communication and the necessary function of belief and persuasion (πίστις/πειθώ) in the reception of utterance.

The speech itself concentrates on the *ponoi* of the warriors. These toils someone may declare (τις ἂν λέξειεν) to be in some ways good, in some ways bad, in the length of time (551–3). In the passage of time, for mortals, such predications are not simply fixed (as, indeed, the victory here proclaimed will be seen to be part of the pattern of Agamemnon's downfall). For 'who but a god is without suffering for his whole lifetime's length?'. Only a god's acts can be so defined at once and clearly without the possibility of opposite predication (in time). In the need for definition in the describing of events once more there is developed a link between the control of language and the control of narrative – and theology (cf. 813ff.).

But after his description of the war on the Trojan front, he says:

τί ταῦτα πενθεῖν δεῖ; παροίχεται πόνος   (567)

[89] Clay 1969, p. 3.

This stands in ironic contrast to the misgivings of the chorus, their description of μίμνει...μνάμων μῆνις τεκνόποινος, and the watchman's prayer for release. As with his naive faith in the transparency of language, so here his naive belief in the τέρμα, the *telos*, of action, and of πόνοι in particular, is undercut by its juxtaposition to the statements of the chorus.

> παροίχεται δέ, τοῖσι μὲν τεθνηκόσιν
> τὸ μήποτ' αὖθις μηδ' ἀναστῆναι μέλειν   (568-9)

This is refuted by the famous statement of the slave at *Cho.* 886: τὸν ζῶντα καίνειν τοὺς τεθνηκότας λέγω. The sense of reciprocity of suffering and gain is continued with νικᾷ τὸ κέρδος, πῆμα δ' οὐκ ἀντιρρέπει: ἀντι- suggests, as before, the force of opposition/exclusion: ῥέπει, as with ἐπιρρέπει (251) expresses a sense of incline, tilt, rather than balance. Finally, the motive force of the action against Troy is once more stated to be from Zeus:

> χάρις...
> Διὸς τάδ' ἐκπράξασα   (581-2)

Fraenkel says of this speech that the messenger shows 'an unqualified optimism'. But this attitude, contrasting sharply with the tone of the elders, is undercut not only by the recognition of his simple belief in the end of πόνοι but also, and this is particularly important, by his assertion of a straightforward, transparent, communication function, his faith in logos, which is nevertheless undercut at the beginning and end of his speech.

The uncertain status of language in messages is further brought to the fore by the speech of Clytemnestra that follows, where she sends with the messenger a notably hypocritical (untransparent) message to her husband. Clytemnestra's misrepresentations form an uneasy dialectic with the two messenger speeches between which they stand. After the complexities of the beacon-signal and leading towards the power-play of *peitho* in the carpet scene, Clytemnestra's message-sending in the messenger scene marks the complexity and danger of the exchange of language, and undercuts the possibility of the constitution of the messenger's message as simple, referential, or representational language. Clytemnestra's manipulation of language echoes in and around the scene of message giving and receiving.

The queen makes it plain from the start that she regards the messenger merely as confirmation of the signal of the beacon:

> ἀνωλόλυξα μὲν πάλαι χαρᾶς ὕπο
> ὅτ' ἦλθ' ὁ πρῶτος νύχιος ἄγγελος πυρός,
> φράζων ἅλωσιν Ἰλίου τ' ἀνάστασιν   (587-9)

ὁ πρῶτος ἄγγελος, 'the first messenger', indicates that she regards the herald merely as second. ἄγγελος πυρός is reminiscent of her long speech (288ff.), where the possibility of a signal in/of language was set in play. φράζων here points to that possibility: φράζω can mean 'to indicate'. So in Homer: it is used, for example, in the *Odyssey* (19.250; 23.206) of a god 'showing' σήματα. It is used in the play later specifically to contrast communication with speech and without speech:

σὺ δ' ἀντὶ φωνῆς φράζε καρβάνῳ χερί   (1061)

Yet it also comes to mean 'to declare', 'to tell' – it is not, however, the same as λέγω in range of meaning and is used in contrast to it on occasion (cf. L.–S.–J.). φράζειν, then, can imply communication *both* in speech *and* without speech. As the phrase ἄγγελος πυρός juxtaposes the possibilities of language (saying) and beacon-light (showing), so φράζων offers the deconstruction of the opposition of saying and showing, φράζων writes through the opposition. This ambiguity is significant as she rebukes the chorus for their 'sexism':

φρυκτώρων διὰ
πεισθεῖσα Τροίαν νῦν πεπορθῆσθαι δοκεῖς;
ἦ κάρτα πρὸς γυναικὸς αἴρεσθαι κέαρ   (590–2)

For by the use of πεισθεῖσα, which need not imply language although it usually does, and the ambiguity of φράζων which need not imply language although it often does, the semiotic function of the beacon chain, the difference between the signal and the languaged message, is obscured.

She continues to remind the chorus that the basis of their distinction was sexual: γυναικείῳ νόμῳ (594); and that all the women reacted in the same way (595–6). This widens the opposition to men v. women in the city, not merely Clytemnestra and the chorus. She regards herself now as patently justified:

καὶ νῦν τὰ μάσσω μὲν τί δεῖ σ' ἐμοὶ λέγειν   (598)

λέγειν, last word in the line, is picked up by λόγον (599), in the same metrical position. She will learn the 'whole story' from the king himself. πάντα λόγον (599) echoes the messenger's πάντ' ἔχεις λόγον (582). The phrase represents on both occasions the desire to control language, to give and receive πάντα λόγον; but with Clytemnestra, as opposed to the messenger, it is fixed within her recognition of the play of language, the possibilities of falsification, as the speech that follows (600–14), in its hypocrisy and blatant misrepresentation, shows. The repetition of the phrase serves to site the difference of the approach of Clytemnestra and the messenger.

It is interesting to note how Clytemnestra refers to Agamemnon:

τὸν ἐμὸν αἰδοῖον <u>πόσιν</u>
σπεύσω πάλιν μολόντα δέξασθαι...   (600–1)

The ironies of her desire to receive her returning husband (πόσις) have been long noted. She generalises the situation, and it is once more in the juxtaposition of male and female, light and dark:

τί γὰρ
<u>γυναικὶ</u> τούτου φέγγος ἥδιον δρακεῖν,
ἀπὸ στρατείας <u>ἄνδρα</u> σώσαντος θεοῦ
πύλας ἀνοῖξαι;   (601–4)

Here the terms are ἄνδρα and γυναικί, as often before. She returns to the particular situation, and Agamemnon is once more called πόσις:

...ταῦτ' ἀπάγγειλον πόσει   (604)

It is as if Clytemnestra, while she talks generally of the pleasure of a woman seeing her man return, in referring to the particular situation terms Agamemnon more specifically in his socially defined role as 'husband', 'spouse', πόσις – rather than the more sexually charged ἀνήρ.[90] Is there a suggestion that she is unwilling to name Agamemnon as πόσις because of her ἀνήρ, Aegisthus? So over the corpse of the king there seems a particular emphasis in Clytemnestra's proclamation οὗτός ἐστιν Ἀγαμέμνων, ἐμὸς | πόσις νεκρὸς δέ (1404–5), where the name of Agamemnon marks specifically her societal relation with him, the societal relation she has corrupted by her adultery with Aegisthus. Similarly, in her long speech of welcome to Agamemnon (855–912), when he is actually face to face with her, and where her hypocrisy has been often noted, she refers to him as ἀνήρ (867, 896), and calls her manner φιλάνορας. But the irony of that term lies precisely in her suggestive use of -άνορας, which can also imply here 'paramour', 'lover'. The process of naming is precisely that by which society delineates and defines social, sexual, and political relationships, and is often seen as a prophetic, directive device, from which the naming of children takes on a significance for their future characters or abilities, as we will see in the choric ode 681ff. This assertion of the power of names is an assertion of the classificatory process of society and is a necessary condition for the functioning of

[90] L.-S.-J. say πόσις refers to 'especially a lawful husband as opposed to ἀνήρ, a paramour', and quote Soph. *Tra.* 550 μὴ πόσις μὲν Ἡρακλῆς | ἐμὸς καλῆται τῆς νεωτέρας δ' ἀνήρ. There is not, however, a precisely defined category of legal marriage in Greek thought (according to Vernant 1973) and the difference between husband/man/lover/consort is not quite so clearly defined since ἀνήρ is often used of 'husband'. πόσις, however, seems not to have been used except with regard to a recognised relationship, and it is the difference in the use of πόσις/ἀνήρ in Clytemnestra's language that I am trying to trace here.

society. The redefining of the Erinues will be one of the final acts of the trilogy, the assimilation by society through the power of the name, the word. The final reassertion of society will come from the assertion of its power in language.

Clytemnestra continues her speech, emphasising her qualities as a wife, a woman: γυναῖκα πιστήν (606),[91] γυναικὶ γενναίᾳ (614). When she calls herself, however, δωμάτων κύνα ἐσθλήν (607–8), there is an interesting ambiguity. For although κύων in this context of a master's return in particular recalls Argos, Odysseus' dog (who dies on his master's return), it is also precisely what Helen calls herself at *Il.* 6.344, 'shameless hussy', and indeed at *Il.* 6.356, and she calls herself κυνῶπις as a term of reproach at *Il.* 3.180, and at *Od.* 4.145, and it is how Hephaestus describes Aphrodite when he catches her *in flagrante delicto*, committing adultery with Ares (*Od.* 8.319). So there is a certain moral ambiguity about the use of the term here (particularly as it is connected explicitly with acts of adultery – and Helen's – in Homer), even when qualified by ἐσθλήν – in fact, the adjective follows the noun almost *para prosdokian*. Indeed, the only occasion, apart from this passage, quoted in L.-S.-J. of κύων being used as a favourable term (e.g. 'watchdog') is later in this play (896), in Clytemnestra's speech of welcome to Agamemnon where she calls him τῶν σταθμῶν κύνα, which we read as a favourable term because it stands in apposition to σωτῆρα ναὸς πρότονον κτλ. But there, too, there is a considerable ambiguity, which perhaps allows Clytemnestra to utter a veiled insult to the returning king, as the term here colours her speech with a trace of the 'shamelessness' into which she has fallen.[92]

She concludes her message:

> τοιόσδ' ὁ κόμπος, τῆς ἀληθείας γέμων
> οὐκ αἰσχρὸς ὡς γυναικὶ γενναίᾳ λακεῖν (613–14)

τῆς ἀληθείας γέμων indicates once more the problem of the signifier and the signified in communication: for to describe her language as 'stuffed full', 'loaded' with truth implies the possibility of its opposite, that the language may have no truth content – as indeed in this case it has not. Words are separated from a referential function and seen for Clytemnestra, like the beacon-lights, as signifiers with an arbitrary and controllable relation to the signified within the system. Yet the ambiguity of κύνα indicates that language escapes

---

[91] Vernant and Vidal-Naquet 1972 (p. 112, n. 10 (p. 103, n. 9)) suggest that in saying γυναῖκα πιστήν 'she is really saying the opposite...γυναῖκ' ἄπιστον'.

[92] Cassandra uses the term of Clytemnestra at 1228, where it is usually regarded as insulting (thus pointing to the ambiguity here). For more on dogs see Harriot 1982; Lilja 1976; Stanford 1939, p. 149; Redfield 1975, pp. 193ff. Below pp. 204–5.

even her (absolute) control. The gap between signifier and signified by which Clytemnestra's hypocrisy and lying function (it is the condition of their possibility), evades her *kratos*, language still e-ludes her.

The chorus comment critically but in a veiled manner on her speech: εὐπρεπῆ λόγον (616),[93] 'a fair-seeming speech'. πρεπ- refers back to the element of the visible in the watchman's speech and throughout the play, and implies, as before, here particularly through the irony of the chorus, the possibility of speech having an opposite predication. 'Visible' seems here to imply 'appearance' as opposed to reality, as it did with δόξα/φάσματα. We see the need, then, on which we have already commented, for a figure to bridge the gap between speech and reception, the interpreter, and one who is accurate: τοροῖσιν ἑρμηνεῦσιν.

The chorus turn to the messenger and ask for information on Menelaus. He replies:

οὐκ ἔσθ' ὅπως λέξαιμι τὰ ψευδῆ καλά   (620)

This, in juxtaposition to Clytemnestra's speech, is markedly an opposite position, which, as with Clytemnestra's repetition of πάντα λόγον, serves to site (and emphasise) the difference between the messenger's and the queen's language. The chorus, commenting on the herald's remark, turn to a construction equivalent to a wish, πῶς δῆτ' ἄν...τύχοις; or rather, a construction almost the equivalent of a wish, for in such a construction 'the interrogative word serves to express the possibility of the notion so that the underlying idea is: in what way is it conceivable? Is there no way by which you might bring it about? Could you not somehow or other?'.[94] In other words, this construction both asserts a wish (that the messenger might speak both good and true things) and puts its possibility under question. For, as they go on to explain, 'truth' and κεδνά, when separated, are not well/easily hidden. This is precisely the state of affairs with the language of Clytemnestra: a disjunction between κεδνά and truth content. The underlying question has already been answered.

The messenger tells them that Menelaus has disappeared and that no one except the sun knows where he is (again the concept of μάρτυς, the one who *sees*, is central to knowledge). The chorus ask (634–5) how the storm came and ended, suggesting divine wrath as cause. This is, on the one hand, an indication of their theological view of natural events which attempts to explain through anthropomorphised

---

[93] Fraenkel's text. Page obelises εὐπρεπῶς.
[94] Ameis–Hentze, *Anhang zu Homer* 3rd ed. Leipzig 1899–1900 (on *O*. 195), quoted in Fraenkel.

divinities a passage of cause and effect for an otherwise apparently randomly caused and stopped phenomenon; on the other hand, within the form of the open equation that we saw earlier, of sin and punishment through divine action, it expresses the misgivings of the chorus who had feared some retribution for the now realised fear that the army might destroy the shrines. The messenger, however, does not immediately answer the question, but talks about the nature of giving messages. Once again, then, the stichomythic process of question and answer, rather than exchanging information in transparent language, breaks down to consider the nature of language exchange. The narrative is self-referential.

His first reason for wanting to impart only good news is:

> εὔφημον ἦμαρ οὐ πρέπει κακαγγέλῳ
> γλώσσῃ μιαίνειν   (636–7)

He asserts what we saw in Lévi-Strauss' analysis of the prohibitions of the Malay Peninsula, that it is a misuse of language (a function of the misuse of exchange) that leads to disaster. μιαίνειν has the religious overtones of the instructions quoted by Lévi-Strauss. Not only in traditional societies is a misplaced, misomened word regarded with fear, but throughout the Classical world the need to have εὔφημον στόμα is seen. The conjunction of 'light' and 'language' (ἦμαρ...πρέπει...-αγγέλῳ...γλώσσῃ) harks back to the prologue (e.g. 30, and elsewhere), which again places parallel (in their differences) the message of the beacon and the herald. Here, the messenger intimates his fear to mix good-omened and bad-omened terms:

> πῶς κεδνὰ τοῖς κακοῖσι συμμείξω, λέγων   (648)

– a fear to lose distinctions in language (λέγων), mutually to pollute and thus erase not only meaning (for meaning is constituted in difference) but also the structures of society based on those distinctions. The storm he describes owes much of its force precisely to this mixing of what was previously and properly kept apart:

> ξυνώμοσαν γάρ, ὄντες ἔχθιστοι τὸ πρίν
> πῦρ καὶ θάλασσα, καὶ τὰ πίστ' ἐδειξάτην   (650–1)

The γάρ seems also to suggest a direct explanatory relation between 648–9 and 650: the mixing of distinctions through misuse of language on a human level is made parallel to the loss of distinctions on the natural level between the elements: in either case, it leads to disaster, to κακά:

> ἐν νυκτὶ δυσκύμαντα δ' ὠρώρει κακά   (653)

As the speech continues, the lack of control increases as each explanation consists of either divine intervention or chance, the negative of narrative control, which is almost personified:

ἤτοι τις ἐξέκλεψεν ἢ 'ξητήσατο
θεός τις, οὐκ ἄνθρωπος, οἴακος θιγών,
Τύχη δὲ σωτὴρ ναῦν θέλουσ' ἐφέζετο   (662–4)

And as we may now expect, this leads to a series of prayers and optatives culminating in a recognition that if it turns out as he expects or hopes it is through the power of Zeus, who does not wish to destroy the Atreid house: Zeus, the house, ἐλπίς: the text maintains the focus we have seen:

μηχαναῖς Διὸς
οὔπω θέλοντος ἐξαναλῶσαι γένος
ἐλπίς τις αὐτὸν πρὸς δόμους ἥξειν πάλιν   (677–9)

When you have heard such things, he concludes, you know you have heard the truth: lack of control, inability to see a passage of cause and effect, finally prayers, and hope. This is τάληθῆ (680).

So there is here a general move in the scenic action from control, certitude, even joy, through a realisation particularly of the non-transparency, non-controllability, over-determinacy, of language, to a recognition of lack of control, misgiving, and finally prayer, hope. This is particularly marked in a 'messenger scene', episodes which are normally centred on the assumption of the exchange of referential language. The questioning and undercutting of that exchange here (and the messenger scene comes earlier in this play than in many) colours, stands in juxtaposition to, the future processes of communication in the work.

The explanatory origin?

The chorus, following on from the story of the sufferings of the Argive expedition and an uncertainty of the fate of one of the kings of their house, turns to consider the origin of the war whose outcome has just been narrated. But as we will see, it is more than the origin of the Trojan War that is at stake.

The chorus open the second stasimon by considering the nature of naming in language, τίς ποτ' ὠνόμαζεν ὧδε. First the process of naming is described as perfectly accurate, ἐς τὸ πᾶν ἐτητύμως, a phrase reminiscent of the absolute nature of Zeus in the hymn to Zeus (also concerned with naming and accuracy, ἐτητύμως, 166). Certainly they are loth to suggest any mortal[95] has such a control in language,

---

[95] Or rather 'anyone who can see'. This may imply the dead.

a control which is linked to the power of prediction, a foreknowledge of what must happen: προνοίαισι τοῦ πεπρωμένου γλῶσσαν ἐν τύχᾳ νέμων. The name itself (following ὧδε) is delayed until the last word of the sentence, and as I have mentioned earlier, this is the first time that Helen is named. It is as if now that Troy has been announced as destroyed and society has revenged itself on the adulteress, she can be safely rehabilitated as a member of society, named. Society has reasserted itself and can once again classify, delineate, define Helen safely. The reason for this perfect naming, however, is a punning etymology, ἑλένας ἕλανδρος ἑλέπτολις. As we saw with Clytemnestra's opening speech (264–5), which punned on εὔφρων/εὐφρόνης, the play on words indicates the use of the signifier as a sound image linked now to one, now to another, signified. The etymon, however, asserts the natural relation of signifier and signified, it asserts that the name as a sound image is significant and, moreover, directive. The cledonomantic[96] argument is an attempt to control language and narrative by an affirmation that the relation between the signifier and the signified is not arbitrary, and thus if one can trace the word to its root then the natural effect will be perceivable; it will have a precise meaning.[97] As with the postulation in the hymn to Zeus of a transcendental signified to stop the sliding of the chain of signifiers, the play of metaphors, so here the assertion of a natural relation between sound image and signification is an attempt to 'master the word', ἐς τὸ πᾶν ἐτητύμως, 'completely', 'in its truth', its etymon. Noticeably, however, it is juxtaposed to a metaphor, a *griphos*, which not only undercuts the simple, certain link of signifier and signified in the play of sign for sign, as I argued on pp. 21ff. but also is a metaphor expressly concerned with the process of tracking, of one sign standing (as a trace) for another, a trace which is 'unseen':

κυναγοί
κατ' ἴχνος πλατᾶν ἄφαντον   (694–5)

As the chorus continues, the process of naming, the relation between the signifier and signified, is put into further question by the claim that the duality of a *jeu de mots*, the recognition of the collection of two normally distinct and exclusive meanings in one sound-image, is, in fact, also significant, and that the relation between two lexical definitions of the same sound image, in this case at least, has a directive function:

[96] On cledonomancy, see n. 152, p. 98.
[97] This argument was used explicitly and in great depth by the eighteenth-century neoclassical grammarians. See Foucault 1973 (1966) particularly pp. 78–120, 328–35. For a different view see Aarslef 1982, and for a good general bibliography, Hewes 1975.

Ἰλίῳ δὲ κῆδος ὀρ-
θώνυμον τελεσσίφρων
Μῆνις ἤλασεν (699–701)

'Wrath which brings to pass her thoughts drove on what is *rightly named* a marriage-tie/sorrow.' Here, too, even the ambiguity of the noun/name (ὄνομα) is subsumed to a natural, ordained relation between signifier and signified, in the desire to control narrative and language, to see a pattern. The name/noun has the quality of ὀρθότης.[98]

Language, in the form of song, remains the focus of the action,[99] as they express the fortunes of Troy first as the singing of τὸ νυμφότιμον μέλος...ὑμέναιον (705–7). But as their fortunes change, this song must then be changed, μεταμανθάνουσα δ' ὕμνον, to the singing of πολύθρηνον μέγα που. It is after the event that the hopes of the ὑμέναιον are seen to be falsely predictive, and consequently, the Trojans must repredicate, redefine in new words:

κικλήσκουσ-
α Πάριν τὸν αἰνόλεκτρον
†παμπρόσθη πολύθρηνον (712–14)

Language is seen as directive only after the events: it remains a hope for control based on the possibility of gaining sufficient clarity, knowledge, in language. The desire for clarity in language and, thus, narrative (that is, accurate prediction or accurate description of the past, the present) is parallel to, for example, the prediction of Calchas, and returns notably in the form of directive or predictive etymologies at later points in the play:

ἰὼ ἰή, διαὶ Διὸς
παναιτίου πανεργέτα (1485–6)

This play in language is particularly important as it is concerned explicitly with Zeus as transcendent responsible force, παναιτίου, and as transcendent power, πανεργέτα. As Zeus is seen as a cause of all action, παναιτίου, which thereby assumes a source, an origin, and thus coherent pattern for events (which thus denies the randomness of events), so a word expressing the general power of agency διαί 'through', 'by', is connected etymologically with the power of Zeus, asserting a non-arbitrary relation between sound-image and signification – or perhaps the name Διός, one might say, is applied because of its relation to the sense of agency in διαί. Either way, the relationship in language between διαί/Διός, agency and Zeus, is

---

[98] *Orthotes* was becoming, or was to become a key word in the Greek philosophical discussions of language and naming. Cf. e.g. Kerferd 1981, pp. 68ff.

[99] 'ὑμέναιον is to provide the key note of what follows' Fraenkel op. cit., p. 335.

asserted as being in some way natural (and thereby definable outside the chain of signs) which implies the possibility of control in narrative (i.e. a coherent pattern of cause and effect / agency) and language (the escape from the sliding of signs i.e. absolute definition).

A similar play occurs in the *Choephoroi*, considering the motive force of δίκη – of reciprocal action. As many critics have noted, there is a strong desire in the trilogy to escape from the reciprocity of action and counter-action,[100] to redefine δίκη as the function of δικαστής rather than δικηφόρος (cf. *Cho.* 120 and Kitto's analysis, which is followed in perhaps slightly different form by many critics). At *Choephoroi* 948–51, δίκη is broken down etymologically as Διὸς κόρα

> ἔθιγε δ' ἐν μάχᾳ χερὸς ἐτήτυμος
> Διὸς κόρα, Δίκαν δέ νιν
> προσαγορεύομεν
> βροτοὶ τυχόντες καλῶς   *Cho.* 948–51

The process of etymological derivation is marked by the use of ἐτήτυμος and τυχόντες καλῶς with the word of addressing, naming. This phraseology has also been shown[101] to be connected also with the religious need for correct language, as with εὔφημον στόμα. Here, as Orestes is in the process of killing his mother, the act regarded both as the supreme and necessary act of δίκη, and at the same time as the most unnatural and criminal act (ἄδικος) that a person can perform (συμφορὰν διπλῆν *Cho.* 931), the chorus attempt to reach a definite and absolute position by defining δίκη from its imagined etymon, which is, in this case, a literal origin (i.e. father) and which is, as with διαί, linked to Zeus, the transcendental signified; an attempt to control the ambivalence of the δίκη of matricide by finding its natural meaning, its supracontextual sense: Διός, 'from/of god', is to provide the irreducible origin.

In the following stanzas of the second stasimon (716–82) there is a dominating image of parents handing on characteristics to children, the 'birth' of faults: τίκτει and words derived from it occur at 724 τέκνου, 728 τὸ πρὸς τοκέων, 754 τεκνοῦσθαι, 759 τίκτει, 763 τίκτειν, 767 τόκου, 771 τοκεῦσι; παῖς and connected words at 721 εὐφιλόπαιδα, 754 ἄπαιδα, 762 καλλίπαις; γένος κτλ. at 755, 760.

---

100 πρασσομένα is translated here (705) as 'revenging', 'exacting account'; generally it implies 'doing (something to someone)' – it is almost as though any action is reciprocal, as though one cannot 'do' without 'revenging'.

101 Kranz 1933, pp. 287ff. Pease (ed.) Cic. *de div.* 1.102 (Illinois, 1920). Cf. also Schmid, *Gesch. d. griesch. Lit.* 1.2. (Munich 1934), p. 297, n. 3. Pauly-Wissowa, *RE* XVIII pp. 376ff. Also N. Austin 1972. Zeitlin (1982b). Below (pp. 252–4) we will discuss further the desire for a single point of origin, and its undercutting in the plays of doubling and difference in the text.

The extended allegory of the lion in the house (notice the focus even there on the household: οἶκος, 732; οἰκέταις, 733; δόμοις, 718; δόμοις, 736) centres around the proposition χρονισθεὶς δ' ἀπέδειξεν ἦθος τὸ πρὸς τοκέων (727–8), 'In time' (as the derivation of Helen's name became clear *only after* the war) 'he showed the character of his parents.' This search for an origin of character, a cause for action, is parallel to the search for the etymon for words, the desire to stop the infinite play of language/action by fixing a point from which things may be said to derive. It shows the chorus' desire for narrative control: to fix the πρώταρχον ἄτην from which other events may be said to proceed in a relation of cause and effect.

As the narrative itself will turn on child–parent relations, for example in the trial scene of the *Eumenides*, so again and again throughout the trilogy we shall return to the informing model of childbirth and child–parent similarities as providing the explanatory structuring of events by the postulation of an origin and a descent. In this stasimon, then, the language of childbirth joins the interlocking narratives of Troy's fall, the naming of Helen, the structuring of moral events, in the postulation of an origin as a fixed point in the structuring of explanation.

The stanzas 718–36, the story of the lion cub, have been well analysed by Bernard Knox,[102] where he shows that this passage 'is a knot of suggestions which evoke simultaneously all the principal figures of the *Oresteia*' (1952, p. 18) not only in the further suggestive descriptions of characters as lions (cf. e.g. 1224, 1258–9), but also in the return in time of parental characteristics, in the delay and reversal of revenge, in the imagery of breeding and nourishing, and in the imagery of sacrifice and feasting (always important in the Atreid dynasty). The *ainos* is, as Knox notes, marked by a strong disruption of the discourse. It is introduced merely by οὕτως, which is delayed until seventh word, and is not explicitly linked to what follows by any particle but the elided δέ at 738. This helps to constitute the *ainos* as a unit of signification strongly, and Knox has shown well the echoing connotations of this important passage. We shall indeed have cause to return to it again in the reading of the trilogy.

Strophe γ is the apparently primary significance of the *ainos* of the lion. So the early calm of πάραυτα δ' ἐλθεῖν... φρόνημα... γαλάνας seems juxtaposed to the bitter end of ἐπέκρανεν δὲ γάμου πικρὰς τελευτάς (745), as the pre-sacrifices of the lion's life, ἐν βιότου προτελείοις, are to the final recognition, χρονισθεὶς δ' ἀπέδειξεν (727). λέγοιμ' ἄν, 'I would say', 'offer a logos', adds by the optative a doubt

---

[102] 1952, *passim*.

to the certainty of the reading of the allegory, to the example of its generality, which opens the way to Knox's extended reading.

The motivation of this passage is again stated to be Zeus Xenios: πομπᾷ Διὸς ξενίου. But interestingly, what Zeus sends, delayed until last word of the stanza, is Ἐρινύς, when the expected subject of the feminine participle is perhaps Helen. Is she, then, to be understood as an Erinys? Is the sending of the Erinys hinted at at 59 in fact earlier than the expedition from Aulis? Once again we see a confusion of motivation, of suspected divine causalities, a doubt as to the beginning of the pattern of cause and effect, crime and punishment. Indeed, as the following three stanzas, which Fraenkel calls the 'general problems', show, the stress is on cause, source, parentage, particularly of hubris but also (762-3) of good fortune. It is the desire to find an origin which will stop the apparent infinite regress of action, here depicted in moral terms.

> φιλεῖ δε τίκτειν ὕβρις
> μὲν παλαιὰ νεά-
> ζουσαν ἐν κακοῖς βροτῶν
> ὕβριν τότ' ἢ τόθ' ὅτε τὸ κύ-
> ριον μόλῃ φάος τόκου   (763-7)

Looking forward, these stanzas refer also to the revenge of the son; in general terms, the opening of the equation, the expectation: the actions of Clytemnestra will lead to what similar actions in her children? Also, in a more local sense, particularly through the emphasis on wealth and prosperity as a dangerous success, their warnings awaken misgivings seen to be fulfilled in the carpet scene:

> μέγαν τελε-
> σθέντα φωτὸς ὄλβον
> τεκνοῦσθαι μηδ' ἄπαιδα θνῄσκειν
> ἐκ δ' ἀγαθᾶς τύχας γένει
> βλαστάνειν ἀκόρεστον οἰζύν   (751-6)

Indeed, wealth actually encourages sin:

> Δίκα δὲ λάμπει μὲν ἐν
> δυσκάπνοις δώμασιν
> τὸν δ' ἐναίσιμον τίει
> τὰ χρυσόπαστα δ' ἔδεθλα σὺν
> πίνῳ χερῶν παλιντρόποις
> ὄμμασι λιποῦσ'...   (772-8)

These stanzas stand directly as a prelude, and a threatening one, to the entry of Agamemnon. We also find the image of the false coin again – false value, false signification.

> δύναμιν οὐ σέβουσα πλού-
> του παράσημον αἴνῳ   (779-80)

This leads into the chorus' warning about hypocrisy. The element of exchange in this economic imagery is linked to the exchange of language: the power of wealth is 'falsely stamped by praise'. This seems an important prelude to the carpet scene, where the language of Clytemnestra could well be described as a 'false stamping with praise', a corrupted exchange, a distorted use (παρα) of signs in praise. The queen's argument will also be involved with the power of wealth.

The antistrophe ends with a statement that seems to sum up both the chorus' search for coherence and their vague feelings of fear, of unstated worry:

[Δίκα] πᾶν δ' ἐπὶ τέρμα νωμᾷ   (781)

Justice directs everything (though not without Zeus, as we have seen, Διὸς κόρα/διαὶ Διός) but directs it to an end, τέρμα. The process of movement towards the end remains under the direction of Justice, hidden to the chorus. The end, like an origin, becomes a point that by fixing is used to try to control narrative, to control the chain of signification by fixing a *telos*.

As the chorus turn to address Agamemnon, they call him 'king', βασιλεῦ, his formal role; Τροίας πτολίπορθ', that is, his role as successful general, his actions;[103] 'Ατρέως γένεθλον, his position in the family, his origin; and then they ask πῶς σε προσείπω; 'How am I to address you?' Parallel to this is the question:

πῶς σε σεβίξω
μήθ' ὑπεράρας μήθ' ὑποκάμψας
καιρὸν χάριτος;   (785-7)

This would seem to imply that the difficulty of naming comes from a difficulty in hitting καιρόν, the exact measure. Juxtaposed to this are eleven lines on hypocrisy, on how expression may falsify emotion. After the different namings of Agamemnon (what Hartman with customary flourish has called 'the disseminating movement of antonomasia'),[104] here we are further reminded of the process of one sign standing for another, as we were with Clytemnestra's ὄμματα σοῦ...κατηγορεῖ (271). ὄμματα...εὔφρονος here particularly recalls that earlier scene, which seems a significant irony as a prelude to Clytemnestra's hypocritical falsification of emotion through language. So too the contrast of τὰ δοκοῦντα and 'reality' seems to point back to the δόξαι which the chorus imputed as a ground of argument to Clytemnestra. The chorus express how expression may falsify emotion, but a good προβατογνώμων is not easily

---

[103] This, after their prayer not to be, precisely, a πτολιπόρθης (472), increases the misgivings of the passage.   [104] 1981, p. 81.

deceived.[105] This too looks forward to the carpet scene. Indeed, as many critics from Schütz onwards have noted, these lines can be read as a warning to the king of his coming dialogue with Clytemnestra. πόνος εὖ τελέσασιν (806), as with the herald's παροίχεται πόνος (567), indicates the end of a particular action, but neither the end of the implications of the action (as we shall shortly see) nor indeed the end of *ponos* in a more general sense. As the stanzas of the second stasimon have developed the notion of an origin as control in narrative, language, so the chorus return here to the end-point as a similar fixed moment of control. But as we have seen and will see further, the ἀρχή and the τέλος are terms whose certainty of determination is rendered problematic in this trilogy.

The floating text-ile

Agamemnon's first speech after his long prepared entrance is an extensive formal address, which moves from greetings and thanks to a version of the logic of Troy's destruction, and to a general statement of his proposed action, now that he has returned. His first words pick up and answer the chorus' first question:

> πρῶτον μὲν Ἄργος καὶ θεοὺς ἐγχωρίους
> δίκη προσειπεῖν   (810–11)

He rejects or qualifies their πῶς <u>σε</u> προσείπω by an appeal to the authority of the gods as τοὺς ἐμοὶ μεταιτίους | νόστου δικαίων θ' ὧν ἐπραξάμην πόλιν | Πριάμου; the 'theologised' narrative. A reason is offered for this:

> δίκας γὰρ οὐκ ἀπὸ γλώσσης θεοὶ
> κλύοντες ἀνδροθνῆτας Ἰλιοφθόρους
> ἐς αἱματηρὸν τεῦχος οὐ διχορρόπως
> ψήφους ἔθεντο   (813–16)

'The gods hear *not from the tongue*' – that is, 'not by way of speeches' (Fraenkel). They have direct access to the signified without recourse to an intermediary of communication by a removal of the function of the exchange of signifiers: once again we see that a transcendental – and a divine transcendental – is postulated above and beyond language (and in opposition to the human world of words).

This 'superior knowledge' (Fraenkel) allows them to vote οὐ διχορρόπως – as Clytemnestra prayed τὸ δ' εὖ κρατοίη <u>μὴ</u> <u>διχορρόπως</u> ἰδεῖν (349) – 'without oscillation', 'without inclining in

---

[105] On these lines, see Harriot 1982.

opposite directions'. Here, διχορρόπως retains its derivation from the 'balance', 'the scales', and implies votes all on one side, that is, the sense of opposition and exclusion we have seen earlier. At 1272 διχορρόπως is used, however, in what appears to be a more meta-phorical sense (as it was at 349): φίλων ὑπ' ἐχθρῶν οὐ διχορρόπως, 'by enemy friends without oscillation, precisely'. It seems to be employed almost ironically: for the conjunction of φίλων/ἐχθρῶν, words normally kept in opposition, is qualified by a word implying precisely the opposition and exclusion undercut by the conjunction. As with the scene between Agamemnon and Clytemnestra, the impossibility of distinguishing friend from enemy (φίλων/ἐχθρῶν) comes from the possibility of hypocrisy and lying, from the nature of the semiotic system based on signifiers and signifieds. The gods escape this because οὐκ ἀπὸ γλώσσης...κλύοντες: because they can bypass the process of signification in language. Thus the gods οὐ διχορρόπως ψήφους ἔθεντο. Opposed to this (τῷ ἐναντίῳ κύτει) stands ἐλπίς, the (human) mediator between present and future, which is necessarily open to doubts and uncertainties.

The version of the end of Troy that Agamemnon tells by way of preface for the gods is dominated by bold physical (in particular, bestial) images, set around the statement:

> τούτων θεοῖσι χρὴ πολύμνηστον χάριν
> τίνειν ἐπείπερ χάρπαγὰς ὑπερκόπους
> ἐπραξάμεσθα   (821–3)

This summation of events in juxtaposition and contrast to the chorus' misgivings and confusions seems somewhat ingenuous. Even so ἄτης θύελλαι ζῶσι (819), while implying simply that the winds still encourage the flames in Troy, points also to the fact that, as the rest of the play will show and as the ominous expressions of the chorus have led us to expect, ἄτη lives yet in a more general sense; particularly when juxtaposed to ξυνθνῄσκουσα δὲ σποδός. The force that destroyed Troy is still vital, though 'the embers die'. The imagery of wealth returns (820) also, picking up the chorus' reflections and worries of the second stasimon. So, too, we are prepared for the exchanges of the carpet scene.

As to the chorus' warning on hypocrisy, Agamemnon agrees. The tenor of his remarks is different, however. For rather than picking up the element of falseness, of an expression not standing for an emotion, he stresses the unlikelihood of feeling happiness at another's success:

> παύροις γὰρ ἀνδρῶν ἐστι συγγενὲς τόδε,
> φίλον τὸν εὐτυχοῦντ' ἄνευ φθόνων σέβειν   (832–3)

The irony of his 'certain knowledge of the incertitude of social intercourse' (838–9) before his exchanges with his wife, is marked; as is his example of Odysseus, the renowned liar. Agamemnon turns to his house (ἐς μέλαθρα καὶ δόμους) with a prayer that his victory (νίκη) may remain (μένοι) firmly set. It is precisely νίκη that he will yield to Clytemnestra (941–2).

Although she has not been mentioned in the king's speech, it is Clytemnestra who offers a reply. She opens her speech with an address to the citizens; Agamemnon is addressed in the third person until 879–80, where σῶν is joined to ἐμῶν (with reference to Orestes), and is not addressed in the vocative until 905. The ironies and hypocrisy of her exaggerated joy are clearly marked and have been commented on by many critics.[106] We have already noted the double layers of φιλάνορας τρόπους. It is interesting to note further how much of the speech is concerned with false language, the lying reports which return from Troy: 863 κληδόνας παλιγκότους, 865 λάσκοντας δόμοις, 868 φάτις, 869 ὡς ἐπλήθυον λόγοι, 872 ἐξηύχει, 886 τοιάδε...σκῆψις; and how much with the process of speaking itself: 857 λέξαι, 859 λέξω, 872 ἐξηύχει, 896 λέγοιμ' ἄν, 903 τοίοισδ'... προσφθέγμασιν. It is more even than 'it is almost as if she was challenging Agamemnon to see the truth, if he can'.[107] It is drawing attention by these continuing references to the process of the exchange of language: the speech is about speaking (the self-referential text) and the heuristic gap between signifier and signified, listener and speaker, the condition of falsification in language.

The conclusion of her speech literalises what had been read as a metaphor at 371–2: ὅσοις ἀθίκτων χάρις | πατοῖθ'. The religious and economic significance of the act (which 'all decent men' (Denniston–Page) would detest) has been discussed by others at some length.[108] There is something further here. Metaphor, if we are to use the term, is determined, classified, as we have seen, by a recognised process of 'deviation'. Critics normally adopt a notion such as 'violation of the language code', 'play upon the message'.[109] The notion of substitution (sign for sign) as outlined first by Aristotle[110] depends upon a sense of 'narrative contract',[111] that is, a level of accepted referentiality in the text beyond which we define the code as metaphorical, symbolic, fantasy, and so on. A text (in other words) defines its *effet du réel*.[112]

---

[106] 'Almost every word she says...lays bare her insincerity' (Fraenkel).

[107] Kitto 1956, p. 23.

[108] Cf. e.g. Jones 1962, pp. 72–96. On the act of stepping, Gernet 1981, pp. 177–9. On the tapestry, Lanahan 1974. On the colour of the tapestry, Goheen 1955.

[109] Cohen 1966, pp. 114, 115.

[110] Cf. e.g. *The Rhetoric*, discussed by Ricoeur, 1978, Study 1.

[111] Culler 1975, p. 190.   [112] Barthes' phrase.

The 'literalisation of metaphor'[113] challenges that process of production of meaning by challenging the produced level of referentiality. It resists the move through language to a stable referentiality, forcing us by such realignments of referentiality to recognise the literariness of the text as an unstable verbal object, with a self-produced level of referentiality – or rather to recognise *our* production of the levels of referentiality.

Agamemnon's reply and the following stichomythia and speeches, the so-called carpet scene (wrongly, according to Denniston–Page, since the εἵματα are more like tapestries, hangings), are dogged by an aggressive debate, the very terms of which are fraught with difficulty. Perhaps the most quoted words of Fraenkel's commentary have been: 'the king is, at least up to now, completely composed; he speaks with the gracious dignity of a great gentleman'.[114] Rather than attacking, however rightly, the anachronism of the terminology of his judgement, critics would do well to turn first to Fraenkel's methodological statement for the reading of this passage:

The clue to Agamemnon's behaviour must be found in the play itself. As he nowhere reveals his motives explicitly, we must draw our inferences from the general picture of his personality. This may seem a risky undertaking and exposed to the fallacies of a subjective interpretation. All that a conscientious reader can possibly do is to try to outline the characteristic features as they present themselves to his mind. Other readers must be allowed to reach different conclusions, provided, however, they do not neglect or distort any piece of clear evidence in the words of the play (p. 441).

As often with Fraenkel's methodological position, this is difficult to analyse because, mainly, of the vagueness of his terms. What is the relation between 'general picture' and the play itself? How can a 'general picture' of Agamemnon's personality/behaviour be a *starting*-point ('draw inferences from') for the analysis of his personality/behaviour in this scene? A 'general' picture without, and to define, this scene? A picture of the general from the *parodos* perhaps? How general a general(-ity)? What constitutes 'clear evidence'/'a clue'? How do features '*present themselves*'? Or is that an attempt to mask the work of interpretation, the teleological hermeneutic of clue/solution? What is the unclear evidence (of)? Does not the interpreter's selection of 'clear evidence' predetermine, as it is predetermined by, its 'answer'? Verrall also offers a concise statement

---

[113] Cf. Kitto 1956, p. 23: 'What was a metaphor when applied to Paris comes to life in a startling fashion.'

[114] P. 414. Not an isolated remark. Cf. 'sentiment of a true gentleman'...'the *gentilezza* of the utterances of the king and queen' (p. 425).

of how to read this scene:[115] 'Our reading of the scene will depend on the view we take of the king's state of mind in relation to his wife' and (somewhat more brusquely than Fraenkel) 'The impression that his language makes upon me is that he hates her.' Their arguments have, it seems, certain similarities. Both treat words as 'evidence' or 'clues' of something (knowable) behind the text, 'personality' / 'state of mind', which is then proved by an appeal back to the words (the circularity of which is marked) and which, furthermore, is regarded as an *origin* for the words, a transcendental source: thus the inconsistencies of language, the play, are limited by an appeal to the (in-)consistency of human character; language becomes transparent; thus for Fraenkel the openness of language, the production of meaning in difference, despite his earlier claim that other readers must be allowed to reach different conclusions (how can these passages be reconciled?), must be limited and defined precisely *according to* this (already) postulated character: on 936, 'He answers the question in the affirmative very emphatically, but quite quietly without a trace of contempt or irritation which would certainly have been understandable.' ἐν ποικίλοις ἂν κάρτα μοι βῆναι δοκεῖ is defined in its tone, strength, motive process of thought, even volume (!) according to an assumption of what Fraenkel postulates as a gentlemanly way to behave: reading through transparent language for a (true) origin of words in the complexity of the human(ist) mind.

Opposed to this view of character is what P. E. Easterling calls 'the new orthodoxy' of 'no character'.[116] This finds its modern apologists in J. Jones and the textual critic R. D. Dawe.[117] Dawe is, following Tycho von Wilamowitz, concerned with inconsistencies. These are not, he claims, inconsistencies with regard to an external reality, but with regard to what he calls 'poetic reality': a postulated internal coherence. This is linked to the poet's intention: 'When inconsistencies occur, they may arise *from carelessness or indifference*. Alternatively, they may be part of a *deliberate technique*.'[118] The choice is between an inconsistency that the poet put there or an inconsistency that the poet didn't notice! The recognition of inconsistency itself by the reader is an assumption that Dawe presumably regards as self-evident or straightforward: certainly no discussion is forwarded in his article. How can one tell the difference between deliberate and careless inconsistencies? This question, which would, one may hope, lead to a recognition of the intentionalism fundamental to his article,

---

[115] Appendix R.
[116] 1973, p. 3. See also Garvie 1969, p. 132 n. 2.
[117] Dawe 1963. Jones 1962, sections 1 and 2.
[118] P. 25 (my emphasis). Cf. also pp. 27, 31.

is answered or masked by an appeal to 'major' and 'minor' inconsistencies. Major inconsistencies are inconsistencies 'in the dramatic logic of the plays themselves' (1963, p. 25). Does this imply that they are so major that they must be regarded as significant and not mere carelessness? Where is the borderline? Is it a continuum of inconsistencies (if that is possible) only the upper end of which is to be regarded?

Let us consider, however, one of Dawe's examples of an 'inconsistency'. 'In reality no person of whatever quality would try to glorify his warlike deeds by emphasising that the whole enterprise was undertaken for the sake of a woman. Aeschylus has here (823–4) shattered the dramatic illusion to put a damning phrase into the mouth of the king' (p. 48). 'Shattered the dramatic illusion' would seem to indicate the inconsistency in the poetic 'reality', a lack of internal coherence. Yet this seems to be proved by an appeal to precisely the external reality Dawe claimed to reject: 'In reality no person...'! If this inconsistency is not to test the reader, a sort of joke, 'inconsistency', would seem to be here something contrary to the expectations of 'reality' that Dawe brings to the play (that is, ignoring the produced and played-with levels of referentiality discussed above), or that he considers all readers must bring to the play: does his term 'dramatic logic' imply a prior set of rules, external to the narrative against which the narrative is to be judged, and judged here, for Dawe, as falling short?

We are all familiar with Klytemnestra as a masterful, ruthless, even demonic figure. But when she delivers her beacon speech she is not a wronged mother or a faithless wife: she is – and I know some will recoil in horror from this sentence – little more than a mouthpiece for Aeschylean iambics. His passion for geography thus indulged, Aeschylus makes her next speech describe the scene in the ruined city of Troy. She cannot possibly have known what conditions were actually like there but she speaks with the authority of a messenger and the insight of Kassandra. Only at the end of this speech is she the Klytemnestra that we know from her scenes with the king and his captive (pp. 50–1).

Although this may at first read as though Dawe recognises the importance of language itself in these scenes, the dismissive contrast between 'a wronged mother or a faithless wife' and 'little more than a mouthpiece for Aeschylean iambics' indicates a generalised form for the terms of his discussion: 'not *a* wronged mother' or '*a* mouthpiece'; the words (language) seem to be opposed (though how can they be kept separate?) to something behind the words (character), something with which 'we are all familiar'. Dawe desires to make the text familiar, to dismiss and thus control what he terms inconsistencies by a process of normalisation to his notion of the familiar, a form of non-reading.

On *Cho.* 691ff., Clytemnestra's reaction to the news of Orestes' death, a notoriously difficult passage (see below pp. 167–9 for a further discussion), Dawe marks the steps of his argument for us (p. 54):

(2) nothing in the speech (691–700) suggests insincerity.

(3) Kilissa tells us that Klytemnestra is secretly glad at the news of her son's death.

(4) There is no straightforward way of reconciling the queen's reported reaction...with the reaction which we have seen on stage some fifty lines earlier – which is a mother hearing tidings of her son's death.[119]

(5) Each reading is appropriate[120] to the immediate context.

(6) Conclusion that the poet has subordinated character to plot in quite a violent manner, so that each scene can be played for all it is worth. To achieve this end the poet is even willing to use the same speech twice for contrary purposes.

The fact that Cilissa describes Clytemnestra's verbal reaction as indicating an emotional response different from that which Dawe indicates we must have accepted, received, is a disruption that points to the heuristic gap in speech, the failure of communication / possibility of falsification. This disruption is indeed sited within the hermeneutic discourse I have been tracing. One cannot say Clytemnestra's reaction is false, Cilissa's interpretation genuine, or vice versa: the tension between the two possibilities is what is significant. For (and this is what Dawe in his extraordinary last sentence seems to hope to evade) 'repetition produces difference'[121] and it is in difference that meaning is constituted. A speech *is used* an infinite number of ways, signifying as it does by its contextualisation in the syntagmatic order of the play.

So Dawe's text on inconsistency seems to be (self-referentially) inconsistent in its denial of and then constant appeal to a generalised external reality. Is it a major or minor inconsistency? Is it 'deliberate technique' or 'careless indifference'? How can we tell? How can we read this text on its own terms? It erases the possibility of its own (consistent) reading.

119 '*A* mother'. Again Dawe uses a generalised expectation of reality without a consideration of the model. This example is a particularly poignant conceptual naivety in a play which considers what constitutes a parent.

120 Cf. pp. 5–6. Appropriate to what? What is an 'appropriate...reading', or an 'appropriate reaction'? Even in Dawe's terms, it seems extraordinary that he cannot conceive of the possibility of a person on stage falsely interpreting what has happened, is happening. Especially with regard to the carpet scene!

121 Said 1974, p. 33.

Inconsistency and character remain a continuing theme of classical criticism:[122] Mrs Easterling attempts to find a middle line, rejecting Fraenkel and Dawe. But she replaces character with 'human intelligibility': 'for human intelligibility in the carpet scene is not at all the same as attributing motives to Agamemnon in terms of his character' (1973, p. 10). What does 'human intelligibility' mean? It is a 'relation between this scene and the way people behave in real life': that is, again an appeal to a generalised, external referentiality. This leads us to 'supply a colouring of motive'. For example, of the beginning of the carpet scene, 'it is easy to imagine a highly successful person in his moment of triumph being simplistic in this sort of way' (p. 10). As with Dawe, a reading through language, appealing to the familiar ('*a* highly successful person', 'it is easy to imagine', and even 'real life'), without considering (because 'it is easy') the problematic relation between literature and the familiar, or literature and 'real life'. Thus the unfamiliarity of literature is dealt with, controlled, and the language itself is normalised (or ignored).[123]

Gould (1978) further develops with some subtlety the notion of 'human intelligibility' to include notions of 'discourse', 'poetic language': he recognises that 'we have only language' (48) and talks of 'the texture and continuity of metaphor and imagery rather than...a kit of clues on the basis of which to reconstruct their motivation' (48). He maintains a shifting criterion of 'human intelligibility'; but the move to personality is still followed: 'we cannot do without the concept of personality here' (41). This is supported by 'Indeed, the attenuation of personality, the gradual bleaching out of all its colours, that takes place in her confrontation with the chorus after Agamemnon's murder...would be unintelligible in terms of dramatic strategy, if the thing itself had not been so palpable a factor hitherto in the play' (42). The apparent tautology, or self-referentiality, of defending the need for the presence of the concept of personality by an appeal to its already being there marks the problematic movement from his emphasis on language to the development of personality, character, a move marked, concluded, by such statements as 'we feel it in the physical aura that surrounds Klytemnestra'; but marked in its absence, for there is no indication beyond the 'we feel', of how he moves from the language, which constitutes the character, to 'the physical sensual presence' (beyond

[122] There are numerous other critics who have commented on these problems. Among classicists, see Anderson 1929 and 1932, Betensky 1978, Earp 1950, Garton 1957, Michelini 1979, Scott 1969, Simpson 1971. For an interesting cross-section of views from non-classicist critics and further bibliography see *New Literary History* 5 (1974).

[123] Mrs Easterling has told me that she would not now have published this article in its present form.

language?). Indeed, he concludes 'We do best to approach the intelligibility of his dramatic persons...*through* their language' (47, my italics). They are 'parts of a world of metaphor' (47),[124] parts of the 'metaphorical colouring of the whole language of the play' (45), and yet 'we have a very strong sense of her *as a person*' (59). Both part of language (though by a gesture of supplementarity added to the plenitude of the 'whole language of the play') and yet a person. The link: 'We cannot quite detach Klytemnestra from what I have called the play's "world"' (45). The 'quite' seems to point to the difficulty of the connection between 'personality' and 'language' here, the difficulty of defining boundaries of personality, and boundaries between personalities, in the 'world of metaphor', the shifting 'possibility of non-sense'.

I will be approaching these problems of character and consistency and reading – problems which are raised not only in Aeschylean criticism – in two ways. I shall first offer a reading of this complex scene moving towards an investigation of how the difficulties outlined in and through the critics discussed above arise. Secondly, these more specific conclusions will be developed more abstractly in the second chapter (pp. 167–9), when I consider the scene of Clytemnestra's reaction to the news of Orestes' death. The reading itself, however (since methodology and reading are mutually implicative), stands in contrast to the readings of the critics discussed above.

In his reply to Clytemnestra (914–30), Agamemnon addresses her as Λήδας γένεθλον (914). This seems particularly significant after the discussion of naming and the significance of πῶς σε προσειπῶ and after the chorus which considered the production of events in terms of 'parentage', the character of the parents returning in the children. Clytemnestra had been called Τυνδάρεω θύγατερ (83–4) by the chorus. Here she is addressed through her mother's name rather than her father's. This difference points to the uncertainty of her genitor, since Leda had slept with both Zeus and Tyndareus. The implications of the adulterous nature of Clytemnestra's mother are obvious.[125] On δωμάτων ἐμῶν φύλαξ, Fraenkel, attacking Headlam, rightly quotes *Odyssey* 19.525–6, but not the lines around it, which are significant:

ὡς καὶ ἐμοὶ δίχα θυμὸς ὀρώρεται ἔνθα καὶ ἔνθα,
ἠὲ μένω παρὰ παιδὶ καὶ ἔμπεδα πάντα φυλάσσω,
κτῆσιν ἐμὴν δμῷάς τε καὶ ὑψερεφὲς μέγα δῶμα

---

[124] Gould rightly notes his debt to Traversi and others in this notion.
[125] Which is not to say we must read it with Verrall as a deliberate slur by Agamemnon, nor by denying Verrall must we accept Fraenkel's reading of 'a respectful form of address': in its juxtaposition to the previous chorus, say, and in contrast to her previous appellation, the language has the possibility of the implication.

εὐνήν τ' αἰδομένη πόσιος δήμοιό τε φῆμιν
ἣ ἤδη ἅμ' ἕπωμαι 'Αχαιῶν ὅς τις ἄριστος
μνᾶται

In this famous passage of Penelope speaking to her husband, who is disguised as a beggar, of her choice between fidelity and remarriage, we see the terms of the choice of action (δίχα θυμὸς ὀρώρεται) offered: Penelope decides on the former course and is renowned as the exemplum of the faithful wife: Clytemnestra, on the other hand, does not stay παρὰ παιδί but sends Orestes away: she does not guard the possessions of the home but lays them out to be walked on; she enters into conflict with the servants who resent her; she does not respect her husband's bed, and, as we shall shortly see (937–9), she rejects δήμοιο φῆμιν. So while δωμάτων φύλαξ is not in itself an insulting phrase, it does point to the difference between Penelope and Clytemnestra, to the way in which Clytemnestra is *not* a φύλαξ.

The 'gentle irony'[126] of the beginning of Agamemnon's reply, 'Your speech is suited to my absence: for you have drawn it out to great length', is interesting. As Fraenkel claims and Denniston–Page are willing to allow, this may have seemed 'conventional' and 'entirely without offence' to the Athenian audience, however odd and ungracious a remark it may seem to us. (We have also seen reasons why Fraenkel should be concerned to look for evidence to prove this remark 'entirely without offence'.) The play on words, however, depends not on a single sound-image referring simultaneously to different meanings, as with Clytemnestra's pun, but on the predication of a single adjective in the same sense to two different nouns. It is the juxtaposition, parallelism of 'the speech' and the 'Trojan War' that constitutes the ironising. Clytemnestra's word play, like her beacon lights, depends on a recognition and manipulation of the signifier, as does her hypocrisy, her falsehoods. Agamemnon's irony works on a different level, which does not challenge or manipulate the relation between signifier and signified. It is, of course, precisely Clytemnestra's manipulation of language, mastery of words, that comes to the fore in the stichomythia, as she persuades Agamemnon to walk on the tapestries: his opening comment indicates immediately the difference between their language, which we will see played out in the stichomythia.

His request to be praised παρ' ἄλλων, which is glossed from the scholiast by Fraenkel as μὴ παρὰ τῶν οἰκείων, rejects Clytemnestra's fulsome praises. ἄλλων, 'others', is in opposition to ἐμῶν. ἐμοί (920), ἐμέ (925) – both are last word in the line – and ἐμοὶ μέν (924:

---

[126] Fraenkel's description.

the μέν *solitarium* emphasises ἐμοί considerably) seem to pick up this sense of self, which is placed in opposition first to γυναικός, then to βαρβάρου and finally to the gods, who are to be praised in such a way – as he said in his opening words. φόβου (924) is his reaction to an act not suited to his mortal nature: the recognition of the φθόνος of the gods, that malevolent force we saw in the *parodos* (ἐπίφθονος Ἄρτεμις, 134) as the motive force leading to the sacrifice of Iphigeneia. There the adjective was used in its active sense, 'bearing a grudge against'; here it is used passively, 'likely to cause a grudge'. As Artemis feeling a grudge was seen as a cause of the events leading towards Agamemnon's death, so his action of walking on the carpet is seen as a cause of a grudge on the divine level: this active/passive play obscures a pattern of cause and effect, helping to create the over-determination often noted in the carpet scene.

τὸ μὴ κακῶς φρονεῖν (927) refers back to τὸν φρονεῖν βροτοὺς ὁδώσαντα (176–7) and the repetitions of φρονεῖν in the hymn to Zeus, and to τὸ παντότολμον φρονεῖν μετέγνω (221) where Agamemnon's action is described precisely in terms of a negatively judged φρονεῖν. The statement here (927) appears, then, to point to a further cause of Agamemnon's impending doom, which end is hinted at by his own phrase, χρὴ βίον τελευτήσαντ'. τελευτήσαντ' picks up γάμου πικρὰς τελευτάς (745) and its connection with τέλος with its religious overtones. τέλος was how Clytemnestra described the strewing of the tapestries (908). It is how he describes the act of walking on the tapestries as completion of a vow. It is to Zeus Teleios that she prays as Agamemnon enters the palace, a prayer τὰς ἐμὰς εὐχὰς <u>τέλει</u> (973). Both 'bring to completion' and also 'perform a sacrifice', 'do'. Action becomes seen within a religious framework of ritual which not only seems to increase the sense of over-determination of the carpet scene – θυσίαν ἑτέραν – but also is to be seen within the 'theologised' narrative we have commented on before. When the pattern of events is regarded in terms of divine forces of the ethico-religious terminology, such as, say, hubris, an action of murder becomes seen as an act of sacrifice, a ritual act of communication, exchange, between gods and men. That the ambiguity also exists between the sense 'an end' and this sense of sacrifice helps to undercut (as we have seen before) the notion of a definable point of end, since the act of 'bringing to an end' is seen as *part* of a (communication) process.

Fraenkel's masterly exposition of the stichomythia, followed with caution by Denniston–Page, considers the opposite views held on this controversial passage: his main cause for speculation remains the first two lines (931–2). μὴ παρὰ γνώμην ἐμοί: the sense of 'not contrary to your true opinion' gives a clear train of thought. But the sense of 'will', taking γνώμην closely with ἐμοί (the repetition at the end of three lines of ἐγώ, ἐμοί, ἐμέ gives an 'undertone of strife between two wills' (Headlam)) and its connection with an assertion of κράτος cannot simply be dismissed as Fraenkel does, 'there is no room for the view generally held since Schütz...noli ea adversus sententiam meam dicere'. For as we will see, in answering according to his opinion, Agamemnon yields to Clytemnestra's will: her final comment (943), unfortunately corrupted, seems to stem from a juxtaposition of κράτος and παρίημι. κράτος, as we have seen, had been the description of Clytemnestra's power, both in the watchman's speech, and when she first speaks (258): here, she regards her πειθώ (πίθου), her power in language as the assertion of her κράτος. The tension between the sexes is a power-struggle – a power-struggle played in the scene of language. So any ambiguity between 'will' and 'opinion' in Clytemnestra's request to Agamemnon to speak is significant.

Clytemnestra's argument is based on the use of potentials, on undercutting Agamemnon's assertion by showing him that under certain circumstances walking on the tapestries would be the right thing to do: it is based on an idea of manipulation of the signifying function of the act of walking on the tapestries: if there was a preceding vow, the act would be a duty (τέλος), and not ἐπίφθονον πόρον. A different person (Priam) would walk on tapestries, if he had achieved such success. φθόνος: where there is no φθόνος there is no ζῆλος, which, of course, does not mean (logically) that therefore ζῆλος implies the necessity of φθόνος. The negatives do not prove the positive statement she seeks. What we read is the force of πειθώ, the art of persuasion, the manipulation of signifiers, the recognition that the act of walking on the embroideries could imply more and opposite things to the implications Agamemnon drew. This force aims at victory (940–2: once again the assertion of the sexual determinants of the argument οὔτοι γυναικός, 940) and significantly the first and emphatic word of her last line of persuasion is πίθου: her victory is by/in words; it is for Agamemnon to admit that the act of walking on the tapestries has differing, variable significances; that the act of walking on the tapestries has a floating significance. A floating signifier...

This openness of signification has led many critics to try to develop a scheme of motivation and to 'cash out' the 'true' signification of the act of walking on the tapestries – correcting foolish Agamemnon, or blaming his pride. But while it may be possible to emphasise implications of the act (as J. Jones successfully does with the economic significance of the crushing of fine things) and while it may prove advantageous for *an* actor to produce *a* scheme of motivation for himself in *a* production, the ambiguities of *telos* in this scene, and the play in γνώμη, and the way the clash between the king and queen is almost *depersonalised* by its fixing upon an external object and by the marked lack of explicit motivation, and in particular the argument from potentialities, all function towards the production of meaning, and it is this process of the production of meaning that is important. For the openness of the process of signification itself signifies. The shifting signifier–signified relation (its potentialities), the dangers of which societies (must) control, is the condition of possibility, indeed the *form* of Clytemnestra's *peitho*, as it was of her deceptive falsehoods. Indeed, the manipulation of the signifier (by Clytemnestra), its very constitution as floating signifier *undercuts as it makes possible* each attempt (the critics' and Agamemnon's) to reduce the over-determination, the openness. As Segal has recently written 'The tapestry...is itself the emblem and the instrument of disruption in the sign system on which all civilised order rests.'[127] In the carpet scene, the interwoven systems of language, economics, religion and sexuality are set at risk, placed *en jeu*.

The wealth of the house, as Jones notes (1962, pp. 87ff.), is an important consideration (cf. 948–9, 957), as Agamemnon steps down. But again Clytemnestra dismisses his concern with a magnificent (and sibilant) appeal to the wealth of the seas:

> ἔστιν θάλασσα. τίς δέ νιν κατασβέσει;   (958)

'The sea is there. Who will drain it?' Her faith in continuing prosperity seems more than somewhat hubristic; the house of Atreus does not know how to be poor:

> ...πένεσθαι δ' οὐκ ἐπίσταται δόμος   (962)

This will be picked up markedly in the fears and worries of the third stasimon. Her description of her husband as τελείου (972) indicates finally Clytemnestra's use of multivalent language once more, the net of words in which she has enveloped Agamemnon. τελείου means 'full-grown', 'perfect', and applied to ἀνήρ it seems to imply almost 'paterfamilias' (L.–S.–J.). But as Verrall remarks, it is the word used particularly of sacrificial (τέλος) animals. And as Zeitlin points out, the killing of Agamemnon is imaged as a sacrifice.[128] So it is not in any innocent way that the queen prays as they exit to Ζεῦ τέλειε. 'Fulfilment' is no straightforward object.

So the manipulation of language by Clytemnestra, her disruption of communicational exchange, itself signifies in the carpet scene. And

---

[127] 1981, p. 55.
[128] 1965, pp. 475ff. On these lines see also Goldhill 1984.

the argument of potentialities, redefining the significance of the act of stepping on the tapestries by redefining contexts and connotations, opens the text to the complex over-determination often noted by critics and, moreover, such openness, such over-determination, undercuts attempts (the critics' and Agamemnon's) to control the signification absolutely. The floating text-ile cannot be pinned down. The manipulation of signs and corruption of exchange that we saw particularly in the beacon-speeches scene and the messenger scene become here the instrument and means towards the murder of the king, the collapse of the 'civilised order' of the hierarchies of society. As the order of society depends on its powers of discourse control, so here it is the weapon of deceitful language that is depicted as Clytemnestra's force. The fact that Agamemnon's murder itself is not depicted on stage (though there is but little on-stage violence in our surviving corpus of tragedies) draws further attention to the violent drama of logos being played out in this scene.

'Between the...and the...falls the...':
gaps and hesitations

The third stasimon, which follows the dramatic exit of Clytemnestra and Agamemnon into the palace, is (not surprisingly?) a song of intense worry and uncertainty. It begins with a statement of the chorus' fear,[129] which is connected explicitly with hope (991, 999), as we saw earlier, as the link between present and future, and is depicted in terms of soothsaying, prediction: δεῖμα προστατήριον καρδίας τερασκόπου...μαντιπολεῖ. These three modes of seeking for, or expressing a lack of, narrative control, of telling what will happen, fall significantly between the expectation of the murder of Agamemnon and its depiction (1343) as a prelude to the long scene concerned explicitly with foretelling the future, the scene between Cassandra and the chorus. It delays the fulfilment of expectation, prediction, fear, by discussing the nature of expectation, prediction, fear: the writing is in a sense self-reflexive. The chorus also refer back to their altercation with Clytemnestra at 274–5:

> οὐδ' ἀποπτύσαι δίκαν
> δυσκρίτων ὀνειράτων
> θάρσος εὐπειθὲς ἴ-
> ζει φρενὸς φίλον θρόνον;   (980–3)

εὐπειθές here, however, refers to θάρσος, the courage to reject dreams, whereas at 274 it had referred to ὀνείρων φάσματ', the

---

[129] De Romilly 1958 remains an important study of fear in Aeschylus.

quality of persuasiveness in dreams. This tension between dreams as
a false or a true omen makes them δυσκρίτων[130] and will return in
the *Choephoroi*, where Clytemnestra's dream is treated as an omen,
and where the language of true soothsaying, accurate prediction
returns also: τορός...ὀνειρόμαντις (*Cho.* 32–3), κρῖται...τῶνδ'
ὀνειράτων (38–9), and where Orestes says of Zeus: πέμπειν ἔχοις ἂν
σήματ' εὐπειθῆ βροτοῖς (*Cho.* 259). This dream is connected with
fear by the chorus:

ἔκ τ' ὀνειράτων
καὶ νυκτιπλάγκτων δειμάτων   (*Cho.* 523–4)

and then expounded by Orestes:

κρίνω δέ τοί νιν ὥστε συγκόλλως ἔχειν   (*Cho.* 542)

to which the chorus respond:

τερασκόπον δὴ τῶνδέ σ' αἱροῦμαι πέρι   (*Cho.* 551)

Here, then, too, the functions of the interpretation of omens (prediction, soothsaying), fear, and dreams (as a predictive sign) are linked
at a central moment of expression of expectation: that is, at the
statement of Orestes (554ff.) of his plan of action. As a preface to
Apollo's entry in the *Eumenides* to expound his plan to save Orestes,
we have:

ἰατρόμαντις δ' ἐστὶ καὶ τερασκόπος
καὶ τοῖσιν ἄλλοις δωμάτων καθάρσιος   (*Eum.* 62–3)

Similarly, the ghost of Clytemnestra, a dream (ὄναρ, *Eum.* 16), says,
motivating the Erinues in opposition to Apollo's plan:

εὕδουσα γὰρ φρὴν ὄμμασιν λαμπρύνεται
ἐν ἡμέρᾳ δὲ μοῖρ' ἀπρόσκοπος βροτῶν   (*Eum.* 104–5)

where the value of the dream as an omen, giving an insight into the
future, normally hidden, is made clear.

So we see that, as with the third stasimon of the *Agamemnon*, at
a significant point of expression of advancement of future narrative,
the text is concerned with the prediction of future narrative, how it
may be clearly seen, by what signs, how it subsides into fear or hope
as an expression of the lack of narrative control: Apollo in his function
as ἰατρόμαντις, τερασκόπος, sends Orestes off with the words:

μέμνησο, μὴ φόβος σε νικάτω φρένας   (*Eum.* 87)

To return to the third stasimon of the *Agamemnon*: πεύθομαι δ' ἀπ'
ὀμμάτων νόστον αὐτόμαρτυς ὤν (988–9) continues the structure of
imagery of witness/sight as the criterion for κρίνειν. It is set in
opposition (δ'...ὅμως, 990) to the feeling of foreboding. Sight is

---

[130] See also, for the chorus' inability to decide between opposites, 1561:
δύσμαχα...κρῖναι.

once again questioned as a mode of judgement, as what is seen with their own eyes, that is, Agamemnon's *nostos*, will be realised to have been a source of false expectations, expectations of falsehood – ἐς δῶμ' ἄελπτον (911).

The second strophe is badly mutilated: it picks up, however, the last sentence of the antistrophe α (ἐς τὸ μὴ τελεσφόρον) and talks of avoiding shipwreck by throwing freight overboard. This is couched in the terms of fear of excessive wealth and sickness,[131] and then of an evil 'the worst consequences of which could still be averted at the last moment' (Fraenkel). This is placed in contrast[132] to death, the spilling of blood, which cannot be stopped or changed: it is the ultimate lack of narrative control. This notion returns importantly throughout the trilogy (cf. e.g. *Eum.* 263, *Cho.* 48, *Eum.* 647–8). Death is claimed as a fixed point in the narrative (even if the ghost of Clytemnestra, the prayers of the *kommos* to Agamemnon, seem to belie this) as is birth, origin: τέλος and ἀρχή. As we saw with the etymologising and with τέρμα πόνων, πόνος οἴχεται, the narrative searches for control by the postulation of limits.

The stasimon ends with a further expression of this lack of control:

νῦν δ' ὑπὸ σκότῳ βρέμει [sc. καρδία]
θυμαλγής τε καὶ οὐδὲν ἐπελπομένα ποτε καίριον ἐκτολυπεύσειν
ζωπυρουμένας φρενός   (1030–3)

ὑπὸ σκότῳ continues the imagery of light and dark, linking darkness, lack of clarity once more to lack of control. οὐδὲν ἐπελπομένα: 'hope', the mode of extension into the future, is here without possibility of the desired accuracy, οὐδὲν...ποτε καίριον. ἐκτολυπεύσειν, 'to finish off', 'end': it is completion, τέλος, that is aimed at, but which cannot be fixed with any accuracy.

The clear metaphor...

The scene with Cassandra and the chorus and, at first, Clytemnestra, is the longest scene of the play and it is of corresponding importance. As with the πειθώ and hypocritical deception of the carpet scene, as with the messenger scene and its undercutting of the process of referential language, as with the beacon-speeches scene and its concentration on the process of signification, so too this scene is focused on the problematic of the exchange of language, but now, as opposed, say, to Clytemnestra's manipulation of signs to engender

---

[131] Cf. Vickers 1973, especially pp. 364ff. – sickness presaging the threats of the Erinues.
[132] It also stands in contrast to their own actions 'at the last moment' where their indecision is marked.

a reception of words that is misleading, the viewpoint of the heuristic process is reversed, so that we have referential language, language that is not only true, but also capable of accurate prediction; but language that is incapable of being received. The focus shifts from the manipulation of utterance to the failure to be received.

Clytemnestra's first speech is an example of her manipulative language of deceit. She asks Cassandra to take part in the sacrifices (κοινωνὸν εἶναι). It is, of course, as a victim. The chorus respond significantly:

σοί τοι λέγουσα παύεται σαφῆ λόγον   (1047)

The ambiguity is marked: 'She has stopped speaking and what she was saying was clear, transparent' or 'she has stopped speaking clearly'. Fraenkel says, to avoid the ambiguity, that 'σοί τοι λέγουσα παύεται contains a complete thought in itself...and σαφῆ λόγον is added as a characterizing afterthought'. Thus he punctuates with a comma after παύεται. Even with Fraenkel's attempt to demarcate the sentence to a clear expression (σαφῆ λόγον?), the irony of σαφῆ does not cease.[133] The chorus' language continues to emphasise the process of communication:

πείθοι᾽ ἂν εἰ πείθοι᾽· ἀπειθοίης δ᾽ ἴσως   (1049)

The threefold repetition of (α-)πειθ- picks up Clytemnestra's πιθοῦ (943), and refers back ultimately to ἀγγελίας πειθοῖ (86–7) and points to the process of communication as a bridging of the gap: as Clytemnestra now says:

...λέγουσα πείθω νιν λόγῳ   (1052)

The function of speech is emphasised by the pleonastic λέγουσα... λόγῳ and the function of communication by the assertion πείθω νιν. As we saw in the carpet scene, Clytemnestra's persuasion is precisely in λέγουσα...λόγον. The chorus also exhort πείθου (1054). Clytemnestra hints at the unexpected nature of the sacrifice (ὡς οὔποτ᾽ ἐλπίσασι τήνδ᾽ ἕξειν χάριν) and then with a 'suggestive though unusual' (Fraenkel) phrase points precisely to the nature of the communication process in question:

εἰ...μὴ δέχη λόγον   (1060)

As Kennedy says, 'correlative (to this expression) is δοῦναι λόγον'. It is the process of 'giving' and 'receiving' λόγον, between which

---

133 On σαφής and its connections with sight and knowledge, cf. Xenophanes F. 34: καὶ τὸ μὲν οὖν σαφὲς οὔτις ἀνὴρ ἴδεν οὐδέ τις ἔσται | εἰδὼς ἀμφὶ θεῶν τε καὶ ἄσσα λέγω περὶ πάντων. | εἰ γὰρ καὶ τὰ μάλιστα τύχοι τετελεσμένον εἰπών | αὐτὸς ὅμως οὐκ οἶδε. δόκος δ᾽ ἐπὶ πᾶσι τέτυκται. Another example of a constellation of terms important in the *Oresteia* in an earlier poet. Cf. p. 7 n. 17.

there is a possibility of breakdown (εἰ... μή). Clytemnestra, after her λέγουσα πείθω νιν λόγῳ, resorts to

σὺ δ' ἀντὶ φωνῆς φράζε καρβάνῳ κερί.   (1061)

She resorts to the non-voiced signifier (as with the beacons etc.) to which the chorus respond:

ἑρμηνέως ἔοικεν ἡ ξένη τοροῦ
δεῖσθαι   (1062–3)

The interpreter stands, as we saw above, precisely in the gap between δοῦναι and δέχεσθαι λόγον.

As prelude to the 'Cassandra scene', then, we see emphasised the process of communication and the heuristic gap in communication and the means of bridging that gap (πειθώ, ἑρμηνεύς) and the desire for clarity (σαφῆ, τοροῦ). The silence of Cassandra (the indication of lack of reception) emphasises the process of utterance (ἀντὶ φωνῆς, λέγουσα... λόγῳ, λέγουσα... λόγον). After Clytemnestra leaves, however, Cassandra begins to speak (in Greek) bewailing Apollo. The chorus ask her twice why she addresses Apollo in such terms: significantly they call Apollo Λοξίου (1074), τὸν θεόν (1078): for the reason that Cassandra offers (γάρ, 1082) is an etymology of the name Apollo, as ἀπόλλων, 'destroyer'. As we saw, the use of etymology is an attempt to ground language in a point of origin, to relate signifier and signified in a not necessarily arbitrary relation. Cassandra's appellation is thus fixed and repeated with force: the chorus address the god not only differently from Cassandra, but by two different appellations. Thus we see the first indications of the true language of Cassandra not being fully received.

Cassandra asks 'to what house' Apollo is leading her; the chorus, emphasising the process of question and answer (εἰ σὺ μὴ τόδ' ἐννοεῖς, | ἐγὼ λέγω σοι. καὶ τάδ' οὐκ ἐρεῖς ψύθη: 'You will not call it false'), say πρὸς τὴν Ἀτρειδῶν – 'to the house of the Atreids'. But Cassandra, accepting but correcting (μὲν οὖν) their answer (which stands in contrast to the chorus' assumption of a simple opposition of truth and falsehood – she precisely does not 'not call it false') offers an extraordinary description of the house running with blood:

μισόθεον μὲν οὖν, πολλὰ συνίστορα
αὐτόφονα κακὰ †καρτάναι†
ἀνδροσφαγεῖον καὶ πέδον ῥαντήριον   (1090–2)

Cassandra ('tracking' (1093–4) – judging by signs) begins her prophecy with a reference to the past, that the chorus understand (ἐπιπείθομαι, 1095), as they had understood the significance of Helen's name after the event. They describe Cassandra as a soothsayer and prophet (1098) which recalls the third stasimon, Calchas, the discourse of prediction that I have been considering. The chorus, however, cannot understand her prophecies (1105). Cassandra with an ambiguity especially significant in the description of Clytemnestra's actions uses the term τελεῖς (1107), τέλος (1109), which, followed by the explicit noun θύματος (1118), continues the ambiguity of 'complete', 'accomplish', 'perform a rite', 'sacrifice'. But the chorus still do not understand Cassandra's utilisation of the ambiguity:

> οὔπω ξυνῆκα. νῦν γὰρ ἐξ αἰνιγμάτων
> ἐπαργέμοισι θεσφάτοις ἀμηχανῶ   (1112–13)

ἐπαργέμοισι links us back to the imagery of sight, light, and darkness, and the desire for clarity: her language is more than not believed, it is not received, understood, οὔπω ξυνῆκα. Cassandra's language seems to be referential: as things *appear* in front of her, she describes them:

> τί τόδε φαίνεται;
> ἦ δίκτυόν τί γ' Ἅιδου   (1115–16)

But the chorus hearing the words revert to what has become a common reaction for them, faced with the passage of narrative over which they have no control, namely, fear:[134]

> οὔ με φαιδρύνει λόγος
> ἐπὶ δὲ καρδίαν ἔδραμε κροκοβαφὴς
> σταγών   (1120–2)

The parallel to the third stasimon is obvious, particularly as the chorus slip here into a more passionate lyric metre after the iambics of their previous interjections in this scene. It is noticeable that after Cassandra talks of what she sees, what appears, the chorus talk of λόγος: it is in their reaction to λόγος that they enter lyric intensity. Theirs is a fear for what might happen, (κακῷ δέ τῳ προσεικάζω τάδε, 1131), fear from the φάτις (1132) of soothsayers; Cassandra's fear is for what will happen. The chorus go on to say (1133–4) κακῶν γὰρ διαὶ πολυεπεῖς τέχναι θεσπιῳδῶν φόβον φέρουσιν μαθεῖν: as before, fear is the reaction bridging present and future narrative, a sort of prediction, and it is here linked to language: it is the 'wordy arts' that bring fear.

Cassandra's use of μίμνει (1149) recalls the reported words of Calchas (154–5) μίμνει γὰρ φοβερὰ παλίνορτος οἰκονόμος δολία κτλ. and perhaps μένει δ' ἀκοῦσαί τί μου μέριμνα (459–60). In both cases, the vagueness of that worry stands now in contrast to the specific fear of Cassandra; it emphasises the clarity of her terror, the precision of her prediction. It is only when she sings of the marriage

---

[134] Cf. Winnington-Ingram 1983, pp. 208–16, Scott 1969, Conacher 1974 on the chorus.

of Paris and then (in iambics), in vaguer terms, of her death that the chorus seem to understand:

Κα. νῦν δ' ἀμφὶ Κωκυτόν τε κ'Αχερουσίους
ὄχθους ἔοικα θεσπιῳδήσειν τάχα

Χο. τί τόδε τορὸν ἄγαν ἔπος ἐφημίσω;
νεογνὸς ἂν ἀίων μάθοι   (1160–3)

Indeed, the chorus conclude in their lack of understanding:

τέρμα δ' ἀμηχανῶ   (1177)

which as well as showing the failure of reception of Cassandra's prophecy, indicates also the lack of narrative control which we have seen focused around the sense of end (τέλος, τέρμα).

It is interesting that as Cassandra promises to speak clearly (1178ff.) she expresses herself in three similes: 1179 νεογάμου νύμφης δίκην, 1180–1 λαμπρὸς δ' ἔοικεν...πνέων ἐφήξειν, 1181 κύματος δίκην. Of this dense texture, Silk says[135] 'This intense concentration seems not merely apt for a prophetess versed in oracular equivocations, but somehow suggestive of her unique access to the complexities of events that are now reaching their fulfilment.' For λαμπρός can be seen with four separate senses, 'clear' of oracles, 'bright' of the bride's complexion, 'keen' of the wind, and 'bright' of the sun-light. Lucid...or ludic? This multivalency of word and interlocking of vehicles (to use Silk's and Richards' terminology) seems to suppress the tenor: the expression of clarity comes through an extremely complex interplay of meanings of the central term for 'clear', which, through the cumulative refraction of the structure of the similes, undercuts the very desire for clarity, and emphasises not simply 'unique access to the complexities of events' but the language to find and express the complexities of events. For it is through her prophetic language that she reaches the clarity in narrative: and significantly her true prophecies (marked by μαρτυρεῖτε, 1184; ἐκμαρτύρησον, 1196; μαρτυρεῖτε, 1317 (cf. 1095), 'witness', the basis of proof) stem from her expression of the πρώταρχον ἄτην, the postulation once more of an origin, in this case an origin for the narrative of ἄτη in the confusion of sexual boundaries by the adultery of Thyestes. The significant ambiguities of Cassandra's language play also in her use of τέλει (1202) where the sense of *munus* is to be qualified by the notion of 'rite', 'sacrifice', 'end'. This is perhaps picked up at 1253–4 where the chorus in their confusion say:

τοῦ γὰρ τελοῦντος οὐ ξυνῆκα μηχανήν.

and Cassandra rejoins

καὶ μὴν ἄγαν γ' Ἕλλην' ἐπίσταμαι φάτιν

[135] 1974, p. 197.

The ἄγαν γε, 'aye, all too well', applied to her understanding may (as well as merely pointing to the failure of communication despite the common tongue) be seen as referring also to the chorus' unwitting use of τελοῦντος in the sense of 'perform a rite', which points to the rites in the palace. It is because Cassandra sees the relevant ambiguity of the term (itself pointing, as we have seen, to the ambiguity of action) that she can talk of understanding language 'too well'.

Cassandra explains her plight:

ἔπειθον οὐδέν' οὐδὲν ὡς τάδ' ἤμπλακον   (1212)

To which the chorus reply, with great irony:

ἡμῖν γε μὲν δὴ πιστὰ θεσπίζειν δοκεῖς   (1213)

πειθώ leading to πίστις: but immediately, as if to test the chorus' remarks, the prophetic πόνος comes upon Cassandra. This juxtaposition to the chorus' statement of belief is marked; for, as we shall see, the chorus neither believe nor understand.

Her vision is firstly of the children of Thyestes, οἰκείας βορᾶς (1220), which is linked causally to the plot of Aegisthus:

ἐκ τῶνδε ποινάς φημι βουλεύειν τινὰ
λέοντ' ἄναλκιν ἐν λέχει στρωφώμενον   (1223–4)

The recognition of the causal pattern is indicative of the control sought for by the chorus. Agamemnon's error is described, however, as a misinterpretation of language:

οὐκ οἶδεν οἷα γλῶσσα μισητῆς κυνός,
λέξασα κἀκτείνασα φαιδρόνους δίκην   (1228–9)

A misunderstanding of the words a tongue said: the use of γλῶσσα,[136] the means of the production of sound (but not sense), indicates the gap between expression and feeling, the gap between the signifier and the signified. κυνός used in a derogatory sense seems to refer to Clytemnestra's own flattering use of the word, pointing once more to a significant ambiguity in language, and Cassandra's utilisation of it.

The conflict is expressed clearly in sexual terms:

θῆλυς ἄρσενος φονεύς
ἔστιν   (1231–2)

The use of the generic terms 'male' and 'female' indicates the generalised opposition of the sexes. Clytemnestra is referred to as ἀμφίσβαιναν ἢ Σκύλλαν, which, as Zeitlin notes,[137] emphasises the unnatural (female) character of the queen, that is recalled particularly

---

[136] This is picked up in the chorus' reaction to Clytemnestra's hypocrisy (1399).
[137] 1978, p. 55.

in the first stasimon of the *Choephoroi*, with its catalogue of corrupted females. She is also called παντότολμος (1237) which refers back to the description of Agamemnon's sacrifice of Iphigenia τὸ παντότολμον φρονεῖν μετέγνω (221) and this emphasises the parallelism between their actions which Clytemnestra herself will claim strongly (1417ff., 1431ff., 1525ff.) in her appeal to the sacrifice of Iphigeneia as motive for her regicide.

The perfect vision (language) of Cassandra, however, shows her what will happen, but changes (persuades) nothing: τὸ μέλλον ἥξει (1240). Her 'perfect' language, the accuracy that the chorus sought for, leads to accurate prediction – as the chorus hoped it would – but *not* (ironically) to narrative control.

As Cassandra feared, her language does not persuade the chorus of the future. Again the sexual antithesis is brought into focus by the misunderstanding of the chorus turning on a mistaken gender:

Χο.   τίνος πρὸς ἀνδρός...
Κα.   ἦ κάρτα ⟨μακ⟩ράν παρεκόπης χρησμῶν ἐμῶν   (1251–2)

παρεκόπης, as with παρακοπά (223), παράσημον (780), connotes a 'false coining', the wrong value, wrong signification.

As Cassandra predicts her own death (1258–63), her sense of lack of control grows into rage at her prophetic trappings:

τί δῆτ' ἐμαυτῆς καταγέλωτ' ἔχω τάδε
καὶ σκῆπτρα καὶ μαντεῖα περὶ δέρῃ στέφη;
σὲ μὲν πρὸ μοίρας τῆς ἐμῆς διαφθερῶ.
ἴτ' ἐς φθόρον   (1264–7)

After her prediction of the revenge of Orestes (again in the opposition of sexuality, mother and father, μητρόκτονον φίτυμα, ποινάτωρ πατρός (1281; see also below 1318–19) and the prediction of her own death once more (1290–1), the chorus still noncomprehending ask (with considerable irony) how she can go 'like an ox to the altar'. Cassandra's answer again points to this lack of control, the inevitability of τὸ μέλλον:

οὐκ ἔστ' ἄλυξις...
ἥκει τόδ' ἦμαρ. σμικρὰ κερδανῶ φυγῇ   (1299–1301)

The irony of the chorus' failure to understand the nature of the sacrifice continues (1310–12), showing again the difference in their recognition of language. Cassandra's final prediction sums up the future action in terms of a reciprocity and sexual tension:

...γυνὴ γυναικὸς ἀντ' ἐμοῦ θάνῃ
ἀνήρ τε δυσδάμαρτος ἀντ' ἀνδρὸς πέσῃ   (1318–19)

The juxtaposition of γυνή/γυναικός, ἀνήρ/ἀνδρός, the use of ἀντι-, the morally charged sexual term δυσδάμαρτος, as we have seen throughout the *Agamemnon*, is pointed and as we shall see in Chapter 2 is essential to the narrative structure, what Zeitlin has called 'the dynamics of misogyny'.

The chorus pick up her final comments on the changing future of mankind and apply it (in the potential structure of εἰ...) to Agamemnon, connecting it to the sense of reciprocal action:

> νῦν δ᾽ εἰ προτέρων αἷμ᾽ ἀποτείσῃ
> καὶ τοῖσι θανοῦσι θανὼν ἄλλων
> ποινὰς θανάτων ἐπικράνῃ
> τίς ἂν ἐξεύξαιτο βροτῶν ἀσινεῖ
> δαίμονι φῦναι τάδ᾽ ἀκούων;   (1338–42)

'But if he (Agamemnon) should pay for the blood of those slain before and give to the dead by his own death the recompense of other deaths, what man could boast himself born with fortune without harm, when hearing this?' As they sing this, comes to their hearing the cry of the dying Agamemnon.

The chorus' deliberation[138] (1347–70) stands in stark contrast to the attitude of Cassandra: without the ability to say what has happened or to predict what will happen, they are unable to act: one asks ἢ γὰρ τεκμηρίοισιν ἐξ οἰμωγμάτων | μαντευσόμεθα τἀνδρὸς ὡς ὀλωλότος; (1366–7), where the use of the word μαντεύειν (in the question) marks precisely the non-mantic process. As the next lines say: σάφ᾽ εἰδότας χρὴ τῶνδε μυθεῖσθαι πέρι. With Cassandra's accurate language (which language – ironically, after the apparent desire for univocality as accuracy/clarity – was itself metaphoric, allusive, ludic language), with her knowledge to predict accurately came (and this is one of the greatest ironies of the trilogy, essential to any discussion of 'free will' in the *Oresteia*) only a recognition of the inevitability of the future. Knowledge of the future constitutes a lack of free will. Nevertheless, paradoxically, for the chorus without an accurate knowledge or language to predict a sequence of cause and effect, action becomes something to be feared and even impossible for them. The ineffectuality of the chorus is the logical outcome of their lack of narrative control, their fear that stems from their inability to predict, from their lack of control of the risks of language. Their inability to see the beginning or the end with certainty, which seems as a lack of control to be a lack of free will, is in ironic tension with Cassandra's predictive vision of the inevitability of things.

---

[138] Cf. Winnington-Ingram 1983, pp. 208–16. Wills 1965. Taplin 1977, pp. 323ff.

The triumph of rhetoric / the rhetoric of triumph

Clytemnestra pre-empts their deliberations. With knowledge after the event (as with prescriptive etymologies) their possible action is too late. Now she appears[139] with the bodies of the king and Cassandra. She revels in the power of language which she claims as the means of her revenge:

πολλῶν πάροιθεν καιρίως εἰρημένων
τἀναντί᾽ εἰπεῖν οὐκ ἐπαισχυνθήσομαι   (1372-3)

αἰσχυνή/αἰσχύνεσθαι is that by which society seeks to repress and control the desire of transgression. Referring to women, it is commonly applied to sexual behaviour. Here its conjunction with τἀναντί᾽ εἰπεῖν marks again the association between Clytemnestra's adultery and verbal deceit, between sexuality and language as objects of (her) shamelessness. Moreover, her willingness to 'say opposite things' and 'to have spoken καιρίως' stand in contrast to the chorus' and Cassandra's desire for accurate language, their search for the right name as control. Clytemnestra's κράτος and lack of αἰσχυνή has been in the manipulation (perversion) of those desired boundaries. καιρίως, furthermore, not only implies language to fit her intentions, but also recalls the καιρίαν πληγήν by which Agamemnon was struck καιρίως οὐτασμένος (1344), that is, the fulfilment of those intentions. This links the murder of Agamemnon to the nets of language Clytemnestra here boasts of weaving καιρίως, those necessary nets of hypocrisy, of seeming:

πῶς γάρ τις ἐχθροῖς ἐχθρὰ πορσύνων, φίλοις
δοκοῦσιν εἶναι, πημονῆς ἀρκύστατ᾽ ἂν
φάρξειεν ὕψος κρεῖσσον ἐκπηδήματος;   (1374-6)

Her boasts continue as she moves into a description of the act of murder in a most blasphemous (perverted) parody of a libation to Zeus. This too is set within the imagery of the regicide as sacrifice, the double sense of *telos*. The sense of an end (the third libation being the last) comes to the fore:

τοσῶνδε κρατῆρ᾽ ἐν δόμοις κακῶν ὅδε
πλήσας ἀραίων αὐτὸς ἐκπίνει μολών   (1397-8)

As we have seen before and will see again, the expression of an end to reciprocity as closure is undercut. The idea of the third act providing a point of conclusion, completion, is deeply set in the language and form of the trilogy,[140] but its very repetition (cf. *Cho.*

---

[139] There has been much discussion of the staging of this 'macabre tableau' (Taplin). See Taplin 1977, pp. 324ff.   [140] Cf. Clay 1969, *passim*.

577–8, 1060; *Eum.* 589) challenges that fixed point: which third? Indeed, Clytemnestra's description of her act as ὑπερδίκως (1396) marks its excessive, transgressive nature (picked up by the chorus at 1426–7) which further suggests her coming punishment – thus undercutting her desire for an end. Similarly, her description of the blood as δρόσου and χαίρουσαν οὐδὲν ἧσσον ἢ διοσδότῳ | γάνει σπορητὸς κάλυκος ἐν λοχεύμασιν (1390ff.) is, as Peradotto and Vickers in particular have noted, a demonstration of her corrupt view of nature, the perversion of her political/social/sexual actions seen in the reversal of natural world imagery. Her act of murder, however, is seen mainly in its social implications, both in terms of sexual opposition and how this affects society: first, we see a further juxtaposition of ἀνήρ and γυναικός (1400–1), as the terms of the opposition between Agamemnon, the chorus and Clytemnestra, an opposition centred on her use of language against her husband:

> θαυμάζομέν σου γλῶσσαν, ὡς θρασύστομος
> ἥτις τοιόνδ᾽ ἐπ᾽ ἀνδρὶ κομπάζεις λόγον   (1399–1400)

It is her boldness in language, the desire to transgress, her daring against her husband that causes their outrage. Picking up ἀνδρί, Clytemnestra rejects (as she had at 275–7) 'the application to her of accepted ideas as to what is womanly' (Fraenkel): πειρᾶσθέ μου γυναικὸς ὡς ἀφράσμονος (1401). Moreover, as she triumphantly displays the corpse, ἐπ᾽ ἀνδρί is not the terminology of the queen:

> οὗτός ἐστιν Ἀγαμέμνων, ἐμὸς
> πόσις, νεκρὸς δέ...   (1404–5)

As we saw before, the difference between ἀνήρ and πόσις is sexually charged. The social role implied by *posis* leads to the chorus' exclamation that Clytemnestra has put herself outside society, and will be rejected by society (as we saw with Helen) for her anti-social act.

> δημοθρόους τ᾽ ἀρὰς
> ἀπέδικες ἀπέταμες; ἀπόπολις δ᾽ ἔσῃ
> μῖσος ὄβριμον ἀστοῖς   (1409–11)

This is repeated by Clytemnestra (1412–13)

> νῦν μὲν δικάζεις ἐκ πόλεως φυγὴν ἐμοί
> καὶ μῖσος ἀστῶν δημόθρους τ᾽ ἔχειν ἀρὰς

But she cites against this Agamemnon's action of killing her daughter, and their inactivity over that sacrifice (ἔθυσεν, 1417, enforces the parallelism of her (sacrificial) killing of Agamemnon and his (sacrificial) killing of Iphigeneia). The chorus brought no charge against *him* (ἀνδρὶ τῷδ᾽, 1414). Ought they not have chased him (ἀνδρηλατεῖν,

1419) from the land? ἀνδρηλατεῖν seems to echo the uses of ἀνήρ, suggesting a further link in her argument. She accuses them of being harsh judges (her argument is similar to Orestes' and Apollo's defence against the Erinues), and finally she threatens them with γνώσῃ διδαχθεὶς ὀψὲ γοῦν τὸ σωφρονεῖν (1425). This seems to echo the hymn to Zeus as though Clytemnestra were the δαιμόνων... χάρις βίαιος. Does this apparently ironic repetition mark her opposition to the male, to the order of Zeus? Her turning of the chorus' remark against its user? The corruption in the term σωφρονεῖν from Clytemnestra's lips? The chorus' reply is significant:

μεγαλόμητις εἶ,
περίφρονα δ᾽ ἔλακες   (1426–7)

It is the element of excess, μεγαλο-/περι, as with παντότολμον, that they blame. περίφρονα is picked up with φρὴν ἐπιμαίνεται (1428). As with παντότολμον φρονεῖν (221) of Agamemnon, it is precisely her power of φρονεῖν that is depicted to be at fault. Asked to judge, they note the opposition and exclusion stemming from an overvaluing which will lead to further opposition, rather than an end:

...σε χρή...
τύμμα τύμματι τεῖσαι   (1429–30)

This argument of cause and effect, the opposition first of Clytemnestra and the chorus, with Clytemnestra's position (as many critics have noted) shifting, suggesting various patterns of motivations, and then of Aegisthus and the chorus, adding a further structure of causality, suggests an over-determination that stands in contrast to the lyrics of Cassandra where the course of narrative and its interrelations of cause and effect were expressed with a prophetic clarity (though not without complexity or over-determination). The obscurity of action, the lack of control, vision, returns: δύσμαχα δ᾽ ἐστὶ κρῖναι.

Clytemnestra offers (1431) her murder as recompense for the death of her daughter: μὰ τὴν τέλειον τῆς ἐμῆς παιδὸς Δίκην, but adds Ἄτην and Ἐρινύν to Δίκην, both of which we have seen to be unclear, shifting causal agents (cf. on 749; on 1192; cf. 1119, 1190). Nor, she claims, does 'hope walk the house of fear'. Here, at the moment of rationalisation of the past narrative and threat for the future, we see the juxtaposition of two modes of projection I have been tracing. Her lack of fear is while Aegisthus lights the 'fire of her hearth': this is in contrast to 601–2, where she used such imagery of the returning king (now we realise what φέγγος ἥδιον might be?), and it is also in contrast to 522 – Agamemnon 'bringing light into darkness'. She also attacks Agamemnon and Cassandra for their sexuality (Χρυσηΐδων μείλιγμα, 1439; κοινόλεκτρος, 1441; ξύνευνος, 1442; and, if we

follow Koniaris and Tyrrel, ἱστοτρίβης, 1443;[141] φιλήτωρ, 1446)
which seems to emphasise the sexual basis of the discourse, which,
indeed, Orestes will recall as he too justifies a killing with φιλεῖς τὸν
ἄνδρά (*Cho.* 894), ἐπεὶ φιλεῖς | τὸν ἄνδρα τοῦτον, ὃν δὲ χρῆν φιλεῖν
στυγεῖς (*Cho.* 906–7).

The problematic of the right, allowable, suitable object of sexual
desire, as we saw with the discussion of Helen, and as we will see in,
for example, *Cho.* 585–651, is fundamental. Clytemnestra, after
professing her love for Aegisthus again, offers the relationship
between Agamemnon and his lovers as an example of unacceptable
sexuality: the chorus simply retort that they would rather die because
their guardian (φύλαξ stands in ironic contrast to Agamemnon's
δωμάτων ἐμῶν φύλαξ, 914) has suffered 'on account of', 'through'
a woman; γυναικός διαί picks up διαὶ γυναικός (448), linking Helen
and Clytemnestra. Indeed, the repeated use of γυναικός 1453/4
strengthens the sexual reference, which is immediately picked up by:

> ἰὼ
> παράνους Ἑλένα,
> μία τὰς πολλάς,...
> ψυχὰς ὀλέσασ'   (1454–7)

It was Helen's illicit sexual alliance, seen as a wrong judgement,
valuing, παράνους, that was the cause of the Trojan war. This
juxtaposed to the death of Agamemnon γυναικὸς διαί, πρὸς γυναικός,
demonstrates the parallelism between the destructiveness of the
wrong female desire of Clytemnestra and of Helen, which will be
further drawn by the entrance of her lover, Aegisthus, the object of
her illicit and damaging sexual desire. Agamemnon is described as
πολλὰ τλάντος, whereas Helen is ἄτλητα τλᾶσα (408): the difference
is marked and points to the distinction between illicit sexuality and
its results, and societally defined sexuality.

Clytemnestra explicitly rejects this description of Helen, however,
challenging the causal/moral status of Helen's adultery:

> μηδ' εἰς Ἑλένην κότον ἐκτρέψῃς
> ὡς ἀνδρολέτειρ'   (1464–5)

The use of ἀνδρολέτειρ', however, again emphasises the opposition
of the sexes, regulation of which forms the basis of the parallel
between Clytemnestra and Helen. The chorus suggest 'you daimon'
(Clytemnestra? cf. 1497–1504) is the cause (the shifting pattern of
causality, as well as their postulation of a further divine motivation,
is indicative of their desire for control over the over-determinism).
But the chorus also maintains as a cause ἐκ γυναικῶν...κρατύνεις

---

[141] Neither article observes that this sense of ἱστοτρίβης had been denied as possible by
Diggle 1968.

(1470–1), 'You have your power through/by women'. So Clytemnestra will claim (1497–1504) that it was the daimon in the shape of a woman who is to bear the blame for the sacrifice. Indeed, the queen here (1475–80) notes their change of opinion in their invocation of the 'thrice-gorged daimon'. As it was she that invoked the third libation to Zeus, this seems to link Zeus, daimon, and Clytemnestra more closely in the patterning of cause and responsibility. Indeed, the chorus immediately revert to Zeus as the origin responsible for all action – but the echo of γυναικὸς διαί in διαὶ Διός reverberates uneasily in the absoluteness of παναιτίου.

τελεῖται (1487) implies the action of murder with the religious overtones of sacrifice but also refers back to τελεῖται δ' ἐς τὸ πεπρωμένον (68), which was the conclusion of the passage describing Zeus' sending of the Atreids to avenge Helen's transgression; this echo brings that sense of fate[142] to bear here also: every action is seen as fated, determined, but also, as the differing patterns of causality suggest, to the human observer, over-determined, with an excess of causal significations. It is this tension that leads to their expressed lack of clear vision, their inability to control events; or perhaps in their belief in god's plan (determinism), we see the expression of a search for an origin to rationalise the lack of control to a coherent force, albeit one outside their own powers.

They mourn for the king, questioning for the right words (1490ff.) in terms which will be picked up and extended in the *kommos* in the *Choephoroi*. So δολίῳ μόρῳ (1495) will be echoed in Orestes' πειθὼ δολίαν (*Cho.* 726). What will be seen to have been hints of the future and the gradual multiplication of suggested agencies thus prepare us for the reciprocal punishment to come.

Clytemnestra's statement that the *alastor* of Atreus in the shape of a woman 'made the sacrifice' further confuses the pattern of causality: not merely ἐκ γυναικῶν but φανταζόμενος...γυναικί. This the chorus cannot accept:

> ὡς μὲν ἀναίτιος εἶ
> τοῦδε φόνου τίς ὁ μαρτυρήσων;   (1505–6)

μαρτυρήσων: the act has a witness, that is, the proof of causality is through the presence of one who sees. ἀναίτιος, however, is in play with παναιτίου (1486). The similarity of the sound points the paradox of supplementarity between Zeus παναιτίου, and the yet unacceptable οὐκ ἀναίτιος εἶ. The polarisation of responsible/irresponsible is here broken down in the problematic of obscured causality.

---

[142] Also θεόκραντον recalls ἔπραξεν ὡς ἔκρανεν.

Clytemnestra (1521–9, unfortunately some words are lost) again seems to assert that her action is to be seen as direct retribution for the death of Iphigeneia. Her death is described as a δολίαν ἄτην οἴκοισιν. After δολίῳ μόρῳ δαμείς (1519, repeated from 1495), this argument, in marking the parallel between Iphigeneia's and Agamemnon's death in a further way, seems to offer some further justification or rationalisation of the regicide. The chorus, at a loss (ἀμηχανῶ . . . μέριμνα again) and terrified, pick up the reference to the house (οἴκοισιν) with πίτνοντος οἴκου (1532) and with the following image of the house being 'slipped up' (δομοσφαλῆ, 1533), damaged by the storm, the cloudburst, of blood, which also refers back to Clytemnestra's almost sexual boast 1389ff.[143] – the continuing perversion of natural imagery after the death of the king. But the chorus still suggest the reciprocal punishment to come: Fate whets *dike* to 'another action':

Δίκαν δ' ἐπ' ἄλλο πρᾶγμα θηγάνει βλάβας
πρὸς ἄλλαις θηγάναισι Μοῖρα   (1535–6)[144]

They turn to bewailing the king and the fact that no one will bury him, which looks forward to the *Choephoroi* and the *kommos* in particular, where the king will receive his ἐπιτύμβιον αἶνον:

τίς δ' ἐπιτύμβιον αἶνον ἐπ' ἀνδρὶ θείῳ
σὺν δακρύοις ἰάπτων
ἀληθείᾳ φρενῶν πονήσει;   (1548–50)

πονήσει also echoes the general description of the afflictions of the house with which the play opened, which have not ceased, despite the herald's and others' hopes. ἐπ' ἀνδρί reiterates the determination of the conflict in sexual terms (cf. e.g. 1400). αἶνον . . . ἰάπτων ἀληθείᾳ φρενῶν with its focus on φρενῶν and more particularly on sincerity of expression, utterance matching feeling, recalls the constitution of Clytemnestra's hypocrisy and such phrases as ὄμμα σοῦ κατηγορεῖ. Fraenkel may be right that 'questions like these . . . are common in Aeschylean laments', but the terms are woven into a network of references forwards and backwards in the text, refusing a simple delimitation of sense (particularly by a notion of 'traditionality').

Clytemnestra refuses[145] to allow them to see this death as the bereavement of the *oikos*: οὐχ ὑπὸ κλαυθμῶν τῶν ἐξ οἴκων (1554) but again, with a grimly ironic picture of father kissing daughter in Hell, which may recall the earlier pathetic picture of father and

[143] Cf. Moles 1979.
[144] Fraenkel's text (using Auratus and Hermann) which Page in his apparatus also suggests might be preferable.
[145] The alliteration of κάππεσε κάτθανε καὶ καταθάψομεν is strongly marked. The inevitable connection between the events described?

daughter before her sacrifice (cf. 243ff.), she depicts it rather as revenge for the killing of Iphigeneia:

> ἀλλ' Ἰφιγένειά νιν ἀσπασίως
> θυγάτηρ, ὡς χρή,
> πατέρ'...
>
> ...φιλήσει   (1555–9)

The ironical reminder of moral duty, ὡς χρή, by the regicide and adulteress is marked. But the sense of revenge as opposition and exclusion is impressed upon the chorus:

> ὄνειδος ἥκει τόδ' ἀντ' ὀνείδους,
> δύσμαχα δ' ἐστὶ κρῖναι.
> φέρει φέροντ', ἐκτίνει δ' ὁ καίνων   (1560–2)

They generalise this sense in the phrase παθεῖν τὸν ἔρξαντα, which, as many critics have noted, is picked up at *Cho.* 313 δράσαντα παθεῖν, and which expresses tersely the active/passive reciprocal nature of the action. How, then, to escape? The race seems 'glued to *atē*'.

Clytemnestra sings in reply of making a bargain with the daimon to rid the house (δόμων, 1565; δόμων, 1572; μελάθρων, 1576) of its curse on the race of Pleisthenes.[146] Her fear of reciprocity (μανίας μελάθρων ἀλληλοφόνους ἀφελούσῃ) ends her speech with a foreboding of punishment which is in contrast to her strongly expressed intention of making a verbal contract with the daimon. Her power of words is set against the θέσμιον (1564), the predictive χρησμόν of opposition and reciprocity.

This scene moves, then, from the queen's boasting assertions and the chorus' outrage to a lyric exchange of high intensity, where as the positions of the chorus and Clytemnestra shift and interrelate, a complex network of uncertain and over-determined expressions of causality and responsibility is suggested – which leads finally to Clytemnestra's hope to form some bargain with the daimon that seems to threaten her future punishment and death. As often before in this play, even as Clytemnestra queens it over the dead bodies and the chorus keen in response, there is marked the movement from certitude and assurance to doubt and unease.

---

[146] Pleisthenes' name darkens the obscure pattern of cause and effect. Hesiod (Papathomopoulos 1980, pp. 11–26; Vernant 1982, n. 21) makes him the hermaphrodite parent of Agamemnon and Menelaus. His genealogical place is uncertain, however (Fraenkel). This challenges Cassandra's πρώταρχον ἄτην as a fixed point, in its resiting of the possible origin of πόνοι, the possible parentage.

Man's talk

The lyric intensity is brought to a close by the entrance of Aegisthus, which many critics have felt to be an anticlimax, though not Winnington-Ingram, who writes: 'The entry of Aegisthus is an effective piece of bathos. The stage, which has held only Clytemnestra and her victims, now fills with soldiers. The queen stands silent while Aegisthus, who has had no share in the emotional tension of the preceding scene, makes a forensic speech.'[147] As we will see, this 'effective...bathos' is also sited within the discourse of communication and exchange that I have been discussing, as well as offering a further explanatory patterning of events. As we shall see later (especially pp. 183ff.), this reducing the role of Aegisthus is an essential part of the dynamics of the *Oresteia*.

Aegisthus' opening words echo Clytemnestra's own first speech: εὖφρον is seen by Peradotto[148] as a repeat of that double meaning and claims the connotation here of 'night' which, he says, indicates the perversion of nature on a subtextual level by the confusion of night and day (ἡμέρας). There is, however, a contrast between the manipulation of language in Clytemnestra's punning echo of the chorus' speech and the simple ambiguity of Aegisthus' use of the term.[149] For throughout this short last scene Aegisthus is seen precisely as possessing no manipulating skill with words, no πειθώ: his explanation of his case (δίκη) is treated with scorn by the chorus (Αἴγισθ' ὑβρίζοντ' ἐν κακοῖσιν οὐ σέβω, 1612). When he attempts to argue with the chorus, they merely call him 'woman' (γύναι, 1625). His first threat is also treated with scorn: ὡς δὴ σύ μοι τύραννος 'Αργείων ἔσῃ (1633). His promise to use money to persuade shows the failing process of the exchange of language being replaced by the exchange of money. When this fails (τὸν...μὴ πειθάνορα, 1639), he threatens force, the collapse of communication. When they return his threat with the threat of Orestes, he is forced to vague aggression (γνώσῃ τάχα) and then to threaten death at the hands of his soldiers. At this point Clytemnestra enters the dialogue and balances the situation, restraining Aegisthus and sending the old men home: significantly, she concludes ὧδ' ἔχει λόγος γυναικός, εἴ τις ἀξιοῖ μαθεῖν (1661). This is in contrast to τὸν ἄνδρα τόνδε (1643), ὦ φίλτατ' ἀνδρῶν (1654) and refers back to her previous arguments on male and female language: and although the bickering does not stop immediately, it

---

[147] 1983, pp. 112–13.   [148] 1964, p. 390.

[149] Nor does Peradotto comment on such 'confused expressions' as ὀρφναίου πυρός (21), λαμπτὴρ νυκτὸς ἡμερήσιον φάος (22–3), though perhaps he would claim that these too indicate that there is something rotten in the state of Argos.

remains without the threatened physical violence and after her next speech the play ends, with Aegisthus accepting her advice 'not to mind the barkings' of the old men, yielding to the λόγος γυναικός.

The explanation of events that Aegisthus offers (which he characterises as ὡς τορῶς φράσαι!) after the differing and shifting patterns of motivation and causal agencies that we have been reading, seems notably insufficient, particularly in its conclusion ἐκ τῶνδε σοι πεσόντα τόνδ' ἰδεῖν πάρα. The assumption of a direct and straightforward relation between events (ἐκ τῶνδε) is in marked contrast to the complexities of the previous lyric dialogue, or Cassandra's intense metaphoricity. Aegisthus' reduced role in the regicide (which I will discuss at length in Chapter 2) seems parallel to his reductive view of events and the exchange of language.

Aegisthus' language is described thus by Denniston–Page: 'After a grandiose opening, he lapses into a glib, leisurely flatness, enlivened by an occasional proverb or cliché, puns, and bombastic grandiloquence.' The examples of the 'puns' are 1591, and 1629–30. In 1591, there is no word play bar the jingling repetition of two adverbs ending in -ως:

'Ατρεύς, προθύμως μᾶλλον ἢ φίλως πατρί

which is clearly not a play on words, a pun, at all! At 1629–30, there is not even a similarity of sound:

'Ορφεῖ δε γλῶσσαν τὴν ἐναντίαν ἔχεις.
ὁ μὲν γὰρ ἦγε πάντ' ἀπὸ φθογγῆς χαρᾷ
σὺ δ' ἐξορίνας νηπίοις ὑλάγμασιν
ἄξῃ.   (1629–32)

It is a rather weak βωμολοχία based on the well-attested εἰκάζειν form.[150] But here the opposition (ὁ μέν, σὺ δέ) is worked on the same word, in the same sense, merely a different tense and mood. There is none of the expected play of meaning by manipulation of signifiers, no indication of the sort of control evinced by Clytemnestra. Similarly, when she used a cliché/proverb, she marked it as such (ὥσπερ ἡ παροιμία) and used it to make a pun. Aegisthus' speech is not so much 'enlivened' by cliché, but by this very use of cliché is determined in its flatness, its lack of πειθώ, its lack of manipulation: it is because of the failure of his exchange of words, that he resorts to the exchange of money, and then to force. There too, following Fraenkel's distribution of the lines,[151] the failure of his communication process is marked by his unfortunate (for him) omen of οὐκ ἀναίνομαι

---

[150] See Fraenkel, who calls this example 'vulgar'.
[151] Denniston–Page attribute 1651 to Aegisthus on the grounds that the chorus 'do not have swords'. Fraenkel's arguments refute Denniston–Page convincingly.

θανεῖν (1652), the ambiguity of which is immediately picked up by
the chorus, utilising the predictive nature of words/speech/names.[152]

δεχομένοις λέγεις θανεῖν γε   (1653)

The use of δέχομαι refers back to εἰ μὴ δέχῃ λόγον (1060) and marks
the heuristic gap in communication, the 'reception' of speech;
Aegisthus cannot bridge the gap between speaker and listener, he has
no πειθώ – except by this κληδών: Halliday writes that it is essential
for all such κληδόνες 'that... the spoken word may produce an effect,
not indeed irrespective of its meaning, but other than the meaning
or intention of the person who carelessly uttered them'. It is precisely
the failure of Aegisthus' use of language, speech, that stands as a
prelude to his intended reduction of the exchange of language to the
exchange of physical gesture – that is, fighting.

Aegisthus, then, attempts to reduce language exchange first to
economic exchange and then to physical violence. As he corrupts the
exchange of marriage by his adultery with Clytemnestra, so he
corrupts the exchange of language. By his breaking of the rules of
society he stands outside society – lack of sexual identity (γύναι),
rejected as were Helen and Clytemnestra by the citizens (δημορριφεῖς,
σάφ' ἴσθι, λευσίμους ἀράς, 1616; χώρας μίασμα καὶ θεῶν ἐγχωρίων,
1645). His loss of recognition by society is parallel to his corruption
and loss of the exchange of language.

The play ends with a future tense: once again looking forward,
predicting narrative.

So we have seen that the workings of communication as an exchange
of signs are considered in various forms in the *Agamemnon* and reach
various points of breakdown and corruption, centred around the
heuristic and hermeneutic processes, and the gaps between signifier
and signified, addresser and addressee. The functions of reciprocity,
exchange and control also inform the structuring of the sexual
differential, the regulation of which is a fundamental ordering of
society. The orderings of language, the orderings of sexuality –
mutually implicative – are seen as breaking down in adultery, female
dominance, 'misuse' of language. It is this misuse of signs, the
corruption of the process of exchange, that constitutes the threat to
the *oikos* and to society.

---

[152] Technically known as 'cledonomancy', cf. Peradotto 1969b.

2

Definition, paradox, reversal: τοῦ πατρός in the *Choephoroi*

denn wir leben wahrhaft in Figuren.

Rilke

I catch myself defining the threshold
As the geometric locus
Of arrivals and departures
In the House of the Father.

Barrault

This turning away from the mother to the father signifies a victory of intellectuality over the senses.

Freud

Paradox, inversion, logos: the system in turmoil?

First, a problem of stagecraft, of 'significant action' and of 'visual meaning'.[1] When Orestes appears with the bodies of his mother and Aegisthus as Clytemnestra had appeared with the corpses of Agamemnon and Cassandra, he calls on an unspecified second person plural (the Argives? the chorus? the audience?) to witness:

ἴδεσθε χώρας τὴν διπλῆν τυραννίδα
πατροκτόνους τε δωμάτων πορθήτορας   (973–4)

This command to 'see' is repeated (980–1) ἴδεσθε δ' αὖτε...τὸ μηχάνημα – the redisplay, bringing to light, of the devices of Agamemnon's murder. As Orestes talks of his approaching madness, he says καὶ νῦν ὁρᾶτέ μ' (1034). Orestes further calls on the protection of the Sun, who will be a witness (I mentioned the connection between vision and the process of witnessing in its wider, authorising sense in the *Agamemnon*, p. 32, pp. 36ff., and it will be increasingly important throughout the trilogy). This protection is depicted by the role of the sun as ὁ πάντ' ἐποπτεύων τάδε (985), 'he who over*looks* all these things'. (Divine forces as determining powers will be regularly referred to through words of sight, cf. 1, 11, 126, 246 etc.) When madness (and we will have cause further to discuss some implications of the connections between 'madness', 'vision', 'reason' later) overtakes Orestes, he talks of δμωαὶ γυναῖκες αἵδε... The chorus respond τίνες σε δόξαι...στροβοῦσιν; (1051–2), 'What *visions* disturb you?' δόξαι recalls the uncertain status of δόξα in the

[1] Taplin's terms. See Taplin 1977, especially pp. 12–39.

99

Agamemnon (*Aga.* 275, 421 etc., cf. pp. 37, 46–7) where the ambiguity of 'opinion', and 'vision' (in the sense of 'that which appears', 'is seen') and the sense of 'appearance' (as opposed to reality) helped to constitute the suggested inconstancy of the visions of dreams. Orestes here retorts, however, οὐκ εἰσὶ δόξαι τῶνδε πημάτων ἐμοί. | σαφῶς γὰρ αἵδε μητρὸς ἔγκοτοι κύνες (1053–4). They are not visions, he declares. He denies inconstant status to his vision – σαφῶς <u>γάρ</u>: he sees '*clearly*'. This term σαφῶς, so often applied in the *Oresteia* in a metaphorical sense, implying the possibility of fixedness, surety, is undercut here by the challenging of the certainty of the object of/in the visual mode, indeed, a challenging of the most radical binary fashion: ὑμεῖς μὲν οὐχ ὁρᾶτε τάσδ' ἐγὼ δ' ὁρῶ (1061), 'You do not see these women, but I see them.' The inconstancy of the vision of the madman (and we will see how this inconstancy is placed within a series) puts in question, however, not only the ontological status of the object of (his) vision, but also the very power of reference in language: γυναῖκες <u>αἵδε</u>...σαφῶς γὰρ <u>αἵδε</u>...ὁρᾶτε <u>τάσδε</u>: these deictics are challenged in their simple referential function by the exclusive, binary opposition of the possible 'truth-content' of the statements of the chorus and Orestes. Which 'this' is referential? The very possibility of denying the referentiality of the deictic in language points to the gap between signifier and signified, a gap which constitutes the problematic of 'referentiality', a gap the closure of which seems to be attempted by the assumption of the full presence of the deictic 'this is' (especially as a model for communication).

How, then, to read the words of Orestes ἴδεσθε...ἴδεσθε...ὁρᾶτε? Where, if we can, do we try to draw the boundary, the point, where madness destroys the referentiality of language? Is it just madness which puts referentiality under question? When, for example,[2] Orestes says (997) τί νιν προσείπω; 'What shall I call νιν?', to what does the νιν refer? Does it refer to Clytemnestra, the subject of τί σοι δοκεῖ, looking back to his metaphorical description of his mother (a metaphorical reference?)? Or is it looking forward to the following suggested descriptions of the weapons of Agamemnon's death (998–9)? This problem results in the attempted transposition of lines by Proctor, Scholfield, Lloyd-Jones. How, then, can we even assume a simple referentiality of Orestes' words to say 'Orestes appears with the bodies of the διπλῆν τυραννίδα'? How are we to read the

[2] I choose the example from this scene to mark the difficulty of defining a point of transition from 'sanity' to 'madness' by a criterion of referentiality, or of defining referentiality by a criterion of 'madness' and 'sanity'. We will find many examples from earlier passages challenging the object in the visual mode and its possible description in language.

stagecraft of this scene? How does the (significant) action signify? How are we to perceive its 'visual meaning'? The apparent clarity of the showing (to sight) of the bodies of the tyrannicides seems challenged not only by the complex over-determination of meaning which Orestes' doubling of Clytemnestra's tableau evokes (How are we to *understand* the sight? Its 'visual meaning'? The clarity of deictic showing becomes the questioning of interpretation) but also by the undermining of the criterion of the specificity of sight itself. How simple can we regard seeing what one sees in this scene?

This radical challenge to the ability, power, of language to indicate with certainty, clarity, will be seen to be within a series also. Not merely in its referentiality... Orestes calls on the sun

ὡς ἂν παρῇ μοι μάρτυς ἐν δίκῃ ποτέ,
ὡς τόνδ' ἐγὼ μετῆλθον ἐνδίκως φόνον
τὸν μητρός (987-9)

The conjunction of μάρτυς ἐν δίκῃ would seem to suggest a context of the law-court: indeed, to look forward to the *Eumenides*. In the same metrical position, however, ἐνδίκως. This word, while having its 'etymology' of ἐν-δικ- suggested by the use of the preposition and the noun in the previous line suggests not the opposition of δίκη to δίκη (case to case), not the institution of the law-court, but an absolute moral system; not the opposition of actions (with both the legal and non-legal senses) but the criterion of distinction between them. Orestes continues:

Αἰγίσθου γὰρ οὐ λέγω μόρον·
ἔχει γὰρ αἰσχυντῆρος, ὡς νόμος, δίκην. (989-90)

Here δίκη, juxtaposed to ὡς νόμος, 'as the law [has it]' and the defining genitive αἰσχυντῆρος suggests the outcome of the action or deciding, that is, 'the punishment', 'retribution', as in such phrases as δίκην διδόναι. This shifting of the signifier δίκη, the difficulty in defining it, limiting it, accurately is followed by the questions τί σοι δοκεῖ...τί νιν προσείπω. This desire for finding, fixing, the correct word is undercut by (as it is constituted by) the shifting of the signifier in language, as well as in vision. Indeed, as Orestes speaks of seeing the Erinues, he says:

δμωαὶ γυναῖκες αἵδε Γοργόνων δίκην
φαιοχίτωνες καὶ πεπλεκτανημέναι
πυκνοῖς δράκουσιν (1048-50)[3]

---

[3] δμωαί M, δμοιαί Lobel (followed by Page and Fraenkel), which is an emendation of a word found only in Hesychius, ἁμοιός. κακός. Σικελοί. An emendation to an otherwise unattested... emendation. The phrase δμωαὶ γυναῖκες is a common phrase in Homer. Lobel's emendation would reduce the syntactical ambiguity I am discussing. The echo of δίκη (noun) in this phrase may still be unsettling.

δίκην is normally construed here as *ceu*, an adverbial or prepositional usage, 'like Gorgons'. That is, the sound image δίκην is kept separate from the problematic of the noun δίκη, the shifting meanings we considered briefly above, by its syntactical function. Thus it points, particularly here approaching the end of a play in which δίκη will have been seen to be so important, towards the split between signifier and signified; that is, as in a pun (a use of a signifier with varying signifieds), it points towards the materiality of the signifier. It marks precisely that relation between signifier and signified that constitutes the ambiguity of the noun δίκη, the difficulty of fixing its meaning. The phrase under discussion, however, has no main verb. Could not δίκη be construed as the object of the missing verb, taking δμωαὶ γυναῖκες and Γοργόνων together: 'the hand-maidens of the Gorgons [e.g. want, promise, threaten] δίκην'? The aposiopesis opens the possibility of δίκην having the wide implications of its legal, moral sense as a noun, *or* as a preposition having a specifying function for the connection between δμωαὶ γυναῖκες and Γοργόνων. The possibility of ambiguity between the two lexical constellations confuses the boundaries of definition, the definition of boundaries. And the choice between δίκην (noun) and δίκην (adverb) is precisely both the fixing of meaning and the 'arbitrary' imposition of categories – a choice strangely but normally seen as the 'objective' measure in the play of language. How, then, do we read Orestes' important assertion:

κτανεῖν τέ φημι μητέρ' οὐκ ἄνευ δίκης   (1027)

How can we attempt a definition of δίκης in this series of differences, how can we limit the play of the signifier? And the play is further problematised by the double negative. Is it an emphasising litotes or a suggestion of doubt (effort of repression) through the marked possibility of ἄνευ δίκης – if these two are in fact alternatives and not always in play in a double negative? The discourse of defining, the search for the power to limit, and find the right word, juxtaposed to the shifting play of language, will be considered in some depth in this chapter. For what was seen as an essential dynamic of Clytemnestra's trickery in the *Agamemnon*, the manipulation of the relation between signifier and signified, is essential to the discourse of the *Choephoroi* not only in the adoption of πειθὼ δολία as a means of revenge – which reversal of values will be seen in a series of further paradoxes revolving around the paradox of the assertion of the validity of the ties of society by an act of transgression of those ties – but also in the shiftings of many of the oppositions and terms which are major referents for the discourse. The development of this discourse, its relation to (and, indeed, constitution in) the opposition of male and female, focused on the terms of parenthood, particularly τοῦ πατρός (I use the genitive to indicate the senses of what belongs to the father, comes from the father, consists in the father),[4] will be seen to develop the relation between language, sexuality, and narrative discussed in the *Agamemnon*. The extremely short consideration of fragments of the final scene I have offered by way of introduction to the paradoxical inversions of this play, an exemplum of the difficulty of this most difficult work, which has not received the attention of the *Agamemnon*. In the coming analysis, I shall have further cause to discuss the complex interrelations of the language of definition and the language of sight, with which I began this chapter. I shall also be discussing the important topic of the relation of the *Oresteia* to Homer, as well as two of the most difficult scenes in the trilogy, namely the *kommos* and the recognition scene – as well as the psychoanalytic and other readings to which these difficulties have given rise.

Return of the native: saying what he sees

As the *Agamemnon* opened with a prayer for release, the *Choephoroi* opens, as we glean from Aristophanes (see n. 5), with Orestes, returned to his native land, praying. As with the watchman's speech, this prologue introduces a series of important terms and relations. The prayer (to Hermes, god of deception and guile) constitutes, as we saw with the opening prayer of the *Agamemnon* (αἰτῶ, *Aga.* 1; αἰτουμένῳ, *Cho.* 2), the mode of desire: for narrative control, for assistance, to oversee (ἐποπτεύων) what is to happen. Hermes, however, unlike the generalised θεούς of *Aga.* 1, is named; and called χθόνιε, as god of the underworld (which will be a particular force in the *kommos*), the god who guides transition from life to death (the liminality of which function will also be important). The god is overseeing πατρῷα... κράτη: κράτη, as with κρατεῖ used of Clytemnestra (*Aga.* 10, 258), implies both the sense of political power ('realm' Tucker), and the wider 'authority', 'influence', 'power'; and, in a more general sense, 'capability' – which is connected with the desire for control of events as well as control of the house. The ambiguities of πατρῷ'

---

[4] πατρός (in the genitive) occurs twenty-three times in this play: 19, 99, 106, 108, 180, 200, 235, 237, 247, 256, 264, 273, 293, 300, 435, 540, 572, 829, 905, 915, 918, 925, 927. πατήρ (in all other cases) occurs twenty-nine times: 4, 8, 14, 88, 95, 130, 139, 143, 164, 240, 315, 329, 332, 346, 364, 456, 479, 481, 489, 491, 493, 495, 500, 762, 783, 865, 978, 981, 984. πατρο- (in compounds): 1, 77, 126, 251, 253, 284, 315, 443, 444, 909, 974, 1015, 1028. This, with the other words for parentage (τίκτειν etc.) is sufficient indication of the generative play of the genitive function.

have provoked much discussion[5] centred on the question[6] whether it refers to Zeus or Agamemnon. This ambiguity is, however, significant: the unspecified form πατρῷα[7]...κράτη, 'the/a father's authority/power', which links Agamemnon and Zeus in a more general structure of paternal authority, is situated within the opposition of male and female, as seen often in the *Agamemnon*, an opposition here between the κράτος[8] of the father and what Bachofen terms 'das Mutterrecht'. I will return to the debate initiated by Bachofen's polemic later (pp. 193ff.). ἐποπτεύων, 'watch over', 'oversee', is an interesting term: not only does it look back to the discussion of sight and appearance revolving around the terms φάσμα/δόξα/φαίνω/πρέπει/τέκμαρ in the *Agamemnon* and forward to the heightened emphasis on the modality of the visible in the *Choephoroi*, but also, as with ἀπαλλαγὴ(ν) πόνων (*Aga*. 1, 20), it is a technical term from the mysteries – to become an ἐπόπτης, to complete the mysteries with the final epiphany. This indication of initiation will also be seen to be of importance later on.

While it is not an uncommon epithet of tutelary gods, σωτήρ, particularly after the vocative χθόνιε, recalls τοῦ κατὰ χθονὸς... σωτῆρος (*Aga*. 1386–7), Clytemnestra's blasphemous and ironic parody of a libation: that her son echoes these words is the first in a series of correspondences between the murder of Agamemnon and its revenge by Orestes, leading towards the appearance of Orestes over the bodies of Aegisthus, and his mother, as she had appeared over the corpses of Agamemnon and Cassandra. This system of references, this parallelisation, informs the narrative, refusing at any point a simple, forward-moving linearity, demanding a strategy of (re-)reading which considers such structuration.

The military metaphor of σύμμαχος (2), 'fellow-fighter', maintains the sense of conflict (cf. e.g. *Aga*. 940, *Aga*. 1561 and below p. 132), and αἰτουμένῳ, in the middle voice, emphasises the more particular

---

[5] From the citation of the lines in Aristophanes, *Ran*. 1119ff. Lloyd-Jones says 'there is little doubt that the interpretation of the Aristophanic Aeschylus is right'. An ambiguity, which is the constitution of the citation, can be 'solved' for Lloyd-Jones, removed (although 'some scholars say...' otherwise) by an appeal to the author-ity of...whom? It seems to be by an appeal to his reading of Aristophanes' Aeschylus' reading of a line not in the manuscripts collected under the signature 'Aeschylus'. The common strategy of Classical critics in referring to an authorial origin to restrict the play of language seems parodied, or at least thrown into a confusion, a regress, of signatures, by the appeal to 'the Aristophanic Aeschylus'. Whose 'Aeschylus' does 'Lloyd-Jones' read at *Cho*. 1?

[6] See Tucker's seven-page appendix for this.

[7] πατρῷε McNaughton, Verrall.

[8] κράτος, as we have seen and will see further, is specifically linked to the house and the opposition of the sexes.

nature of this opening prayer. It is a prayer 'for himself', 'on his own behalf'. The watchman prayed simply for an unspecified release; Orestes is involved in a personal action of retribution and regaining his position in the *oikos* – the sense of return (from exile) to a former position implicit in the verb κατέρχομαι.

From the fragments of the next lines, we may shore up the continuation of χθόνιε with τύμβου δ' ἐπ' ὄχθῳ, and the repetition πατρί, πάτερ after πατρῷ'.

τί χρῆμα λεύσσω; 'What thing do I see?' This direct question, apparently a question about a simple object (χρῆμα), is followed first by an expression of what he sees (though still in the form of a question) and then by the phrase ποίᾳ ξυμφορᾷ προσεικάσω; (12), 'to what occurrence am I to liken it/them?' So, in such a questioning of the criterion of vision juxtaposed to a prayer for a divine overlooker the play's opening anticipates its ending (cf. 1061–3). For even in Orestes' apparently simple phraseology, it seems as if sight is being placed in doubt, open to interpretation, within a metaphoric structure. Things are not simply perceivable but must also be interpreted. This seems also reminiscent of the opposition of showing/saying, of the difference in the opening speech of the watchman between the stars and the beacon-light in a communicative function. Indeed, there are echoes: ὁμήγυρις...πρέπουσα (10–12), ὁμήγυριν...ἐμπρέποντας (*Aga.* 4–6), πρέπει (*Aga.* 30); χοὰς φερούσαις (15), καὶ τοὺς φέροντας (*Aga.* 5), φέρουσαν (*Aga.* 9). The opposition of saying/showing was undone by the term φράζω, 'to indicate' (both in language and without words); here, the opposition of 'sensible'/'intelligible' is put in doubt by the suggestion of the uncertainty, the interpretability of the sense (meaning/faculty) of vision. Indeed, the repetition of πρέπουσα(ν) (12/18) in the same metrical position but with the different implications of first 'noticeable in itself', *conspicienda* (Tucker), and then 'pre-eminent' (Tucker, 'sc. ἐν αὐτοῖς') offers varying characterisations of the object seen, pointed by the use of the same word with different emphases. For πρέπει can mean both 'shine', i.e. *source* of light – juxtaposed with μελαγχίμοις pointing to the recurrent opposition of light and dark in the trilogy – and also 'be distinctive/distinguished', an object of vision. This ambiguity suggests a breakdown of a simple subject/object of sight and thus further implies a radicalisation of the visual mode.[9] Indeed, the question τίς ἥδε (10), 'What is this?' and its answer ἥτις ἥδε (21)

---

[9] This may seem too bold a conclusion to too extensive an analysis of the question of the sense (in all its senses) of sight. It will become, however, increasingly important in my investigation of this theatrical spectacle. As often in Aeschylus, the first hints of major concerns may seem barely hints.

mark the differing characterisations of the woman as προστροπὴ
γυναῖκων / ὁμήγυρις γυναῖκων, suggesting the difficulty of language
applied to vision: in λεύσσω...φάρεσιν μελαγχίμοις πρέπουσα /
δοκῶ...πένθει λυγρῷ πρέπουσαν the connection between the
'object of sight' and its 'interpretation', the move λεύσσω...δοκῶ,
'I see...I think', is marked by the repetition of πρέπουσα(ν), then,
but marked as a play of difference.

With a prayer to Zeus also to be his σύμμαχος (the linking of Zeus,
Hermes, Orestes to avenge the fate of the father, as they will be linked
in the prayers of the second stasimon, just before the revenge) Orestes
with Pylades moves aside ὡς ἂν σαφῶς μάθω. σαφῶς, as we saw in
the *Agamemnon*, is connected with images of light and dark and of
blindness and sight, and used to describe knowledge, interpretation.
Here, however, juxtaposed to the difficulty of πρέπουσα(ν) and the
turning-to-metaphor of vision, the metaphor of 'clear' in the sense
of 'certain', 'accurate' knowledge, as we saw above with Orestes'
σαφῶς γάρ at the ending of the play, becomes itself part of the
structure of interpretation, conceptualisation, rather than the standard of interpretation. The assertion of clarity in this play will be
seen to be an uncertain claim.

This prologue of Orestes, then, echoes the prologue of the *Agamemnon*, not only in offering in important terms a prayer for the future
action, but also in the development of the opposition of saying and
showing by the first hints of a further questioning of the mode of the
visual, a structure of imagery leading towards Orestes' visions of the
final scene of the play.

Recollection/dislocation

The *parodos* of the entering chorus further sets the situation of the
drama (as did the prologue) in terms which recall the language of the
Agamemnon; but it is a recollection which marks the dislocations of
Clytemnestra's rule and the coming revenge.

The chorus, who have been sent by the queen (as with ὧδε γὰρ κρατεῖ
Aga. 10, we meet the effect of Clytemnestra's commands before her
entrance), march in full mourning: πρέπει, used now by the chorus
to describe themselves, further removes the possibility of at least the
expression of a 'simple perception', not only by their reflexive use
(the recognition of oneself being seen)[10] but also by its conjunction
with the hyperbolic metaphor of ἄλοκι νεοτόμῳ, 'fresh-cut furrow',
'ploughland', to describe the scratches on their cheeks. With the

---

[10] Cf. Sartre, *L'Être et le néant*, quoted in Lacan 1977b, p. 84.

entry into language, the 'innocence' of perception, or rather, the possibility of an innocent perception is lost.

After Orestes' speech interpreting the sight of the approaching women, the connection between sight and interpretation is stressed in the antistrophe also with the references to Clytemnestra's dream, a vision that demands interpretation (ὀνειρόμαντις, 33; κριταί, 38). This also refers back to *Aga.* 274–5 where Clytemnestra dismissed dreams as φάσματ᾽ εὐπειθῆ, and to *Aga.* 491, where dreams, connected with light that deceives the mind, were opposed to 'truth'. Now, however, the queen accepts, and is terrified by the appearance of the dream. τορός, both 'thrilling', 'piercing', and also 'accurate' was used, like σαφής/ἐτήτυμος/ὀρθός, in the *Agamemnon* to describe interpretation, speech, and it is here predicated of ὀνειρόμαντις – μάντις being one of the prime words for interpreter, the figure between present and future, signifier and signified. In juxtaposition with ὀρθόθριξ, however, both significations of τορός are brought into play. ὀνειρόμαντις, a *hapax legomenon*, draws attention to precisely the function Clytemnestra had disclaimed at *Aga.* 275 – but there remains a doubt about the subject of the sentence. Who or what the ὀνειρόμαντις is remains unclear: κότον πνέων, ...ἐν δώμασιν βαρὺς πίτνων suggests some form of spirit, the daimon with which Clytemnestra claimed to be filled: the chorus said there, echoed in this passage: δαίμον, ὃς ἐμπίτνεις δώμασι (*Aga.* 1468). The scream, the dream, however, appear to be connected with Clytemnestra: γυναικείοισιν ἐν δώμασιν. This confusion of possessed and possessor, similar to Clytemnestra's relation to the daimon (*Aga.* 1433, 1497ff.) suggests a similarly complex pattern of causality, which would in no way be diminished by the reading of φόβος or Φοῖβος in 32. The role of fear as a reaction to interpretation and lack of narrative control was stressed in the *Agamemnon* – indeed, the cluster of words central to the *Agamemnon* is marked here: τορός, δόμων, ὀνειρό-, -μαντις, νύκτον, φόβῳ, γυναικείοισιν ἐν δώμασιν. Φοῖβος, which either may imply Apollo, or, as Verrall suggests, 'inspiring possession', with a play (Tucker) on φόβος and φοῖβος as 'clear', 'shining', would also look forward to the end of the *Choephoroi* and the *Eumenides*, where Apollo/possession and, indeed, 'clear interpretation' are closely linked. The chorus do not tell here, however, the substance of the dream, merely its interpretation by κριταί. They offer as explanation for the dream the 'reproach of those underground': once again we are in the area of vague causality, postulated divine emotions as reasons. Despite the words for 'accuracy' and 'judging', the chorus' description of events is shrouded in an aura of uncertainty and darkness – suited perhaps to the terrors of the world of dreams.

Thus the chorus come with Clytemnestra's offerings 'to turn away evils' – a connection between causality and 'magic' – in the sense of rites particularly of a piacular nature as proposed by Durkheim.[11]

But the chorus are afraid to speak (of) such offerings (48): this fear of the uncertainty of language, as we saw in the *Agamemnon*, is the fear of the power of the word to prophesy, define, beyond the author-ity of the user, as well as the fear of blaspheming. The chorus' fear, they say, stems from (γάρ, 48) the questioning of the possibility of 'atonement for spilt blood'. This image of a poured-out liquid will return again and again (cf. e.g. 66, 95, 109, 152, 185) – libations, blood, tears.

The lament for the house bereaved of its δεσπότης, which is expressed in the emotive language of the *Agamemnon* (ἑστία, δόμων, darkness/light), turns to general moralising reminiscent in particular of the second stasimon of the *Agamemnon*. ἄμαχον, ἀδάματον, ἀπόλεμον seem to refer to (Orestes') sense of conflict in σύμμαχος (2, 19). ἀφίστασαι indeed often implies 'to have a revolution', 'be deposed from power'. σέβας has fared as did Agamemnon himself: σέβας is connected closely with a reaction to authority, one in power (cf. πῶς σε σεβίξω; (*Aga.* 785); τὸν εὐτυχοῦντ' ἄνευ φθόνων σέβειν (*Aga.* 833); σεβίζων...κράτος (*Aga.* 258)). The overthrow of the δεσπότης and σέβας are simultaneous and mutually implicative. This too leads to fear – φοβεῖται δέ τις. As with the watchman's speech and the chorus' warning to Agamemnon, the cause of fear is unexpressed, or rather, deliberately repressed: here even the subject of the verb is impersonal. But revenge is hinted at in ῥοπά...Δίκας (61), 'the downward tilt of *dike*' (not the balance) which 'overlooks', ἐπισκοπεῖ. And that imagery of sight is further extended in the description of the outcome of the 'tilt of *dike*' in terms of three realms of light and dark (62–5).

δι' αἷματ' ἐκποθένθ' ὑπὸ χθονὸς τροφοῦ (66) reiterates the sense of 'blood fallen to the ground' (48) but ἐκποθένθ' links it with the libation (cf. *Aga.* 1384ff.) – as often in Aeschylus, events are 'sacralised', depicted with a structuring of religious terminology. The earth, which naturally receives the libation and the blood, is termed τροφοῦ, 'nurse', 'feeder', 'nourisher'. This, which looks forward to the argument of the *Eumenides* (658ff.), and also to the speech of the nurse in the *Choephoroi*, and to Clytemnestra's baring of her breast (εὐτραφὲς γάλα, 896–8), is strangely inverted by its connection with ἐκποθένθ' which suggests 'feeding' rather than 'feeder'. Similarly, φόνος, 'gore', is termed τίτας, 'avenger', when

---

[11] *The Elementary Forms of Religious Life.* Trans. by Swain. London, 1976, p. 363.

we might have expected 'needing to be avenged' (as Verrall, Tucker, Sidgwick translate, though Sidgwick suggests 'vengeful', later used by Lloyd-Jones). This confusion of subject and object, acted on and acting, suggests the complexity of cause and effect, of narrative desire and fulfilment, that we have noted before as so important to the doubling narrative of revenge. The blood which is first depicted as 'drunk away completely' ἐκποθένθ᾽, leaves 'gore', which is clotted, fixed οὐ διαρρύδαν – '*not* slipping away'. The stain, the trace, remains.

διαφέρει (68), the verb which specifies the relation between *ate* and the man responsible or guilty, is difficult. Indeed, δι(α) (66), διαρρύδαν (67), δι(α)-αλγής (68), three differing senses of διά – 'by' (agency), 'through' (passage), 'very' (intensive) – suggest a difficulty of specifying the relation between δια and φέρει in διαφέρει (the splitting of the signifier through the prefix – suffix relation). The scholion suggests διασπαράσσει, 'tears in pieces', followed by L.-S.-J., Conington, Schütz: 'mad destruction tears the one responsible in pieces'. Hermann, followed by Sidgwick, Lloyd-Jones, suggests *differt*: 'mad destruction puts off the punishment of the guilty'. Verrall suggests φέρεται διὰ τοῦ αἰτίου as a gloss: '*ate* rushes on the guilty'. The range of meanings from 'sustain' to 'tear to pieces' would seem to leave the relationship between ἄτα and τὸν αἴτιον without clarity; and this lack of clarity in that relationship looks back to the various delayings of δίκα, expressed as it was in the structure of light/dark imagery. The end, the *telos*, however, is certain sickness – †παναρκέτας† νόσου βρύειν (69). As we saw in the *Agamemnon* (*Aga.* 68, for example), it is in the transition from postulated ἀρχή to τέλος, that passage of narrative, where doubt and lack of control are expressed, here by the lexical variations of a single word – which often means also 'it differs'!

Antistrophe γ, looking forward with some irony to the argument of the Erinues and Apollo's defence, concludes that there is no purification for spilt blood – θιγόντι...νυμφικῶν ἑδωλίων (71). This summons up both the individual examples of adultery, the transgressions of the marriage bower (Paris/Helen, Clytemnestra/Aegisthus, Atreus, Thyestes) and also, within the imagery of flow and irretrievability, 'a virgin's blood', the hymen. All waters, they continue, cannot clean the stain of χερομυσῆ φόνον – the flow (of blood) is the cause of the stain, the flow (of water) the suggested cure.

So the *parodos* recalls many of the problematics of the *Agamemnon* within the setting of the situation of their expedition to present apotropaic offerings from the now dream-scared Clytemnestra at the tomb of her husband. Specifically, it echoes the earlier focus on communication, on interpretation, particularly on the interpretation of the visual object (the dream – like the beacons), on the structure of authority within the house (which is marked after Orestes' prayer for a return to κράτος); and also it echoes the tension between the reciprocity of action and the confusions of cause/effect, subject/object, possessor/possessed. In its questioning of the value of offerings for spilt blood, however, the chorus also look forward to the problem of Orestes' purification. Moreover, in such interests it functions as an important prelude to Electra's first speech, which concentrates on finding the correct words for a prayer (language as directive) and on the difficulties of a simple view of reciprocal action.

Sees, seems, semes: signs and sight

The first scene after the short *parados* and prologue, is a long and extremely complex episode. In the opening passages, Electra and the chorus discuss the terms in which to make the prayer Clytemnestra has requested, and then Electra makes the offering at the tomb – but for Orestes' return; and the chorus sing a short *paian*. At the tomb, Electra spots the lock of hair that Orestes left, and the recognition process is acted out. Orestes comes forward. After the joyful reunion, Orestes goes on to expound Apollo's motivation of the revenge. In the discussion of the correct language to use in the dangerous moment of addressing a divinity, in the following process of sign-reading which constitutes a proof towards recognition, and in the explanation of the complex motivations of a pattern of cause and effect, this scene has evident links with the trilogy in the terms I have already been outlining; indeed, this scene is an extremely important development of the interrelations of signs and sight as well as an important and exciting moment in the narrative.

First, then, the movement towards Electra's prayer and the chorus' *paian*.

The language of prayer

Electra's opening speech emphasises the difficulty of using language safely, particularly in this religious context, and her desire for the right word: τί φῶ (87), πῶς εὔφρον' εἴπω (88), πῶς κατεύξωμαι (88), πότερα λέγουσα (89), ἢ τοῦτο φάσκω τοὔπος (93), ἢ σῖγ' (96), οὐδ' ἔχω τί φῶ (98 (91)). Her first question (87) strengthens this uncertainty by the use of κηδείους. Sidgwick's rendering of this adjective as 'funerary'[12] glosses over the inherent pun on 'connection

---

[12] Although κῆδος in Homer is often connected with care for the dead. Cf. *Il.* 5.156; 22.272. Cf. also κηδέμων.

by marriage' (Clytemnestra to Agamemnon) and 'care', 'worry', which was made explicit in the play at *Aga.* 699–700. The irony of offerings 'of loving duty' (Tucker), an extension from κῆδος in the sense of *cura*, is pointed by a reference to precisely the bond (κῆδος) broken by the murder of Agamemnon, as well as by the more general sense of κῆδος as 'distress',[13] and as a (social) act of funerary obligation. Such polysemy provokes πῶς εὔφρον᾽ εἴπω; πῶς κατ-εύξωμαι πατρί; Even εὔφρον᾽, which is significantly both active and passive ('well-meaning', 'kindly', and also that which will be well-received, 'welcome' (Tucker), 'acceptable' (Verrall)),[14] points to the difficulty of simply controlling a word (even in a request for control).

The word order of 89–90 is turned to the juxtaposition φίλης/φίλῳ and γυναικός/ἀνδρί. φίλης φίλῳ emphasises the relation of φιλία, which is precisely the relationship disturbed by Clytemnestra's adultery, and subsequent interreaction with her children and *oikos*: 'φιλεῖν has an obligatory character and always implies reciprocity,'[15] – a reciprocity which is the centre of the marriage/exchange system (society). φιλεῖν thus becomes the expression of the relations within the family (often weakly translated 'love'): 'The whole vocabulary of moral terms is strongly permeated by values which are not personal but relational.'[16] Thus Orestes:

φιλεῖς τὸν ἄνδρα;   (894)

ἐπεὶ φιλεῖς

τὸν ἄνδρα τοῦτον, ὃν δὲ χρῆν φιλεῖν στυγεῖς   (906–7)

At the moment of tension immediately before the matricide, the repetition of this term is not merely a reaction against his mother's sexuality,[17] but an expression of the damage done to the family, the *oikos*, by the corruption of the bonds of φιλία. We shall see the transgression of the bonds of φιλία expressly recalled again and again in this play.

The juxtaposition γυναικὸς ἀνδρί (90) emphasises (again) the sexual opposition. This is also formed in a generational structure by the addition of τῆς ἐμῆς μητρὸς πάρα (90). These interwoven oppositions between male and female, children and parents are

---

[13] Cf. *Il.* 1.455; 2.69; 18.55.

[14] Lloyd-Jones translates it 'wise', which seems to miss the point.

[15] Benveniste 1973, p. 280 (= 1969, p. 344).   [16] Ibid., p. 277 (= 1969, p. 340).

[17] For this view, see, for example, the rather unsatisfactory psychoanalytic criticism of the *Oresteia*, which is discussed below pp. 137–40. The most developed psychoanalytic reading is perhaps that of André Green. He writes of these lines, however, 'She is seeking to arouse sexual temptations' (1975, p. 48), 'the revenge...has the nature of a substitute coitus carried out in his father's place' (p. 52). *Philein* does have undeniable sexual connotations, but it extends beyond simply sexual connotations.

central referents for the discourse of the *Choephoroi* as for the *Agamemnon*, as we move towards the conflict of mother and son.

ἵσ' ἀντιδοῦναι τοῖσι πέμπουσιν τάδε (92(94)) indicates the stress on reciprocity (cf. ἀντι-, 94, 121, 123, 133, 135, 142, 144), which is to be viewed not only as a basis of societal forms but also with regard to the increasing parallelisation of events in terms of narrative expectation: revenge itself as a reciprocity. The revenge against Clytemnestra's and Aegisthus' crossing of the norms of reciprocity is by an act depicted as having a reaffirming reciprocal nature.

Electra (100) repeats her request for advice and asks them not to hide their opinions because of their fear (as at 57–8, 83). The reason she suggests (γάρ, 103) is that 'Fate' awaits both free and enslaved. What will be, will be – an expression reminiscent of the tautologies of the *parodos* of the *Agamemnon* (67ff., p. 15). μένει: as with Calchas' prophecy (*Aga.* 154) and elsewhere, the passage of waiting is the connection between narrative, inability to predict, and fear.

The stichomythia that follows (106–24), a series of questions and answers, offers further discussion of the problematic terms of prayer, as, in particular, Electra questions the reciprocity of revenge, the simple *dike* of killing in return. This movement proceeds through a constant checking and shifting imposed on the terms by the dialectic of questioning and answering; the terms of the dialogue are linked, too, in a network of allusions and references which further undercut the possibility of any simple definition. This stichomythic exchange is especially marked after Electra's repeated questions as to what to say. As often in the *Agamemnon*, this stichomythic dialogue highlights the situation of language exchange as well as augmenting and developing the movement of the scene.

The dialogue begins with the chorus stating (in answer to Electra's request) their reverence for the tomb of Agamemnon (note πατρός, 106, repeated in the same metrical position, 108) and they promise to speak τὸν ἐκ φρενὸς λόγον: the possibility of speech οὐκ ἐκ φρενός, of dissimulated language, is also linked back to the play on φρήν/προφρόνως/σωφρονεῖν/φρονεῖν (*Aga.* 165–81, 351 etc.) and thus to the role of 'thought', 'conception' and the principle of Zeus (and the male: cf: pp. 27, 37–8). Electra reiterates this connection between their speech and reverence, λέγοις ἄν, 'So you may speak', i.e. ἐκ φρενός – ὥσπερ ἡδέσω τάφον πατρός (108), 'As you have expressed reverence for the tomb of father'. Because of their reverence for πατρός, they may offer advice ἐκ φρενός – the sandwiching of the participial phrase (αἰδουμένη) and the explicative ὥσπερ ἡδέσω, emphasises the significant juxtaposition of ἐκ φρενός and (αἰδώς) πατρός.

The chorus express their first command:

φθέγγου χέουσα κεδνὰ τοῖσιν εὔφροσιν   (109)

κεδνά is, like εὔφρον᾽, a word of both active and passive senses, which implies both 'careful', 'diligent', and 'dear', 'cared for'. It has even been translated as 'joyful', as at *Aga.* 622, where it is juxtaposed to τἀληθῆ and characterises things spoken to advantage which may not be true: this use, from another passage discussing the way to utilise language, indicates the non-absoluteness of the term. It indicates an ambiguity beyond the lexical possibility of active/passive construction, specifically an ambiguity as a relational term within the communicational model. τοῖσιν εὔφροσιν, as we saw at 88, may also be active and passive: εὔφρων picks up ἐκ φρενός, suggesting the connection between φρήν and the force of Zeus/the male (as in the hymn to Zeus, *Aga.* 165) – as indeed we saw also at *Aga.* 351: κατ᾽ ἄνδρα σώρρον᾽ εὐφρόνως λέγεις. But εὐφρόνως/εὔφρων also may be seen as referring back to the beginning of the scene of which *Aga.* 351 is the concluding speech, where Clytemnestra puns on the words εὔφρων/εὐφρόνη, (recalling the possibilities of miscontrol of the term). Furthermore, the command φθέγγου χέουσα κεδνὰ τοῖσιν εὔφροσιν echoes Electra's questions τί φῶ χέουσα τάσδε κηδείους χόας; | πῶς εὔφρον᾽ εἴπω; (87–8) – κεδνά/κηδείους, a verbal similarity pointed by the repetition of χέουσα and εὔφρων, suggests an echoing connection between the two words[18] which not only recalls with κεδν- the complex associations of κῆδ- (particularly in the sense of family tie, as will be picked up by φίλων, 110) but also by the play itself suggests the openness of language, its resistance to univocality. So the network of allusions and elusiveness of words prompts further questioning. It is τοῖσιν εὔφροσιν that Electra seeks to define further:

τίνας δὲ τούτους τῶν φίλων προσεννέπω;   (110)

They are regarded as a 'subset' of τῶν φίλων, picking up φίλης φίλῳ (89) which implies that there are φίλοι who are not εὔφρονες. Indeed, the chorus' naming of herself (αὐτήν) and χὤστις Αἴγισθον στυγεῖ, despite the generality of the second phrase, points also towards the unstated name of Clytemnestra: the emphasis is on Aegisthus, who has been and will be comparatively unstressed in the trilogy, but it is an emphasis on Aegisthus as the object of a verb with a sense opposed to that of φίλων (defining φιλεῖν/φίλος by its 'opposite',[19] στυγεῖν). This not only suggests the possibility of the chorus, for example, as the unstated subject (as proposed by Electra, 112), but

---

[18] Accepted by some etymologists, in fact.
[19] That is, a word often placed in opposition to it, particularly in general ethical, social statements.

it also hints towards Clytemnestra, who, since she is Electra's mother, would be regarded as φίλη, but who does not hate Aegisthus. Clytemnestra, that is, is suggested as the implied subject of the negated sense of the phrase – which looks towards Orestes' question, φιλεῖς τὸν ἄνδρα; (894), and, with a strong echo of this passage, ἐπεὶ φιλεῖς | τὸν ἄνδρα τοῦτον ὃν δὲ χρῆν φιλεῖν στυγεῖς (906–7). It is, in Barthes' terms, a hermeneutic sentence, the riddle being the unstated subject, the answer constituted in terms of a relationship to Aegisthus. Clytemnestra, then, as one of the φίλων who is *not* εὔφρων?

Electra asks, then, (τἄρα) if she is to pray for herself and the chorus. Again the non-naming of either Clytemnestra or Orestes is noticeable; and again the chorus refuse to be more explicit:

αὐτὴ σὺ ταῦτα μανθάνουσ᾽ ἤδη φράσαι   (113)

Despite the chorus' previous remark, Electra continues with another question – and the chorus finally state the name of Orestes. Verrall comments 'we are not to suppose that Electra who has but one near friend in the world really needs to be reminded of her brother'. The movement from 'speaking darkly' to the statement of the name (and the assumption of status involved in the announcement of a name); the expectation of Orestes' name (he has just left stage), its delay, and then fulfilment, is a prior expression, a version,[20] of the drama to follow, of Orestes' deceiving (a withholding of his name) and final revealing of himself, and his move towards accession of status.

The chorus turn to mention of revenge – or at least begin to (117): τοῖς αἰτίοις νυν τοῦ φόνου μεμνημένη, but Electra interrupts with:

τί φῶ; δίδασκ᾽ ἄπειρον ἐξηγουμένη   (118)

The expression of revenge is divided by the interruption into two phrases. First, the expression of guilt, responsibility τοῖς αἰτίοις. This recalls the recurring problematics of causality, and definition in language. Who are, and how are we to define, οἱ αἴτιοι? This constitutes a significant point of interruption – again with a question 'What am I to say?' and a request for further knowledge expressed also in religious terminology, ἐξηγουμένη, to 'prescribe a correct form of language'. The second phrase is the prayer that some δαίμων or βροτός should come. δαίμων or βροτός seems to refer not only to Orestes and the support of Hermes/Zeus/Apollo/Agamemnon but also to the passages after the murder of Agamemnon where the problematic of causality revolved around attribution of motivation to daimon or Clytemnestra. The word αὐτοῖς (119) glosses over the difficulties of αἰτίοις and attribution of responsibility by saying

---

[20] It could be seen as an expression of the desire of the chorus and Electra for the appearance of Orestes – a 'fort/da' game with his name.

merely 'they themselves'; but also it 'suggests and anticipates
ἀνταποκτενεῖ (121)' (Verrall) by the suggestion that they are to be
done to as they did. Electra's interruption separates then, the
expression of guilt from the expression of punishment with the desire
for accurate expression. Electra requests indeed a further definition:

πότερα δικαστὴν ἢ δικηφόρον λέγεις;   (120)

This distinction, looking back towards *Aga.* 525 – the pickaxe of
δικηφόρου Διός which destroyed Troy – and *Aga.* 1577, where
Aegisthus greeted the day of Agamemnon's murder as δικηφόρου,
and looking forward also to the *Eumenides* and the jurors and final
resolution, implies an opposition between opposition itself, the
reciprocity of retribution (which Electra questioned at 91–3 (93–5))
and mediation, decision between oppositions. But this distinction
(which Kitto,[21] for example, sees as central to the dynamics of the
trilogy) is glossed over by the chorus:

ἁπλωστὶ φράζουσ᾿ ὅστις ἀνταποκτενεῖ   (121)

ἁπλωστὶ φράζουσ᾿, after the complexities of the preceding dialogue
and, indeed, the immediate distinction on which they are asked to
comment, seems an almost ironic assurance of the possible sim-
plicity/singleness of language: to speak, indicate 'simply', ἁπλωστί,
with its connection with 'single' despite the duality offered by
Electra, as with the herald's assumption in the *Agamemnon* of πάντ᾿
ἔχεις λόγον (*Aga.* 582) and its reduction, is in marked juxtaposition
to the movement of attempted definitions, the network of allusions
and references, the repeated questions, πῶς εἴπω etc., which refuse
the assumption of univocality for language. Furthermore, ἀνταποκτενεῖ is a simplification of the uncertainties of Electra's questioning
of the right to revenge at, say, 91–3(93–5). Indeed Electra asks if
theirs is a pious wish from the gods: εὐσεβῆ, referring back to the
chorus' words at 55ff., implies by its prefix εὐ- the further possibility
of δυσσέβεια which had been the chorus' fear. And the chorus, relying
on the almost proverbial ethical stance of φιλεῖν φίλους, ἐχθαίρειν
ἐχθρούς and the desire for reciprocal punishment ἀνταμείβεσθαι,
assume certainty for their position:

πῶς δ᾿ οὐ; τὸν ἐχθρὸν ἀνταμείβεσθαι κακοῖς;   (123)

But it is precisely the opposition of φίλος/ἐχθρός that was in doubt,
at risk, in the opening lines of stichomythia and in Electra's questions
(89–90), and it is precisely this problem of defining τῶν φίλων that
stands in contrast to the chorus' assertion.

Electra's prayer, then, is preceded by a stichomythic exchange

[21] 1961, pp. 79ff.

explicitly concerned with the problem of definition, and of reciprocity; before the religious invocation, with its predictive, dangerous, cledonomantic, force that we saw in the language of the *Agamemnon*, we see a discussion of, and a search for, a possible univocality of language, but a search undercut by the shifting interplay of signifiers, the difficulty of controlling language.

Electra's prayer opens with an address to Hermes, which is parallel to Orestes' opening prayer: so the repetitions of language, the doublings, bridge the separation of brother and sister, associating them together: Ἑρμῆ χθόνιε (1), Ἑρμῆ χθόνιε (124b), κλύειν (6), κλύειν (125). The prayer's context is the relations in/of the *oikos*: she calls the daimons πατρῴων δωμάτων[22] ἐπισκόπους (126, picking up the divine overseers, 1, 61). The plural δωμάτων maintains the general sense of πατρῴων, and ἐπισκόπους continues the metaphors connected with vision. The daughter's address of Earth as 'parent' and 'rearer' (127–8) marks and overlays the associations of 'generation'/'maternity' (not only in the *oikos* relations), and after the doubt concerning the characterisations φίλος/ἐχθρός in the *oikos* she calls Orestes φίλον with regard to herself and their father unquestioningly. φῶς τ' ἄναψον ἐν δόμοις refers back to Clytemnestra's (sexual?) boast that Aegisthus will light the fire in her hearth (*Aga.* 1435–6), which contrasted with her insincere delight at her husband's return to the hearth, like heat in winter (*Aga.* 968–9): Electra prays for the return of the paternal light in the house, a rectification of Clytemnestra's insincerity. The economic imagery of the *Agamemnon* returns in the 'expressive and contemptuous' (Sidgwick) metaphor of πεπραμένοι: it is not merely 'as if they were in some way slaves', but linked to the economic basis of the *oikos* in inheritance. Engels suggests influentially[23] in this light that inheritance is concomitant with the rise of paternal authority and the transformation of women into 'commodities' (of exchange). Certainly here the lack of the father separates Electra from her social role[24] and Orestes from his economic rights.[25] Clytemnestra, however, is still not named but termed τεκούσης, 'she who bore me'. This term will become central in the debate in the (re)definition of the emotive term μήτηρ,

---

[22] Interestingly M reads δ' ὀμμάτων (*correxit* Pearson; Sidgwick calls it an 'obvious correction'). ὄμμα is what Electra calls Orestes at 238 and how Athene characterises the final procession of the *Eumenides* (1025): ὀμμάτων ἐπισκόπους offers a nice play on the active/passive fields of vision, 'overseers of the eyes'.

[23] Cf. for a critique of Engels and his influence Coward 1983, Pembroke 1967, and Coward's bibliography.

[24] That is, as a 'slave' she is an object of exchange, but not in the marital system.

[25] As in the commonly voiced fear in the ancient world on the part of stepchildren of dispossession by their stepmother in favour of her own children.

which is itself used in the *Choephoroi* only with careful qualification
up to the confrontation between Clytemnestra and Orestes, and only
by Electra: first, in the problem of the definition of φίλος in her
present position (89–90); to be rejected as a model at 141; rejected
as a suitable term for Clytemnestra (190); used to describe Orestes
as having taken over her mother's role (240). Significantly, Orestes
does not use the word μήτηρ until the highly emotive question (899)
μῆτερ' αἰδεσθῶ κτανεῖν; But afterwards, as madness overcomes him,
he uses the term on several occasions (986, 989, 1027, 1054) to
describe, and defend, the committed action. Here (133), the specificity
of the biological function and the resultant undervaluing of the
social/emotive force of either μήτηρ or even Κλυταίμηστρα, is
pointed by the juxtaposition of τῆς τεκούσης with ἄνδρα... Αἴγισθον
– social role (husband/paramour) and name (full status). As in the
Agamemnon, the function of naming is invested with circumspections
and projections, particularly here in the predictive/predicative language of prayer, preceded as it was by the series of questions
concerning the correctness of the language to be uttered. Note too
that Aegisthus is called φόνου μεταίτιος (134), as the chorus were to
be βουλῆς...μεταίτιαι (100). The chorus had referred merely to
αἰτίοις (117), glossed by αὐτοῖς (119). Electra, however, distinguishes
Aegisthus from Clytemnestra as an 'accomplice', a supplementary
causality, showing the complex doubts and recessions in the patterning of responsibility that we read in the *Agamemnon*.

As for the εὐχή itself: (1) Electra prays that Orestes should
ἐλθεῖν...σὺν τύχῃ τινι. The irony of this coincidence, the answer to
the prayer coming before the prayer – the tense of the infinitive also
allows the sense that Orestes 'has come' (cf. ἥκω, 3) – invests her
prayer with the sanction of success, and Agamemnon with having
heard and brought about the fulfilment of the prayer. (2) For herself,
she wishes to be (a) σωφρονεστέραν πολὺ μητρός (140–1): σώφρων
(as at *Aga.* 181) indicates the restraining of what might oppose
φρονεῖν/φρένες; it often occurs particularly in a sexual context, where
it indicates the qualities opposed to unlicensed sexuality (cf. the first
stasimon, particularly 622ff.). Clytemnestra's behaviour is rejected
because of its failure to be σώφρων, to σώζειν φρένας; (b)
εὐσεβεστέραν: the qualities of being εὐσεβῆ (122), of showing σέβας
(55–6), as we have seen, are placed in a position of value, but also with
an undetermined, uncertain sense: the paradox, in Lebeck's words,
is that 'On the lips of Electra and Orestes the traditional piety
(εὐσέβεια) of this prayer [for vengeance] is sacrilege.'[26]

[26] 1971, p. 103.

Electra prays further for the epiphany of her father (πάτερ, 143;
cf. 130, 139) as 'avenger' against τοῖς ἐναντίοις. After the specificity
of ἡμῖν μέν, this phrase, 'those opposed', markedly does not specify
the form of the opposition or even name Clytemnestra or Aegisthus.
Nor is τοὺς κτανόντας ἀντικατθανεῖν (144) quite simple. For the
qualification of ἀντικατθανεῖν with δίκῃ marks an interesting development: at 121 the chorus had said ἁπλωστὶ φράζουσ' ὅστις ἀνταποκτενεῖ in reply to Electra's question about δικαστὴν ἢ δικηφόρον;
Electra now prays for the killers to ἀντικατθανεῖν (note 'die', 'be
killed in return' rather than 'kill' – passive rather than active), but
she does not pray ἁπλωστί; she adds the adverbial δίκῃ (retained
accusative δίκην M). *Dike* not only implies both sides of her
opposition between δικαστής and δικηφόρος (i.e. *dike* in its legal
sense of 'trial', 'law-suit', that at which a δικαστής arbitrates; and
dike in the sense of 'punishment', 'satisfaction', 'penalty', as those
who read the retained accusative translate, e.g. 'receive death as a
penalty', Verrall); but it also suggests the more general sense of
'justice', i.e. what is right morally. Particularly in the strong position
of last word in the sentence and line, it implies the doubt seen earlier
about the action prayed for, and opens up the possibility of the
opposite characterisation ('without *dike*') for ἀντικατθανεῖν. So, far
from 'simply/singly saying to kill in return', Electra opens again,
dis-covers, the possibility of incertitude. Indeed, she goes on:

> ταῦτ' ἐν μέσῳ τίθημι τῆς καλῆς²⁷ ἀρᾶς
> κείνοις λέγουσα τήνδε τὴν κακὴν ἀράν   (145–6)

Here, the assumption is that her prayer for success is not necessarily
identical with the prayer for the death of Clytemnestra and Aegisthus
as the one may be characterised as κακή, the opposite of the other
(καλή). The strict reciprocity of the chorus' ἀνταποκτενεῖ is undone
by the non-identity of her prayers (a) for herself and Orestes; and
(b) against the murderers of her father.

Indeed, she concludes with the hope that Agamemnon will be the
transporter of good things, blessing for them:

> σὺν θεοῖσι καὶ γῇ καὶ δίκῃ νικηφόρῳ   (148)

'With the help of the gods and earth and *dike* bringing victory.' The
chorus had implied that δικηφόρος 'bringing retribution' (especially
regarding the parallelisation of action and the references to the fall
of Troy and the death of Agamemnon, cf. p. 115) was the figure to
pray for: here Electra ends the prayer with δίκῃ νικηφόρῳ, where

²⁷ As read by Page, Thomson, Sidgwick. M's κακῆς is not defended well by Verrall or
Tucker. The different senses of τῆς κακῆς ἀρᾶς / τήνδε κακὴν ἀράν show the relational
quality of the moral terms well.

one might have expected (especially considering the battle imagery)
νίκη δικηφόρῳ. δίκη, even with the adjective νικηφόρῳ, is open to
the ambiguities we saw on 144 – νικᾶν, for example, is often used in
the contexts of councils, debates, courts, for a prevailing opinion. The
paragram δικηφόρῳ/νικηφόρῳ, pointed strongly by the juxtaposition
of the latter term to δίκη, emphasises the openness of the moral terms,
the rejection of a simplification of the question raised by Electra
δικαστὴν ἢ δικηφόρον, and the rejection of ἁπλωστὶ φράζουσ', the
possibility of univocality.[28] The prayer itself, then, flirts with the
dangers of language that her questions for definition (87 ff.) were to
control.

The *paian*, Apollo's hymn, which the chorus now sing, reiterates
the sympathetic connection between the pouring of tears, libation and
the pouring of blood with the figure δάκρυ...ὀλόμενον ὀλομένῳ,
'the tear fallen for our fallen master'. The text of the *paian* is
uncertain[29] but even the boundaries of the apparently binary opposition of κεδνῶν/κακῶν, after the play κεδνά/κηδείους, are rendered
less clearly defined, transgressed. Here too, the apparent simplicity
of the chorus' use of moral terms ('good', 'bad') is in contrast to
the problematic definings, the shifting, of the stichomythia, and
Electra's questioning of the terms of the reciprocity of revenge and
the simplicity of *dike*. This apparent naivety, or misprision, of the
chorus we will also see later, particularly at the end of the play (cf.
1044, pp. 201–2). If, as Vernant suggests, the chorus of Greek tragedy
is in some way to be depicted as rehearsing, representing a traditional,
social, communal viewpoint, it can only be within the recognition that
the dialect of shifting terms, as here, undercuts any attempt at
hypostatisation of the chorus as a repository of a certain wisdom or
truth: 'tragédie...ne reflète pas cette réalité; elle la met en question'.[30]
'En jeu', he might have said.

They call Agamemnon σέβας (157) – at 55 the chorus had sung of
the absence of σέβας because of the δεσποτᾶν θανάτοισι (53–4).
Now with the two vocatives σέβας/δέσποτ', the absence of σέβας
and the absence of δεσπότης are equivalent, as though mutually
implying each other's presence/absence.

ἐξ ἀμαυρᾶς, as we saw at *Aga.* 546, indicates both 'dark' and
'blind', working within both the structure of light and dark imagery,
and the problematic of the visual. At *Aga.* 546, it was connected with

---

[28] Kristeva writes on the semiotics of paragrams (1969a), on how they emphasise the
materiality of a text, a signifier as a combination of letters: 'The expression of a
particular signifying function which dispenses with the word and the sign as the basic
units of meaning, throughout the whole signifying material of a given text' p. 293.

[29] See Dodds 1953, especially pp. 13ff.

[30] Vernant and Vidal-Naquet 1972, p. 25.

the repressiveness of Clytemnestra – that force is now linked more explicitly with the absence of the male figure of authority. The 'darkening', 'blinding' of the φρενές is through the absence, the murder, of the father. Indeed, they end their song with a prayer for a 'spear-strong man', who will free the house. The relation is forged once more of maleness and its military function and the control of the *oikos*.

Electra concludes ἔχει μὲν ἤδη γαπότους χοὰς πατήρ. In 14–15 πατρί is separated from χοάς (in the same sentence) by nearly a whole metrical line. So at 87–8 χοάς; | πῶς εὔφρον' εἴπω; πῶς κατεύξωμαι πατρί; So too at 92: χέουσα...πατρός. And at 97 πατήρ... ἐγχέασα...χύσιν, 106–9 πατρός...πατρός...χέουσα, 129–30 χέουσα...πατέρ', 139–49 πάτερ...πάτερ...ἐπισπένδω χοάς. Now at the conclusion of the rite, we see for the first time the immediate juxtaposition of χοάς and πατήρ: Agamemnon has his offering.

Cognition and recognition

Electra spots the lock of hair. From her offering to Orestes': so the passage towards recognition...

The following short scene of dialogue between Electra and the chorus (introduced by the offer and request for the exchange of language μύθου τοῦδε κοινωνήσατε...λέγοις ἄν) begins the complex process of recognition. This stichomythia parallels their earlier exchange at 106–134,[31] but the roles of questioner and questioned are reversed. As before, the name of Orestes is delayed. Again we will see the process of judging (by) signs, of interpreting signifiers; indeed, the hermeneutic process of the recognition scene through the reading of signs towards the recuperation of a present identity stands in its length and complexity as an extremely important paradigm of the hermeneutic discourse of the *Oresteia*, and must be considered in some depth:

> ὁρῶ τομαῖον τόνδε βόστρυχον τάφῳ   (168)

ὁρῶ, 'I see' – the basis of the proof/hope placed as first word – recalls specifically the problematic of τέκμαρ/ὄψις in the earlier scene of discussion of a σύμβολον, the beacon-speeches scene. The chorus want to know the hair's origin. Electra replies:

> εὐξύμβολον τόδ' ἐστὶ παντὶ δοξάσαι   (170)

σύμβολον at *Aga.* 8, the term for the beacon light (as we saw also

---

[31] Cf. Lebeck 1971, pp. 106–7.

at *Aga.* 315) was constituted in the opposition of perception/conception, showing/saying; it was placed in juxtaposition to τέκμαρ/τεκμήριον as a basis of knowledge – the problematic we read of one thing standing for another, or of the half-token awaiting completion, as Electra awaits Orestes, as the hair is a 'half-token' of Orestes completed in its similarity to Electra's hair.[32] After ὁρῶ, δοξάσαι (which perhaps suggests, like δόξαν, *Aga.* 275, both 'judging' and 'vision') marks the move from sight to interpretation, that seems to invade even the object of vision, since the further marker of judgement, εὐ-, actually qualifies the σύμβολον itself rather than simply the verb of interpretation. Is seeing believing...?

Electra, however, follows the request for further knowledge (171) with 'There is no one except me who would cut it' – a remark which withholds the suggestion of her brother; she is reluctant to put the name to her hopes (as in the earlier dialogue the name of Orestes had been delayed, cf. 109ff.). The openness of her remark is further pointed by the general plural of the chorus' response: ἐχθροὶ γὰρ οἷς προσῆκε πενθῆσαι τριχί. προσῆκε not only means 'it is fitting, right', but also has the implications of 'related to', 'akin'. Clytemnestra and Aegisthus, who as kin have a moral obligation to mourn, nevertheless are 'enemies': the continuing definition of the relation of φίλος/ἐχθρός. The recognition is the recognition of a *philos*.

---

[32] It is interesting to recall here what Aristotle says Empedocles says: *G.A.* 722 b 11: φησὶ γὰρ ἐν τῷ ἄρρενι καὶ τῷ θήλει οἷον σύμβολον ἐνεῖναι, ὅλον δ' ἀπ' οὐδετέρου ἀπιέναι, ἀλλὰ διέσπασται μελέων φύσις ἡ μὲν ἐν ἀνδρός...διὰ τί γὰρ τὰ θήλεα οὐ γεννᾷ ἐξ αὐτῶν εἴπερ ἀπὸ παντός τε ἀπέρχεται καὶ ἔχει ὑποδοχήν; This is part of the argument concerning male and female seed which as E. Lesky 1951 has shown, continues to be debated strongly from the earliest philosophic material into the medieval and Renaissance writers. The insistence in the *Oresteia* on φίλ- words, the explicit reference by Apollo to the role of male and female in procreation (and the possibility that σύμβολον was the term used by Empedocles to describe the relation between the sexes in procreation) may suggest a more involved interrelation between Aeschylus and the philosopher-poet than just as background to the specific 'scientific' argument of Apollo. This may be further developed in consideration of the emphasis on the senses (particularly of sight) that I have been tracing in the *Oresteia*, with regard to such fragments of Empedocles: (3.10ff.): ...μήτε τιν' ὄψιν ἔχων πίστει πλέον ἢ κατ' ἀκουήν | ἢ ἀκοὴν ἐρίδουπον ὑπὲρ τρανώματα γλώσσης | μήτε τι τῶν ἄλλων, ὁπόσῃ πόρος ἐστὶ νοῆσαι, | γυίων πίστιν ἔρυκε, νόει δ' ᾗ δῆλον ἕκαστον. This is also written with Parmenides as intended opposition. The empirical value of the senses was a continuing debate in Greek writers. So too, the vocabulary of 'genesis' and that of intelligibility is highly suggestive in the *Oresteia* with regard to the Presocratics.

So, we may recall in the first stasimon of the *Choephoroi* Empedocles' monsters (cf. Diels–Kranz, *Die Fragmente der Vorsokratiker*, 6th ed. (1951–2), 31A72), especially since the opening strophe divides the sources of the horrors into the four ῥιζώματα of earth, sea, fire, and air, though this need not refer solely to Empedocles. As I indicated in my introduction (n. 17), there is a tendency in Aeschylean criticism to underplay the interplay with earlier Dichter. As Heidegger says: 'dichterisch wohnet der Mensch'.

Electra: καὶ μὴν ὅδ᾽ ἐστὶ κάρτ᾽ ἰδεῖν ὁμόπτερος (174). καὶ μὴν, a deictic particle, and the relation of similarity of ὁμόπτερος, qualified by the epexegetic ἰδεῖν, emphasise the visual basis of proof. The similarity of ὁμόπτερος further suggests the completion of the recognition tokens, the *tesserae*. The chorus interrupt (or does Electra hesitate?) with a desire for knowledge (cf. 118), and Electra leads further towards a statement of Orestes' name – αὐτοῖσιν ἡμῖν κάρτα προσφερὴς ἰδεῖν. The masculine plural, the idiom for self-reflexive feminine expression in Greek (cf. Sidgwick), also allows the sense of 'ourselves', i.e. 'my own family' (Verrall, Conington) – suggesting the name of Orestes? And the relation of visual resemblance is emphasised by the repetition of the epexegetic ἰδεῖν with προσφερής. προσφερής was also connected with the visual mode at *Aga.* 1218, where in a striking phrase of Cassandra it described things 'like to the shape of dreams' – dreams, the privileged example of the inconstancy of the visual, cf. *Aga.* 274 etc. The chorus finally ask if it could really be a gift of Orestes. Electra replies:

μάλιστ᾽ ἐκείνου βοστρύχοις προσείδεται   (178)

'It looks like particularly his hair'. προσείδεται, the visual term, seems placed in a metaphoric structure, 'to look like' – not the possible metonymy of σύμβολον, to stand for, or the simple partitive relation of ἐκείνου and βοστρύχοις. As we have discussed in part (p. 37), this opposition of metaphor to metonymy in the definition of the visual is highly suggestive (not just in a theatrical context), and it will be important in the definition of the role of *genitor/pater*. We shall return to it shortly.

It is the sight (187) of the offering of Orestes that leads Electra to cry (his offering is εὐδάκρυτα the chorus say, 181), as the offering of Electra had led to the falling of tears (152ff.): the sympathetic libations. Electra proceeds to reject two other possible sources for the lock of hair: first, another citizen, secondly, Clytemnestra, who is denied in striking language:

ἀλλ᾽ οὐδὲ μήν νιν ἡ κτανοῦσ᾽ ἐκείρατο
ἐμή γε μήτηρ, οὐδάμως ἐπώνυμον
φρόνημα παισὶ δύσθεον πεπαμένη   (189–91)

ἡ κτανοῦσ᾽ is in interesting juxtaposition with ἐκείρατο. κείρω can mean 'cut down', 'ravage' as well as 'cut' hair for an offering. It seems, then, to be both in direct opposition to ἡ κτανοῦσ᾽, 'murderer'/'mourned', but also connected subtextually 'murderer'/'cut'. This is also brought out in the ambiguity of the referent for νιν, which, for example, Conington refers to Agamemnon, but Sidgwick to the lock of hair. The word 'mother', μήτηρ, is used only to be qualified: οὐδάμως ἐπώνυμον φρόνημα...πεπαμένη. The name as referent slides (marking the gap) as the word itself as signifier breaks into a play of syllables: οὐδὲ μὴν...ἐμὴ γε μήτηρ...

The queen is not in fact called by her name[33] in the *Choephoroi* except as she is called to meet Orestes by the servant (883). Her children and the chorus on each occasion use a limitative, selected appellation, such as, here, ἡ κτανοῦσ'. The queen's φρόνημα is depicted as being παισὶ δύσθεον. δύσθεον, as part of the rhetoric of opposition, implies a corruption of Clytemnestra's relation to the gods, which seems especially significant after the expressions of the queen's motivations for sending offerings, and the children's prayers to the gods for assistance (so Electra calls on the knowing gods, 201ff.). δύσθεον also anticipates not only the *kommos*' further attempt at mustering daimonic aid, but also the *Eumenides* court-case, that instantiation of the complexity of divine and human linkages. So too, applied to Clytemnestra, δύσθεον recalls the complexity of the relations with the divine in Clytemnestra's justification of the regicide (*Aga.* 1460ff.). φρόνημα, too, will be seen to be an important term in the rhetoric of opposition and control. Here, it describes the force of will, desire, of Clytemnestra's acts, which is opposed to σωφρονεῖν. These lines, then, mark the terms in which Clytemnestra is rejected as a *philos*. A further recognition...?

Electra returns, however (picking up the implications of ἐπώνυμον), to a question of language, of accurate statement: ὅπως μὲν ἄντικρυς τάδ' αἰνέσω. This recognition of the need for accuracy is opposed (μέν...δέ) to ἐλπίς (σαίνομαι δ' ὑπ' ἐλπίδος – 'perhaps the most beautiful of the many ἀποσιωπήσεις in Aeschylus' (Fraenkel)). Whereas in the *Agamemnon*, then (and generally in the trilogy), ἐλπίς expressed an attitude to the relation between present and future which was connected with prediction/precision in language, ἐλπίς here seems to be a barrier to 'accurate' language. And despite her questioning ὅπως...ἄντικρυς...αἰνέσω she says of the lock:

εἴθ' εἶχε φωνὴν ἔμφρον' ἀγγέλου δίκην   (195)

'If only it had a voice...' The assumption that the possession of a voice, language, would make things clear and accurate stands in contradiction to her own repeated questions on the way to speak (of which πῶς...ἄντικρυς is only the most recent) and to the rejection of univocality or even over-simplification of language. Indeed, ἀγγέλου δίκην seems to recall precisely the undercutting of simple,

---

[33] Cf. Schaps 1977 for a discussion of the taboos involved in speaking a woman's name: the use of the woman's name seems to imply a bond of *philia*, which the revengers are keen to avoid.

referential language in the messenger scene of the *Agamemnon*. Nor is it simply the assumption that an inanimate, non-human object could speak most clearly (as at *Aga.* 37), that it could reduce communication to the clarity of showing. For ἔμφρον' places this φωνή within the structurings of φρεν/φρον/σωφρονεῖν – a voice with sense, mind, expression, a voice of a *speaking subject*[34] (which involves the problems of control and indeterminacy that I have been tracing).[35]

Electra's doubt, however (δίφροντις, a further play on ἔμφρον'), is expressed in terms of the opposition of ἐχθρός and (now) συγγενής, 'kinsman' (198–9), despite the fact that both Aegisthus and Clytemnestra are 'kinspeople' to Electra. συγγενής, which expresses a less general relation than φίλος, points precisely to the paradox of Electra's desire for vengeance, the need for redefinition of the opposition φίλος/ἐχθρός in familial conflict, in which this recognition is sited. This further undercuts the possibility of the accuracy of the φωνή of the lock of hair. For the opposition συγγενής/ἐχθρός is not sufficient to answer Electra's incertitude – it cannot, as suggested, εὖ σάφ' ἥνει (197).[36]

This search for definition of and through the verbal sign (particularly with regard to the terms of kin relations φίλος/ἐχθρός/συγγενής etc.), which is made necessary and challenged in its absoluteness by the sliding, slipping relation of signifier to signified, interlocks on this semiotic level with Electra's strange movement of proof we have been reading, that is, the movement from the lock of hair as signifier to its signified. For on the one hand this movement seems as if it should be simply metonymic: there are three possessors of the lock suggested in answer to the question τίνος ποτ' ἀνδρὸς ἢ ... κόρης; (where the genitives suggest the metonymic relation of part, ownership); namely, ἐκείνου (178) ('Ορέστου, 177), ἀστῶν τιν', and μήτηρ. Is it part of, parted from, which person? On the other hand, the connection of the tress with Orestes is traced by the metaphorisation of similarity (which is not simply reducible to the doubling of *tesserae*): ὁμόπτερος, προσφερής, προσείδεται. What does the lock look like? This is the point – the assumed family resemblance – that critics have found so difficult.

---

[34] The 'speaking subject' is a term used by Kristeva and others to indicate a relation between the subject and language – or rather the construction of the subject in language. On the 'subject', cf. Coward and Ellis 1977, Silverman 1982, and their bibliographies.

[35] For Kristeva, the speaking subject *supposes* the gap between signifier and signified: 'The subject of enunciation takes shape within the gap opened up between signifier and signified, that admits both structure and interplay within' (1980, pp. 127–8).

[36] On this clear knowing cf. Ch. 1, n. 133, p. 82.

The piece of hair as an object of vision, the empirical perception
of the lock, seems stressed by the repeated deictics τόνδε (168), ὅδ' ἐστὶ
(174), τόδε (177), τόνδε (187), τόδ' (193), τόνδε (197), τήνδε (226).
'Here is a lock', 'this is a lock', seem the simplest of assertive
statements. In such light, I have already characterised the deictic
'this is' as aiming towards the closure in present referentiality of the
signifier/signified gap in language. But recognition is not just the
seeing but the interpreting also. There is a marked passage from the
lock to its meaning, and the passing from the tress to its significance,
the analysis of the lock, trespasses on that aimed-at unity, that
simplicity of the 'this is'. Passing from the signifier towards signified
restresses the irreducible difference in the sign, the absence that this
trace (of Orestes) inscribes – the absence (gap) that instigates and
constitutes the problem of reading the tress as trace. As with Calchas'
prediction (for example), the movement of sign to sign, sign for sign,
cannot totally erase the gaps in their linkings.

Can the 'second proof' (δεύτερον τεκμήριον – Orestes had left
δεύτερον...πενθητήριον, 7), which is often regarded as stranger
than the first, help locate this recognition process? The footprints she
sees (καὶ μήν) are commensurate with her own (μετρούμεναι | εἰς ταὐτὸ
συμβαίνουσι τοῖς ἐμοῖς στίβοις, 209–10); they are ἐμφερεῖς, 'like',
'answering to' (as with προσφερὴς ἰδεῖν, 176). More strongly (hence
the critics' greater unease), a relation of similarity is put forward as
significant: συμβαίνουσι: 'they coincide'. Despite ὑπογραφαί/περι-
γραφά which seem to imply a signifier–signified relation whereby the
mark stands for, represents,[37] the foot, the relation between the
foot-mark and the significance of the mark (the presence of Orestes)
is approached *non-causally*, *obliquely*, that is, by means of an analogy,
a similarity. To use Roman Jakobson's 'generic matrices' again,[38]
the one is a relation of metonymy, the other of metaphor. We shall
return to this puzzling interplay of metaphor and metonymy again.
First let us consider how this passage has been regarded by critics.

This scene, parodied so well by Euripides, has resulted in critical
confusion. Sidgwick defends against the charge of absurdity thus:
'The resemblance of the hair is a perfectly legitimate and natural
point in the tale...the resemblance of the foot-marks is certainly not
reasonable; but the improbability is not a point for surprise in a poet
to whom certainly no-one would attribute realistic detail.' Lloyd-
Jones follows this with a rejection of naturalism, with a plea for the
undeveloped state of tragedy at that time: 'the technique of Tragedy

---

[37] This representation as re-presentation is problematised by Derrida, with regard to the
interpretation of a picture of boots by Van Gogh (1978, pp. 293–436).
[38] Scholes' (1974) phrase. Cf. Jakobson and Halle 1956.

in Aeschylus' time was of a simplicity utterly removed from modern naturalism'. Conington, following Blomfield (and Seidler) says 'Electra reasons...like a drowning person clutching at a straw', while also 'we need not be much concerned to vindicate Aeschylus from the ridicule of Euripides'. He throws scorn on Butler, who joins 'issue on the question of the comparative size of male and female feet'. Verrall defends Aeschylus against Euripides, who 'misinterprets it [the *Choephoroi*]...with an apparatus of error'. Kitto claims psychological realism for the over-emotional Electra. Tucker, who is in agreement with Kitto, states 'She is after all acting as women habitually do. There is as much intuition as logic in the process.'

Yet the charge (if it is a charge) of 'absurdity' is not to be reduced by an appeal to an external reality, to 'credibility'. For 'absurdity' and 'credibility' are mutually constituted, and thus, for these critics, the discussion, rather than a consideration of the proof-process, becomes a comparison of constructions of reality, nature, reason, treating the text as a simple example of that unquestioned naturalness (or lack of it). So: 'perfectly legitimate and reasonable'/'no-one would attribute realistic detail' (Sidgwick); 'most extravagant absurdity'/'reasonably accurate...perfectly natural' (Verrall); 'absurd'/'dramatic veracity...sufficiently secured' (Tucker). Nor is the challenge of this scene to be reduced by an appeal to psychological verisimilitude, a strategy of limiting the plurality of the text by an assumption of a complex emotional production of and behind the words which explains (away) the words: 'a picture of Electra's inner emotions...a more intense, quasi-lyrical performance might *justify the illogicalities*' (Kitto).[39] How justify? To whom? In what way? How are inner emotional illogicalities a 'justification' for the words? Is it the circular argument of 'the words are illogical *because* (the justification) they are spoken by an illogical person (who is to be recognised by her illogical words)'? This strategy too returns to nature with an appeal to what we all know about human character: 'She is *after all* acting *as women habitually do*' (my emphases).

As we have already indicated, the problematic shift in this passage between signifier (the tokens of recognition) and signified (what Electra recognises in and by them) is set within a complex structuration of relations with the rest of the trilogy. In particular (and this particularising will not be able to exhaust the complexity), it is structured in relation to the process of proof in the beacon-speeches scene (where we also saw a basis in the manipulation of signifier/signified, saying/showing, seeing). This recognition also recalls the

[39] 1961, p. 82.

recurrent vocabulary of proof and witnessing that we will see instantiated in the trial scene of the *Eumenides* (and we should remember the connection between sight and the idea of witnessing). It is also sited within the problematic modality of the visible that we have been trying to view, the opposition set up and challenged between the perceptible and intelligible (which stands as an elusive criterion for 'witnessing' and 'proof'). The difficult linkage between events, the confused chain of responsibilities and causation (of which this scene offers a constitutive link) also structures these passages importantly. So, too, this scene may be seen through these connections with proof, causality, responsibility, the sensible/intelligible as anticipating in a significant way the determination of paternity (that further recognition process) on which the trial scene turns. The hermeneutic discourse of the recognition scene is to be read not on its own, but within this plural series of relations, the interlocking and interpenetrating languages of the sexual, political, linguistic codes, looking towards Apollo's rejection of the visible connection between mother and child, his denial of a significant or causal relation between them (with all that implies).[40]

For the act of recognition in all its senses is invested in the plurality of social language: indeed, 'the task of legitimating the established order', writes Bourdieu, 'does not fall exclusively to the mechanics traditionally regarded as belonging to the order of ideology, such as law'.[41] Rather, in the more stable system of doxa, the recognition which legitimates is linked to a necessary misrecognition of the arbitrariness and limits of the system. 'Schemes of thought and perception can produce the "objectivity" that they do produce only by producing the misrecognition of the limits of the cognition that they make possible, thereby founding immediate adherence...to the world of tradition experienced as a "natural world" and taken for granted.'[42] But in the challenged system, it is the recognition of the previously misrecognised limits, boundaries, arbitrary relations, which leads to the antagonistic clash of languages in stasis. As for Bourdieu, kin-relations form a paradigm of this interplay of structures, habitus, power, so here, as we have seen, it is the recognition of her special relation with Orestes, a symbolic linking, *that goes together with* a rejection of the kinship tie with her mother. Sited (linguistically, as it were) between Clytemnestra's metonymic use of τὸ σύμβολον (her manipulation of the chain of signifiers) and Apollo's authorisation of the 'paternal metaphor', Electra's metaphoric reading of the signs

---

[40] These implications have been discussed in great detail since the middle of the nineteenth century in particular. For a sound survey of the debate see Coward 1983.

[41] 1977, p. 188.   [42] Ibid. p. 164.

does not merely look towards the 'institutionally organised and guaranteed misrecognition'[43] that structures the symbolic functions (capital) of maintained social organisation, but also looks towards the redefinition of kinship terms in the inaugurated civic discourse (as in the matricide, and its justification). After her prayer, which discussed the right language to use with regard to φίλος/ἐχθρός and *dike*, and before the *kommos*, the appeal to the father, this scene of recognition is important both in how the recognition takes place and in what is recognised: in the movement of how she recognises, Electra's strange metaphoric linking marks (in its challenge to accepted boundaries) the possibilities of arbitrariness, transgression and redefinition, essential both for the justification of matricide and for the development of a civic language beyond traditional kin-ties.[44] Here, the relevance of the earlier linguistic analysis of the recognition is marked. The scene is further important in what Electra recognises – with regard to the specific redetermination of the links between herself and members of her family. So the linguistic analysis of the process of recognition as marking the condition of possibility of this shifting is more than contingently related to the legal, political, social discourses of the trilogy, as we move towards Apollo's rejection of the mother in a trial before the city.

The process of Electra's recognition is emphasised in Orestes' speech in which he asserts his identity. He marks her metaphoric movement of proof – but only in close juxtaposition to the metonymic:

αὐτὸν μὲν οὖν ὁρῶσα δυσμαθεῖς ἐμέ,
κουρὰν δ᾽ ἰδοῦσα τήνδε κηδείου τριχός,
ἀνεπτερώθης κἀδόκεις ὁρᾶν ἐμέ
ἰχνοσκοποῦσά τ᾽ ἐν στίβοισι τοῖς ἐμοῖς
σαυτῆς ἀδελφοῦ σύμμετρου τῷ σῷ κάρᾳ
σκέψαι τομῇ προσθεῖσα βόστρυχον τριχός
ἰδοῦ δ᾽ ὕφασμα τοῦτο   (225–31)[45]

---

[43] Ibid. p. 171.

[44] Civic language notably adopts kin terms for itself: the city is mother/father, it nourishes/educates/brings up etc.

[45] The order and authorship of these lines has been often questioned. I have printed the manuscript order. While it is an awkward sentence structure, it scarcely merits Fraenkel's solution, which is the excision of these lines, as well as 205–11 and Eur. *El.* 518–44. His arguments for wholesale removal (which he opposes to others' 'arbitrary changes') have been tellingly criticised by Lloyd-Jones 1961. Fraenkel calls 229 'miserable and clumsy verbiage'. I hope my attempt to read the importance of being σύμμετρου in this scene (as in the functioning of σύμβολα) and the importance of the role of sight and metaphorisation goes beyond Lloyd-Jones' defence of 'typical Aeschylean pleonasm'. With characteristic critical insight, he writes that Aeschylus 'was by no means a polished or sophisticated writer'.

αὐτόν...ὁρῶσα δυσμαθεῖς ἐμέ – she can see[46] the author himself
(αὐτόν) but 'fails to recognise'. δυσμαθεῖς, a *hapax legomenon*,
expresses the failure of her process of mathesis. 'But' (δ') 'when you
saw' (ἰδοῦσα) 'the lock of hair' and 'when you *looked at* the tracks'
(ἰχνοσκοποῦσα – another very rare word) ἐδόκεις ὁρᾶν ἐμέ, 'you
thought you saw me'.[47] This is in contrast to Electra's speech where
she notably did not treat the 'trace', ἴχνος/στίβος, as a sign of
Orestes directly, nor the hair simply as part of the whole man, but
compared the footprint and lock with her own. But he then offers
the βόστρυχον from a brother('s head), συμμέτρου τῷ σῷ κάρᾳ
'*like* in measurement *to your* head', which echoes Electra's
μετρούμεναι...συμβαίνουσι (209–10). His questioning of her doubt
about his identity, then, seems to point her argumentation first in
contrast to it (assumption of a simple metonymy) then in agreement
with it (process of comparison).

Electra, however, does not immediately accept Orestes' self-
proclamation as the answer to her prayers.[48] Rather, in a short passage
of stichomythia, in which the delaying of her use of the name of
Orestes, the hesitation around his identity, seems parallel to the two
earlier exchanges of the chorus and Electra (106ff., 212ff.), Orestes
leads his sister towards the speech quoted above (225ff.), after which
(its accumulation of proofs), Electra turns to joyful apostrophe.
Indeed, in her doubt even the self-referential deictic by which
Orestes asserts his presence, ὅδ' εἰμί 'This is me', 'Here I am', is
questioned by Electra.

> ἀλλ' ἢ δόλον τιν', ὦ ξέν', ἀμφί μοι πλέκεις;   (220)

---

[46] Cf. Verrall. μὲν οὖν seems to oppose 'sight' to 'naming'.

[47] This speech, with its challenge to the simplicity of vision, that is, to the relation between
'recognising' and 'seeing' (and the possibility of mistakes in that process), looks
forward to the last scene of the play.

[48] The line which presages the charged moment of Orestes stepping forth πάρεστι δ' ὠδὶς
καὶ φρενῶν καταφθορά (211) is regarded by Fraenkel as an 'interpolator's link', and
Taplin regards it as wrongly placed. It is, however, well analysed by Lebeck (1971,
pp. 107–9): 'Electra's speech (183ff.) immediately precedes the entrance of Orestes and
it too is filled with words of unconscious prophecy...The violent emotions experienced
by Electra at thought of Orestes' return are expressed in metaphors which presage his
madness, the outcome of his return...Her last line is still more ominous. Towards this
line, the entire speech builds; it is a *kledon*, a "presage contained in chance
utterance"...she says "There's present here a painful birth and sanity's downfall."
At that moment Orestes, the child whose birth ends in his mother's death and his own
madness, appears...' (She also notes ὠδὶς in the sense 'child', cf. *Aga.* 1418.) So, too,
Thomson writes (p. 33) 'It is as though these words were addressed to him and they
are an unhappy augury.' This adequately answers Fraenkel's and Taplin's point here,
I think. Lebeck's and Thomson's analyses question the criterion of effectiveness even
on its own terms. Taplin does not mention Thomson or Lebeck. For a further comment
on ὠδὶς and this line, see the stimulating article of Loraux (1981c).

The rejection of his use of 'Ορέστην (217) by ξέν', and the further
suggestion of falsification (δόλον) of reference – even of self-
reference – seem to point once more to the separation of word and
object. So, indeed, her last doubting question focuses on recognition
as naming: ὡς ὄντ' 'Ορέστην γάρ σ' ἐγὼ προσεννέπω; (224), 'Am
I to address you as...?', 'Am I to use the *name* Orestes?' In
questioning the assertion 'Here am I', 'This is me' (how can one
challenge the statement 'This is me'?), the exchange ὅδ' εἰμί...
ὦ ξέν' marks the ego of self-reference as a 'shifter' (the condition of
possibility of recognition) – that entry into language which instigates
the ever-failing search for the self-presence of the 'Here am I'.[49]

Indeed, the identifying of Orestes is an identification with Electra,
a strange extension of the complementary relation of likeness already
stressed, the σύμβολα combining...

> 'Ορ. ὅδ' εἰμί. μὴ μάτευ' ἐμοῦ μᾶλλον φίλον.
> 'Ηλ. ἀλλ' ἦ δόλον τιν', ὦ ξέν', ἀμφί μοι πλέκεις;
> 'Ορ. αὐτὸς κατ' αὐτοῦ τἄρα μηχανορραφῶ.
> 'Ηλ. ἀλλ' ἐν κακοῖσι τοῖς ἐμοῖς γελᾶν θέλεις;
> 'Ορ. κἀν τοῖς ἐμοῖς ἄρ'   (219–23)

Orestes tells her to seek no one more φίλος than himself. Electra is
suspicious of a trick – αὐτὸς κατ' αὐτοῦ τἄρα...'then *I myself* plot
against *myself*'. The association is so close that they are as one: ἐν
κακοῖσι τοῖς ἐμοῖς (222) – κἀν τοῖς ἐμοῖς, 'Then mine too'. The bond
of φιλία extended in sense through the relation of affinity between
Electra and Orestes is depicted as making them identical: in the
house of Atreus, *philia* seems to link as excessively as its disjunctions
are severe! Orestes says, however, after his conclusive proof of
identity:

> τοὺς φιλτάτους γὰρ οἶδα νῷν ὄντας πικρούς   (234)

The oxymoron φιλτάτους/πικρούς expresses the paradox of φιλία
here, where the mother is both (traditionally, at least) φιλτάτη and
the enemy, none the less. And Electra says in the next line:

> ὦ φίλτατον μέλημα δώμασιν πατρός   (235)

φίλτατον refers back to μὴ μᾶλλον φίλον (219), τοῦ φιλτάτου
βροτῶν 'Ορέστου (193–4), but in juxtaposition with φιλτάτους...

[49] On the important notion of the shifter, which was developed first by Jakobson, see Eco
1976, pp. 115–21. With regard to personal pronouns as shifters, see the important and
influential analysis of Benveniste 1966, pp. 225–88. The background to this paragraph
is the series of attacks on the Cartesian 'cogito' and the notion of the unitary self that
have been so stressed particularly in twentieth-century Continental philosophy. This
material has become a familiar topic of modern debate. See Coward and Ellis 1977,
Rorty 1980, Wilden 1972, for introductions and bibliographies for this extensive
critique.

πικρούς it also shows the necessary qualification, the ambiguity, of this moral term in familial conflict.

The final proof that Orestes presents, introduced by ἰδοῦ (231; cf. αὐτὸν μὲν οὖν ὁρῶσα, 225), the woven textile of Electra, offers a further supplement to his assertions. It is a shared possession, this handiwork of Electra, and, like the περιγραφὰ ποδοῖν, ὑπογραφαὶ τενόντων, it points to its representational force: θήρειον γραφήν. The hunt itself, too, is a significant motif in the trilogy, as Vidal-Naquet has analysed, and here in particular, as we will see at 251ff., there is a wider sense of hunting suggested – a hunting for the return to his role (social, financial, political) in the *oikos*. A hunting for recognition, one might say.

This complex and suggestive scene, then, develops no one univocal hermeneutic process to effect the recognition – itself a complex term. The process of shifting from signifier to signified, or sign to sign (which echoes earlier sign readings) in its metaphoric linking may suggest the linking of σύμβολα – a closeness between brother and sister developed in the language of φίλος/ἐχθρός etc. The process of recognition marks the conditions of possibility of redefinition essential both to the justification of matricide and also to the realignment of kinship vocabulary in a civic discourse. The specific recognition of the relation of *philia* with Orestes and rejection of such ties with Clytemnestra (which we will see further) marks the sphere of redefinition. But a simple model of subject, object and 'process' of recognition is problematised not only in the shifting definition of the subject and the interpretability of the flighty signifier, but also in the way in which object and process imply each other: the defining of the object cannot assume a non-problematic process of perceiving it, just as a questioning of the process of perception cannot simply assume the signifier as simple. Recognition is both object and process.

The recognition scene, then, not only develops the problematic of the sign and the reading of the sign which we read as so important to the *Agamemnon*, but also marks the importance of such a topic in the discussion of a relation between language and discourse, between a subject and society's language.

Figuring it out

Electra accepts that this is indeed Orestes, and her expression of thanks reiterates many of the central terms of the work so far; and specifically the terms of her relation with Orestes and her family: δώμα(σιν) πατρός (235/7) depicts the house still in terms of 'of-the-father'. The 'weeping' of δακρυτός (236) is both in the sense

of εὐδάκρυτα (181) and 'bewailed'; ἐλπὶς σπέρματος σωτηρίου –
ἐλπίς, 'expectation', 'hope', has been linked both to the narrative
prediction (cf. 187, 194) and, as here, to the forthcoming generation,
the (future) seed, σπέρματος, which picks up 204, her seed of hope.
And σωτηρίου picking up σωτήρ (2) recalls the link between Orestes
and the gods. ἀλκῇ πεποιθώς is reminiscent of a phrase used several
times in Homer, ἀλκὶ πεποιθώς,[50] often of men likened to wild beasts.
This not only helps to emphasise the intertextuality[51] with the
Odyssey, but acts as a pointed foreword to the allusions in the
following lines, which recall in particular *Il*. 6.429ff.,[52] the lines
spoken by Andromache to Hector (who is depicted as ἀλκὶ πεποιθώς,
Il. 18.158, the only time a man is directly alluded to by that phrase)
in order to make the bulwark of the Trojans retire from battle out
of consideration for his family.

In the *Choephoroi*, however, it will be a sending to battle (-μαχ-,
2, 19, 489, 874, 890, 946, 948, etc.) in order to continue the
generational line of the family but the 'battle' will be one of a
'cunning hunter'[53] and victim, a trick rather than a fair fight: it will
be returning into his home rather than leaving it; it will be against
a woman rather than a man. This reference, then, to Hector marks
the difference of Orestes from Hector. The language of Electra shows
a marked development also in terms of her relation to Orestes:

> ὦ τερπνὸν ὄμμα τέσσαρας μοίρας ἔχον
> ἐμοί. προσαυδᾶν δ' ἔστ' ἀναγκαίως ἔχον
> πατέρα σε καὶ τὸ μητρὸς ἐς σέ μοι ῥέπει
> στέργηθρον, ἡ δὲ πανδίκως ἐχθαίρεται,
> καὶ τῆς τυθείσης ὁμοσπόρου.
> πιστὸς δ' ἀδελφὸς ἦσθ' ἐμοὶ σέβας φέρων.   (238–43)

She does not assert her dependence on Orestes as a simple identity
as does Andromache (*Il*. 6.429–30 σύ μοί ἐσσι πατὴρ καὶ πότνια
μήτηρ | ἠδὲ κασίγνητος...), but her address is marked as a function of
language, of naming, προσαυδᾶν δ' ἔστ'..., and thus as a relational
expression ('One never names...one classes')[54] rather than as the
property of an individual.[55] The syntax of the sentence does not
continue as one might expect with καὶ μητέρα but with τὸ
μητρός...στέργηθρον – ἡ δὲ...ἐχθαίρεται. This emphasises that
it is the relation, the bond of affection between Clytemnestra and

---

[50] E.g. *Il*. 5.299; 18.158; *Od*. 6.130.
[51] 'Intertextuality', a term coined by Kristeva, is glossed by her as 'the transposition
of one or more systems of signs into another, accompanied by a new articulation of
the enunciative and denotative position'. Cf. n. 34, n. 35 above. 'Intertextuality' is
not simply a new piece of jargon for 'influence', 'reference'.
[52] Quoted here first by Schütz.   [53] Vidal-Naquet 1968, p. 63.
[54] Lévi-Strauss 1966, p. 240.   [55] Lévi-Strauss 1969, p.482.

Electra that is important. ἐχθαίρεται once more is a passive expression of ἐχθρός – Electra does not say she hates her mother, but that 'her mother is hated' – the unstated subject avoiding and emphasising the problematic of φίλος/ἐχθρός, a problematic marked by πανδίκως, which recalls the difficulties of defining, controlling δίκη (120, 144–8) with regard to the object of revenge (φίλον/ἐχθρόν). Such a problematic is recalled also in the reference to Iphigeneia, the daughter of Agamemnon (φίλη), who was sacrificed νηλεῶς, 'pitilessly', overlooking the bonds of φιλία (cf. *Aga.* 245–7 πατρὸς φίλου...φίλως ἐτίμα), to aid the revenge of Menelaus (φίλος) on Paris (ἐχθρός) who seduced Helen (φίλη/ἐχθρά?). Electra's address to her recognised brother, then, marks the shifting terms of recognition in the family in conflict.

In these extended expressions of kinship, Orestes is fourthly her πιστὸς ἀδελφός who brings σέβας – which refers back to the connection of σέβας and δεσπότης δόμου (157–8), their mutual constitution and absence, and the need and prayer for εὐσέβεια (122). Orestes, the figure of male authority, by his return brings back σέβας. She ends with a prayer for the assistance of κράτος – force, authority – referring back (in the first instance) to ὧδε γὰρ κρατεῖ (*Aga.* 10), and the control of the house (cf. *Cho.* 1); and for the assistance of δίκη – the ambiguities of which have been discussed above; and for the assistance of Zeus, the greatest of all, τῷ τρίτῳ, 'the third'. This seems to refer back to Clytemnestra's blasphemous parody of the libation (*Aga.* 1385ff.), the juxtaposition of which two prayers suggests the parallelisation of events, and also a relation between the two, the second being the rectification of the travesty of the norm of the first.

Orestes continues with a prayer also to Zeus:

Ζεῦ Ζεῦ θεωρὸς τῶνδε πραγμάτων γενοῦ   (246)

Unlike the more common form of a prayer, which requests the hearing of a god (*Cho.* 5, 125, 157) here Orestes calls on Zeus to *see*, to be an 'observer', θεωρός, of events, picking up the imagery of the prayers at *Cho.* 1 ἐποπτεύων, *Cho.* 126 ἐπισκόπους. He continues:

ἰδοῦ δὲ γένναν εὖνιν αἰετοῦ πατρὸς
θανόντος ἐν πλεκταῖσι καὶ σπειράμασιν
δεινῆς ἐχίδνης   (247–9)

The command ἰδοῦ, picking up θεωρός, is followed by the object of sight, which is, however, an extended metaphor or γρῖφος; the object of vision with entry into language is structured like language, as a system ('a mobile army' (Nietzsche)) of metaphors, open to the sliding, the free play of signifiers. This playfulness is marked here by the allusiveness (elusiveness) of the terms: αἰετοῦ, the bird of Zeus, refers back to the omen of the eagles and the hare at *Aga.* 110ff. which was interpreted by Calchas (linking the Atreidae and Zeus) as referring to Menelaus and Agamemnon (πατρός, 247, the common term, with γένναν εὖνιν, marking the ground of comparison). It also refers to the description of the Atreidae setting forth like vultures who have lost their children (*Aga.* 49–54); and moreover, juxtaposed to δεινῆς ἐχίδνης, which itself looks forward to the dream of Clytemnestra and its verification (928–9), it echoes *Il.* 12.200ff., another omen of battle to come. This complexity of allusions denies the possibility of a simple relation between the signifier and the signified in the metaphoric structure, placing here the object of vision within a structure of interpretation denying the possibility of an innocence of perception. One cannot simply see such a complex metaphor.

Hunger oppresses the nestlings for:

οὐ γὰρ ἐντελεῖς
θήραν πατρῷαν προσφέρειν σκηνήμασιν   (250–1)

θήραν πατρῷαν within the context of the metaphor indicates the object hunted by the father, but with the implication for Orestes and Electra of their patrimony, and also of their need to hunt[56] (and their present incapability: οὐ...ἐντελεῖς – to have not reached a *telos* – an indication of the teleological structure of the metaphor, the aiming at a *telos*). σκήνημα, a rare word, with the hint of σκήνη (' = σκήνη' (L.-S.-J.)) not only implies 'dwelling-place', used normally of expressly human habitation, but also the stage itself (or rather the wall at the back of the stage depicting the house of Atreus) which not only involves the invasion of the vehicle by the tenor (to use Richards' terms), the regrounding of the metaphor in a level of reality, or the metaphorisation of the metaphor (describing the children's 'nest' in terms of human habitation) but also by the association with the σκήνη of the theatre draws attention to the representational nature of the house in question, to the play as play.

We leave this prayer, however, as if it had been a Homeric simile, οὖτω δέ... (The scholion remarks in order to harmonise the expressions, ἰδοῦ ἡμᾶς ὡς γένναν εὖνιν...οὖτω δέ...) This odd shift of syntactical emphasis suggests for the metaphor of the eagles a different referential structure, 'as if he had described a real eagle without a figure of speech' (Paley); what was read as a metaphorical description of the children (where 'eagle's brood' in some way *referred* to Orestes and Electra) now becomes realigned as a play of language on some conceived similarity between children and 'eagle's

---

[56] Cf. Vernant and Vidal-Naquet 1972, pp. 151ff.

brood'. 'Eagle's brood' no longer *refers* to the children. So there is added the specificity of direct indication: κἀμὲ τήνδε τ᾽ Ἠλέκτραν λέγω | ἰδεῖν (252–3). This phrase is, however, a strange continuation. Such a construction as Ἠλέκτραν λέγω is 'always used for some clear effect, e.g. to play upon a name, to instruct the audience, to avoid ambiguous reference' (Tucker), but here, after τήνδε, it seems to emphasise the difficulty of the deictic expression of indication, as if τήνδε needed further clarification, needed the *added* specification of speech, λέγω (as if the present shifting syntax were not in awkward tension with the implied specificity of λέγω!). Even the phrase οὕτω δὲ...ἰδεῖν πάρεστί σοι (252–3), 'It is possible to see *in this way*', seems to point to the possibility of seeing in different ways, of the non-transparency, non-innocence of perception.

This shifting status of the referential/representational function of the image of the eagle continues as Orestes further asks καίτοι θυτῆρος καί σε τιμῶντος μέγα | πατρὸς νεοσσοὺς τούσδε ἀποφθείρας πόθεν | ἕξεις...γέρας; (255–7) where νεοσσούς, 'chicks', 'young birds', seems to refer to Electra and Orestes both through the deictic τούσδε, and through νεοσσούς picking up γένναν...αἰετοῦ, the children of the father θυτῆρος καί σε τιμῶντος μέγα. θυτῆρος, particularly after τυθείσης (242), recalls the sacrifice of Iphigeneia, which juxtaposed to σὲ τιμῶντος μέγα depicts Agamemnon as the agent of Zeus again. This use of νεοσσούς, however, is juxtaposed to:

οὔτ᾽ αἰετοῦ γένεθλ᾽ ἀποφθείρας πάλιν
πέμπειν ἔχοις ἂν σήματ᾽ εὐπιθῆ βροτοῖς   (258–9)

which suggests the eagle now as the bird Zeus (linking Agamemnon and Zeus) the bird as omen, which is, however, linked back to the house (οὔτ᾽...οὔτ᾽ suggesting parallel phrases) by:

οὔτ᾽ ἀρχικός σοι πᾶς ὅδ᾽ αὐανθεὶς πυθμὴν
βωμοῖς ἀρήξει βουθύτοις ἐν ἤμασιν   (260–1)

This *glissement* of reference/representation, what one might term the breakdown of a simple referential language, significantly marked by ἰδοῦ, ἰδεῖν, seems to set the mode of the visual in a structure of interpretation, which is important to the practice of reading a theatrical script not only in its suggestion of the need of interpretation for visual significance, but also in the specific difficulty of defining a fixed level of reference – an instability in the basis of a representation of the text on stage?

As the recognition process suggested the difficulties of defining an identity in shifting language relations, Electra's and Orestes' first speeches on recognition set their relations in a complex system of metaphors. 'Denn wir leben warhaft in Figuren...'

Causality and motivation

After the passion of the recognition, the chorus advise 'the saviours of the father's hearth' to maintain a circumspect quiet. Orestes, however, offers Apollo as his protection and goes on to give the story of the oracle.

The subject of the verbs of speech in this story (κελεύων, 270; ἐξορθιάζων, 271; ἐξαυδώμενος, 272; λέγων, 274) is χρησμός, 'the oracle' itself and not Apollo. And the instructions reported seem to ignore precisely the problems of definition raised by Electra's speech:

εἰ μὴ μέτειμι τοῦ πατρὸς τοὺς αἰτίους
τρόπον τὸν αὐτόν, ἀνταποκτεῖναι λέγων   (273–4)

Behind the command is a threat of dire punishment (275–7). τῇ φίλῃ ψυχῇ recalls the problematic of φίλος/ἐχθρός for Orestes in his relationship[57] with Apollo, but fails to recognise the paradox of his relation with his mother. Apollo's threats are further outlined and summed up as προσβολὰς Ἐρινύων | ἐκ τῶν πατρῴων αἱμάτων τελουμένας (283–4). The double-bind finds ironic expression here in this fear of the Erinues: it is his mother's (not father's) blood which will set the Erinues in motion; τελουμένας, 'being finished', 'perfected', 'initiated', marks (in its ambiguities) again the sought-for telos of the narrative. For the unavenging kinsman, however, there wait madness, fear (cf. μίμνει...φοβερὰ μῆνις, *Aga.* 155), which will drive him from the city divorcing him from his social role, which is defined (291ff.) in terms of the rituals of libation and sacrifice. He will be banned from social intercourse, ἄτιμον κἄφιλον (the relations of exchange and reciprocity which, like the libation and sacrifice, have been corrupted by Clytemnestra). His fears of what would happen if he failed to avenge his father are what will happen to him for killing his mother – the logic of the double-bind.

τοιοῖσδε χρησμοῖς ἆρα χρὴ πεποιθέναι;
κεἰ μὴ πέποιθα, τοὔργόν ἐστ' ἐργαστέον   (297–8)

'An ironic appearance of doubt to a question which is really meant to contain a pointed and emphatic assertion' (Conington). πεποιθέναι, both 'believe' and 'rely upon', restresses the oracle as a motive force[58] for the action – as indeed he continues with a series of motives for the action, which he calls 'desires', ἵμεροι: 'constraint

---

[57] Following here Benveniste's cogent attack on the traditional view of *philos*, seen here in Sidgwick's comment on this line, 'epic use'.

[58] NB the etymological pun, χρησμοῖς χρή, linking 'oracles' with 'necessity': χρή with the implication of 'must' (compelled by circumstance), 'what it is right to do', and also 'what is fated' – this complex of associations endows χρησμοῖς with a considerable force of necessity. Cf. Lebeck 1971, p. 111 n. 2.

and choice converge: in man's own will the gods find fate's accomplice'.[59] After those instructions of a god, and grief of/for the father, comes an economic pressure (the desire to regain the patrimony, cf. p. 116) and the desire to return the Argives to the rule of males. Aegisthus and Clytemnestra are both termed women (cf. *Aga.* 1625) – the opposition of gynarchy to patriarchy. θήλεια γὰρ φρήν (305), within the range of ideas around the terms φρεν-/σωφρονεῖν, Zeus, masculinity (cf. pp. 27, 37) – that is, the charged opposition of male and female – is almost an oxymoron, or rather the *corruption* of φρήν is marked by the predication of the adjective θήλεια.

The conclusion of this long and difficult scene of recognition and prayer with the description of Apollo's divine support stands as a prelude, then, to the *kommos* (the recognition of the son before the invocation of the father) – where we will see the further conjuration of supernatural aid.

Kommos for the father: *in hoc signo vinces*

The *kommos*, formally a strange mixture of a mourning song, and a conjuration of the dead Agamemnon through invocation and prayer, revolves around the appeal for supernatural support and the need for correct language to achieve the end of matricide. For mourning and language cannot be easily separated, as we will see, in what Pucci has called the 'remedial discourse' of mourning. Much of the extensive criticism of the *kommos* centres on the question of 'psychological reading', and I shall take the opportunity of this invocation of the father (rather than the moment of the son's off-stage penetration of his mother's body with powerful sword) to discuss something of this exchange of views.[60]

Wilamowitz,[61] Schadewaldt,[62] and Lesky[63] debate concerning the relation between (psychological) 'inner conflict' and 'ritual'. Does Orestes show a struggle of conscience? Is he being emboldened to the deed of matricide which he finds repugnant? Or are the expressions of despair ritual motifs? Is it only a traditional (and thus less personal) lyric of lamentation and mourning? Others since have joined the debate in much the same terms, some finding with Lesky a middle

---

[59] Lebeck 1971, p. 111.

[60] On Classicists' attitudes to psychoanalysis – see the work particularly of Caldwell, Devereux, Slater, Pucci, Simon, Segal (particularly 1978/9), Vernant 1977, pp. 77–8 (a good critique from a position different from mine). For a different sort of Classicist rejection of any form of psychoanalytic readings, see Dawe's edition of Sophocles' *Oediupus Tyrannus* (Cambridge, 1982), pp. 2ff.

[61] *Griechische Tragödien*, 7th edn (Berlin, 1913) II, pp. 143–4, 148.

[62] *Hermes* 67 (1932) 312–54.   [63] Lesky 1943.

line between the extremes of Wilamowitz's and Schadewaldt's positions.[64] The relation between ritual, mourning and what the critics have called 'inner conflict' is, however, more complex than the polarising terminology (even as mediated by Lesky) can delineate. For the system of allusions, the definition and redefinition of terms, already important in the text, goes beyond the simple, developmental argument, beyond the attempted control which the formalism of ritual offers. As we have seen, even an apparently traditional prayer becomes charged with its siting in the complexity of the trilogy. It moves, moreover, beyond the 'psychological orientation'[65] of Lesky and of Srebrny, who as Lebeck quotes with approval 'stresses the meaning *hidden behind Orestes' words*',[66] as if the postulation of a character beyond and behind its constitution in language could determine the language except by a circular reductionism. In its terminology, then, the opposition of 'ritual' to 'psychological development' will be seen to be not sufficient to the textual play of signifiers. Nor, however, in its status as an opposition. For (to make psychoanalytic writing at first work for us), as Lacan says

The work of mourning is accomplished at the level of the logos...the work of mourning is first of all performed to satisfy the disorder that is produced by the inadequacy of the signifying elements to cope with the hole that has been created in existence, for it is the system of signifiers in their totality which is impeached by the least instance of mourning.[67]

Ritual introduces some mediation of the gap (*béance*) opened up by mourning.[68]

The inadequacy of the signifying elements, then, the search to mediate the *béance* ('the projection of the missing signifier'), the summoning of the support of the father by calling his name (signifier), the recalling of his sufferings, all these signs of the developing grief of Orestes find 'some mediation' in ritual: ritual *presupposes* the psychological disorder; ritual presupposes the psychological development inherent in the work of mourning. Ritual cannot, as formulated by the critical debate mentioned above, be simply opposed to a psychological development in mourning.

[64] Lebeck 1971, pp. 93–5, 110–30; Kitto 1961, pp. 83–4; Cf. also S. Srebrny, *Wort und Gedanke bei Aischylos* (Wroclaw, 1964) pp. 55–94.
[65] Lebeck 1971, p. 93, n. 4.   [66] Ibid. (my emphasis).
[67] *YFS* 55–6 (1977, p. 38).
[68] Ibid. p. 40. He adds, 'more precisely ritual operates in such a way as to make this gap coincide with that greater béance, the point *x*, the symbolic lack' – the gap as site for projection of the veiled phallus: which makes the young man's mourning for a dead father when about to kill his mother and her lover, particularly significant. This role of the *kommos* has been missed by the psychoanalytic critics who follow this sort of line.

Thus the discourse of psychoanalysis might be further brought
into play to develop a reading along the lines that the *kommos* in its
literal 'summoning' of Agamemnon attempts to assert the word-
of-the-father in the discourse – the missing signifier being precisely
that of the father. This has clear implications towards the assertion
of paternity by Apollo. Lacan writes, 'the attribution of procreation
to the father can only be the effect of a pure signifier, of a recognition
not of a real father but what religion has taught us to refer to as the
name-of-the-father'.[69] Thus a psychoanalytic approach might state
that the *kommos* suggests that we 'link the appearance of the signifier
of the Father, as author of the Law, with death even to the murder
of the father – thus showing that if this moment is the fruitful moment
of debt through which the subject binds himself for life to the Law,
the symbolic father is, in so far as he signifies this law, the dead
father'.[70] The *kommos*, indeed, the mourning rite, is 'part of the
necessary passage he [Orestes] must cross to call himself the son of
Agamemnon'.[71] Since the name-of-the-father is implied in and
implicated with the entry into language, the *kommos*, linked to the
initiation motifs (cf. pp. 193ff.), indicates the necessary prelude to the
full assimilation of Orestes as a male subject, an adult, a sexed male,
into society. Through the role of the name-of-the-father in the
Oedipal triad,[72] this would offer a theoretical connection between
language and sexuality and patriarchal authority – the link, in other
words, between the initiation of Orestes into the role of his father and
the role of language so stressed in the play. So psychoanalytic
discourse, rather than simply suggesting that Orestes' revenge, say,
'has the nature of a substitute intercourse',[73] could lead towards a
recognition of possible links in the trilogy between, say, the *kommos*,
the killing of Clytemnestra, the role of paternity, and the authority
of the father of gods and men, Zeus. But the locking of the literary
text into some sort of psychoanalytic structuring involves its own
repressions: for, to re-cite Lacan: 'the work of mourning is accomplished *at the level of the logos*' (my emphasis) and it is precisely at
the level of the logos that the assertion of 'the effect of a *pure signifier*'
(my emphasis) is at risk. For not only have we seen the materiality
of the verbal signifier in puns, paragrams, etymological plays, and
even the radicalisation of the visual object, but also the very iterability
of the signifier 'a priori introduces into it a dehiscence and a cleft,
which are essential'[74] and 'dehiscence (like iterability) limits what it

---

[69] Lacan 1977d, p. 199.   [70] Lacan 1977a, p. 199.   [71] Green 1975, p. 80.
[72] Green talks of the 'Oedipalization of the *Oresteia*', p. 59 in the chapter entitled
'Oedipus and Orestes: from oracle to law'.
[73] Cf. n. 17 above.   [74] Derrida 1976b, p. 192.

makes possible, while rendering its rigor and purity impossible'.[75]
The citation of the name-of-the father, then, as a means towards un-
veiling a structure of truth falls, for Derrida, under what he calls the
logic of *différance* and the trace: the word-of-the-father in as much
as it is a word is at risk. This refuses the closure of the text in the
promised truth of the teleological structure.[76] The language of the text
eludes finally the talking cure.

The *kommos* opens with an imprecation to the Fates to end through
Zeus[77] ἦ τὸ δίκαιον μεταβαίνει, which seems to suggest that τὸ δίκαιον
changes position (μετα-) or at least that the differing claims for *dike*
are in conflict (cf. 461). This sense of conflict is brought out in the
strict reciprocity of ἀντὶ μὲν ἐχθρᾶς γλώσσης ἐχθρὰ γλῶσσα τελείσθω
(309–10) (note the sense of an end in τελείσθω picking up τελευτᾶν,
307) and ἀντὶ δὲ πληγῆς φονίας φονίαν πληγὴν τινέτω, where
τινέτω, 'pay', links the economic imagery (of exchange) to the
reciprocity of punishment. So too with the phrase τοὐφειλόμενον
πράσσουσα, where τοὐφειλόμενον implies both an economic and a
less specific sense, and πράσσουσα (as at *Aga*. 705; cf. p. 62, n. 100),
implies both 'doing' and 'revenging'. This suggestion of a necessary
reciprocity of action is made explicit with the tag δράσαντα παθεῖν
(313), called τριγέρων μῦθος.[78] So the 'light' (319) is called σκότῳ...
ἀντίμοιρον (320). It is noticeable, however, that these generalisations
or proverbs are cited as the words of *dike*: δίκη μέγ' αὐτεῖ (which
places them within the structure of communication as verbal objects
of exchange); and cited as the words of μῦθος – μῦθος τάδε φωνεῖ.
The apparent tautology of μῦθος...φωνεῖ points to the non-
transparency of μῦθος as the medium of communication. 'Die
Sprache spricht...'? It points to the materiality of the text of μῦθος as
constituted in words. In the invocation, the right deeds and words
are needed. τί σοι φάμενος ἢ τί ῥέξας τύχοιμ'. As we saw with Electra

---

[75] Derrida 1977, p. 197.

[76] Derrida, whom I have here set all too easily against Lacan, writes extensively on
the teleology of psychoanalytic thought, especially 1975. For a superb critique of
Lacan, and of Derrida's critique of Lacan, see Johnson 1977. For an excellent
discussion of psychoanalysis and attempts to master the text, see Felman 1977: she
writes: 'Here then is the crowning aberration which psychoanalysis sometimes
unwittingly commits in its mêlées with literature. In seeking to "explain" and *master*
literature, in refusing, that is, to become a *dupe* of literature, in killing within literature
that which makes it literature – its reserve of silence, that which, within speech, is
incapable of speaking, the literary silence of a discourse ignorant of what it knows – the
psychoanalytic reading, ironically enough, turns out to be a reading which *represses the
unconscious*, which represses, paradoxically, the unconscious which it purports to be
"explaining". To master, then,...is, here as elsewhere, to *refuse to read* the letters'
(p. 194).

[77] So the trilogy will end with (all-seeing) Zeus and Fate coming together (*Eum*. 1045–6).

[78] Cf. Clay 1969.

(87ff.) the power of prayer instils the desire for correct language and action. ῥέξας also has the religious sense of sacrifice: action as religious rite. Such power, such desire, are especially important if mourning is accomplished at the level of the logos. Indeed, the γόος εὐκλεής is *called*,[79] κέκληνται, an object of beauty / source of thanks (χάριτες): again, the process of naming slips towards the fore.

The chorus assert the consciousness of the dead:

τέκνον, φρόνημα τοῦ θανόντος οὐ δαμάζει πυρὸς μαλερὰ γνάθος　　　　　(324–5)

φρόνημα does not simply mean 'thought', however, but a particular disposition[80] of thought: it was used to describe the atmosphere in Troy when Helen arrived (*Aga.* 739), it was used for Clytemnestra's attitude towards her children (*Cho.* 191), it will be used to describe the force of mind leading to adultery and similar acts of violence to the bonds of society (*Cho.* 595; cf. below p. 160). Here, it looks forward to φαίνει δ' ὕστερον ὀργάς (326). ὀργή shows a similar shifting in sense from 'disposition as resulting from impulse' to, in particular, 'wrath', 'passion': indeed, at *Aga.* 215–17 ὀργᾷ περιόργως ἐπιθυμεῖν θέμις was Agamemnon's depiction of the coming sacrifice of Iphigeneia, which led to τὸ παντότολμον φρονεῖν (*Aga.* 221), which is recalled by ὑπέρτολμον...φρόνημα...παντόλμους ἔρωτας (*Cho.* 594–7), picking up also πάντολμε μᾶτερ (430) and ἡ παντότολμος (*Aga.* 1237, spoken by Cassandra of Clytemnestra). φρόνημα/ὀργή/τόλμα, then, not only suggest Agamemnon at the act of sacrificing his daughter but also the mental state involved in the actions of Clytemnestra and Helen: it will be that which is summoned for the revenge; it is how Orestes describes Clytemnestra's actions (996); it is how Orestes describes the matricide (1029) – once more the vocabulary of transgression draws a parallelisation of actions, a reciprocity hinted at also in the symmetry of

ὀτοτύζεται δ' ὁ θνῄσκων
ἀναφαίνεται δ' ὁ βλάπτων　　　　　(327–8)

ἀναφαίνεται also refers to φαίνει (326): the syntactical reversal of active and passive suggests a causal connection beyond the immediate semantic context between the display of anger and the bringing to light of ὁ βλάπτων (note the masculine gender). γόος ἔνδικος (picking up γόος εὐκλεής, 321) is personified (ματεύει ποινάν), maintaining the emphasis on the power of the word.

πατέρων τε καὶ τεκόντων, the genitive dependent on γόος, is an interesting phrase. Conington and Tucker call it 'merely a pleonasm',

[79] NB the play -κλεής/κέκληνται: it points to the etymology of εὐκλεής, as well as the function of naming.　　[80] Cf. Fraenkel, pp. 343–4.

while Verrall at least notes the possible generality of the plural πατέρων set off against the specific τεκόντων: but the phrase also looks forward to Apollo's argument in the *Eumenides* which centres on the definition of the status of μήτηρ/τοκεύς, on who can be said to τίκτειν; the difference of roots[81] (πατρ-/τικτ-) here draws attention to the possible separation of 'biological' and 'social' definitions of paternity (although as Barnes notes, the determination 'genitor' itself can be regarded as a *social* status).

Electra (antistrophe α) calls on her father, ὦ πάτερ (332) as does Orestes (315), ὦ πάτερ; the chorus call Orestes (324) τέκνον, Electra παῖ (372), which not only suggests the generational structure (cf. δίπαις, 334, and the repetitions of πατερ-/τεκν-, e.g. 346, 349, 364, 379, 385, 419, 435, 443, 444, 457) but also by situating Orestes and Electra in a relation to the chorus of παῖς/τέκνον (note τέκνον-τεκεῖν and παῖς connected at least homophonically to πατ-) suggests a *Spaltung*[82] of the parental function, which again looks forward to the nurse and Clytemnestra, to Apollo's arguments: the multiplication of possible relations expressed by the term τέκνον opens the way for the rejection of the mother as τοκεύς.

The subject of ἀναστενάζει (335) is θρῆνος – again a personification of the hymn. τί τῶνδ' εὖ τί δ' ἄτερ κακῶν is reminiscent of Agamemnon's τί τῶνδ' ἄνευ κακῶν (*Aga.* 211) (a further parallel between the avenging of Agamemnon and his sacrifice of Iphigeneia rather than his death), as οὐκ ἀτρίακτος ἄτα (338) is reminiscent of the divine generational conflict at *Aga.* 171 (and with τρι- it seems to refer to τριγέρων μῦθος, and the third libation to...ἄτη).[83] This network of allusions and implications is set in juxtaposition to the power of the word, and particularly to the predictive/predicative force of language, so stressed in the following stanza (340ff.), where a depiction of change of fortunes is expressed in terms of a change in voice (as with the fortunes of Troy, cf. *Aga.* 709ff.): θείη εὐφθογγοτέρους. The change of song from the *threnos* to the *paian* suggests that the god who is the subject of θείη may possibly be Apollo. The *paian*, which remains the subject of its clause, brings νεοκράτα φίλον, 'a new fledged loving-cup' (Tucker), which seems to hark back to the libations of Clytemnestra and of Electra – and to the sacrifice of Iphigeneia. φίλον indicates the field of conflict. This interreaction between the power of the word and its continuing dissemination constitutes the tension of the desire for control in narrative and language.

[81] Benveniste 1969, pp. 209ff.
[82] On the psychoanalytic connotations of *Spaltung*, see (for example) Laplanche and Pontialis 1973, pp. 427–30.
[83] Cf. Clay 1969.

Orestes laments the fact that Agamemnon did not die in war (the male sphere of action) where he would have left a τάφον... δώμασιν εὐφόρητον (352–3). δώμασιν, where he did in fact die, is that which is afflicted by his death; his death affects the generational continuity of the house (*qua* house): τέκνων τ' ἐν κελεύθοις ἐπιστρεπτὸν αἰῶ κτίσας (349–51). The chorus picks up the idea of death in Troy as a link, but expresses the relation between Agamemnon and the dead in Troy in terms of a mutual bond of φιλία – φίλος φίλοισι (354). This adds a further (military) implication to the opposition φίλος/ἐχθρός.[84] This stanza continues to build up the authority of the dead father – σεμνότιμος ἀνάκτωρ (356), πρόπολός τε τῶν μεγίστων χθονίων ἐκεῖ τυράννων (359), βασιλεύς (360), βάκτρον (362). Electra also stresses the preference for death in warfare μετ' ἄλλῳ δουρικμῆτι λαῷ (365), and deprecates the instruments of his death. The expression for his 'killers', οἱ κτανόντες, a masculine plural, as with the masculine singular ὁ βλάπτων (328), draws attention to the sexual differential particularly in terms of the reversal of normal spheres of action (whereby the king was killed by a woman and not in battle). And as a summation, τῶνδε πόνων refers back to *Aga.* 1, 20 etc., constituted there in the opposition of the sexes, showing/saying, light/dark; continuing problematics. As the mourners recall the earlier events, the terms of mourning echo the earlier vocabulary.

The chorus retort:

> ταῦτα μέν, ὦ παῖ, κρείσσονα χρυσοῦ
> μεγάλης δὲ τύχης καὶ ὑπερβορέου
> μείζονα φωνεῖς. δύνασαι γάρ   (372–4)

These expressions of the power and possibilities of her language of prayer are followed by the assertion of the success of the *kommos*: δοῦπος ἱκνεῖται· τῶν μὲν ἀρωγοί... γῆς ἤδη (376–7). The subject of the verb ἱκνεῖται is, however, difficult. διπλῆς... τῆσδε μαράγνης δοῦπος is referred by some to the double affliction of Orestes and Electra, i.e. either death of Agamemnon and impiety of Clytemnestra, or Aegisthus and Clytemnestra (δυοῖν γυναικοῖν) (Schütz, Dindorf, Peile and the scholion). Conington, however, and Klausen take the scourge to be the appeal to the dead 'lashing up the sluggard vengeance' (Sidgwick). Paley and Lloyd-Jones literalize this as the beating of the hands on the tomb. διπλῆς suggests by this ambiguity also the wider doubling, the parallelizations of Aegisthus/Clytemnestra, Orestes/Clytemnestra etc., or the murder of Agamemnon, the murder of Clytemnestra, the 'doubling' of the text in the sense of constitutive oppositions, the 'doubling' of the text of the

---

[84] Although one may remember μόνος δ' Ὀδυσσεύς... ἕτοῖμος... σειραφόρος (*Aga.* 841–2).

kommos itself.[85] This continual doubling resists the possibility of a
simple linear reading, of simply reducing the plurality of the text.
They conclude with παισὶ δὲ μᾶλλον γεγένηται (379): as Rose notes,
μᾶλλον is without reference: it leaves the nature of the 'more', 'the
victory' (Tucker) of the children without specificity, (although
'children' itself may hint towards the relation involved in the
abhorred and unnamed crime of matricide).

This pierces Orestes' ear ἅπερ τε βέλος, 'like a weapon': an image
looking forward to the conflict of Clytemnestra and Orestes, as it
recalls the chorus' prayer (160–3) for a man with a weapon – the
weapon is here words. He appeals to Zeus to send up against mortals
ὑστερόποινον ἄταν (cf. *Aga.* 58–9 ὑστερόποινον πέμπει παραβᾶσιν
Ἐρινύν). But this general expression is broken off without a main
verb,[86] and the stanza concludes, when one might have expected
syntactically a command, request (for punishment, say), with the
highly suggestive and ambiguous phrase τοκεῦσι δ' ὅμως τελεῖται.
τελεῖται is a passive, 'it will be accomplished', 'brought to an end',
'performed as a rite'; and either τοκεῦσι, 'for/to/with parents', is
to be connected with ὅμως, an ellipsis for καίπερ οὖσι τοκεῦσι,
'although they are parents', or ὅμως is to be taken closely with
τελεῖται, 'nevertheless it will be done', etc. The plural, 'parents',
as Lebeck notes, is significant: it opens itself not only to a general
statement about punishment that is to be meted out even to parents,
but also, as Verrall and Tucker read, in the metaphorical context of
'punishment as child of crime' to the sense of offspring resembling
parents; moreover, as a plural for singular, it may suggest a reference
to (severally) Agamemnon *and* Clytemnestra, that is, it must be paid
(etc.) *for* Agamemnon and *against* Clytemnestra. The plural which
terms both Agamemnon and Clytemnestra τοκεύς, connected as it is
to the ambiguities of τελ-, is woven in the paradox of Orestes' desire
for vengeance with regard to the emotive term τοκεύς, the need for
redefinition of that term. As we have seen, the normal moral kinship
vocabulary is insufficient in the present circumstances; and the
ambiguities of this phrase suggest precisely those uncertainties.

This uncertainty is further brought out in the chorus' desire to
raise the ὀλολυγμόν over:

[85] Verrall suggests διπλῆς refers to the text of the *kommos* itself; 'its elaborately duplicate
construction which is now for the first time apparent. This group of anapaests is the
centre of the whole system: two triplets have preceded; two are to follow.' This, he
says somewhat disarmingly, 'is, I think, certain'.

[86] 'Orestes breaks off because he seems to avoid a more direct imprecation against his
mother...The idea is almost stated, then suddenly replaced with a vaguer formulation'
(Lebeck 1971, p. 119). The causal connection of the first part of the quotation is
difficult: one would have expected 'because he breaks off, he seems...', as indeed
Sidgwick writes.

ἀνδρός
θεινομένου γυναικός
τ' ὀλλυμένας   (387–9)

The specificity of the sexual role (ἀνδρός/γυναικός, recalling Cassandra's prediction, *Aga.* 1318ff.) stands in contrast to the moral problem inherent in τοκεῦσι δ' ὅμως τελεῖται. Indeed, the chorus ask why they should restrain their ἔγκοτον στύγος (392); στυγεῖν may easily express the relation between slave and evil tyrant, but it ignores the bond of *philia* between son and mother. The chorus' expression τί γὰρ κεύθω (as at 123) avoids, then, and emphasises the difficulty of, the expression of the emotion of στυγεῖν, of οὐ φιλεῖν for Orestes and Electra towards Clytemnestra.

Electra maintains this avoidance of stating the necessary act of Orestes by both questioning when *Zeus* will enact the punishment (linking Zeus and Orestes) and by leaving unstated the object of χεῖρα βάλοι, the noun on which κάρανα (396) would be dependent. Zeus is termed ἀμφιθαλής (which was used ironically at *Aga.* 1144), which is translated 'rich' (Sidgwick), 'strong on both sides' (Verrall), 'mighty' (Lloyd-Jones). ἀμφιθαλής most often means (ironically in a prayer for a parent's death) 'with both parents still living' (cf. Plat. *Leg.* 927d, *Il.* 22.496). This applied to Zeus draws attention again to Zeus as an example of intergenerational conflict. ἀμφι- as with διπλῆς, doubleness: two parents, two children, two lovers. She concludes with a double prayer to two forces:

πιστὰ γένοιτο χώρᾳ
δίκαν δ' ἐξ ἀδίκων ἀπαιτῶ.
κλῦτε δὲ Γᾶ χθονίων τε τιμαί   (397–9)

So she requests assurances from the gods and δίκαν ἐξ ἀδίκων, both 'right instead of wrong' (Verrall) and 'punishment, retribution from the unrighteous' (Conington) – the continuing ambiguity of δίκη as an object of desire.

The chorus again avoid any difficulties of definition of δίκη by asserting the strict reciprocity of punishment (as at *Cho.* 121, 123) in terms of blood flowing for blood (as at *Cho.* 48, 66, 151ff.), of ἄτην …ἐπάγουσαν ἐπ' ἄτῃ (403–4). The vagueness of τῶν πρότερον φθιμένων (403) and the sense of repetition in ἑτέραν (cf. θυσίαν ἑτέραν, *Aga.* 150) suggest the extended series of events leading towards the πρώταρχον ἄτην, that resists the possibility of depicting the act of revenge as a τέλος. So indeed this ominous note is enforced by the ironic forewarning of βοᾷ γὰρ λοιγὸς Ἐρινύν (402). Orestes, indeed, appeals to the πολυκρατεῖς…φθιμένων Ἀραί (406), which are the forces that will chase him after the matricide. He demands that the

Curses observe the remnants of the Atreid house: ἴδεσθ' Ἀτρειδᾶν
τὰ λοίπ' ἀμηχάνως ἔχοντα καὶ δωμάτων ἄτιμα (407–8). Ἀτρειδᾶν τὰ
λοίπ' invokes the generational continuity of the house of Atreus;
δωμάτων ἄτιμα, the children's deprivation of status (-τιμ-) in the
oikos. So δύσελπις (412) follows from this as an expression of fear for
the future (of the house); a 'bad hope' arising from what they *hear*,
κλύουσαν (411) πρὸς ἔπος κλυούσᾳ (414), and expressed in the
metaphoric colouring of dark and light, κελαινοῦνται / φανεῖσθαι† μοι
καλῶς. Again the language of prayer recalls the earlier prayers of the
trilogy.

Indeed, Electra continues with a question which echoes all the
earlier demands for accurate language in such a religious context:

$$\text{τί δ' ἂν φάντες τύχοιμεν;} \hspace{3cm} (418)$$

'What must we say to hit the target' (Lloyd-Jones), 'to gain our end'
(Lebeck)... She suggests an answer:

$$\text{ἦ τάπερ}$$
πάθομεν ἄχεα πρός γε τῶν τεκομένων;
πάρεστι σαίνειν, τὰ δ' οὔτι θέλγεται·
λύκος γὰρ ὥστ' ὠμόφρων ἄσαντος ἐκ
$$\text{ματρός ἐστι θυμός} \hspace{3cm} (418\text{–}22)$$

A complex passage: 'Are we to say those things of harm which we
suffered from the very ones who gave us birth? It is possible to fawn
but these things are not charmed away. For like a wolf cruel-minded
and not to be fawned on / unfawning is the nature from/out of a/the
mother.' Lebeck has an excellent lengthy analysis of the ambiguities
of this passage: the active/passive play of ἄσαντος implies not only
the childrens' rage, like a cruel wolf, which they inherited from their
mother (as did the lion in the house): it will brook no flattery to avoid
its purpose, however she may try (πάρεστι σαίνειν). It also implies
that the children may fawn before the mother, but crimes do not
become charmed away, and so behind words of flattery lurks, like a
wolf, an unfawning nature. Lebeck concludes, 'The confusion here
created by the omission of a personal pronoun abetted by an adjective
either active or passive, brings out the likeness of child to parent.
They may fawn, she may fawn; theirs is her nature which will not
fawn, cannot be fawned upon.' (1971, p. 123). This also brings
forward the parallelisation of events once more; πρός γε τῶν τεκομένων
suggests 'origin', 'descent': Electra and Orestes have inherited the
dilemma which forces them to take vengeance for Agamemnon's
death, itself depicted in some degree as a punishment for the curses
of his father. ἄχεα πρός γε τῶν τεκομένων can connote the
necessity of crime and punishment passed from one generation to the

next' (Lebeck, p. 123). But more than this: as we saw (above pp. 62ff.) in the second stasimon of the *Agamemnon* in the αἶνος of the lion cub and particularly in the stanzas following (*Aga.* 750–71) there was a search for an origin of narrative, particularly moralised narrative (that is, the pattern of sin and punishment), in an extended metaphor of childbirth. The search for an origin in action stood parallel to the search for the etymon in words, an attempt to control the play of language and narrative by fixing a point from which things could be said to derive: the model of childbirth, the character of the parents appearing in the children, provided the (metaphorical) structure of this discourse: here in the 'origin or descent' (Lebeck) of πρός + the genitive (418) and in ἐκ ματρός (421–2) connoting 'the necessity of punishment and crime passed on from one generation to the next' we find a similar development of childbirth / child–parent relation as a model of (causality for) narrative, as the metaphor of the lion cub is realised here in the revenge of Orestes on Clytemnestra (χρονισθεὶς δ' ἀπέδειξεν, *Aga.* 727). Childbirth / child–parent relation is no longer (if it ever was) simply a metaphor for moral action, for narrative in general, but is precisely the sphere of actions on which morality bears: 'The non-discursive event is...the incarnation of a discourse; reality is a realisation.'[87] But as we have seen (pp. 122ff.) and will see there is a continuous (re-)definition of the terms and the model of procreation leading towards Apollo's assertion that only the male is to be termed τοκεύς. The redefinition of the role of the mother, the female, asserts also the redefinition of the model of narrative towards its authorisation of/by the word of the father – οὐπώποτ' εἶπον...ὃ μὴ κελεύσαι Ζεὺς Ὀλυμπίων πατήρ, *Eum.* 616ff.; τούτων ἐπῳδὰς οὐκ ἐποίησεν πατήρ, *Eum.* 649. This authorisation of narrative, however, by the situating of its origin in the word of the father (the birth of the text, its paternal origin) can also be questioned by marking the word within that 'graphics of iterability',[88] its capability of being repeated, cited. Apollo's *citation* of the word of Zeus as authority, enshrines its own deconstruction. It is in the dynamics of this tension between the authorisation of the word of the father and its undercutting questioning by the Erinues that the trial of Orestes and the ending of the trilogy will be constituted.

The chorus continue, ἔκοψα κομμόν (423). This may refer to the hymn just passed (Conington, Peile *et al.*) or to the time of

---

[87] Todorov 1977, p. 64.

[88] Derrida also writes of the alteration that repetition inscribes: 'Iterability alters, contaminating parasitically what it identifies and enables to repeat "itself"...limiting the very thing it authorizes, transgressing the code or the law it constitutes, the graphics of iterability inscribes alterity irreducibly in repetition' (Derrida 1977, p. 200).

Agamemnon's death (Verrall) or to the *parodos* (Lloyd-Jones) – once more the openness of the reference allows the implication of the repetition of events: Electra, however, recalls the non-burial of Agamemnon, which suggests a narrowing of reference. The queen's πάντολμε nature (cf. p. 141) is seen in that she dared (ἔτλας) to conduct the burial without the citizens' presence, without the ritual mourning. Orestes picks up this lack of social respect with ἀτίμως (434), which is followed with ἀτίμωσιν...τείσεις (435; cf. also 445): once more the reciprocity of action is expressed in economic terms. ἕκατι μὲν δαιμόνων ἕκατι δ' ἁμᾶν χερῶν, however, points to the doubling of responsibility, the doubling of causality, which despite the symmetry of syntax (ἕκατι μὲν...ἕκατι δέ...) stands opposed to any simple symmetry of action implied in ἀτίμως...ἀτίμωσιν... τείσεις. After the specificity of ἁμᾶν χερῶν, he concludes with a rhetorical expression of despair: ἔπειτ' ἐγὼ νοσφίσας ὀλοίμαν (438), 'when I have killed, then let me die'. The suppression of the object of the verb of killing, despite the now single object implied by τείσεις, ἔλεξας[89] (after Electra's apostrophe ἰώ...μᾶτερ 430) marks the recognition of the extraordinary nature of the act to be performed, a silence in the discourse concerning Clytemnestra's death, similar to that in the *Odyssey*[90] (although the final conflict will be so different from the emphasis in the *Odyssey*). Once more, the specific horror of matricide is all but named.

The command ὄργα (454), as we saw 324–6 (cf. p. 141), as an expression for the attitude to revenge, refers back to Agamemnon at Aulis which further parallels Orestes' killing of Clytemnestra and Agamemnon's sacrifice of Iphigeneia. Orestes then calls on his father to be of assistance (ξυγγενοῦ picking up 2, 19 ξύμμαχος γενοῦ, connecting Zeus, Hermes, and Agamemnon) to φίλοις. As if φίλοις were not specific, Electra continues ἐγὼ δ' ἐπιφθέγγομαι, 'I join my voice to his', and the chorus furthers it with στάσις δὲ πάγκοινος ἅδε, 'and this whole company echoes the call' (Lloyd-Jones), and adds:

> ἄκουσον ἐς φάος μολών,
> ξὺν δὲ γενοῦ πρὸς ἐχθρούς   (459–60)

The delimited φίλοις are opposed to ἐχθρούς: the chorus, Orestes, and Electra are opposed to Aegisthus and Clytemnestra, cutting across the normal filial boundaries of the opposition φίλος/ἐχθρός.

> Ἄρης Ἄρει ξυμβαλεῖ, Δίκα Δίκα   (461)

This expression, as many critics have noted,[91] with the emphasised

---

[89] ἔλεξας M, ἔρεξας Herwerden and Page: Page's unnecessary change does not effect the point I am making here.   [90] Cf. below p. 191.

[91] Perhaps Kitto is the most forceful of these (1961, p. 84).

military implications of Ἄρης Ἄρει ξυμβαλεῖ, shows the tension in term *dike* – opposing sides, both of them with δίκη. Electra, however, cries:

> Ἰὼ θεοί, κραίνετ' ἐνδίκως ⟨λιτάς⟩ (462)

κραίνετ', 'fulfil', suggests the result of the battle, the conclusion of the opposition Ἄρης Ἄρει, a deciding between the opposition Δίκᾳ Δίκα. It is qualified, moreover, by ἐνδίκως, where the implication of a single standard of δίκη stands in contradiction to Δίκᾳ Δίκα of the previous line (cf. 987–9). This tension in the discourse of δίκη, which is repressed by those who wish to read a simple developmental structure towards enlightened 'Justice', will continue through the trilogy.

The chorus conclude the lyric section of the *kommos* with four short stanzas recalling many of the tensions and terms of the preceding passages:

> τρόμος μ' ὑφέρπει κλύουσαν εὐγμάτων
> τὸ μόρσιμον μένει πάλαι,
> εὐχομένοις δ' ἂν ἔλθοι (463–5)

As we saw in the Cassandra scene, there is a marked and ironic tension between the belief in the fixedness of fate, and the belief in the efficacy of language as a predictive force – if fate waits, why pray? The irony is especially seen in the fear surrounding the cledonomantic use of language, a fear that stems from the lack of control in language being seen as a lack of control in events, and from the belief that a total control of language would remove this apparent lack of free will.[92]

πόνος ἐγγενής (466), as an expression of events, refers back to 'these toils' at 371 (and thence to the *Agamemnon* and its use in the language of the mysteries). ἐγγενής connotes not only the sphere of action for the πόνος, the γένος, but also the connection between narrative and childbirth, generation. So indeed ἄτας (467) referring to ἄτην...ἐπ' ἄτη (403–4) and πληγή (468) to ἀντὶ...πληγῆς... πληγήν (312–13) recall the expressions of reciprocity of punishment between the generations, and κήδη (469) recalling the play at 87 and 109 and *Aga.* 699, the connection between grief and marriage-tie. So too, ἄφερτον recalls μόρον...ἄφερτον αἰῶνι (441–2). The chorus continue to emphasise the internal familial nature of the strife, which is linked also to the imagery of sickness and cure – an organicism with the inherent valuing of sickness and health:

---

[92] Lloyd-Jones writes here 'The philosophical problem of determinism had not at this time presented itself to the poets, and we must beware of supposing that they took either a determinist or an antideterminist view.' My analysis suggests that while one certainly cannot characterise this text as simply determinist or antideterminist, it does not follow that the discourse does not set in play notions of (lack of) control, and desire for control, and the tensions that arise from such notions.

δώμασιν ἔμμοτον
τῶνδ᾿ ἄκος οὐκ ἀπ᾿ ἄλλων
ἔκτοθεν, ἀλλ᾿ ἀπ᾿ αὐτῶν
δι᾿ ὠμὰν ἔριν αἱματηράν   (471-4)

But it is a sickness to be cured by the patient, not by outside help,[93]
which looks forward with some irony to the court-scene of the
Eumenides, as well as suggesting the perversion of the binary values
of self and other (φίλος/ἐχθρός) involved in the inversions of familial strife. The cure is seen in terms of 'bloody strife', opposition not
mediation; αἱματηράν invokes the images of flow and the implications
of reciprocal punishment – the action is a battle, for which they
request ἀρωγὴν ἐπὶ νίκῃ (477-8). This is reminiscent of the plays
between δίκη and νίκη, as well as the continuation of the imagery of
Ἄρης Ἄρει ξυμβαλεῖ (461). So προφρόνως (478), situated within the
structure of φρεν-/φρον-/σωφρον- recalls more specifically, in its
juxtaposition to ἐπὶ νίκῃ, the hymn to Zeus:

Ζῆνα δέ τις προφρόνως ἐπινίκια κλάζων
τεύξεται φρενῶν τὸ πᾶν   (*Aga.* 174-5)

So Agamemnon's assistance for Orestes is linked to the supporter of
Zeus, in the possession of φρενῶν as opposed to the φρόνημα...
δύσθεον (191) of Clytemnestra. So ends the lyric *kommos*, with the
assertion of a prayer for victory with the help of Agamemnon, the
father, in terms recalling Zeus the father of the gods, as throughout
the *kommos* the terms of the prayer of invocation of the male force
of the father in the house recall the vocabulary and images of the
earlier transgressions in the house of Atreus. So the conjuration/
invocation/mourning of Agamemnon asserts and projects the role
of the father.

In the following trimeter scene, however, the invocation to the
father (πάτερ, 479; πάτερ, 481; πάτερ, 491; πάτερ, 493; πάτερ,
495; πάτερ, 500) and to the Earth and the gods of the underworld
(ὦ γαῖ᾿, 489; ὦ Περσέφασσα, 490) continues for some forty lines.
Continues? How continues? The 'repetition' of ideas in a different
metre? Is Gould's analysis of 'modes of presentation' enough?[94]
Why now, after the gift of Clytemnestra's offerings and the chorus'
short lyric (153ff.), where Electra said only ἔχει μὲν ἤδη γαπότους
χοὰς πατήρ, does the prayer, the invocation, go over the boundaries
of the lyric? Is this to mark the continuation of the lack and the
continuing attempt to fill it (unlike Agamemnon 'having his offer-

---

[93] Note the play οὐκ᾿ ἀπ᾿ ἄλλων ἀλλ᾿ ἀπ᾿ αὐτῶν.
[94] 1978, pp. 50ff., following Jones 1962 and Dale 1969a. See also W. Schadewaldt,
Monolog und Selbstgespräch (Berlin, 1926), p. 144.

ings', the 'end' of the rite) through the play until Orestes takes up
the position of the father in the house and in the view of society? The
references in the trimeters back both to the earlier prayers and to the
kommos certainly mark the continuation of the mode of desire.[95] The
chorus, who do not otherwise speak in these trimeters, conclude it
with τόνδ' ἐτείνατον λόγον (510, cf. *Aga.* 916) marking the crossing
of the lyric–trimeter boundary by the two children who will effect the
re-establishment of the home, by further crossing of boundaries –
with Pylades (πύλας). The *Choephoroi* as play of the *limen*...

Certainly, these trimeters echo the language of the lyric *kommos*
markedly: τρόποισιν οὐ τυραννικοῖς θανών (479) emphasises the
non-military death, not fitting to the status of a king, to which status
Orestes wishes to pass:

αἰτουμένῳ μοι δὸς κράτος τῶν σῶν δόμων   (480)

κράτος, as in the *Agamemnon*, involves status, power, authority – as
in πατρῷ'...κράτη (1). So μοι...αἰτουμένῳ (2), δόμοισι (13), δός
(18) – the repetition of the words of the opening prayer marks the continuing projection of the *kommos* and the earlier prayers, together in
the desire for πατρῷα κράτη. The house is still Agamemnon's,
τῶν σῶν. Orestes cannot call it his house until he has achieved his
role within it. This will result also in the due honour for Agamemnon
in the Underworld (483–5) – the exchange of food for help,[96] the offer
of sacrifice, a ritual exchange, as opposed to his present status of ἄτιμος,
cf. 434, 435, 443, 445.

Electra, too, will pour offerings *then*, offerings from her marriage
ceremony: γαμηλίους (487). These offerings contrast with the offerings she has made, and the offerings she was asked to make by
Clytemnestra, whose adultery transgressed and perverted the exchange of marriage and whose rule keeps Electra from her role as a
woman – to be married.[97] Married, however, she will return to the
system of reciprocity. πατρῴων ἐκ δόμων (487), then, is a charged
phrase: it will be not only from the ancestral home but also from the
home returned to the rule of the father – and with the rule of the father
the role of the woman in marriage as object of exchange between men
is re-established.

Orestes asks the earth that his father may ἐποπτεῦσαι μάχην. This
connects Agamemnon with Hermes and Zeus (cf. 1, 126) as the
overseers of events (depicted once more as a μάχη). Electra in her

---

[95] What Hartman has well called 'the interminable work of mourning' (1982, p. 103),
where he writes interestingly on 'the scene of nomination' and its relation to
psychoanalytic readings, which is relevant to this analysis of the *kommos*.

[96] Cf. 255–7, where a similar promise was made to Zeus.

[97] Cf. Vernant 1965.

turn prays to Persephassa to give εὔμορφον κράτος – εὔμορφον in implied opposition to the present κράτος of Clytemnestra. On the one hand, this may be read (after ἄνες μοι πατέρ', 489) as referring to the power Agamemnon needs; on the other hand, after δός κράτος ...δόμων (480), it could refer to Orestes' regaining of κράτος. This ambiguity for κράτος stresses the parallelisms of role between Orestes and Agamemnon in the power struggle for the house.

The children go on to recall Agamemnon's death again: the method by which he was *hunted* is both in contrast to the king's status as a warrior, and also parallel to the manner of Orestes' revenge (cf. 274 τρόπον τὸν αὐτόν). This paradox, as Vidal-Naquet[98] and Zeitlin[99] point out, is situated within a system of reversals similar to the reversals of the initiand.[100] Orestes, indeed, prays to get 'a similar hold' (it is not so much the *same* hold, αὐτὰς λαβάς, as a '*similar* move'). A similar strategy is to be used against Clytemnestra (ἀντίδος, 498; ἀντινικῆσαι, 499). This strategy is, however, *opposed to* the assistance of δίκη: Orestes in his pursuit of δίκη (punishment, retribution), in his fight for νίκη in the μάχη, will adopt the same standards of trickery, lying, deception, which have been characterised as ἄδικα (cf. e.g. 398), i.e. as the transgression of δίκη in the sense of moral standard. There is a continuing paradox, then, in his acceptance within the parallelisation of events of the need for exactly *reciprocal* punishment while condemning the basis of the parallelisation, that is, the mode of attack on Agamemnon which he will use against Clytemnestra also. It is a paradox which falls within the structure of reversals that not only follow from the reversal inherent in Clytemnestra's gynarchy (rule-reversal/role-reversal); but also such reversals are important to any structure of initiation. Does the suggestion of choice between δίκη σύμμαχος and ὁμοίας λαβάς as moves towards νίκη express the paradox of the initiand whose moral standard is to be that of the hoplite, the warrior, but whose initiation requires actions of a reversed standard?

Electra calls on their father to hear their last cry, in words which recall 247–56 (cf. pp. 133ff.), the emotional prelude to the *kommos*:

ἰδὼν νεοσσοὺς τούσδ' ἐφημένους τάφῳ
οἴκτιρε θῆλυν ἀρσενός θ' ὁμοῦ γόον[101]   (501–2)

---

[98] 1968, *passim*. Also Vernant and Vidal-Naquet 1972, *passim*.   [99] 1978, *passim*.

[100] Cf. also van Gennep 1960, for the first formulation of this. Cf. also Girard 1972, Bleeker 1965, Leach 1964.

[101] An interesting change from 'child(-production)' to 'language(-production)'. ἀρσενος γόνον is not without point: ἀρσενος is called a genitive of description by Verrall (i.e. periphrasis for ἀρσενα) but it also opens the possibility of precisely the distinction between male and female parentage so important for the *Eumenides*.
   The production of children and language were linked in the metaphor of τίκτειν (etc.)

The juxtaposition θῆλυν ἄρσενος draws attention not only to the sexual differential but also to the parallelisms of the text. As Cassandra said: ὅταν γυνὴ γυναικὸς ἀντ' ἐμοῦ θάνῃ | ἀνήρ τε δυσδάμαρτος ἀντ' ἀνδρὸς πέσῃ *Aga.* 1319–20. They will be effected by a woman and man also: a further doubling.

Orestes stresses once more the aim of the generational continuity of the σπέρμα Πελοπιδῶν (503), which refers back to the earlier hopes of the house, σπέρματος...πυθμήν (204), ἐλπὶς σπέρματος σωτηρίου (236). This continuity (οὐ τέθνηκας οὐδέ περ θανών, 504) is expressed by Electra (505) as a continuity of the word κληδόνος, the name. Indeed, Orestes' words of the invocation are ἄκουε...αὐτὸς δὲ σῴζῃ τόνδε τίμησας λόγον (508–9) – salvation comes through an honouring (in exchange) of the word. So, the chorus mark the end (510ff.) of precisely τόνδ'...λόγον. And they turn towards the outlining of Clytemnestra's dream and Orestes' plan of revenge.

Sign language: the dream-text

After the recognition scene's sign reading, and the *kommos*' search for the language of prayer (which seems almost summed up in the trimeters which open this scene), Orestes' progression in the narrative of revenge is notably another reading of signs – the dream of Clytemnestra as prophecy.

Orestes begins by questioning the motive of Clytemnestra's offering. His use here of the phrase θανόντι δ' οὐ φρονοῦντι has rightly troubled the commentators. For it appears to be in contradiction to the chorus' φρόνημα τοῦ θανόντος οὐ δαμάζει πυρός... γνάθος (324–5), indeed, to the whole assumption of the preceding *kommos*! Tucker punctuates with a question mark, and translates 'Was it for a dead man that the paltry boon was meant?' Sidgwick translates φρονοῦντι as 'feeling', ignoring any problem of the reference to the chorus' words. Verrall calls it an 'exaggeration of rhetoric' and notes simply the *logical* inconsistency of language. Peile and Conington suggest it is an *argumentum ad hominem* for Clytemnestra, relying on the common view of the insensibility of the dead. But can one avoid the implication of φρόνημα with φρονοῦντι?

used of narrative and story-telling. Here Pauw's and Page's fathering of a new word from an echo in the text – opening the question of a theory of literary production, of a relation between an author and his page of words – is pointed self-referentially in the ambiguity of child-production/sound-production. γόον or γόνον? Whose word(s)? Can one hear the text's difference? Can one tell the difference? As I question in a transgressive way the defensive barrier erected by (father) Page on his page between the apparatus and authenticated, legitimated, text, so (self-referentially) I am defended and undercut by these words' footnote status.

Does Tucker's punctuation avoid the problem? The strange apparent inconsistency of his phrase stands juxtaposed to:

...οὐκ ἔχοιμ' ἂν εἰκάσαι τόδε   (518)

'I can't possibly compare, liken, guess this', which seems to refer back to ποίᾳ ξυμφορᾷ προσεικάσω (12) and the process of judging by analogy. Orestes continues:

τὰ δῶρα μείω δ' ἐστὶ τῆς ἁμαρτίας.

τὰ πάντα γάρ τις ἐκχέας ἀνθ' αἵματος

ἑνός, μάτην ὁ μόχθος. ὧδ' ἔχει λόγος   (519–21)

That poured blood has no purification (as was asserted at 48, 66 etc.) is described as λόγος. Yet it is precisely the veridical value of μάτην ὁ μόχθος that is challenged first by Orestes' purification, and then by his eventual acquittal, where the Erinues echoing this passage ask:

τὸ μητρὸς αἶμ' ὅμαιμον ἐκχέας πέδοι

ἔπειτ' ἐν Ἄργει δώματ' οἰκήσει πατρός;

ποίοισι βωμοῖς χρώμενος τοῖς δημίοις;

ποία δὲ χέρνιψ φρατέρων προσδέξεται;   (*Eum.* 653–6)

The answer to these outraged questions is the speech (657–73) asserting the male role in procreation, (re)defining the function of μήτηρ. οὐ φρονοῦντι, then, an apparent contradiction, stands in juxtaposition to the suggestion of judging by analogy, likenesses, εἰκάσαι, and the assertion of the fixedness of a λόγος, which will be seen – and this contradiction is essential to the dynamics of the trilogy – to be contradicted by an appeal to another λόγος, a λόγος itself based on a gesture of metaphorisation, analogising (ἀναλογία). Reversal, paradox, contradiction cannot be excised from the text.

Indeed, the assertion ὧδ' ἔχει λόγος, the fixedness of the proverbial truth, stands as a prelude to the description and interpretation of Clytemnestra's dream, where the non-referential vision of the dream, the exemplary model of the inconstancy of sight, is in its inscription in language (the 'dream-text') linked to, formed in, the inconstancy of language. To Orestes (550), the dream *speaks*. After that discussion, Orestes states his plan, beginning:

ἁπλοῦς ὁ μῦθος   (554)

This echoes ἁπλωστὶ φράζουσ' (121), where ἁπλωστί stood in contrast to and was undercut by the duality of δικαστὴν ἢ δικηφόρον, as it was by the shifting of δίκη itself. Moreover, the *mythos* that follows is manifestly not 'simple', but 'false', 'double', two people feigning accents, using language deceptively, lying. Furthermore, the speech itself will be seen to be far from ἁπλοῦς: for not only is there a marked silence on the subject of his revenge on Clytemnestra, which will be the central confrontation, but also this remark, for example, is scarcely 'simple':

φόνου δ' Ἐρινὺς οὐχ ὑπεσπανισμένη
ἄκρατον αἷμα πίεται τρίτην πόσιν   (577–8)

The ironic allusion to Clytemnestra's third (implying final) libation (*Aga.* 1385–7), its indication of a telos of reciprocal punishment (undercut precisely by the Ἐρινὺς οὐχ ὑπεσπανισμένη) indicates a complexity beyond the possibility of his asserted ἁπλοῦς ὁ μῦθος. Let us consider this tension between the assumed fixedness and simplicity of language and the *glissement* of ironic allusion in more detail. Orestes questions the basis of the chorus' knowledge of the dream further – πέπυσθε...ὥστ' ὀρθῶς φράσαι (526): ὀρθῶς φράσαι looks back to the desire for clarity, accuracy in communication. Here, however, more precisely, it will be in the report of a report of a vision which itself needs interpreting.

The chorus say:

τεκεῖν δράκοντ' ἔδοξεν, ὡς αὐτὴ λέγει   (527)

τεκεῖν, which was linked before with narrative, is now a signifier in the dream-text, a 'symbol' to be interpreted by Orestes: his interpretation concentrates mainly on the fact that she gives birth to a *snake* (544–51), but Clytemnestra (928–9) realises the force of τεκεῖν in a 'literal' sense, as the point of contact between the allegory (if one may risk the term) of the dream, and the reality (if one may risk that term!) of the confrontation. τεκεῖν, then, not only as a central term in the prediction of events, linking giving birth and narrative, but also as the common point between the dream and events, shifting between its use as a metaphor, a symbol, and its use to express the 'literal' relation between parents and children, opens itself to a process of redefinition, which culminates in Apollo's speech at *Eum.* 657ff., that definition of τεκεῖν so essential for the dynamics of Orestes' acquittal. As we saw with φιλεῖν, the development of the language of familial relations is essential to the appropriating discourse of the city.

ἔδοξεν (527), 'she seemed', 'she thought',[102] looks back to δόξαν at *Aga.* 275, *Cho.* 227 etc. in the sense of 'vision', 'fantasy', explicitly with regard to dreams (*Aga.* 422–3) and of illusions (cf. 1057). The phrase ὡς αὐτὴ λέγει (527), 'her own words', emphasising the textual nature of their presentation of the dream, is picked up by Orestes καὶ ποῖ τελευτᾷ καὶ καρανοῦται λόγος (528). He seeks for the *telos* of the logos here as he does in the play overall: the status

---

[102] L.-S.-J. note the commonness of this expression in relating dreams – opposed to εἶναι.

of this search for closure, however, is placed at risk by the predictive nature of the logos, its relation to the confrontation of Orestes and Clytemnestra, where, for example, the chorus' words, αὐτὴ πρόσεσχε μαστὸν ἐν τὦνείρατι (531), become realised in Clytemnestra's τόνδε δ' αἴδεσαι...μαστόν (896–7). The resultant continuing signification of, for example, Orestes' ἐκδρακοντωθείς...ἐγώ (549), the production of meaning in the relation between the dream-text of confrontation and the (re-)presentation of confrontation, resists in its continuing signification the possibility of *telos* for the narrative, the logos. Indeed, the process of interpretation followed by Orestes, its manipulation of the metaphoric (symbolic?) structure of the dream, places the *telos* of the dream in the future, deferred: ἀλλ' εὔχομαι...τοὔνειρον εἶναι τοῦτ' ἐμοὶ τελεσφόρον: yet it is precisely the production of meaning in the structure of difference and deferral that erases for the logos the possibility of the prayed-for τέλος.

κρίνω (542) marks the interpretation: he selects ὥστε συγκόλλως ἔχειν, 'as it holds, is, glued together'. The process of selection 'so as to', 'in order to', produce a coherent structure: the teleology of the hermeneutic structure is marked by the consecutive conjunction.

The interpretation, as with εἰκάσαι (12, 14, 518, cf. also 174–6, 206) is based on a recognition of similarity, τὸν αὐτὸν χῶρον ἐκλιπών (543), μαστὸν...ἐμὸν θρεπτήριον (545), 'the breast... my nourisher'.[103] But this hermeneutic, the (causal?) connection δεῖ...ὡς ἔθρεψεν ἔκπαγλον τέρας, θανεῖν βιαίως remains open to ambiguities: does it imply that Orestes is an ἔκπαγλον τέρας? ἔθρεψεν (548) seems to pick up ἐμὸν θρεπτήριον (545), and the position of the ὡς- clause in the apodosis, the 'cashing out' of the dream, draws the snake and Orestes closer together. ἐκδρακοντωθείς, then, suggests more than the simple identification of Orestes with the animal; it also implies Orestes as ἔκπαγλον τέρας (ἐκ-δρακοντωθείς / ἐκ-παγλον), as the object of Clytemnestra's rearing.

The chorus accept Orestes as interpreter:

τερασκόπον δὴ τῶνδέ σ' αἱροῦμαι πέρι   (551)

τερασκόπον (cf. *Aga.* 977, 1440) pointed by δή, puns on its etymology: τέρας – σκοπεῖν. For it is not only as a 'diviner' that Orestes is accepted but also as one who looks at, analyses through vision (σκοπεῖν) the τέρας (548): but this re-sites the interpretation of the dream within the structure of interpretation pertaining to the

---

[103] φίλον γάλα: φίλον expresses the bond of 'nature and motherhood' (Sidgwick), the bond which in view of the process of redefinition of the opposition φίλος/ἐχθρός, and μήτηρ/τοκεύς, as well as its application to the suckling of the snake, seems almost ironical.

visual mode (as it was marked as a language act by ἐννέπει, 550; λόγος, 528; λέγει, 527); so the interpretation is open to the finally un-controllable shiftings of metaphorisation (in language and sight). In the very gesture of accepting Orestes' prophecy, then, the etymological play pointing to the materiality of the signifier opens again the gap between signifier and signified which the prophetic present tense of divination was to close (but emphasised?).

The punishment will be based on a similarity: ἐν ταὐτῷ βρόχῳ, but the command of punishment (termed a deceit) is also marked as a communication: ᾗ καὶ Λοξίας ἐφήμισεν...Apollo, who is, like Orestes a τερασκόπος, like Cassandra, Calchas, a μάντις: does this throw doubt on the absoluteness, the 'truth' (note ἀψευδὴς τὸ πρίν) of Apollo's command? Is it the expression of the gods' power to do precisely that which escapes the sublunary world, to reduce the gap between signifier and signified, the present and the future, or is it significantly juxtaposed to the interpretation of the dream-text as another example of an interpretation of a text, unable to control the sliding, shifting of signifiers? On the one hand, the failure of Apollo's protection at a primary level (the pursuit of Orestes by the Erinues, the failure of the purification, the need to go to an external judgement system – the difficulty felt by many readers about his arguments there) would suggest the latter, that is, a *similar* attempt to find control in language and narrative as marked by the use of μάντις/ μαντεύω for Apollo, Calchas, Cassandra, the chorus of the *Agamemnon* (*Aga.* 1367). On the other hand, the final reconciliation of the Erinues and the acquittal of Orestes seem to suggest the former. The truth of Apollo, both suggested and opened to doubt by ἀψευδὴς τὸ πρίν, constituted here in the ambiguity of the status of Apollo's words, has been debated by numerous scholars: Wilamowitz[104] conceived of the *Choephoroi* and *Eumenides* as a polemic against Apollo; Winnington-Ingram,[105] less aggressively polarized in his opinion, places Apollo between the Erinues and the Areopagus and says 'I believe that Aeschylus meant to criticise this code [Apollo and the Delphic code of vengeance] as an inconsistent compromise.'[106] Kitto talks of the 'radiance that plays around Apollo; there is purity, beauty, order; and this has its human counterpart in the purity of motive shown by the new avengers';[107] this he further opposes, however, to the spirit of reconciliation of Athena. Lebeck assumes 'that the trial is a parody which does not present the Athenian law-court in its most attractive light',[108] and thus Apollo's words are

---

[104] *Griechische Tragödien*, 7th edn (Berlin, 1913) II, pp. 143–4, 148.
[105] See particularly his article of 1933.   [106] 1933, p. 101.
[107] 1961, p. 92.   [108] 1971, p. 137.

considered only within this rhetoric. The paradox of Apollo's role seems, however, to be strikingly interwoven with the paradox ξυμβαλεῖ Δίκᾳ Δίκα...κραίνετ' ἐνδίκως and its implication of *both* a non-absolute *and* an absolute standard of δίκη. For Apollo's development of the patriarchal discourse is problematised precisely in that it is sited both in opposition to (δίκᾳ δίκα), and thus open to the questioning of, the discourse of the Erinues; and also, despite (because of ?) this polarisation, it is hypostatised as a truth and an absolute: the terminology of Apollo's discourse cannot be sufficient both to the interplay of opposition (Δίκᾳ Δίκα) and to its own authority as word-of-the-father, Law, Truth (κραίνετ' ἐνδίκως). The court case, the tied vote of the jurors, the instantiation of ξυμβαλεῖ Δίκᾳ Δίκα, is thus sited *in opposition to* Apollo's assertion that he has performed, as Electra had asked, ἐνδίκως, i.e. according to the dictates of an absolute Justice, δίκη.

It is significant that Orestes will pretend to be (note εἰκώς- making himself *like*) a ξένος. It was precisely the transgression of (the relation of) *xenia* – the significance of the bracketing will become clearer by the end of the paragraph – that was the cause of the Trojan war and it was Zeus Xenios who was depicted as sending the Argive expedition: Orestes will pervert the bonds of *xenia* by lying, murdering his hosts in order to reassert the ties of society. This paradox will be seen again and seen to be important. For as Hillis Miller has argued, *xenia* as host/parasite *is* transgression as relationship:

The uncanny antithetical relation exists not only between pairs of words in this system, host and parasite, host and guest, but within each word as itself. It reforms itself in each polar opposite when that opposite is separated out. This subverts or nullifies the apparently unequivocal relation of polarity which seems the conceptual scheme appropriate for thinking through the system. Each word in itself becomes divided by the strange logic of the 'para'-membrane which divides inside from outside and yet joins them in a hymeneal bond, or which allows an osmotic mixing, making the stranger friend, the distant near, the *Unheimlich heimlich*, the homely homey, without, for all its closeness and similarity, ceasing to be strange, distant and dissimilar.[109]

That which joins to separate, separates to join – the disjunctive sign as limen: a ξένος with Πυλάδης, the man of the gate.

Orestes ends this speech first with an instruction γλῶσσαν εὔφημον φέρειν which (as with the messenger at *Aga.* 636ff., cf. above pp. 58ff.) in its fear of the cledonomantic power of language, stands in contrast to his assertion of ἁπλοῦς ὁ μῦθος (554) and ὧδ' ἔχει λόγος;

---

[109] 1979, p. 221.

secondly, with an injunction to τούτῳ (a deictic without clear reference – Agamemnon? Pylades? Hermes? Zeus? Apollo? – the connection of the male forces) to τὰ δ' ἄλλα... ἐποπτεῦσαι. ἐποπτεύω refers back to 1, 126 etc., the appeals for the gods to oversee events. As 'seeing' becomes more and more uncertain as a simple category, does the prayer to 'oversee' become equally problematised? The unnamed power is to 'set aright', ὀρθώσαντι, the 'spear-carrying contest' (again the military nature of the action is stressed). But the ethic dative μοι (584), as it is construed above, could also be taken as agreeing with ὀρθώσαντι (as read by Verrall). This implication further confuses the lines of causality: is it on an outside power or Orestes' own activity that the outcome depends?

His final instruction to Electra and the chorus returns Electra to the inside of the house (the woman's position which is now made 'savage' (Zeitlin) by Clytemnestra and is to be returned to normality by Orestes' 'most savage act') and returns her also to silence, and to the mass of the chorus, from whom she had been separated. Now he takes Pylades (and the Phocian tongue) as his helper: σὺν ἀνδρὶ τῷδ' (561) ... ἄμφω δὲ φωνὴν ἥσομεν (563). The moment of confrontation becomes thus sharpened as an opposition of male and female. Πυλάδης: the man of the gate; the boundary to be crossed; who offers entry to this language as he offers entry to the matricide (by his ratification): the limen which joins to disjoin. In this play of boundaries and crossing of boundaries, significantly the name of Orestes' assistant etymologically suggests the function of precisely the limen, πύλη.

This scene, then, after the great *kommos* and invocation, the healing/binding in/of language, revolves around first the interpretation of the dream as a predictive sign (as the scene before revolved around the interpretations of the signs of Orestes), and secondly around Orestes' description of his plan. It revolves, that is, around two attempts at projecting narrative towards a *telos*, at seeking for control in and through language, as did the *kommos*. So, the interplay between Orestes' projections and what follows, in the fulfilment and non-fulfilment of his predictions marks the desire for control in narrative and language as it marks the lack of such control.

This monstrous regiment...

The first stasimon, which separates the projections of the previous scene from their realisations, opens with a priamel-like structure (585–92), leading towards the statement of the ode's general thematic (594–601). The monsters of the four elements stand as an introduction to the monstrous women. For after the great invocation of the father and the indication of the plan of matricide, the chorus significantly turn to sing of the host of despised, corrupted and corrupting females: and from its last word, Ἐρινύς, Orestes will knock on the door of the palace to assure Clytemnestra's place in the catalogue.

The earth breeds monsters. τρέφει (585), used commonly of the earth, is also to be read within the structure of imagery of τεκεῖν (after the invocation of the father), and as a preparation for the two scenes that follow, namely, Clytemnestra's reaction to the news of Orestes' death, and the nurse's further reaction. It deepens the already complex associations around the notion of generation and rearing, as does the bold metaphor πόντιαι...ἀγκάλαι. Who is the mother, who the τροφεύς? How are they to be distinguished? The main theme of the ode (marked by ἀλλ'...τίς λέγοι 594–5) is stated first as ὑπέρτολμον ἀνδρὸς φρόνημα (594–5): it is a disposition of mind to dare to go beyond, too far, ὑπερ-, to transgress. Parallel to this is γυναικῶν φρεσὶν τλημόνων παντόλμους ἔρωτας: the 'inflation' of ὑπέρ-τολμον to παν-τόλμους (picking up 430) is marked: women's passions go the whole hog...These women are τλημόνων – both 'wretched' and 'daring'/'reckless', as though the two ideas connected to ἔρως imply each other – and their passions are 'mated[110] with mortal woes' (Sidgwick). These transgressive desires are the theme that is picked up and continued:

> ξυζύγους δ' ὁμαυλίας
> θηλυκρατὴς ἀπέρωτος ἔρως παρανικᾷ
> κνωδάλων τε καὶ βροτῶν   (599–601)

θηλυκρατής both connotes 'ruling females' (θηλυ-, the specific generic term of sexual differential) in the sense of loss of personal control (the opposite of σώφρων); and also, in the context of κράτος as power in the *oikos*, it suggests 'leading to domination by females' (cf. 480, 490). ἀπέρωτος ἔρως, 'a passion that is "away from passion"', expresses a sense of deviation picked up by the prefix παρα-νικᾷ, 'subvert by conquest'. The subverted object of ἔρως is ξυζύγους...ὁμαυλίας, 'yoked together dwelling together', the widest possible reference to the bonds of societal structures, not just the ties of marriage. The effect of the φρόνημα/ἔρως which transgresses the definition of its correct object, affects the whole of society (cf. p. 14, 'a scale that is virtually cosmic' – here both monsters and mortals).

The first example of this transgressive desire, however, is the story of Althaea, ἁ παιδολυμάς, 'the child-destroyer', in which there is

---

[110] Note the metaphor is drawn from precisely the field under discussion.

no direct reference to sexual passion, but which rather involves the depiction of the mother as both giver (μολὼν ματρόθεν, 608–9) and taker of life, which looks forward to Clytemnestra's call for ἀνδροκμῆτα πέλεκυν (889). The denial of generational continuity, the procreation of children to continue the *oikos*, which we have seen threatened and deprecated again and again, is a denial of society, of the *oikos* itself: it is this continuity (and the constitution of such terms as inheritance, legitimacy, paternity) that is threatened by indiscriminate sexuality:[111] in this example, however, the threat is widened to an ambiguity in the figure of the mother herself – an ambiguity which has finally in the restoration of Orestes to the *oikos* an outcome in the *Oresteia* opposite to the example here offered. Rather than the child-destroyer, the story to come will be of the destroying child.

The second example (ἄλλαν δ' ἦν τιν' ἐν λόγοις, 613), the story of Skylla, after the child-killer, offers a father-killer. Again in Aeschylus' version there is no mention of ἔρως (although, of course, many later versions focus on erotic motives): here, persuaded by gold, Skylla corrupts the relation of φίλος/ἐχθρός:

> φοινίαν κόραν,
> ἅτ' ἐχθρῶν ὕπερ φῶτ' ἀπώλεσεν φίλον   (614–15)

Again it is a question of the definition of a correct object, here of φιλεῖν.[112] κυνόφρων (621), used of Helen in Homer (see above p. 56) may suggest an element of sexual licence: but the emphasis here remains on the destruction caused by Skylla's actions.

The third example consists of a series of comments applicable to Clytemnestra and Aegisthus in that they centre on adultery and the murder of a warrior through the plotting of a woman, though noticeably no names are used: outside society's bounds, outside the recognition, the naming process, of society: indeed the relationship is termed a γαμήλευμ' (624–5), a strange coining, which 'seems to parody the honourable name of γάμος' (Verrall). Its strangeness is further marked by δυσφιλές (624), which has the sense of not merely ἐχθρός/στύγ(ερ)ος, opposites of φίλος but a *corruption* of the bond φιλεῖν: 'bad', δυσ-, in its definition of the object of φιλεῖν[113] (cf. 894, 905–6, *Aga.* 1232). This relationship is ἀπεύχετον δόμοις (625) – it is the house that it damages (the plural δόμοις marking the possible generality of the reference). The juxtaposition of γυναικοβούλους to ἀνδρὶ τευχεσφόρῳ continues the opposition of a death suitable for a

---

[111] Cf. Tanner 1980.

[112] The tale is introduced as τιν' ἐν λόγοις στυγεῖν – the reader too is asked to define his/her reaction in terms of φιλεῖν/στυγεῖν.

[113] A rendering such as Conington's 'wedlock where there is no love but hate' seems to miss the point of both the coined term γαμήλευμ' and the force of δυσφιλές.

warrior, a man, and the death of Agamemnon at the hands of a woman
(cf. γυναικείαν, 630), as ἄτολμον presumably[114] rejects παντόλμους/
ὑπέρτολμον. The assault on the king is placed in a series by:

κακῶν δὲ πρεσβεύεται τὸ Λήμνιον
λόγῳ   (631–2)

The Lemnian women, the uprising of the whole female section of
society (the conclusion of the series of individual acts) are depicted
as 'hated' (κατάπτυστον, 633), particularly by the gods, θεοστυγήτῳ
δ' ἄγει (635), and rejected by the society whose rules they have
transgressed, βροτοῖς ἀτιμωθὲν οἴχεται γένος (636). This is generalised in significant vocabulary:

σέβει γὰρ οὔτις τὸ δυσφιλὲς θεοῖς   (637)

σέβει, as we saw on 55ff., 157ff., expresses a relation of 'respect' in
a hierarchised society: δυσφιλές, as at 624, the corruption of the
relation of φιλεῖν, the ties of reciprocity in society; θεοῖς, the
authorising control of the hierarchisation. Which generalisation is
applied to the whole series by:

τί τῶνδ' οὐκ ἐνδίκως ἀγείρω;   (638)

'What of these things do I bring together unjustly, not fitting my
cause?' A hint also of the δίκη towards which this stasimon tends?

τὸ δ' ἄγχι πλευμόνων ξίφος
διανταίαν ὀξυπευκὲς οὐτᾷ   (639–40)

'The sword' seems here to be both the literal sword of Orestes (οὐτᾷ,
an 'inceptive present' (Verrall)), and with διαὶ Δίκας (641) also the
metaphorical revenge of Δίκα,[115] which has been crushed under foot,
πατουμένας. This is reminiscent of *Aga.* 371–2 and its realisation in
that earlier male–female conflict, the carpet scene (cf. p. 68). There
is a similar play here on the *effet du réel* in the ambiguous or dual
status of the sword, which is picked up with:

προχαλκεύει δ' Αἶσα φασγανουργός   (647)

'Fate, the sword-maker, bronzes in advance' suggests a metaphorical
expression; but τέκνον δ' ἐπεισφέρει δόμοις suggests Orestes himself
(cf. 652) – but the delayed dependent genitive αἱμάτων παλαιτέρων
(649) suggests a more metaphorical reading of τέκνον, i.e. the
connection between τίκτειν and narrative, 'sin begetting sin' (which
structure is instantiated, however, in Orestes). τίνειν μύσος χρόνῳ
(650) seems reminiscent of the lion-cub (χρονισθείς) parable; which
further suggests Orestes; but then, delayed for maximum effect, the

---

[114] See Conington, reading τίω with Stanley. The passage is obelised as *desperata* by Page.
[115] Page's capitalisation of *dike* presumably tries to lessen the ambiguity of *dike* which
is once more juxtaposed with ἐνδίκως.

subject of the sentence turns out to be κλυτὰ βυσσόφρων Ἐρινύς (650–1): the revenge of the Erinues (cf. 577ff.), δαίμων as causal agent. This confusion of human and non-human motivation and action, the over-determination of the lines of causality, is further marked by Orestes' immediate knocking at the door, the realisation of τέκνον δ' ἐπεισφέρει δόμοις, and calling παῖ παῖ. The child coming; calling on the child; retribution, the child of former bloods.

A fall story...

As the returning hero Agamemnon came back to a welcome from Clytemnestra that led to his death, so now his exiled son returns (bringing deceptive words instead of spoils), with Pylades (who is imbued with a voice of divine authority, like Cassandra?). Orestes, too, will get his welcome from Clytemnestra, his offer of entrance. As we will see, however, the exchange of words is markedly different. Orestes' is an entrance to reclaim the palace, an entrance of revenge. Significantly, his first words follow the chorus' statement that an Erinus leads the child to the house.

Orestes calls three times (recalling the third libation, the third drink of the Erinues), and he asks pointedly:

εἴπερ φιλόξεν' ἐστὶν Αἰγίσθου διαί   (656)

ξενία, φιλεῖν are the ties[116] of society broken, which have led to the present crisis of action.

The slave asks ποδαπὸς ὁ ξένος; – precisely the question Orestes expected from the lips of Aegisthus (575): the delays to the act of revenge, the differences between Orestes' plan (554ff.) and the events, place the narrative in that unclear area between ἀρχή and τέλος, which we have seen characterised by ἐλπίς/φόβος, the desire for control and σαφῶς μαθεῖν. Orestes seeks τοῖσι κυρίοισι δωμάτων (658), those with κράτος:

ἐξελθέτω τις δωμάτων τελεσφόρος
γυνὴ τόπαρχος ἄνδρα δ' εὐπρεπέστερον   (663–4)

τελεσφόρος is translated by L.-S.-J. and the commentators (following the scholion) as 'one with authority in the house', from the use of τέλος as 'authority', 'position of authority', 'magistracy'. It picks up, however, τοὔνειρον...ἐμοὶ τελεσφόρον (541), which looks back to Clytemnestra's prayer at *Aga.* 973–4 to Zeus Teleios: the ruler of the house is the aim of Orestes also, it is the object that

[116] Cf. Benveniste 1969, pp. 338–53 for links between *philia* and *xenia*.

constitutes the *telos* of his action, the object that can bring (φέρειν) the τέλος (in all its senses).

The reason offered for the greater suitability of a man is interestingly the lack of openness in language, of αἰδώς leading to ἐπαργέμους λόγους. The difficulties of communication are again seen within the opposition of the sexes. 'But a man can be clear with a man': κάσήμηνεν ἐμφανὲς τέκμαρ (667). The signifying of the clear τέκμαρ is placed in opposition to ἐπαργέμους λόγους. τέκμαρ was the word used by Clytemnestra for her description of the beacon chain (*Aga.* 315), that passage of signifiers, 'sure sign(al)s', (rather than the difficult signifier–signified relation of language, cf. pp. 36ff.). And ἐμφανές (φαίνω) is constituted precisely in the opposition of showing/saying as a basis for clarity. These are opposed to the 'cataract-bleared words' – itself an interpenetration of visual and verbal terminology. It is as if the sexual differential is implied as the root of the problematic of communication, the non-equivalence of showing and saying.[117]

It is, however, Clytemnestra who appears: so that the disclaimer of the possibility of clear and straightforward communication between people of the opposite sex stands as a prelude to the deceptive discourse of Orestes; and moreover to the ironies of Clytemnestra's speech (668ff.) and to the problem of her reaction (691ff.). We are to see the failure of communication between the sexes.

Clytemnestra's speech of greeting, like her welcome to Agamemnon, is deeply ironic. The act of deception, however, is with the visitor. The irony is constituted not by the lack of supposed truth value of the statements (as with Clytemnestra's hypocrisy to the returning king) but rather by an excess of signification, an uncontrollable polysemy of reference in the text: πάρεστι γὰρ | ὁποῖάπερ δόμοισι τοῖσδ' ἐπεικότα (668–9); ἐπεικότα connotes both 'what things are fitting to this house' – which stands in juxtaposition to the series of reversals of the norm that we have seen – and also has the sense of 'like', 'suit' (as with προσεικάζω), which, as Sidgwick mentions, points to the series of metaphors that Cassandra (for example) uses to describe the house of Atreus ('human slaughterhouse' etc.). θερμὰ λουτρά, 'warm baths', an offering to a guest in Homer, seems subverted by the reference to the place of Agamemnon's murder (*Aga.* 1108ff.; *Cho.* 1071). πόνων θελκτηρία στρωμνή (670–1): στρωμνή, 'bed', through the adultery of Thyestes, Atreus, Paris/Helen, Aegisthus/Clytemnestra, has been rather a cause of πόνων – which

---

117 Felman again has an interesting comment here: 'sexuality is precisely *what rules out simplicity as such*...sexuality is *the division and divisiveness* of meaning: it is meaning *as* division, meaning *as* conflict' (1977, pp. 111–12).

recalls the specific sense of the toils of the house of Atreus (cf. *Aga.*
1 etc.). Indeed στρωμνή also suggests the 'spreading' (στόρνυμι)
of the purple in the carpet scene. And θελκτηρία is used precisely
in a sexual context at *Il.* 14.215, the well-known description of
Aphrodite's *cestus*:

ἔνθα τέ οἱ θελκτήρια πάντα τέτυκτο.
ἔνθ᾽ ἔνι μὲν φιλότης, ἐν δ᾽ ἵμερος ἐν δ᾽ ὀαριστὺς
πάρφασις ἥ τ᾽ ἔκλεψε νόον πύκα περ φρονεόντων

θελκτηρία, then, evokes the beguilings of sexuality and deceitful
language which act upon <u>νόον</u> πύκα περ <u>φρονεόντων</u>, as φρόνημα,
φρεσί (595, 596 etc.) were the expressed field of corruption.[118]

δικαίων τ᾽ ὀμμάτων παρουσία (671) recalls the problematic
definition of δίκη, and is, linked to ὀμμάτων, reminiscent of the ironic
remark of Agamemnon (*Aga.* 838ff.) on the hypocrisy of social
intercourse, which refers back to, for example, Clytemnestra's ὄμμα
σοῦ κατηγορεῖ (*Aga.* 271) and to the problematic of showing
and saying – indeed to the problems in the sense of sight that we have
been discussing.

Clytemnestra finally indicates she will pass the business over to the
men: ἀνδρῶν...οἷς κοινώσομεν (673). The plural ἀνδρῶν opens
itself to the suggestion of the series of men (Atreus, Agamemnon,
Aegisthus, Orestes) for whom the business of the house is 'something
to be debated further' (672) – and κοινώσομεν ('we/I will communicate, share with') not only recalls the partnership of crime of
Aegisthus and Clytemnestra, and looks forward to their shared deaths
(971ff.), but also through the implication of such terms as κοινωνία,
κοίνωμα suggests the sexual basis[119] of her relationship with the
man/men of the house.

Following on from this dubious welcome, Orestes tells his story.
The plural reference to parents πρὸς τοὺς τεκόντας...εἶπε (681–2),
'say to the parents'..., comes down to <u>τὸν τεκόντα</u> δ᾽ εἰκὸς εἰδέναι
(690) where the masculine singular, while looking forward to *Eum.*
657ff., seems to point to the sexual differential[120] and the absence of
the father once more (particularly after εἶπε...ἀνὴρ πρὸς ἄνδρα,
666–7; ἀνδρῶν τόδ᾽ ἐστὶν ἔργον, 673). Tucker suggests the following
readings of this expression: '(1) But if it is the parent, the parent will
know...(2) Yet it is natural to know one's (my) parent...(3) A man's
father ought to hear news like this...(4) But it is the parent who ought
to be informed.' After εἰ δὲ τυγχάνω | τοῖς κυρίοισι καὶ προσήκουσιν
λέγων | οὐκ οἶδα, it seems also to suggest the failure of the parent

[118] Cf. p. 160 above, and generally on θέλγειν and related terms Kahn 1978, pp. 139ff.
[119] Cf. Sidgwick ad loc.
[120] Sidgwick translates τὸν τεκόντα 'mother', which tries to avoid the problem of gender.

to recognise to whom she is speaking (unlike Electra's recognition of family resemblance) As with Clytemnestra's tales of false reports (*Aga.* 985ff.) as she lies to Agamemnon, this scene of deception points in this play between knowledge and parentage to the constitution of the deception.

The story of the *death* of Orestes, which we find in Sophocles also, is interesting; as Zeitlin points out,[121] the matriarchal/patriarchal tension is linked to a structure of initiation imagery, a point also developed by Vidal-Naquet. Eliade[122] says with regard to the process of initiation, 'a state cannot be altered without being first annihilated' – initiatory death.[123] 'Orestes specifically characterised as on the threshold of maturity in the *Choephoroi* (6), lives out the myth in terms that bear a remarkable resemblance to generalised and widely diffused initiatory patterns.'[124] This death is seen,[125] then, as the representation of the to-be-crossed boundary between states, marking the end of childhood, the entry into 'the sacred time' of initiation ('transitional periods...sometimes acquire a certain autonomy'[126]). As with child-slayer Althaea, it also suggests the outcome of the continuing rule of Clytemnestra, precisely the non-continuance of the *oikos*: indeed Clytemnestra relates her reaction (πορθούμεθα) to the house and the curse:

ὦ δυσπάλαιστε τῶνδε δωμάτων Ἀρά   (692)

The wrestling imagery (cf. *Aga.* 171ff., *Cho.* 339) represents the relation of the house and its characters to the external force of the divine in terms of a struggle, an aggressive opposition. The curse 'watches' (ἐπωπᾷς) – as with ἐπισκόπους (126), ἐποπτεύων (1), of the gods – which further overlays the pattern of causality. So too its weapons are εὐσκόποις, 'well-sighted', 'watchful', ironically an adjective used regularly in Homer[127] of Hermes[128] to whom Orestes and Electra had prayed to overlook events – which also adds to the sense of over-determination.

The curse has stripped Clytemnestra of φίλοι (695). Unlike Electra's and Orestes' determination in the *kommos*, she uses φίλος to express her relation to Orestes in the house; as she will demand αἰδώς before the sword (896). ἐν δόμοισι...ἰατρὸς ἐλπὶς ἦν (698–9): it is

---

[121] 1978, *passim*.   [122] 1963, p. 30.
[123] 'This [initiatory death] is death to the indistinct and amorphous state of childhood in order to be reborn into masculinity and personality' (Turner 1962, p. 177). 'A social return from childhood' (van Gennep 1960, p. 46). '...a moment always comes when apparently by a violent action he [the initiand] is finally separated from his mother' (ibid. p. 74). Cf. Vidal-Naquet 1968 on the initiatory nature of the Ephebe.
[124] Zeitlin 1978, p. 160.   [125] But see below pp. 193–5.
[126] Van Gennep 1960, p. 192.   [127] *Il.* 24.24; 24.109; *Od.* 7.137 (for example).
[128] It is used also of Apollo in an oracle quoted in Herodotus (5.61).

for the house that the hope (as Electra called Orestes, 236) for cure
has been lost.

The contradiction between the expression of grief and what critics
have felt to be the expected reaction of Clytemnestra, which finds
expression in the nurse's accusation of hypocrisy (737–43), has led
to a series of readings in general agreeing with the nurse in some
degree. 'The grief is hollow in Klytaemestra's mouth' (Sidgwick);
'Hypocrisy in the grand manner, a wickedness strictly scrupulous of
appearances' (Tucker, although he also says 'she cannot but feel, at
the least for the moment, some natural pang', which contradiction
is described as a 'consummate realisation of character' – the problem
of distinguishing between 'natural pang' and a 'scrupulous appearance' of 'natural pang' thus skirted). Conington says 'the grief may
be hypocritical, tho'' perhaps that word hardly suits the complexity
of Clytaemnestra's character', where the status of 'hypocrisy' questioned by 'may be' is by a further rhetorical gesture subsumed
(veiling the process of interpretation) to the 'complexity...of
character', as though the predetermined 'complexity of Clytaemnestra's character' were a particular constant by which to judge the
efficacy of the term 'hypocrisy' in this instantiation of 'character'.
The questioning of the status of hypocrisy is followed also by
Lloyd-Jones, who writes cautiously: 'it is not safe to assume that the
emotion Clytemnestra expresses is wholly false'. This speech,
however, cannot be read as simply separate from the scene (play,
trilogy) of which it is a part. For the juxtaposition of Clytemnestra's
reaction to Orestes' speech of deceit and her own first speech of
welcome seems to be playing significantly on the problem of truth
in language, on a sense of referentiality: after Clytemnestra's speech
of welcome where the excess of signification undercuts the possibility
of a simple reference, and Orestes' deceit, which is depicted as
language without truth content, with no referentiality, this speech of
reaction, while seeming to challenge the reader to ground the
language in a referentiality, to judge its truth content (as the critics
and the nurse attempt), resists by the suggestive juxtaposition to such
non-referential language and ironic excess the possibility of the
certainty of the criteria of such judgements. Indeed, the nurse's
explicitly interpretative reading of the scene (or our reading of the
nurse's reading) draws attention to precisely the role of interpretation,
to the *production* of the level of referentiality. It resists therefore a
move through language to (the motivation of) character: for we are
not talking of Clytemnestra as a person as if she had 'a future, an
unconscious, a soul'...[129] 'We are developing connotations not

[129] Barthes 1975a, p. 94.

pursuing investigations.'[130] We are developing connotations of the 'systematics of a (transitory) site of the text: we mark this site (under...[the proper]...name...)...so it will take its place among the alibis of narrative operations in the indeterminable network of meanings, in the plurality of codes'.[131] This speech, then, rather than simply referring to an emotion inside Clytemnestra, contains elements of various languages: the discourse is developed by Clytemnestra's reaction, Clytemnestra's reaction is constituted in the discourse of communication we have been reading.

From a critical point of view, therefore, it is as wrong to suppress character as it is to take him off the page in order to turn him into a psychological character (endowed with possible motives): *the character and the discourse are each other's accomplices*: the discourse creates in the character its own accomplice: a form of theurgical detachment by which, mythically, God has given himself a subject, man a helpmate etc., whose relative independence, once they have been created, allows for playing...[132]

In this case, such interplay of character and discourse creates the ludic potentialities of the reading of Clytemnestra's reaction to the news of her son's death.

Orestes stresses the relation between his adopted role and the house (700–6): ξένοισιν (700), ξενωθῆναι (702), ξένου ξένοισιν (703), κατεξενωμένον (706), a relation expressed also by the term φίλος,

 οὐδ' ἧσσον ἂν γένοιο δώμασιν φίλος   (708)

The word φίλος here in its connection with ξενία is ironically applied by the mother to her unrecognised son: he is φίλος to the house in a way Clytemnestra cannot realise. Now Clytemnestra is on the receiving end of the capabilities of language to go beyond its user.

Clytemnestra orders them to the ἀνδρῶνας εὐξένους δόμων. She herself will tell (κοινώσομεν, cf. 673) the news to τοῖς κρατοῦσι δωμάτων (716): the 'rulers' (those with κράτος) 'of the house' – the masculine plural again masks and emphasises the dynamics of power in the house. οὐ σπανίζοντες φίλων (717), after φίλων ἀποψιλοῖς με (695), seems to suggest Aegisthus as a φίλος (precisely the relation whose validity is challenged by Orestes, 906–7) in the place of the dead Orestes. In the presence of Orestes (whom she regards as absent) this remark is ironical. The redefining of φίλος in the *kommos*, however, also implies that despite being in the presence of one who should be φίλος, Clytemnestra in fact does 'lack φίλων'; yet by the laws of hospitality, Orestes as ξένος places himself in a relation of φιλία

---

[130] Ibid.   [131] Ibid.

[132] Barthes 1975a, p. 178. Further theoretical remarks on the difficulty of the notion of 'character' may be found in Cixoux 1974, Bayley 1974.

(705, 708) to Clytemnestra; that is, to reassert the force of the bond of φιλεῖν, the societal norm transgressed by Clytemnestra, Orestes must not only redefine his relation to his mother as an ἐχθρός – that is, reject the societal norm of the bond between mother and son – but also in enforcing this reassertion ironically must place himself in a further relation of φίλος (as ξένος) with Clytemnestra, a relation that he will transgress. The complex play, then, of φίλος with regard to the relation of Orestes and Clytemnestra (both φίλος and not φίλος) is pointed by these overlaid ironies of οὐ σπανίζοντες φίλων. *Philos* is once more marked as a complex term in the work of redefinition.

Nursing/mother: metaphors and differences

Orestes and Clytemnestra and Pylades enter the palace (as had Clytemnestra and Agamemnon under different circumstances) and the chorus sing a brief ode in marching anapaests requesting help for Orestes. First they ask for στομάτων...ἰσχύν (720–1) 'strength for their mouths' – the force of language brought to the fore. They pray to earth and to the tomb (as in the *kommos*) and for πειθὼ δολίαν: as Buxton notes, this is in contrast to the πειθώ found later in the speeches of Athene (see below Ch. 3); it is 'deception masquerading as peitho'.[133] δόλος, as Vidal-Naquet argues, is the denial of the values of the hoplite warrior.[134] This phrase, followed by the prayer to Hermes, recalls the role of Hermes as trickster, as the deceiver, the god of thieves as well as his function as χθόνιον...νύχιον (727–8).[135] Hermes, the god of transition between life and death, here invoked between the description of Orestes' supposed death and the nurse's recounting of his birth and weaning: as with Odysseus' return home,[136] where the nurse Eurykleia recounts the birth and naming of Odysseus, the return to status in the *oikos* is here preceded by a description of death and birth: the liminality of Orestes' position marked by the points of transition, of 'passage'.

But after this short prayer, from the palace comes surprisingly

---

[133] Buxton 1976, p. 85.

[134] Detienne and Vernant (1978) also argue for the importance of δόλος and related terms in Greek thought.

[135] Also ἐμπολαῖος: the god of trading, exchange – which apart from the 'paradox' of being god of both trading and deceit, places parallel the transactions of economic exchange and the transitions of life and death, the crossing of boundaries (Hermes, the herm, the statue by the front door, the limen). On Hermes, see Kahn 1978, Ramnoux 1955, esp. pp. 138ff.

[136] Cf. Segal 1962b, 1967. Below pp. 184ff. 'When a man who has been thought dead returns home and wants to be reintegrated into his former position, he is required to pass through all rites pertaining to birth, childhood, adolescence' (van Gennep 1960, p. 188).

another character, the nurse. Before the scene of matricide, and looking forward to the debates of the *Eumenides*, the relation of a child to its weaning, feeding, upbringing, is placed outside the mother's sole sphere. As well as being part of the justification of matricide, the splitting and metaphorising of the function of bringing up a child opens the way towards the development of the civic discourse, its appropriation of such language (in the claim that the city is the mother/father/educator/nourisher of its citizens).

The nurse has been sent to call Aegisthus:

> ὡς σαφέστερον
> ἀνὴρ ἀπ' ἀνδρὸς τὴν νεάγγελτον φάτιν
> ἐλθὼν πύθηται τήνδε   (735–7)

Once again the clarity of communication is subsumed to the sexual differential. This desire for 'clearer' language stands juxtaposed to the description of Clytemnestra's feigned emotion, the difficulty of interpreting the queen's words. But the nurse's interpretation of Clytemnestra's reaction is marked as an interpretation, a reading, by:

> φήμης ὕφ', ἧς ἤγγειλαν οἱ ξένοι τορῶς   (741)

For τορῶς, last word in sentence and line, which looks back to *Aga.* 26, 254, 269, 616, 632, 1584 and the problematic of accurate language and clear interpretation, is predicated of Orestes' speech, which is a fabrication, a lie, unclear language. Does her 'misreading' of the clarity of Orestes' message stand significantly, then, in juxtaposition to her reading of Clytemnestra?

After Orestes and Clytemnestra have gone into the house together, as did Agamemnon and Clytemnestra, the nurse's speech on the τροφή of Orestes has a similar effect of delaying the expected action to that of the Cassandra scene: 'expectation...the basic condition of truth...this design brings narrative very close to the rite of initiation'.[137] Through the recounting of 'passage', doubly close! Moreover, as we saw on pp. 146ff., the discourse of τέκνον/τρέφειν constituted a model for narrative, the search for an origin, a pattern of cause and effect: here, then, the delay in the hermeneutic narrative is constituted within the metaphorical structure applied to the narrative earlier. So, then, as well as the change[138] of tone, and the charged contrast between τροφεύς and μήτηρ, the nurse's speech may be read as constituting the self-reflexiveness of narrative.

The chorus ask Cilissa how Clytemnestra ordered Aegisthus to come: she replies τί πῶς; λέγ' αὖθις ὡς μάθω σαφέστερον. Her request for clearer speech in juxtaposition to her own analysis of

---

[137] Barthes 1975a, p. 76.
[138] As noted by many critics: Sidgwick, Verrall, Conington, etc.

Clytemnestra's words and her ἤγγειλαν τορῶς, point once more to the heuristic gap in communication, a gap utilised by the chorus in encouraging the nurse to change the message out of hatred for the master, δεσπότου στύγει (770):

ἐν ἀγγέλῳ γὰρ κυπτὸς ὀρθοῦται λόγος (773)

'In the messenger the bent logos is straightened', a proverb[139] here used with a certain irony since the speech will 'be wonderfully corrected' (Verrall) – the manipulation of the signifier.

Despite the chorus' hints that she has not realised the situation fully, Cilissa continues to talk of the passing of the ἐλπὶς δόμων (cf. e.g. 236, 699). But her fear, hints the chorus, is groundless:

...κακός γε μάντις ἂν γνοίη τάδε (777)

Once again prediction, the projected passage of narrative, linked to ἐλπίς, and the religious connotations of μάντις. The nurse's recognition of some hidden information, τι τῶν λελεγμένων δίχα, is shelved by the chorus:

μέλει θεοῖσιν ὧνπερ ἂν μέλη πέρι (780)

The truth promised by the chorus' enigma turns to a tautology; it creates its own 'jamming' (cf. pp. 9–10). Once more, in stichomythia communication is blocked.

But with a prayer for the future the nurse takes the message.

'...So help me, god...'

The second stasimon is an extensive prayer for success, a further projection: the transition between scenes, the gap between the prediction of Aegisthus' arrival and his presence on stage, is constituted as a desire (παραιτουμένα, 783; cf. *Aga.* 1, *Cho.* 2). This prayer picks up many of the terms and tensions of the previous prayers of the trilogy. As we saw with the continuation of the *kommos*, the projection of desire extends throughout the trilogy.

The first prayer (which is to Zeus, called 'father', linking Agamemnon once again under the general πατρῷα κράτη) marks the need for safe language: διὰ δίκας ἅπαν ἔπος ἔλακον. διὰ δίκας implies 'for the sake of Justice' (Lloyd-Jones); but also 'for the sake of retribution/punishment', and also, as the scholion suggests, δικαίως 'according to justice/punishment'. ἅπαν ἔπος ἔλακον after the shifting of terms, ironies, puns, paragrams, etc. like πάντ' ἔχεις λόγον from the messenger *Aga.* 582 (cf. pp. 52ff.), invokes the (undercut) belief in the controllability of language, the possibility of being univocal.

---

[139] Cf. Tucker for further examples.

For Zeus' help against the enemy 'χθρῶν (790) he will receive (cf. e.g. 483–5) δίδυμα καὶ τριπλᾶ παλίμποινα (792–3): παλίμποινα suggests, however, ὑστερόποινον (*Aga.* 58), and παλίνορτος... τεκνόποινος (*Aga.* 155), the force of reciprocal punishment, which is precisely that by which Orestes is threatened. Immediately, we see the difficulty of ἅπαν ἔπος ἔλακον, the failure to delimit reference in the narrative of repetition and reversal.

The chorus turn to pray (800–2) to the household gods:

<blockquote>
τῶν πάλαι πεπραγμένων
λύσασθ' αἶμα προσφάτοις δίκαις   (804–5)
</blockquote>

The generality of τῶν πάλαι πεπραγμένων opens a reference also to the series of events preceding the killing of Agamemnon; λύσασθ' αἶμα is translated 'cause blood to be paid' (Tucker, Conington – 'the middle is used here as the gods are to bring about the expiation by human hands'), but also (as Lloyd-Jones translates) αἶμα can be taken closely with τῶν πάλαι πεπραγμένων, 'redeem the blood of deeds done long ago'. This ambiguity emphasises the continuing parallelisation of blood for blood – indeed προσφάτοις δίκαις continues this tension. For προσφάτοις means 'lately-*slain*' (hence 'new', 'fresh'), which implies precisely the nature of the act to follow; and δίκαις, a plural, after the singular δίκας (788) suggests at least the two acts of killing to follow, the two acts of revenge on Clytemnestra and Aegisthus, rather than the more abstract notion of Justice.[140] This prayer recalls, however, such expressions as τί γὰρ λύτρον πεσόντος αἵματος πέδοι (48), and the problem of expiation for spilt blood: a threat to Orestes which seems to lead to the chorus continuing:

<blockquote>
γέρων φόνος μηκέτ' ἐν δόμοις τέκοι   (806)
</blockquote>

'Let old man slaughter no longer bear offspring in the house'. τέκοι is once more the metaphor for the passage of events – as, for example, at 648–9 τέκνον δ' ἐπεισφέρει δόμοις αἱμάτων παλαιτέρων and at *Aga.* 750ff., where the truth of ὄλβον... τεκνοῦσθαι is termed a γέρων λόγος, which, as here, suggests the chain of reciprocal sin and punishment back through the household. But connected to the wish μηκέτ'... τέκοι, 'old man' also suggests the 'exhaustion' (Paley) of the curse, the infertility, impotence of old age; the hope (in juxtaposition, however, to προσφάτοις δίκαις) that the slaughter, childbirth, the narrative may reach closure, an end.

The stasimon continues with a prayer to Apollo (807–11, looking forward to his further aid in the *Eumenides*):

<blockquote>
... εὖ δὸς ἀνιδεῖν δόμον ἀνδρός   (808)
</blockquote>

---

140 Lloyd-Jones under-translates this by 'by a new act of Justice'.

ἀνδρός, the unspecified male (Agamemnon/Orestes), opposes the house of the male to the house under the rule of Clytemnestra (cf. 820–1 δωμάτων λυτήριον θῆλυν). The prayer for the house 'to look up' (after ἰδεῖν, 787; ἰδεῖν, 798), the common, inherently judgemental, metaphor of sight and light, is picked up with:

> καί νιν ἐλευθερίας φῶς
> λαμπρὸν ἰδεῖν φιλίοις
> ὄμμασιν ἐκ δνοφερᾶς καλύπτρας　　　　　(809–11)

Is the opposition of ἐλευθερίας φῶς λαμπρόν to δνοφερᾶς καλύπτρας (cf. *Aga.* 1178–80), however, put at risk by the central term ἰδεῖν φιλίοις ὄμμασιν? Does the *qualification* of ἰδεῖν by the adverbial phrase φιλίοις ὄμμασιν (with the marked possibility of ἐχθροῖς ὄμμασιν) suggest again the problematised notion of the visual, that is, its openness to interpretation? The prayer to Hermes[141] the third of the male gods, seems to develop the possibility of such questioning further:

> πολλὰ δ' ἀλά' ἔφανε χρήζων
> ἄσκοπον δέ πως βλέπων
> νυκτὸς προὐμμάτων σκότον φέρει,
> καθ' ἡμέραν δ' οὐδὲν ἐμφανέστερος　　　　　(815–18)

The hermeneutic god 'makes clear', φαίνειν, 'brings to light', 'shows', ἀλά', 'blind things'. The active ἀλά', 'not seeing', when one might expect a passive form, 'unseen', suggests an obfuscation of subject and object in vision, redefining the model of ἰδεῖν. This is further suggested by ἄσκοπον δέ πως βλέπων,[142] 'seeing in a somehow unseen, invisible way' (or 'unseeing'?), the paradox of which is marked by πως, itself punning on φῶς (βλέπειν) – ἄσκοπον φῶς, like ὀρφναίου πυρός (*Aga.* 21), marking the difficulty of a simple opposition of dark/light, clarity/confusion. Hermes the trickster confuses clear sight:[143] νυκτὸς προὐμμάτων σκότον φέρει καθ'ἡμέραν δ' οὐδὲν ἐμφανέστερος. 'Light', 'the day', as a standard of truth, clarity offers no more clarity (ἐμφαν-, root φαίνω) than night. Yet δέ marks the expected opposition of 'day' and 'night'. It is as if the opposition is set up to be paradoxically rejected. This, after the prayer 'to look up'...

The chorus apostrophises Orestes: when it comes to the moment

---

141　He is asked to help ἐνδίκως, which looks back to 462, and which after διὰ δίκας... προσφάτοις δίκαισι points once more to the shifting status of δίκη.

142　Reading Page's text: M and most edd. ἄσκοπον δ' ἔπος λέγων which links sight and language explicitly (even at the level of a single word ἔπος) – the object of sight and the signifier in language depicted in terms of each other, both open to the sliding of metaphorisation and hence unclear.

143　On Hermes as the confuser of sight and communication, see Kahn 1978, *passim*. Significantly, Aegisthus' brief speeches will have many references to his clear vision – as he proceeds to his death. Is that Hermes' help being recalled?

to act, then θροεούσᾳ ''τέκνον'' ''ἔργῳ πατρός'' αὔδα (828–9), 'When she says "child", say "It is the business of the father"' (the openness of πατρός hinting at the association of Zeus and Agamemnon). ἔργῳ πατρός, however, can also be construed (supplying τέκνον) as '[child] of the father in fact / in this deed', which looks forward to the *Eumenides*. 'Child of the father' also, with regard to ἀπέδειξεν ἦθος τὸ πρὸς τοκέων (*Aga*. 727), suggests a parallelisation between Agamemnon and Orestes. 'Of-the-father' is again the motivation of matricide as it is the opposition to Clytemnestra's female rule. And κάρτα δ' εἰμὶ τοῦ πατρός, 'I am especially of the father', will be part of Athene's final reason for giving the deciding vote to Orestes. The matricide is described here, however, also as an ἄταν, 'disastrous ruin', which is ἀνεπίμομφον (830), 'not blameworthy'. This oxymoron is the double-bind in which Orestes finds himself. ἄτα, too, after ἄτα δ' ἀποστατεῖ φίλων seems a difficult term: Orestes is exhorted to commit *ate*, but let *ate* keep away from φίλων! ἄτην ἐπ' ἄτῃ! The race indeed seems glued to *ate*. They further encourage Orestes to perform a 'bloody *ate*' with the spirit of Perseus[144] (831–6), and their final exhortation is:

τὸν αἴτιον
δ' ἐξαπόλλυ' εἰσορῶν   (836–7)

The gender of τὸν αἴτιον is markedly in opposition to that of θροεούσᾳ (828); a prelude, however, to the entrance of Aegisthus. αἴτιος, as we argued on 117ff., seems an expression of responsibility insufficient to the pattern of causality, especially when it is applied in the singular to Aegisthus; here, it is juxtaposed to a word of sight, εἰσορῶν, which has also been set in a shifting model of some complexity. The apparently straightforward assertion here 'as you see the man responsible, kill him' stands in opposition to the problematic of guilt and responsibility (and the questioning of the mode of the visual), but it also stands as introduction to the summary dismissal of Aegisthus. He speaks only some fourteen lines, and is killed with no indication of regret (cf. 989–90). The apparent simplicity, then, of τὸν αἴτιον δ' ἐξαπόλλυ' εἰσορῶν matches the assumed simplicity of the case against Aegisthus and the moral ease of his killing. Such simplicity and ease stand in contrast to the complexity of Orestes' confrontation with Clytemnestra, which involves the shifting redefining of moral terms as we have been reading throughout the play (φίλος/ἐχθρός, τίκτειν/τρέφειν, πατήρ/μήτηρ, σωφρονεῖν/φρόνημα etc.). The chorus' conclusion, then, while functioning

---

[144] Another hero who does battle with a terrible female. Freud, of course, aligned Medusa's snake head with the *vagina dentata*.

as a specific prelude to the immediate entrance of Aegisthus, also significantly fails to mention the more ambiguous confrontation to come.

Babe in arms

The confrontation of Clytemnestra and Orestes is preceded by the entrance of Aegisthus. His few lines in exchange with the chorus strongly emphasise the uncertainties of communication, and the changed message leading him to his death. As the language exchange of the carpet scene (and Clytemnestra's other lies and deceit) brought Agamemnon down, so his revengers are marked as using a similar strategy of deceit and tricky language.

Aegisthus, like Clytemnestra, expresses grief at the message of the death of Orestes (but grief for the house, picking up Clytemnestra's references to the house, 692, 698–9). Paley and Conington see a reference to the odium that will accrue to *him* from such news; Lloyd-Jones says 'even Aegisthus as a kinsman pretends to feel sorrow'. Certainly our expectation (remembering Αἴγισθ' ὑβρίζοντ' ἐν κακοῖσιν *Aga.* 1612) is challenged; as with Clytemnestra's reaction, however, (cf. pp. 167ff.) his expression of grief is preceded and followed by statements implying the difficulty of interpretation, of reading a message: ἥκω μὲν οὐκ ἄκλητος ἀλλ' ὑπάγγελος (838) recalls precisely what the message was, and how it had been changed by πειθὼ δολίαν from the chorus and the nurse to a deceit. This is followed by (839) νέαν φάτιν δὲ πεύθομαι where the hyperbaton of the δέ places great emphasis on the νέαν φάτιν, which as well as simply referring to the newsworthy content of the message of the strangers, recalls the way in which the message from Cilissa was precisely νέαν. The chorus exhort him to ἔσω παρελθών, where it will be possible, πάρα, to learn face to face, αὐτὸν αὐτῶν ἄνδρα, knowledge from one who was present at the death of Orestes παρών. The effort (possibility) of closing the interpretative gap by the presence of the witness, seems both marked and undercut by this repetition of παρ(α), the shifting of the signifier, as it is by the falseness of the 'news'. After his expression of grief, Aegisthus says

πῶς ταῦτ' ἀληθῆ καὶ βλέποντα δοξάσω; (844)

'How am I to judge these things...ἀληθῆ καὶ βλέποντα?' βλέποντα, from such phrases as φῶς βλέποντα, indicates 'alive', which is in opposition to the λόγοι...θνήσκοντες μάτην (845–6). But also βλέποντα is opposed to 'blind', as picked up most markedly in the opposition of ἐξ ἀμαυρᾶς κληδόνος (853) to φρέν'...ὠμματωμένην (854), where the connection between sight and language, thought and vision, the depiction of language in terms of the polarisation of true/false, light/dark, blind/sighted, clear/opaque (as in τί τῶνδ' ἂν εἴποις ὥστε δηλῶσαι φρενί; 847) is placed at risk by the difficulties we have seen in the depiction of the visual mode: indeed, this is marked further by the irony of Aegisthus' <u>ἰδεῖν</u> ἐλέγξαι τ' εὖ θέλω τὸν ἄγγελον (851) in reply to the chorus' double-edged remark:

> οὐδὲν ἀγγέλων σθένος
> ὡς αὐτὸν αὐτῶν ἄνδρα πεύθεσθαι πάρα   (849–50)

After the chorus' previous injunction to kill on sight, and Orestes' own request for a meeting with a ruler of the house 'man to man', Aegisthus' reply seems ironic indeed. Here, as in the *Agamemnon*, Aegisthus is depicted as insufficiently in command of the exchange of words. Here his failure to understand the import of the chorus' words (which makes ironic his final remark at 854, οὔτοι φρέν' ἂν κλέψειεν ὠμματωμένην) also seems to throw further doubt on the opposition of sighted/blind, light/dark. (Is this the instantiation of Hermes' prayed-for help, cf. 815ff.?) His erring points to the role of interpretation of signs, the gap between signifier and signified, which constitutes the difficulty of reading his expression of grief. The attempt to read through the language of Aegisthus' reaction, which the text by challenging expectations has seemed to some critics to invite, is undercut in its possibility of certainty by the juxtaposition of passages emphasising the productive role of interpretation in reading messages, the possibility of deceit, of opaque language. As with Clytemnestra's reaction to the news, it is impossible to repress the interplay of discourse and character.

Aegisthus enters the palace, and the chorus sing a short ode requesting help: as at 152–63, where they requested assistance and fulfilment for Electra's prayer, and as at 719–29 where they requested help (in the form of correct language) to assist and fulfil Orestes' deceit (itself depicted in terms of deceitful language – πειθὼ δολίαν). At three significant points of expectation in the narrative, then, there is a marked change of metre, a punctuation, and a search for control in and of language (as prediction, prayer) and thus in and of narrative: as in the *Agamemnon* – the Cassandra scene – at the moment of expectation, prediction, we see the self-reflexiveness of the recognition of, and attempt for control in, expectation and prediction. This time the request is for assistance of Zeus: it again concentrates on the need for correct language:

> Ζεῦ Ζεῦ τί λέγω; πόθεν ἄρξωμαι
> τάδ' ἐπευχομένη <u>κἀπιθεάζουσ'</u>,
> ὑπὸ δ' εὐνοίας
> πῶς ἴσον εἰποῦσ' ἀνύσωμαι;   (855–8)

Before the act of murder, in this moment of tension between (ἤ...ἤ) the destruction of the house of Agamemnon (860–2) or the 'fire and light for freedom' (863) which will gain πατέρων μέγαν ὄλβον (the plural πατέρων again expressing the generality of the *fathers*, ancestors), the desire for correct language points not only to the predictive power of the word, but also to the role of the discourse, its shiftings and redefinings of such difficult terms as δίκη, φίλος/ ἐχθρός, τίκτειν κτλ., which constitute the drama. Interestingly, they pray εἴη δ' ἐπὶ νίκῃ, as at 478 (the end of the lyric *kommos*), which looks back to the play of Electra's prayer δίκη νικηφόρῳ/δικηφόρῳ. The emphasis remains on conflict (μάχης, 874) rather than the possible judgement or justice of the conflict. The prayer for δίκη νικηφόρῳ has here again become the prayer only for νίκη.

The screams are heard:

πῶς ἔχει; πῶς κέκρανται δόμοις; (871)

The sounds are unclear: πῶς κέκρανται δόμοις, 'How is it fulfilled *in* the house?' and also 'How...*for* the house?': the unity of the house as physical presence and social unit. The chorus stand away from the deed τελουμένου – 'as it is being performed / being sacrificed / being initiated / reaching its end'. This recollection of, say, Clytemnestra's prayer to Zeus Teleios (*Aga.* 973–4) marks Orestes' action as parallel to Clytemnestra's regicide, with the same ambiguities of τέλος, the same desire for an end. He had asked for a τελεσφόρος person to come out of the house: inside an act is constituting a τέλος.

ὅπως δοκῶμεν τῶνδ' ἀναίτιαι κακῶν
εἶναι (873–4)

This recalls the inability of the chorus of the *Agamemnon* to take action (*Aga.* 1346–71), which stands in opposition to this chorus' intervention with the nurse (766ff.). So ἀναίτιαι might prompt the question from the *Agamemnon* (1505–6): ὡς μὲν ἀναίτιος εἶ τοῦδε φόνου τίς ὁ μαρτυρήσων. Once again, the complexities of responsibility are pointed by the naive assumption of their absence; in this case, the pretence of non-involvement by the chorus.

...μάχης γὰρ δὴ κεκύρωται τέλος (874)

τέλος: the sacrifice, outcome, death, initiation, end, of the 'battle', of the πράγματος τελουμένου. But the *telos* looks forward to the conflict of Clytemnestra and Orestes, and his pursuit by the Erinues: indeed, the perfect tense κεκύρωται expresses a sense of continuation which stands in something of a tension with the sense of τέλος as end.

From the palace comes another character. This slave proclaims the news: his third οἴμοι – ἐν τρίτοις προσφθέγμασιν (876) – recalls the

third libation, the third drink of the Erinues. The conflict with
Clytemnestra, however, is to come; the sense of an end is once more
suggested, only to be undermined as a point of closure. He summons
Clytemnestra:

> ἔοικε νῦν αὐτῆς ἐπιξήνου πέλας
> αὐχὴν πεσεῖσθαι πρὸς δίκης πεπληγμένος   (883–4)

'Struck by δίκη' – this is interesting not only for the play on
revenge/justice but also as a metaphor for Orestes, who will strike
her: as though Orestes is the personification of δίκη or indeed
δικηφόρος! A further overlay to the lines of causality; a further shift
in the sense of δίκη. Moreover, after the prayer for νίκη (868) and
before Clytemnestra's expression of the conflict at 890, it constitutes
a further interplay between δίκη and νίκη: the chorus pray for νίκη (as
Clytemnestra depicts the conflict) but the slave describes the outcome
of the battle as πρὸς δίκης πεπληγμένος. The mutual implication of
the terms νίκη/δίκη, the problem of definition of boundaries between
the terms, the logic of the paragram, continues.

Clytemnestra asks what the noise is and receives the reply

> τὸν ζῶντα καίνειν τοὺς τεθνηκότας λέγω   (886)

This riddle can be read in two ways: either 'the dead are killing the
living' or, as Sidgwick notes, with ζῶντα as subject, 'the living is/are
about killing the dead'. (Killing is being killed? – the reciprocity,
play of active and passive, that we have noted before. Cf. 923 'You
will kill yourself'.) Any ambiguity is assisted by the masculine
singular of τὸν ζῶντα (which could refer to Orestes, who is
masculine, singular, and alive). τοὺς τεθνηκότας, which is taken as
the subject, is a generic plural (as Verrall, Conington, Sidgwick, and
Tucker note), and as well as the reportedly dead Orestes, it also
implies Agamemnon, whose help from the tomb has been requested;
indeed the whole pattern of γέρων φόνος, the curse of the series of
murders and revenges.

Clytemnestra interprets the riddle without difficulty:

> οἲ 'γώ, ξυνῆκα τοὔπος ἐξ αἰνιγμάτων·
> δόλοις ὀλούμεθ' ὥσπερ οὖν ἐκτείναμεν   (887–8)

She recognises the inevitable parallelism of action and the reversal
of standards of Orestes' πειθὼ δολίαν: she, too, has been tricked.

> δοίη τις ἀνδροκμῆτα πέλεκυν ὡς τάχος·
> εἰδῶμεν εἰ νικῶμεν ἢ νικώμεθα   (889–90)

ἀνδροκμῆτα, 'man-slaying', points to the specific aim of her
weapon, the opposition of the sexes, and νικῶμεν/νικώμεθα marks
the nature of the opposition itself, the win-or-lose battle for victory.

> ἐνταῦθα γὰρ δὴ τοῦδ' ἀφικόμην κακοῦ   (891)

Thus she marks the failure of her projected restraint from κακά, her hope for a controlled end to troubles, expressed at *Aga.* 1654ff. (referred to here by Conington). The recognition of the pattern of bloodshed arises, the force of τοῦδε κακοῦ leading her into opposition with her son.

Orestes says:

> σὲ καὶ ματεύω τῷδε δ᾽ ἀρκούντως ἔχει   (892)

ματεύω, 'properly of hounds' (L.-S.-J.; cf. *Aga.* 1093 ματεύει φόνον – a significant echo here as prelude to the next act of bloodshed?), is a further image of the 'hunt', which, as Vidal-Naquet points out,[145] is an important part of the double character of Orestes (as initiand): the μάχη is not that of the hoplite but of the hunter.

Clytemnestra reacts to the death of Aegisthus:

> οἲ 'γὼ τέθνηκας, φίλτατ᾽ Αἰγίσθου βία   (893)

and her expression φίλτατ᾽ prompts

> φιλεῖς τὸν ἄνδρα; τοιγὰρ ἐν ταὐτῷ τάφῳ
> κείσῃ   (894–5)

As we have argued above, it is the corruption of the bond of φιλεῖν, the wrong object for φιλεῖν in her adultery that has caused the danger for the *oikos*. Despite the definite article, the openness of the object τὸν ἄνδρα, 'the man', 'the mate', which could suggest both husband and paramour (cf. *Aga.* 856), implies both the adulterous relationship and the broken bond with her husband: this hint is also seen in

> ..θανόντα δ᾽ οὔτι μὴ προδῷς ποτε   (895)

'You will never prove false to the/a dead man' – both the irony of the suggested fidelity (of the grave) to a man to whom none is morally due (and in death to whom none is possible) and a reminiscence of her lack of fidelity to the other dead man, Agamemnon.

Clytemnestra pleads with him to show restraint:

> ἐπίσχες, ὦ παῖ, τόνδε δ᾽ αἴδεσαι, τέκνον,
> μαστόν. πρὸς ᾧ σὺ πολλὰ δὴ βρίζων ἅμα
> οὔλοισιν ἐξήμελξας εὐτραφὲς γάλα   (896–8)

The double vocative παῖ...τέκνον stresses the (over-determined?) nature of the relationship between mother and son: παῖ, 'child', but τέκνον (placed between αἴδεσαι and μαστόν) marks the relation of τίκτειν – and εὐτραφές the role of τροφεύς/τρέφειν. How does the 'mother' relate to the child? αἴδεσαι, which will be picked up by Orestes' question Πυλάδη τί δράσω; μητέρ᾽ αἰδεσθῶ κτανεῖν; is an important term. Benveniste writes

---

[145] Vernant and Vidal-Naquet 1972, pp. 135–58.

φίλος τε αἰδοῖός τε...αἰδώς καὶ φιλότης...αἰδεῖσθαι καὶ φιλεῖν montrent, de toute évidence, une connexion étroite. Même à s'en tenir aux définitions reçues, aidós 'respect, révérence' à l'égard de sa propre conscience et vis-à-vis des membres d'une même famille, associé à phílos, témoigne que les deux notions étaient également institutionelles et qu'elles indiquent des sentiments propres aux membres d'un groupement étroit...aidós éclaire le sens propre de phílos: tous deux désignent en somme des relations de même type.[146]

So Clytemnestra's claim for αἰδώς[147] is also a claim to be a *philos* to Orestes, and Orestes' question, μητέρ' αἰδεσθῶ; particularly with his first highly emotive use of the term μητέρ' (after παῖ...τέκνον... μαστόν...εὐτραφές), is placed within the problematic of φίλος/ ἐχθρός: is it possible *not* to declare the mother–son relation φίλος τε αἰδοῖός τε? Hence the force of Pylades' only speech which, coming from one we have considered up till now a κῶφον πρόσωπον, as Kitto notes,[148] 'has the effect of a thunderclap'.

> ποῦ δαὶ τὸ λοιπὸν Λοξίου μαντεύματα
> τὰ πυθόχρηστα, πιστά τ' εὐορκώματα;
> ἅπαντας ἐχθροὺς τῶν θεῶν ἡγοῦ πλέον   (900–2)

If he respects his mother, he must reject Apollo's oracles, the 'faithful pledges'. But, regard all as ἐχθρούς rather than the gods; that is, within the dialectic of φίλος/ἐχθρός the gods must take priority over the human relationship; a hierarchisation of φίλοι. This sense of *opposition* between following Apollo's words and respecting the normal bonds of society, is seen in Orestes' reply: κρίνω σε νικᾶν (903): νικᾶν has the sense, as with νίκη (868) and νικῶμεν/νικώμεθα (890), of choice between two mutually exclusive possibilities, a μάχη. But Electra had prayed to the gods, with regard to such an opposition (Δίκᾳ Δίκα, 461) κραίνετ' ἐνδίκως (462): κραίνετ'/κρίνω σε νικ- / ἐν-δικ-. The pun, the transposition of letters again, as at 149, seems important: for it is the relation between νίκη and (the here unmentioned) δίκη that constitutes the ambiguity of Orestes' actions. The play σε νικ- / ἐνδικ- marks the avoidance (and thus emphasis) of the problematic of δίκη.

This further reason is given by Orestes:

> καὶ ζῶντα γάρ νιν κρείσσον' ἡγήσω πατρός.
> τούτῳ θανοῦσα ξυγκάθευδ', ἐπεὶ φιλεῖς
> τὸν ἄνδρα τοῦτον, ὃν δὲ χρῆν φιλεῖν στυγεῖς   (905–7)

After the ordering of ἐχθροί, it is the correct definition of the object

---

[146] 1969, Vol. I, pp. 340–1.
[147] She had called Agamemnon τὸν αἰδοῖον πόσιν (*Aga.* 600). Cf. also *Cho.* 106–8.
[148] 1961, p. 86.

of φιλεῖν, specifically in the sexual context of marriage (ξυγκάθευδ'), the failure to follow the correct hierarchisation of respect (νιν κρείσσον' ἡγήσω πατρός) that leads to her punishment.

Clytemnestra recalls her relation to Orestes, ἐγώ σ' ἔθρεψα (which looks forward to Apollo's argument, *Eum.* 659), with a reference also to the standard parental hope σὺν δὲ γηράναι θέλω, quite out of place here, as Orestes notes, reminding her of her crime:

πατροκτονοῦσα γὰρ ξυνοικήσεις ἐμοί; (909)

The killing of Agamemnon places Clytemnestra outside society: she cannot therefore live[149] in society (as Orestes was threatened with excommunication from society if he failed in his revenge, 291ff.).

Clytemnestra suggests Moira is partly to blame, παραίτιος, which once again suggests the confusion of any single pattern of causality; her argument is manipulated against her (as she had manipulated Agamemnon's words against him in the earlier confrontation):

καὶ τόνδε τοίνυν Μοῖρ' ἐπόρσυνεν μόρον (911)

Clytemnestra appeals to σέβας as a restraint (912), which we have seen as an expression of respect in the hierarchy of society, the relation to the δεσπότης, here applied to the parental authority γενεθλίους...τέκνον. Orestes rejects this appeal on the grounds that having given birth (τεκοῦσα picking up τέκνον) she then cast him out. Clytemnestra denies this, since it was to ξένους that he was sent: again, the almost ironic appeal to the status of ξενία from Clytemnestra who has transgressed such ties, to Orestes who is about to. Her appeal is rejected because he was *sold* (the economic imagery looking back to the *kommos*, the motivations of Orestes, 301, etc.), despite being the true son of a free father: ἐλευθερίου expresses his societal status,[150] which is lost by the loss of his position in the *oikos*. And the price for that selling he is ashamed to mention.[151] Clytemnestra attacks him for 'double standards':

μὴ ἀλλ' εἴφ' ὁμοίως καὶ πατρὸς τοῦ σοῦ μάτας (918)

Orestes demands a recognition of the difference of male and female roles – for the male, work outside the house, in this case warfare, and

---

[149] ξυνοικήσεις is a word used commonly of wedlock or cohabitation in a sexual sense, which leads some psychoanalytic critics to suggest a sense of sexual rivalry between Orestes and Agamemnon (within the Oedipal triad), which they claim finds subconscious recognition in the term πατροκτονοῦσα (since Clytemnestra did not kill a father but a husband). Cf. Green 1975 on the matricide, n. 17 above.

[150] Cf. Benveniste 1969, Vol. I, pp. 321–33 on the social sense of freedom.

[151] Psychoanalytic critics have made much of this unwillingness to mention his mother's sexuality. The rhetorical *recusatio*, however, emphasises it quite as much, if in a different way, as a direct statement.

for the female, being inside the house: γυναιξὶν ἀνδρός picked up
by ἀνδρὸς...ἡμένας (921) points to the sexual differential:

ἄλγος γυναιξὶν ἀνδρὸς εἴργεσθαι, τέκνον   (920)

Women–man–child: the generational conflict; the sexual conflict.

τρέφει δέ γ᾽ ἀνδρὸς μόχθος ἡμένας ἔσω   (921)

Man, too, has a role in τρέφει – that which was asserted by Clytemnestra (and the nurse) is seen also as a function of man's work.

κτενεῖν ἔοικας, ὦ τέκνον, τὴν μητέρα   (922)

The rhetorical juxtaposition of τέκνον and the emotive term μητέρα
is rejected by Orestes (another dis-covering of a sense of agency):

σύ τοι σεαυτήν, οὐκ ἐγώ, κατακτενεῖς   (923)

Her death as outcome of her own action: φιλεῖ τίκτειν ὕβρις (*Aga.*
763). Clytemnestra warns Orestes of μητρὸς ἐγκότους κύνας (924);
he places in opposition those of the father, τὰς τοῦ πατρός (925):
male against female, father against mother.

Clytemnestra says:

ἔοικα θρηνεῖν 3ῶσα πρὸς τύμβον μάτην   (926)

This is not just the proverb, as quoted by the scholion, but applied
to Orestes: τύμβον, one who does not hear; Orestes, however, seems
to take this[152] as a reference to her libations for Agamemnon, again
manipulating her words against her cledonomantically:

πατρὸς γὰρ αἶσα τόνδε σούρί3ει μόρον   (927)

'Yes, for the fate of my father marks out this doom for you.' He
further argues the parallelisation of events as a form of causality.
Clytemnestra realises the force of her dream:

οἲ 'γώ. τεκοῦσα τόνδ᾽ ὄφιν ἐθρεψάμην·
ἦ κάρτα μάντις οὐξ ὀνειράτων φόβος   (928–9)

The force of the emphatic τόνδ᾽, as Tucker notes, is hard to construe
with certainty; he suggests '(1) This was the serpent I bore and
brought up. (2) Having borne *this* (child) I brought up a snake; or
(3) Having borne *this* as my serpent I brought him up.' The
association of Orestes and the snake is closely intercoiled (ἐκδρακοντωθεὶς ἐγώ) as marked by τεκοῦσα/ἐθρεψάμην, which are
applicable both to Orestes himself and to the snake in the dream
text – the difficulty again of defining a level of referentiality, the
distinction between metaphor and non-metaphor in the text. Her
φόβος/μάντις express the prediction of narrative (and here the
recognition of the fulfilment of that prediction); and this passage from

---

[152] Surprisingly, the standard reading of this line does not link the shift in sense between
τύμβον and πατρὸς γάρ to the failed offerings of Clytemnestra at the τύμβον πατρός.

present to future is here again connected with τίκτειν/τρέφειν as expressions of causality, the link between events in narrative.

The double-bind, the sense of the reversal of standards to uphold standards is seen in Orestes' climactic words before his and his mother's exit, which emphasise in a striking manner the reciprocity *and* transgression:

ἔκανες ὃν οὐ χρῆν, καὶ τὸ μὴ χρεὼν πάθε   (930)

'You killed whom you ought not, suffer also what you ought not.' This sense of double-bind is picked up by the chorus:

στένω μὲν οὖν καὶ τῶνδε συμφορὰν διπλῆν   (931)

συμφοράν, as we saw at *Aga.* 18 (also with στένω(ν)), *Aga.* 24, and *Aga.* 325 (also with διπλῆς), can indicate both good and bad fortune; it is διπλῆν, 'double': it implies not only, then, the two disasters (i.e. the death of Aegisthus and Clytemnestra) but also the sense of good fortune in Orestes' return to the *oikos* and bad fortune in his matricide; even the good fortune of Orestes and Electra, the bad fortunes of Clytemnestra and Aegisthus; the good fortune of Orestes, the bad fortune of Clytemnestra. As before, then, διπλῆν suggests the various doublings, parallels, of the narrative of reversal and revenge. So, too, the lack of specificity for the specifying deictic τῶνδε opens itself to the plurality of repetitions and doublings. The πολλῶν αἱμάτων, indeed, of which, the chorus assert, Orestes has 'reached a peak': but this συμφορά is subsumed to the safety of the *oikos* (933–4). At this moment of apparent personal, emotional anguish, the mother–son conflict is seen by the chorus within the context of the *oikos*.

This immensely dramatic dialogue, then, before the murder of Clytemnestra shows the continuing development of many of the terms of familial and social relations which have been major referents of the discourse φίλος/ἐχθρός, τίκτειν/τρέφειν, πατήρ/μήτηρ, δίκη/νίκη, οἶκος, αἰδώς, σέβας, ἀνήρ/γυνή – towards the definition and justification of matricide. The interplay of terms which constitute the dramatic action, the opposition of Orestes' and Clytemnestra's language, form a dialectic which constitutes the drama: it is 'the theatre of language'.[153]

Slices (raw and cooked) from Homer's banquet

The focus on the murder of Clytemnestra and on the agency of Clytemnestra in the regicide shows a considerable departure from the

---

[153] M. Lynn-George's phrase, privately communicated.

Homeric tale of Orestes. Indeed, apart from an isolated reference in Pindar, Aeschylus' contemporary, there is no mention of Clytemnestra as the prime plotter and none of her being the sole murderer of Agamemnon and prime object of revenge before the *Oresteia*.[154] The relation of the *Oresteia* to the *Odyssey*[155] is, therefore, of considerable interest. Indeed, the story of an Oresteia is told nine times in the first twelve books of the *Odyssey*,[156] and, as has been often noted, stands as an exemplary model to the actions of Telemachus and his relation to Odysseus, Penelope, and the *oikos*: the interplay of this exemplum (a constitutive part of the discourse) and the network of Telemachus' actions and Odysseus' travels and return is extremely complex, and what I am going to say here will by its generality (and pace) remain necessarily open to the charges of reductionism, over-simplification, of a dangerously formalistic structure; for all its specificity yet unable to describe, delimit the discourse: but despite this recognition of some of the problems of such a truncated reading of the *Odyssey* that is to be offered, there is a need to point towards some factors in the discourse of the *Odyssey* and for some consideration of its structuring, not only because of the exemplary role of Homer in the literary discourse of Greek literature in general, and in this play in particular, as marked by the numerous echoes we have been noting above (which helps justify the historical contraction, the genealogy, linearity of discourse and text), but also because it is in this *transposition* of the one system of signs into the other that is constituted the textual system of the *Oresteia*.

As Segal writes, the *nostos* of Odysseus is 'a return to humanity in its broadest sense';[157] it involves not simply a coming back from the war but a reintegration into society and a redefining of his role in society in general. This is seen by Segal in numerous ways: a defining both positive and negative mediated by a series of liminal images connected to transitions depicted in ritualistic terms: the world of myth (Odysseus' travels) contrasting[158] with the human

---

[154] *Pyth.* 11.17–22, written twenty years earlier in 478 B.C. Cf. also Hesiod (OCT fragment 23a) which contrasts ἀπε[τείσατο π]ατροφονῆα with κτεῖνε δὲ μητέρα (29–30), which, although it mentions the matricide, makes Aegisthus the killer of Agamemnon.

[155] Only a passing mention of Orestes in the *Iliad*.

[156] 1.30ff., 1.298ff., 3.193ff., 3.254ff., 3.303.ff., 4.91ff., 4.545ff., 11.421ff., 11.461ff., Cf. also 24.193ff.   [157] 1962b, p. 20.

[158] The status of these oppositions is a point of difficulty in Segal and Vidal-Naquet. There is the difficulty of the terms 'nature' and 'culture' – which are the general structuring terms of their arguments – as has been questioned by MacCormack 1980c, Strathern 1980, Jordanova 1980, Bloch and Bloch 1980, Gillison 1980 – and indeed by Ortner 1975 and E. Ardener 1975a and b, and problematised by Lévi-Strauss himself, in whose later work the opposition seems to appear as a methodological tool, rather than an organising structure of the human mind. How does the world of

world defining the *condition humaine*, the corrupt world of the suitors contrasting with the world of Nestor and Menelaus; the transition through the world of the Phaeacians (cf. Segal 1962b, 1967), and then through Odysseus' role as the beggar (see below and Segal 1967). For example: the definition of the role of sacrifice and the growing of food, as expounded by Vidal-Naquet (1970b). On his travels Odysseus meets no other human beings, so often described by the adjective 'bread-eating' – which presupposes agriculture. We have instead, e.g., the Lotus-eaters (vegetables), the Sirens (rotten flesh), the Cyclops (raw human flesh – a travesty of hunting), the Laestrygonians (raw human flesh – a travesty of fishing). These encounters are depicted first often in 'human' terms (i.e. terms applied normally in human society, the *oikos*, as seen in the later books and the Telemachy), then overturned: cf. 10.103ff. where the meeting of the girl by the well is turned finally to a travesty, a parody of fishing, a rejection of *xenia*: the interpenetration of languages defining non-society and society confusing the boundaries that Vidal-Naquet and Segal are trying to draw. There is no sign of human work (οὔτε βοῶν οὔτ' ἀνδρῶν φαίνεται ἔργα, 10.98), no cultivation (cf. 9.108–150). In Phaeacia, however, Odysseus on his return to land (after the flux of the sea)[159] shelters under a joint tree of wild and cultivated olive (5.477), marking the moment of transition. The Phaeacians are *hommes parmi les hommes*[160] but there is a magic garden there which does not know the seasons (7.112ff.) and which stands in contrast to the garden of Laertes (24.223ff.). When Odysseus arrives in Phaeacia it is 'as the lion' (that is a wild animal ὀρεσίτροφος, 'brought up, nourished in the mountains'); when he leaves, however, it is as 'a worker tired from toil', the ploughman whose 'oxen have toiled all

Odysseus' travel coincide with our term 'nature'? In what sense can we read transformation between this world of 'nature' and that of Ithacan society as 'culture', except in the physical journey of Odysseus? The journey is, after all, a *nostos*, a return: the sense of oscillation between Odysseus away and the world of Ithaca is important: for the possibility of a secure antithesis between two plenitudes, 'nature' and 'culture', is put at risk by the constant transgressions, the dialectic, the process of construction of meaning in difference, as well as by the interpenetration of vocabularies (worlds) in the text. For example, in the Cyclops passages, we see not merely an opposition of 'culture' and 'nature'. For as much as the Cyclops rejects *xenia*, so does Odysseus have no name, blind his host, lie to his host, which places him on the limen between 'nature' and 'culture', asserting the values of society by transgressing them, breaking down the antithesis. So, then, in following Segal's and Vidal-Naquet's arguments here, it must be with the recognition of their *reading* of nature and culture (not as absolute terms) and with the recognition of the shifting of the antithesis, opposition: the interplay of the system of differences is not simply reducible to an opposition of 'nature' and 'culture'.

[159] Note the need to wash off the brine and put on olive oil (6.128–22). Olive is a standard of culture: olive is used to blind the Cyclops; Odysseus' bed is made around an olive.

[160] Vidal-Naquet 1970b, p. 1292.

day' (13.31ff.). When Odysseus returns to Ithaca and society first it
is to the herdsman's hut, and finally to his father's farm where
Laertes himself is seen working in the fields (24.277ff.). A series or
system of oppositions may be read, then. On the one hand, we see
no work in the fields, no agriculture with its resultant eating of raw
flesh (Cyclops, Laestrygonians – placed parallel to each other explicitly, 10.199–200), or rotten flesh (Sirens), or the plants that lose
the essential human quality of memory (Lotophagoi), or Circe's
drugs, which turn sailors into wild animals and force them to eat
berries, the food of wild animals. These scenes are set in a landscape
described as uncultivated, uncontrolled by man – as wild. On the
other hand, we see the world of Ithaca, Pylos, Sparta, the growing
of crops, herding of animals, society. The human subject is constructed in a series of differences, with regard to his objects of labour;
his position with regard to the savage world of no cultivation, and
anthropophagy (a reversal of the golden age – also without the need
for cultivation); and with regard to the divine world of the gods, who
also do not need cultivation, but who eat ambrosia and nectar:
'L'inhumanité s'y présente à la fois sous la forme de la divinité et
de l'animalité'[161] This pattern is closely connected with sacrifice, a
rite expressing relations of man to the divine and the natural world:
in the Cyclops' cave, it is the guests that sacrifice and not the host;
when the sailors sacrifice the forbidden oxen of the sun, they use oak
leaves, instead of barley groats, the product of agriculture; and water
instead of wine, similarly the replacement of a human product with
a non-produced object: the result is a corrupted sacrifice. The
Phaeacians sacrifice, but the gods are present and visible at the meal
(7.199ff.) – normal sacrifice systematises men and gods; here they
become confused. The suitors significantly are never shown
sacrificing[162] merely slaughtering and feasting. In Pylos and Sparta,
however (which passages precede the examples above in the narrative
through the embedding of the Telemachy) the sacrifices are shown
differently: they use grain and wine, the families are present, guests
made especially welcome, expressions made of their relations to the
gods. These pictures of the 'ordered society' stand before the story
of Odysseus' travels and the future sacrifices are defined in their
relation, their differences, to these rituals (and each other); 'le
sacrifice joue deux fois dans l'*Odyssée* un rôle de critère: entre les
humains et les non-humains, il est critère d'humanité; entre les

---

[161] Ibid. p. 1287.
[162] Despite a reference to a man who led their sacrifices: the absence of the host points
to the corrupt nature of the rites.

humains il est un critère social et moral'.[163] Both these series of relations seem to aim at the constitution in difference of a (relational) model of the subject, of 'human life', of a domesticity of society in relation both to a savagery of the world of Odysseus' travels, and to a beatitude of divinity. This is further seen in an important way (not dealt with by Segal or Vidal-Naquet in any depth, despite its importance), the defining of a sexual object: for it is not by chance that in the Underworld, whereas Aeneas sees the future of Rome, Odysseus observes a procession of women. For Odysseus' travels and sexual adventures function in the same way as a transgression *and* defining of the role of sexuality in society and in the *oikos*. Aeolus, for example, in his floating island (10.1ff.) of Aeolia, married his sons to his daughters, an inward-looking (non-exogamous) non-*oikos* (which is surrounded by a wall of bronze), whose separateness from society is marked by the floating of the island, its sitelessness. In an otherwise perfect community, beloved of the gods, continually feasting on a never-failing store of food, for which they need not work, the incest of the family differentiates them from the human society (as an ideal). Circe, who was often allegorised in earlier readings of the *Odyssey* as a figure symbolising bodily lusts, also lives secluded from the human race in a forest, unmarried yet sexually active. She is mentioned explicitly as a *sexual* threat: not just to Odysseus who is warned that she will 'rob him of his manhood' when he is naked, unless he first extracts a solemn oath (by threatening her with his powerful sword), but even after this the threat remains also to the *oikos*: Odysseus may forget his longing

σαωθῆναι καὶ ἱκέσθαι

<u>οἶκον</u> ἐϋκτίμενον καὶ σὴν ἐς <u>πατρίδα</u> γαῖαν   (10.473–4)

Indeed, his companions have to upbraid Odysseus for forgetting his *nostos* in Circe's company. This relation of unrestricted sexuality is a danger to the constitution of the *oikos*, to the land of the fathers – the inherent sense of continuity denied to his relation with Circe.

With Calypso, where he is first depicted in the *Odyssey*, Odysseus stays seven years; it is the condition from which he must return: Calypso, although she lives in a place

ἔνθα κ' ἔπειτα καὶ ἀθάνατός περ ἐπελθὼν

θηήσαιτο ἰδὼν καὶ τερφθείη φρεσὶν ᾗσιν   (5.73–4)

she inhabits a cave: it is the habitation of the wild; it is, as Hermes says, as far as possible from any human city (5.100ff.). Yet it offers

---

[163] Vidal-Naquet 1970b, p. 1291. The criterion is not an absolute, but a structured opposition, a system, network of differences.

certain signs of domesticity: indeed Odysseus compares Calypso
directly to Penelope (5.215ff.), which gains especial significance from
the fact that by the placing of the Telemachy between the announcement (1.57ff.) and the description (5.1ff.) of Odysseus' circumstances,
the world of Ithaca (without its leader) is juxtaposed with the position
of Odysseus with Calypso. Calypso's sexuality stands to confuse the
relation of mortal and divine (note the need for different food,
5.197ff.); it is a domesticity which is the negative of human life on
Ithaca: no work, no household, no πατήρ, no children, despite the
length of time spent living together. It is not aiming at the generational
continuity of an *oikos* through the procreation of children but at
immortality (5.135–6), the separation from, and denial of, that which
constitutes society, the intergenerational continuity marked by the
Telemachy and the Orestes story with which the Calypso story is
intertwined. With Calypso, Odysseus is societyless.

Significantly, Odysseus' relation to Nausikaa (in what Segal terms
the 'transitional world' of Phaeacia) is characterised in terms of
possible marriage (the sexual tie recognised by society – though the
emphasised role of the mother may mark the separateness of
Phaeacia),[164] and also in terms of a fear of appearing to have an illicit
object of desire:

'ἥρως, μή μοι τοὔνεκ' ἀμύμονα νείκεε κούρην.
ἡ μὲν γάρ μ' ἐκέλευε σὺν ἀμφιπόλοισιν ἕπεσθαι
ἀλλ' ἐγὼ οὐκ ἔθελον δείσας αἰσχυνόμενός τε,
μή πως καὶ σοὶ θυμὸς ἐπισκύσσαιτο ἰδόντι.
δύσζηλοι γάρ τ' εἰμὲν ἐπὶ χθονὶ φῦλ' ἀνθρώπων.'
   Τὸν δ' αὖτ' Ἀλκίνοος ἀπαμείβετο φώνησέν τε.
'ξεῖν', οὔ μοι τοιοῦτον ἐνὶ στήθεσσι φίλον κῆρ
μαψιδίως κεχολῶσθαι. ἀμείνω δ' αἴσιμα πάντα.
αἲ γάρ, Ζεῦ τε πάτερ καὶ Ἀθηναίη καὶ Ἄπολλον,
τοῖος ἐὼν οἷός ἐσσι, τά τε φρονέων ἅ τ' ἐγώ περ,
παῖδά τ' ἐμὴν ἐχέμεν καὶ ἐμὸς γαμβρὸς καλέεσθαι
αὖθι μένων. οἶκον δέ κ' ἐγὼ καὶ κτήματα δοίην'   (7.303–14)

Odysseus is afraid to be seen with the maid because of the jealousy
of the human race in such matters; Alkinoos explicitly agrees (τά τε
φρονέων ἅ τ' ἐγώ περ) and sets in opposition to the jealous anger
of the implied sexual licence the system of marriage: to have Nausikaa
(ἐχέμεν), to fit into the system of naming, καλέεσθαι (society's
defining), as a γαμβρός – he would give Odysseus an *oikos* and
possessions. Odysseus rejoices (γήθησεν, 329) at Alkinoos' speech
but chooses to return to his homeland: ἐγὼ δέ κε πατρίδ' ἱκοίμην

---

[164] A point which has been made much of by some critics, cf. Pomeroy 1975b.

(333) – πατρίδα again with its implication of *pater* stresses the continuation of the *oikos*; it is his 'birthright', the law of succession that is to be upheld, as opposed to the *gift* of Nausikaa, with its subordinating effect, its inversion of patrilocal *exchange* of women. Odysseus desires the return to the house of his fathers, not merely (what was denied him – differently – by Calypso and Circe) an *oikos*.[165]

Penelope the wife at home is pursued by suitors; her choice (cf. above pp. 74–5) throughout her long separation (the model of Penelope stands as a contrast to Clytemnestra at *Cho.* 920) is between upholding the structure of marriage, of protecting the κτῆσιν, δμῳάς, δόμον, εὐνήν (cf. 19.524ff.) or of following one of the suitors: this choice is placed in terms of the continuity of the *oikos* (dependent on the age of the male heir, 19.530ff.). This passage (cf. also 21.113–17 discussed below) is followed by Penelope's dream and her decision to test the suitors through the trial of the bow; and by Odysseus seeing the maidservants and suitors sleeping together (which indiscriminate extra-marital sexuality will be punished by death); by the insulting of the beggar who sits (as Segal notes) on the threshold (liminal status), who has the role of a man without *oikos* (sitelessness). (The interplay of liminality and sitelessness marks the continuing transgressions of Odysseus' reassertion of role.) The juxtaposition of this expression of the choice of Penelope to the sexuality (opposed to her chastity) of the maidservants, and the failure of the suitors to pass the test of the bow is significant: for the bow has (as well as the 'Freudian' overtones (undertones?) of shooting arrows through holes to assert the power of having the woman) the associations of the 'ordered society' – Odysseus obtained it from ξείνοιο φίλοιο (21.40, a criterion of society) and used it only on his own land, ἧς ἐπὶ γαίης (21.41) – sited instead of wandering. 'The bow belongs with the maturity and authority of the prince in a settled community.'[166] To assert the authority of the lord, the father, is to string the bow: Telemachus says:

καὶ δέ κεν αὐτὸς ἐγὼ τοῦ τόξου πειρησαίμην·
εἰ δέ κεν ἐντανύσω διοϊστεύσω τε σιδήρου,
οὔ κέ μοι ἀχνυμένῳ τάδε δώματα πότνια μήτηρ
λείποι ἅμ' ἄλλῳ ἰοῦσ', ὅτ' ἐγὼ κατόπισθε λιποίμην
οἷός τ' ἤδη πατρὸς ἀέθλια κάλ' ἀνελέσθαι   (21.113–17)

---

[165] It must be noted that Alkinoos and Arete are uncle and niece as well as husband and wife (7.54ff.). This incest marks the closeness of the Phaeacians to the gods (as it does with Aeolus). Incest, the denial of the exchange of marriage into a closed circle of family relations, seems connected to the immortality, the fixedness of the gods.

[166] Segal 1962b, p. 50.

If he can handle the bow successfully, his mother may leave without regret since he 'will be left behind, capable of using his father's weapons / winning his father's prizes'. Or, as Merry[167] takes it, 'but should I string the bow,... my lady mother need not then, to my deep sorrow, leave this house, going her way with some other lord, so long as I remain behind, man enough even now to win these splendid prizes of my sire'. The ambiguity of possession and rejection of the mother is seen also in the ambiguity of πατρὸς ἀέθλια, since Penelope is both the prize in question (open to Telemachus) and 'of the father' (closed to Telemachus – a *possessive* genitive). Telemachus goes to the *threshold*, ἐπ' οὐδόν (21.124) to try the bow:

> τρὶς μέν μιν πελέμιξεν ἐρύσσασθαι μενεαίνων
> τρὶς δὲ μεθῆκε βίης, ἐπιελπόμενος τό γε θυμῷ,
> νευρὴν ἐντανύειν διοϊστεύσειν τε σιδήρου.
> καί νύ κε δή ῥ' ἐτάνυσσε βίῃ τὸ τέταρτον ἀνέλκων,
> ἀλλ' Ὀδυσεὺς ἀνένευε καὶ ἔσχεθεν ἱέμενόν περ   (21.125–9)

Telemachus demonstrates finally that he has the power to handle the bow of his father, but this power is restrained by the authority (ἀνένευε – 'nodding' / 'nodding against' – the gesture of the ruler, particularly Zeus) of the father. Indeed shortly afterwards Telemachus asserts himself as master of the house, the man with κράτος:

> τόξον δ' ἄνδρεσσι μελήσει
> πᾶσι μάλιστα δ' ἐμοί. τοῦ γὰρ κράτος ἔστ' ἐνὶ οἴκῳ (21.352–3)

κράτος/οἶκος: the connection we have traced also in the *Oresteia*. This authority is over his mother, whom he orders to her room: the change from the first person ἐμοί, however, to the third person τοῦ, particularly with the disguised Odysseus in the hall, marks the ambiguity of the son – whose authority is it?

Odysseus can string the bow, and does, and from the threshold shoots the arrows successfully through the shafts. His reassertion of authority, as Segal (1966) proposes, shows certain similarities with a generalised pattern of rituals of a man presumed dead returning home, as outlined first by van Gennep.[168] Certainly, in the recurring motif of the bath (for example, the ritual interrupted by Eurykleia dropping the basin, which leads to the recounting of the earliest time of Odysseus and his naming;[169] the ritual which is completed by the bath of purification after the slaughter of the suitors), we may read a structured model of transitions, similar to that of sleep (both dangerous – cf. the loss of the winds of Aeolus – and restorative,

---

[167] *The Odyssey* (Oxford, 1878) ad loc.   [168] Cf. n. 100, n. 123, above.
[169] N. Austin 1972 discusses the important theme of the naming of Odysseus. Such a focus on naming with regard to society and the *oikos* also anticipates the *Oresteia* in an important way.

pleasant); both such sleep and cleansing are common motifs in the rituals of *rites de passage*. This realignment, readoption into the *oikos*, the defining of Odysseus' role, stand parallel to the Telemachy: Telemachus, the adolescent, who also leaves home, is threatened with death, learns to speak in the men's council, returns (a *petit* νόστος) to assert his male authority in the house (even over his mother): he, too, is in the process of defining his role in the *oikos*, in society: Odysseus and Telemachus are placed parallel, father and son. Generational continuity, however, is associated with generational conflict; the authority of the father opposing the growing awareness of the son of his own potency which is not commensurate with his position of inferior standing in the hierarchy of the *oikos*: for Freud – and Lacan – this is an essential model of human growth in the Oedipal triad; for Barthes a paradigm of narratives.

In the *Odyssey* this narrative of Telemachus, Penelope and Odysseus is placed in explicit, interwoven juxtaposition to the model of Orestes, Clytemnestra, and Agamemnon. Clytemnestra takes the course opposite to that of Penelope: her resistance is broken down by the seducer, suitor, Aegisthus. Orestes returns to gain fame: he kills Aegisthus and regains the possession of the *oikos*. Interestingly, there is no mention of the slaying of Clytemnestra – merely an added reference to her funeral:

ἦ τοι ὁ τὸν κτείνας δαίνυ τάφον Ἀργείοισι
μητρός τε στυγερῆς καὶ ἀνάλκιδος Αἰγίσθοιο   (3.309–10)

The specificity of the masculine singular τόν as object of κτείνας, followed by the two genitive phrases, seems deliberately to avoid mention of her manner of death, and Orestes as an agent of it. Here, the submission of the mother to a figure of sexual licence (the parallels between the suitors and Aegisthus have been long noted) results in the overturning of the continuity of power, a transgression of the passing down of authority from father to son. The action of Orestes is to reassert his authority in the *oikos*, when he comes of age, by killing the male usurper. In terms of generational continuity, then, the continuity obtains by the destruction of the older generation, made necessary by its sexual licence, leaving the son in sole (and glorious) control of the *oikos*. This model is held up to Telemachus:

ἦ οὐκ ἀΐεις οἷον κλέος ἔλλαβε δῖος Ὀρέστης
πάντας ἐπ' ἀνθρώπους, ἐπεὶ ἔκτανε πατροφονῆα
Αἴγισθον δολόμητιν, ὅ οἱ πατέρα κλυτὸν ἔκτα;
καὶ σύ, φίλος – μάλα γάρ σ' ὁρόω καλόν τε μέγαν τε –
ἄλκιμος ἔσσ' ἵνα τίς σε καὶ ὀψιγόνων ἐῢ εἴπῃ   (1.298–302)

But how is this model applicable to Telemachus? Is it merely the killing of the suitors? The assertion of the son's right to κράτος? The rejection of the figure of sexual licence, the threat of usurpation? How are these reconcilable with the fact that Odysseus is still alive? How, that is, is a reconciliation of a discrepancy in the potency and authority of the son depicted – a discrepancy which is constituted by the parallelisation of Odysseus' return to the *oikos* and Telemachus' initiation into the *oikos*, both in juxtaposition to Orestes' story? We have already mentioned the willingness of Telemachus to accede to the authority of the father's nod, despite the recognition of his new potency, and his desire (ἱέμενόν περ). Parallel to this willing submission of potent youth to the authority of age is the magic of Athene which makes both figures of the older generation young again:

> ἦ καὶ χρυσείῃ ῥάβδῳ ἐπεμάσσατ᾽ Ἀθήνη.
> φᾶρος μέν οἱ πρῶτον ἐΰπλυνὲς ἠδὲ χιτῶνα
> θῆκ᾽ ἀμφὶ στήθεσσι, δέμας δ᾽ ὤφελλε καὶ ἥβην.
> ἂψ δὲ μελαγχροιὴς γένετο γναθμοὶ δὲ τάνυσθεν
> κυάνεαι δ᾽ ἐγένοντο γενειάδες ἀμφὶ γένειον   (16.172–6)

This rejuvenation (after she had aged him for his disguise) is effected for the recognition scene between Telemachus and Odysseus; the power/potency and authority of Odysseus (both terms suggested by κράτος?) are thereby made equivalent. The former possibility of disjunction between son and father, between father's potency and son's potency in relation to the respective authority of each, is thus partly avoided.

A similar transformation (18.190–6) occurs for Penelope (increasing her potential as ambiguous object of rejection and desire for possession) during a period of sleep (which as Segal mentions, often expresses a sense of transition, 'passage') before she appears to the suitors and Telemachus (and the disguised Odysseus) to hint that she may marry again. And after the slaughter, Odysseus is bathed by Eurynome, and once again Athene beautifies him:

> αὐτὰρ κὰκ κεφαλῆς κάλλος πολὺ χεῦεν Ἀθήνη
> μείζονά τ᾽ εἰσιδέειν καὶ πάσσονα...
> ἐκ δ᾽ ἀσαμίνθου βῆ δέμας ἀθανάτοισιν ὁμοῖος   (23.156–63)

Precisely 'like an immortal in his body'.

So in the discourse of the *Odyssey* the model of Orestes for Telemachus signifies in its differences as in its apparent exemplary similarities. There are set in play differing models of the interrelations of the *oikos*; of the mother as an object of acceptance/rejection; of sexual roles in a family; of the dangers of male usurpers of κράτος; these are all linked with the problem of generational continuity, the reconciliation of potency and authority and the initiation of youth into the world of man. In a wide sense, we are concerned with the defining in this series of differences of the subject in a societal role.

In the *Oresteia*, then, the murder of Agamemnon by Clytemnestra and the concentration on Orestes' revenge on his mother, the queen, change the dynamics of the Homeric narrative in a most marked manner. The imagery of initiation continues; Zeitlin, who follows Vidal-Naquet, argues for these points: the ephebic status of Orestes; his separation from home; his return; his temporarily savage state ('a liminal state as befits his liminal position'[170] – the ambiguities of guilt and innocence also mark this liminality); his banishment in childhood; his return 'at puberty to his home, that space made savage and undomesticated by his mother's action in order to undertake the most savage act of all';[171] the separation (forcible) from his mother – which is followed by 'a second expulsion from the palace...terminated when, reincorporated into society in the third stage of the *rite de passage*, he returns to Argos now as lawful ruler and successor to his father'.[172] To which we may add the vocabulary drawn from the mysteries, a further sort of initiation: ἀπαλλαγὴ πόνων, τελεῖν, ἐποπτεύω, the cutting of the hair. As Zeitlin also notes, developing the arguments of Bamberger, the myth of rejected matriarchy is intimately connected with this structure of initiation, a myth which was set forward in an evolutionary model for the history of all mankind first by J. J. Bachofen, a model which was followed by Marx and Engels (to some degree) and which influenced McLellan, Morgan, and the evolutionists of that period.[173] Zeitlin, following Bamberger, Pembroke, Willets (1959), Vidal-Naquet (1968, 1970a) agrees on a rejection of Bachofen's theories in favour of a discourse whereby this genetic pattern of the myth is seen as a justification, realisation, explanation, of a structure in reality 'giving an invented "historical" explanation of how this reality was created':[174] 'pour la pensée mythique, toute généalogie est en même temps et aussi bien explication d'une structure'[175] – the myth of matriarchy overturned is the expression of patriarchial authority and control. Yet this argument, and indeed the development of the significance of the motif of initiation / *rites de passage*, is not sufficient to the play of the *Oresteia*, and not merely in its failure as a structure to account for, control, describe in its very generality the interplay of signifiers that we have

---

[170] 1978, p. 161.   [171] Ibid.   [172] Ibid.

[173] This material has received much critical attention in the last twenty years. Coward offers a good general introduction. See also G. Harris 1973, Leacock 1981, Detienne 1981, Bamberger 1975, for further general views. We shall return to this material when we consider the political implications of the trial scene of the *Eumenides*.

[174] Bamberger 1975, p. 267.   [175] Vernant 1965, p. 16.

been considering. For even in its own terms this 'narrative structure' signifies through, is constituted by, its relation to the *Odyssey*, through difference, a process of signification which resists the closure, the teleology of such a structure. For the opposition of male and female in the *Oresteia*, the considerably shifted emphasis on the confrontation of Orestes and Clytemnestra, draws their opposition into a series of male–female polarities: we have traced the motivating principles of Zeus and Artemis; we have traced the various oppositions of Agamemnon (constituted as daughter-killer/brother-avenger) and Clytemnestra (as daughter-avenger/husband-killer) and Orestes (as mother-killer/father-avenger); we are to trace the conflict (not only in law) of Apollo and the Erinues, a further divine expression of the conflict. In each case, the male is connected to the valuing of the bonds of society, extra-familial ties and relationships – Zeus Xenios, the ties of *xenia* between houses; Agamemnon valuing the Argive expedition above his daughter; Orestes rejecting the most basic tie of the family to assert his social role; Apollo, the civilising god of state religion. In each case, the female is connected to the valuing of the familial bonds within the *oikos* to the point of the rejection of the ties of society (marriage, law, regards of *xenia*). This results in the developing connection of the male with the values of the *oikos* in relation to a wider society (more than a collection of *oikoi*) and the connection of the female with the overturning of these values, through a valuing of the relations within the family itself. The 'initiation' of Orestes, then, is not so much (though partly) into his role within the *oikos*, of reasserting his κράτος, as also reasserting the role of the *oikos* with regard to the wider society. As the action of Helen led, for society, to 'turmoil on a scale that is virtually cosmic'[176] and resulted in societal action to redress the transgression (the Argive expedition), so Orestes' act of matricide is not only to reorder the disorder of the *oikos*, but also to rediscover the relation of the internal ties of the *oikos* to the wider society of the *polis*. Hence the need for the ratification of his act by a jury from the elders of the whole city. The establishment of this sign system, the transformation of the Odyssean discourse, or rather the establishment of the discourse of the *Oresteia* in relation to that of the *Odyssey* is accompanied, then, by this new articulation of the enunciative position,[177] a new positioning, construction of the

---

[176] Tanner, 1980, p. 27.

[177] Kristeva, whose phrase 'enunciative position' (the position from which the subject speaks) is, uses this term to develop a connection between text and society, which is the aim also of the critics with whom I opened this investigation into the intertextuality of the *Oresteia* and the *Odyssey*. Kristeva writes: 'establishing a sign system calls for the identity of a speaking subject within a social framework which he recognizes as a basis for that identity...countervailing the sign system is done by having the subject

subject. The sexual, political, social, linguistic discourse of the *Odyssey* is essential to the constitution of the text of the *Oresteia*. The fifth-century tragedy is grounded in, as it is sundered from, the epic.

Zeitlin's argument, therefore, under the general term 'misogyny', that the *Oresteia* 'stands as the fullest realisation of an attitude which from its first literary expression in the *Odyssey* is already associated with Clytemnestra',[178] despite the openness of 'fullest realisation', seems insufficient; it does not take account of the production of meaning in difference (as it searches for continuity). The intertextuality of the *Oresteia* and the *Odyssey*, which is so often ignored, is constitutive of the 'dynamics of misogyny' in the *Oresteia*.

'Thus we have seen...'

The ode that follows the exit of mother and son, specifically with regard to the understanding of *dike* and the difficulties of causality and responsibility, retells the events of the trilogy towards finding a patterning of the past which will offer some explanation of the present.

The chorus begin with the revenge visited on Troy: ἔμολε μὲν Δίκα Πριαμίδαις χρόνῳ (935). Δίκα is once again both in the abstract sense of 'Justice' and in the sense of 'retribution' as picked up by βαρύδικος ποινά (936, the sense of reciprocity in ποινά colouring -δικ-). With ἔμολε δέ (937) after ἔμολε μέν (935), the parallelisation of actions is expressed markedly by the syntax, as almost a causal connection. διπλοῦς λέων διπλοῦς Ἄρης, however, which appears through the parallelisation of ἔμολε/ἔμολε to offer a narrative pattern, a recognisable chain of events, is an ambiguous phrase: Conington, Tucker, Lloyd-Jones refer the phrase to Clytemnestra and Aegisthus (cf. the description of Clytemnestra as δίπους λέαινα, *Aga.* 1258, and of Aegisthus as λέοντ' ἄναλκιν, *Aga.* 1224). Sidgwick, however, calls this 'very unlikely' and refers it, with the scholion, to Orestes and

---

undergo an unsettling questioning process; this indirectly challenges the social framework with which he had previously identified and it thus coincides with times of abrupt changes, renewal, or revolution in society' (Kristeva, 'Les traversées des signes', translated and quoted by Roudiez 1980, p. 18). This seems to imply more a question of conditions of possibility than the attempt to ground the text in an external reality of representation: rather a relation of *discourse* and text – 'literary discourse as parody, as a contestation of language rather than a representation of reality...a manipulation of signs that takes the place of an absent reality' (Machery p. 61).

A connection between text and society with regard to the *Oresteia* is spelled out in a somewhat simpler way by the anthropological critics who link this development in discourse from the *Odyssey* to the *Oresteia* to the development of the *polis* from the *oikos*, to the political self-consciousness of the fifth century.

[178] 1978, p. 150.

Pylades. διπλοῦς, however, as we argued before (p. 143), marks the parallelisation of Orestes/Pylades (Electra), Aegisthus/Clytemnestra, the doubling of action, the doubling of doublings. Indeed, διπλοῦς Ἄρης recalls specifically Ἄρης Ἄρει ξυμβαλεῖ. Moreover, in the *Agamemnon*, Troy itself was described as paying διπλᾶ (*Aga.* 537) for their errors, and as struck by the διπλῇ μάστιγι (*Aga.* 642) – to offer two more examples of echoes of 'doubling'.

ἔλασε δ' ἐς seems parallel to ἔμολε δ' ἐς and serves to site Orestes in this series of action and counter-action. It is as ὁ πυθόχρηστος φυγάς, which suggests not only his status before the matricide but also his exile to come, fleeing (as now he hunts – the reversal) from the Erinues.

The chorus raise the cry for the house – for its avoidance of evil from δυοῖν μιαστόροιν, 'a double pollution'. Within the parallelisation of events and the ambiguity of the moral status of Orestes' actions, the phrase is not without irony: does it refer only to Clytemnestra and Aegisthus? Can it avoid the implication of Pylades/Orestes? Such is the logic of the doubling.

ἔμολε δ' (946), the third ἔμολε, constitutes a further parallel for δίκα, διπλοῦς λέων, ὁ φυγάς – now δολιόφρων Ποινά. The adjective δολιόφρων (picking up πειθὼ δολίαν, 726) and the almost oxymoronic nature of κρυπταδίου μάχας (946), 'a clandestine battle', mark the reversal of the face-to-face open fight of the hoplite. κρυπταδίου is a very rare word, used only twice in Homer: once (*Il.* 1.542) by Hera rebuking Zeus, where she calls him also δολομῆτα (540) and says αἰεί τοι φίλον ἐστί... κρυπτάδια φρονέοντα δικαζέμεν (541–2). δολιόφρων seems to pick up this (also δολομῆτα/δολιόφρων, δικαζέμεν/δίκη), suggesting a connection between Zeus and the action made more explicit in the next lines. The second occurrence of the word is as *Il.* 6.161 where, predicated of φιλότητι, it refers to 'clandestine sexual intercourse', 'adultery': κρυπταδίου, then, seems to suggest both the punishment and the crime, the doubleness reflected so often in the text.

In the battle also was the daughter of Zeus, Dike, Διὸς κόρη – δίκαν. This etymological play,[179] as we discussed above pp. 60–2, seems to be searching to control the sliding of the term Δίκα, to fix it by finding a literal origin, a father, in Zeus (the transcendental signified?). But with the opposition of the father to the mother (marked here by ἐν ἐχθροῖς, 952), with the metaphorisation of words connected with childbirth also linked to language (τίκτειν/τρέφειν)

---

[179] ἐτήτυμος, προσαγορεύομεν, τυχόντες καλῶς are words associated with finding the correct form of address, the correct name. Cf. p. 62.

leading towards the definition of paternity, the authority of the logos from the father, even this origin is placed within the problematic: the appeal to paternity, an origin, even (especially?) to the paternity of Zeus, as an attempt to control the discourse, language, inscribes in this metaphorisation of its terminology its own uncertainties.

Apollo is added as a causal agent (ἐπωρθίαξεν, 954–5). The paradox of his instructions is marked by the juxtaposition ἀδόλως δόλια 'deceit undeceitfully' – which recalls the prayed-for πειθὼ δολίαν. χρονισθεῖσα refers back to χρονισθείς (*Aga.* 727), linking Orestes once again with the lion in the house (διπούς λέων?). The justification of following the divine (κρατείτω δέ πως τὸ θεῖον) picked up by ἄξιον οὐρανοῦχον ἀρχὰν σέβειν (960) stresses the hierarchisation of respect (σέβω) put forward by Pylades. It is questioned, however, in its clarity by πως: offered as a fixed cause (a control of narrative) as it is taken away as something certain or clear by the indefinite πως.

The chorus turn to celebrate the house's (οἴκων, 962) revival: the return of imagery of light and sight, τὸ φῶς ἰδεῖν, which looks forward to the final scene of the play (cf. pp. 99ff.). χρονισθεῖσα is now picked up by πολὺν ἄγαν χρόνον (964), παντελὴς χρόνος (965), stressing the sense of generational continuity desired by the house, the temporal span of the narrative, which aims at the *telos* (another causal agent?), παντελής. Their hope for a *telos* here in the purity of the house (916–18) stands as an ironic prelude to the final scene of the play, Orestes' growing madness and pursuit by the Erinues. Does, then, μετοίκοις δόμων recall Cassandra's vision of κῶμος ἐν δόμοις (*Aga.* 1198), as it looks forward to the Erinues' final status as 'metics' (*Eum.* 1011) in the city?

This final antistrophe, then, with its future tenses, looks forward beyond the pattern ἔμολε...ἔμολε...ἔλασε...ἔμολε. The emphasis on change (ἀμείψεται) and chance (τύχᾳ) marks (as so often in the *Agamemnon*) the ending on a note of uncertainty, unfixedness; the inability to look forward with surety (cf. the last chorus of this play). The past may be placed in, read as, a pattern – the present and future remains obscure.

Between the entrance to the house and the outcome of the entrance, then, we see a further passage concerned with narrative itself, with drawing a pattern, which is undercut by its ambiguities and indefinites; concerned with defining causal agents – particularly by the etymological definition, which in its assumption of the questioned paternal metaphor as a model looks back to the problematic definition of τίκτειν/τρέφειν, which involves not only the problem of cause and effect in narrative, but also the particular problem of Orestes' definition of his act of matricide, of the relation of 'child' to 'parent'. This justification comes, then, between the expectation of matricide and the display of the son and the body of his mother.

Seeing and believing

Orestes with the bodies: as we have now seen, his commands ἴδεσθε, ἴδεσθε, ὁρᾶτέ μ', are placed in a series of challenges to the simplicity of the visual mode, the object of sight. The irony now comes into play, that whereas the metaphorisation of vision has played and will play a part in Apollo's discourse of paternity, essential to the defence of Orestes, and has been used by Electra in that strange process of proof of the identity and presence of Orestes, such a rejection of a simple object of sight, what I have termed the radicalisation of the sense of the visual, will constitute through precisely the *sight* of the Erinues also Orestes' madness: the 'final' irony of inversion, of transgression. Seeing is double.

σεμνοί (975), used ironically to express the authority of the usurpers, picks up σέβειν (960), the correct relation; as φίλοι (976), used to express the relation of Clytemnestra and Aegisthus, recalls not only Orestes' rejection of the validity of this relation (906–7), but also the problem of definition of the relation of Clytemnestra to Electra and Orestes in the terminology of φίλος/ἐχθρός – as picked up at 993: φίλον τέως νῦν δ' ἐχθρόν.[180] They have kept faith, he grimly suggests, in dying together.

He displays Clytemnestra's weapons as evidence – to the overseeing sun, called πατήρ (984). This display of the evidence of the weapons is placed by the search for their suitable – and metaphorical – description within the problematic search that we have been reading, the search for the definition of a presence, the presence of a definition beyond (the slidings of) language:

> μαρτυρεῖ δέ μοι
> φᾶρος τόδ' ὡς ἔβαψεν Αἰγίσθου ξίφος.
> φόνου δὲ κηκὶς ξὺν χρόνῳ ξυμβάλλεται
> πολλὰς βαφὰς φθείρουσα τοῦ ποικίλματος.
> νῦν αὐτὸν αἰνῶ, νῦν ἀποιμώζω παρών,
> πατροκτόνον γ' ὕφασμα προσφωνῶν τόδε   (1010–15)

The φᾶρος 'bears witness' (with its assumption of presence as a basis of knowledge) to ὡς ἔβαψεν Αἰγίσθου ξίφος – we may recall the absence of Aegisthus from the murder of Agamemnon. And now Orestes, 'present', παρών, calls upon αὐτόν (referring to which

---

[180] Note the odd rhythm of this line, with such a strong break after the second foot.

masculine singular?), and mourns, 'calling, naming, this cloth...'
(recalling the other ὕφασμα, a different but related proof process)
'...parricide'. It bears witness, yet is called (again a focus on the
predicative quality of language), is *named* precisely that which it is
called on to have witnessed, 'parricide'. This shift from passive
observer to active agent, this over-determination, (particularly after
his emphatic question ἔδρασεν ἢ οὐκ ἔδρασεν; at 1010) challenges,
however, more than a possible simplicity of cause and effect: for not
only is the very presence as the basis of the evidence – implied by
μαρτυρεῖ, explicit in παρών – challenged by this process of naming,
the separation of the signifier and the signified which leaves open the
referential gap; but also, by the play of signifiers, and the explicit
process of naming, the attempt to move to a proof beyond language
is once more grounded *in* language: the *calling* of the woven object
πατροκτόνον marks this proof, the definition of the crime, the
assertion of guilt, as *functions of/in language*, woven into the text of
signifiers. As we saw with the deictics in the recognition scene and
the problem of the δόξαι of the Erinues in the final scene, and as we
saw with the definition of metaphor/reference in the *Agamemnon* and
in this play, we see here both the apparent move through language
to a presence beyond, and the undercutting of that move in the same
gesture: a further search for the fixed point, the delimitation of
definition – a further slippage, however; the de-limitation of
definition.

Orestes likens Clytemnestra to an adder (after ἐκδρακοντωθεὶς
ἐγώ), a snake 'capable of damage':

τόλμης ἕκατι κἀκδίκου φρονήματος;   (996)

τόλμα/φρόνημα, as we saw at 324, 430, 595ff., is the vocabulary of
the cause of her destruction: the wilfulness to transgress the dictates,
the norms, of society; connected to sexual passion; opposed to
σώφρων/σέβειν/αἰδεῖσθαι – a φρόνημα which is ἐκδίκου opposed to
his ἐνδικ- action, 'outside' the boundaries of δίκη.

Orestes needs to find the right word for her, to redefine:

τί νιν προσείπω κἂν τύχω μάλ' εὐστομῶν;   (997)

As Verrall notes, and as Lloyd-Jones (1961) proposes to avoid by
transposing the lines, νιν may also refer to what follows, the
description of Clytemnestra's weapons: the weapons themselves,
used to transgress, also need to be redefined – in the imagery of
hunting. This not only implies an unsuitable death for a king
(1000–2), but also the confusion of that which is outside the house
with the inside, the interpenetration of vocabulary normally kept
separate. Hence τοιάδ' ἐμοὶ ξύνοικος ἐν δόμοισι μὴ γένοιτ' – his

refusal to share his *house* with such a person, a person who has overturned the boundaries defining the house? His prayer that follows, an expression of horror, points once more to the need for continuity in the *oikos* – ὀλοίμην πρόσθεν…ἄπαις (1006): his prayer expresses the possible outcome of the licence of Clytemnestra – the failure of the process of inheritance, the failure of continuity of *oikos*.

The chorus, rather than the expected joy, bewail:

> αἰαῖ αἰαῖ μελέων ἔργων
> στυγερῷ θανάτῳ διεπράχθης
> αἰαῖ αἰαῖ
> μίμνοντι δὲ καὶ πάθος ἀνθεῖ   (1008–9)

The subject of διεπράχθης is uncertain – as indeed are the 'deeds' (ἔργων) to which it refers: is this referring to Clytemnestra (Verrall, Conington, Tucker) expressing the 'natural horror' (Verrall) of matricide? Or does it refer to Agamemnon, picking up the description of the μηχάνημα (981ff.)? Or indeed to Orestes, 'you have been done for by the hateful death', which is then expanded to 'for him who remains, there flowers suffering'[181] – a strong foreboding concerning Orestes. This ambiguity continues the parallelisation and reversal of events, relations – as does the applicability of στυγερῷ (φίλος/στύγος) as at 907, 991ff., to the Clytemnestra–Agamemnon and Orestes–Clytemnestra relations, and as does Orestes' paradoxical oxymoron ἄζηλα νίκης…μιάσματα (1017). μιάσματα recalls the ambiguity of δυοῖν μιαστόροιν (944), looking forward to the μίασμα καὶ…στύγος of 1028, as νίκη recalls the plays on νίκη/δίκη throughout the drama. The prayed-for *nike* after the event becomes inverted to 'unenviable pollutions' – the slippage from the certainty of hope to the confusion of completion.

The chorus lament again, in terms of the passing of life and (ominously) the inevitability of 'toil' reappearing (1020). Orestes expresses his doubts as to the end:

> …οὐ γὰρ οἶδ' ὅπῃ τελεῖ   (1021)

The *telos* is once more suggested as possible but only as a suggested (and unclear) point of narrative. This is in opposition to the chorus' πράγματος τελουμένου (872), κεκύρωται τέλος (874): the non-finishing of what they thought was being finished, the uncertainty of their ratified and certain end. So the onrush of madness is preceded by the uncertainties of language and narrative.

He begins to describe the onrush of madness: φέρουσι γὰρ

---

[181] μίμνειν. Cf. e.g. *Aga.* 154: fear/hope: narrative to come.

νικώμενον – after his victory, he finds he is now defeated – the paradox of reversal. While he retains his wits, however:

κηρύσσω φίλοις
κτανεῖν τέ φημι μητέρ' οὐκ ἄνευ δίκης,
πατροκτόνον μίασμα καὶ θεῶν στύγος.
καὶ φίλτρα τόλμης τῆσδε πλειστηρίζομαι
τὸν πυθόμαντιν Λοξίαν, χρήσαντ' ἐμοὶ
πράξαντα μὲν ταῦτ' ἐκτὸς αἰτίας κακῆς
εἶναι   (1026–32)

There is here a clustering of many of the terms we have been focusing on: the generality of the relation of φίλοις stands in juxtaposition to the specific rejection of μητέρ', which he claims was not without *dike* – marking the term's unresolved signification in this his justification. The crime against the father is a μίασμα (cf. 944), and 'hated of the gods' – στύγος referring to its opposition to φίλοις, and, more specifically, with θεῶν, to Pylades' hierarchisation of the opposition φίλος/ἐχθρός (στύγος) with regard to the gods. His depiction of *his own* act as τόλμης τῆσδε, particularly after τόλμης ἕκατι (996) of Clytemnestra's adultery and murder, places his act as parallel – a similar transgression; the paradox of reversal is marked whereby to assert the values of *xenia, philia*, the *oikos*, he is forced to transgress precisely these values. ἐκτὸς αἰτίας κακῆς – the problematic of causality and responsibility is pointed not only by the naming of Loxias as principal author (πλειστηρίζομαι: the multiplication of agents of causality) but also by the mutual implication of responsibility and accusation in the term αἰτίας: an action implies retribution; and with this foreboding comes the often-stated fear and hesitation surrounding action in the discourse of the *Oresteia*.

Orestes states his intention of going as a suppliant to Apollo, fleeing τόδ' αἷμα κοινόν (1038) – the common blood is precisely that which will be challenged by Apollo. His fleeing and pollution (as Cassandra had hinted, *Aga.* 1282?) make him ἀλήτης τῆσδε γῆς ἀπόξενος (1042). His punishing of the transgression of his mother has placed him outside the society he was asserting. So τῆσδε γῆς (1042) picks up ἐς γῆν τήνδε (3): the second exile.

The chorus, however, claim the goodness of his action, and tell him not to speak badly / say bad things. The description of the act defines it: hence the delimitation they offer: εὖ γ' ἔπραξας (1044). The apparent naivety of their moral vocabulary attempts to mark off the action of the play with as simple, as clean a cut as τεμὼν κάρα: but the genitive phrase δυοῖν δρακόντοιν already marks the sliding in language which stands in opposition to their simple definition εὖ γ' ἔπραξας...τεμὼν κάρα: for although he has freed the Argive city of 'two snakes', he has become a snake (ἐκδρακοντωθεὶς ἐγώ); he is pursued by snakes πυκνοῖς δράκουσιν: this parallelisation expresses the reciprocity and reversal of action; the interplay of signifiers resists the simplicity of definition of δυοῖν δρακόντοιν, resisting the control of their formula to delimit the play.

So, indeed, the madness of Orestes threatens to undo all the attempts at finding and fixing definitions. For how/when is Orestes mad (if he is)? Can we define the point when he becomes mad? His (mad) language seems logical enough, without even the 'symptoms' of madness one might expect from, say, Shakespeare (not to mention Artaud or Nietzsche). Furthermore, the 'vision' of the Erinues is placed in a series of challenges to the simplicity of the object of vision and its (metaphorical) expression in language. Foucault writes in his stimulating work on madness:

The ultimate language of madness is that of reason but the language of reason enveloped in the prestige of the image, limited to the locus of appearance which the image defines...madness...is not altogether in the image which of itself is neither true nor false, nor reasonable nor mad; nor is it, further, in the reasoning which is pure form, revealing nothing but the indubitable forms of logic. Yet madness is in one and the other: in a special version or figure of their relationship...Meaningless disorder as madness is, it reveals when we examine it, only ordered classification, rigorous mechanisms in soul and body, language articulated according to a visible logic. All that madness can say of itself is merely reason, though it is itself the negation of reason.[182]

This contestation, then, of madness as the *supplement* to reason, creating the boundaries of reason as it transgresses them, questions the whole fixing process of reading, of defining – of reason.

By the madness that interrupts it, a work of art opens a void, a moment of silence, a question without an answer, provokes a breach without reconciliation where the world is forced to question itself...the world arraigned by the work of art, obliged to order itself by its language, compelled by it to a task of recognition, of reparation, to the task of restoring reason *from* that unreason and *to* that unreason.[183]

So the 'madness of Orestes' opens a series of questions that question also the space of the critic's enterprise. For the inability of the critic, questioned, provoked, to define the point of turning to madness, an untransgressed boundary between sense and non-sense (despite the critic's avowed procedure of finding, fixing, reading the sense in and of a play) challenges as it sets up – plays with – the whole function

---

[182] Foucault 1967, pp. 95ff. He is writing of what he calls madness in 'the Classical period'.   [183] Ibid. p. 258.

of reading, the function of reading as '*making sense*'. The (indefinable) madness *in* the text is the madness *of* the text.[184]

So this 'madness of Orestes' challenges the secure recuperation of the text by drama critics' simple 'stagecraft'. A stagecraft question: 'Are the Eumenides to be thought of as visible on stage at this point [which point?] in the text?' 'No', answer most critics, with the chorus. 'Yes', say other critics 'though [of course] not to the chorus'. Thus the critics' recuperations, each stressing one potentiality, are forced to repeat (severally) the characters' responses, an uncanny effect whereby 'whichever way the reader turns, he can but be turned by the text',[185] he can but *perform* it by *repeating it in part*, partially. Could not the original (which?) performance give us a simple and direct answer to such an enquiry (which is a strategic gesture important not only to critics of stagecraft)? What evidence is there? What evidence could there be? No critic to my knowledge has talked of more than critical *probabilities*: criticism (reading) even when it attempts to mask itself as historical research, seeking authorisation for its arbitrariness in such a transcendental originary metaphor, can offer only a probable... reading, *a* performance. The constant play of probability and possibility results in the impossibility of exhausting the meanings, the possibilities of the text in a single performance, in performances, in Performance. The (need for) staging itself marks the impossibility of a full reparation of a script in performance. Indeed, the assumed possibility of the univocal recuperation of the text in the performance which its dramatic status requires, is challenged by the shifting and indeterminable levels of reference and metaphorisation, the hovering over the abyss of meaning that we have been analysing *throughout* the text (as we will continue to discover in the *Eumenides*, and not only in the appearance of Orestes' (and Cassandra's?) mad visions as the chorus of the drama).[186] But this goes further in the *Oresteia* than the critical questioning of the text's ability to refer simply, univocally or mimetically, further, too, than the necessary questioning and glossing of the term 'performance' as an adequate criterion in the face of such difficulty. For we have also been tracing the opposition of showing and saying, the problematised notion of

[184] Cf. Felman esp. 1975, 1977. Johnson wrote of Dryden in *The Lives of the Poets* these excellent lines, applicable to more than Dryden's writing: 'He delighted to tread upon the brink of meaning, where light and darkness begin to mingle, to approach the precipice of absurdity and hover over the abyss of unideal vacancy' (p. 194).

[185] Felman 1977, p. 199.

[186] An example: each of the deictics which we found ambiguous in reference, has been reduced by one commentator or another to a univocal, unambiguous expression, usually by the assumption of a clarifying gesture on stage, as if this circular reductionism proved anything more than the arbitrariness of such interpretative strategy.

seeing (its links with expression in language), marked in this final
scene, as we began this chapter by outlining, by the repetitions of the
command 'to see', leading towards the chorus' refusal of Orestes'
vision with τίνες...δόξαι; We have been tracing the prayers to divine
overseers, the hope for a watchful deity, a seen pattern; we have been
tracing the importance of witnessing, its basis in the present onlooker –
the close connection between terms of sight and terms of knowledge,
which is not only of considerable importance in the study of Greek
writing in general, but also of enormous influence on the tradition
it founded, of which we are the heirs. Punned on, glossed, questioned,
nevertheless the vocabulary of sight structures (my) critical discourse.
How, then, does this interplay of notions affect the text as *theatrical*
piece, as *spectacle*, as *opsis*? How does it affect the production of
significance in the theatre, an essential part, it seems, both of the
stagecraft critics' analysis, and of the more formalised work of the
semioticians of drama?[187] It seems to offer more than a further
self-reflexiveness of the dramatic text, more, that is, than the text
pointing to itself in performance as constituted in the speculative gaze
of the spectator, more than 'theatre' marking itself as such through
references to the function of sight in relation to meaning. For the
problematised notion of the visual mode that we have discussed
challenges as it sets up that reference. As the irrepressible role of the
reader (spectator) in the *production* of meaning questions the possibility
of the simple assumption of a coherent, unified, univocal (historically
specific or generalised) 'audience reaction' to which a critic may
appeal as limit, source, or criterion for reading the meaning of the
text, so the text's repeated questioning of the visual mode challenges
the possibility of a simple appeal to coherent, unified, univocal,
'visual meaning'. So, then, comments such as Taplin's 'all but a
lunatic fringe of students of Greek drama would accept the primacy
of performance' seems quite insufficient to the complexity of
Aeschylean drama in particular, and his determination of tragedy as
'a work which is only fully realised in performance' seems inadequate
to the play both in the hope for a 'full realisation' of a/the text (or
can that desire for plenitude be just a figure of rhetoric?) and in its
hope that such a 'full realisation' is to be found through '*the visual
meaning*' of a performance.

Let us return, however, to the lunatic fringe of the *Choephoroi*:
Orestes says his visions are clearly μητρὸς κύνες. κύνες is an
interesting term: the watchman in the *Agamemnon* described himself

<hr>

[187] Cf. Taplin 1977, pp. 12ff. (above n. 1), for 'visual meaning'. For an introduction to
the semiotics of drama, see Elam.

as κυνὸς δίκην (*Aga.* 3). Clytemnestra had called herself κύνα (*Aga.* 607), and called Agamemnon κύνα (*Aga.* 896). The chorus term Cassandra (*Aga.* 1093) κυνὸς δίκην. Electra calls herself κυνὸς δίκαν (*Cho.* 446). The chorus' words at the end of the *Agamemnon* are called 'barkings' (*Aga.* 1672). Once again, we see the difficulty of fixing the level of metaphorisation (reference), to limit the inter-references of the term κύνα/κυνός, which seem to link the characters: in what sense are the watchman, Clytemnestra, Cassandra, Electra, Agamemnon, the Erinues, to be termed dogs, like dogs? The explicit simile with δίκην, the metaphor κύνα applied to Clytemnestra, Agamemnon, finally the certainty of σαφῶς...κύνες, which is challenged by the chorus' τίνες...δόξαι, point in their difficulties (indeed, even – especially – in this attempt to classify them) to the dissemination of κύνα/κυνός, the continuing difficulty of finding a fixed point in or beyond language to limit the play of signifiers.

The Erinues drop from their eyes αἷμα δυσφιλές – δυσφιλές, as of Clytemnestra (624 and *Aga.* 1232), marks the corruption of φιλεῖν involved in the murder both of Agamemnon and of Clytemnestra. Orestes flees and the chorus offer up a prayer for him (the optative mode for future narrative):

> ἀλλ' εὐτυχοίης καί σ' ἐποπτεύων πρόφρων
> θεὸς φυλάσσοι καιρίοισι συμφοραῖς   (1063–4)

συμφοραῖς, even when qualified by καιρίοισι, recalls the doubling, ambiguousness of the συμφοραί of the trilogy – and hence the necessary prayer for good fortune and protection? As the play began with a desire for a god to overlook events, so it ends with a similar prayer. But the repetition of ἐποπτεύων, particularly in juxtaposition to Orestes' exclamation 'You do not see these women, but I do!' marks further implications for the sense in which a god overlooks. Is it through the perfection of divine sight?

The final anapaests sing of the end of a narrative: τρίτος...χειμὼν πνεύσας...ἐτελέσθη. 'The third' picks up the earlier imagery of three as end.[188] ἐτελέσθη, 'has been completed', stands in opposition to Orestes' οὐ γὰρ οἶδ' ὅπη τελεῖ and to the openness of τρίτος: for what are the three storms? The chorus name them: παιδοβόροι μὲν πρῶτον – but what of the adulteries preceding? What of Tantalus? δεύτερον ἀνδρὸς βασίλεια πάθη, λουτροδάικτος δ' ὤλετο – but as the openness of the plural πάθη suggests, what of the Argive expedition? What of Iphigeneia? What of Helen/Menelaus?

> νῦν δ' αὖ τρίτος ἦλθέ ποτε σωτήρ,
> ἢ μόρον εἴπω;   (1073–4)

[188] Cf. Clay 1969.

Even the third storm is not resolvable, but doubles into doubt: the
duality (ἤ) marks the difficulty of defining (εἴπω) the *telos*. σωτήρ,
the prayed-for saviour, at the end remains unclear – the certain
prayer, the uncertain fulfilment. Hence the final questions:

ποῖ δῆτα κρανεῖ, ποῖ καταλήξει
μετακοιμισθὲν μένος ἄτης;   (1075–6)

κραίνω (as of Zeus at *Aga.* 369) means 'accomplish', 'do'; καταλήξει,
'will cease' – the search, here at the end of the play, is for an end
of narrative, another end denied at this point of closing by the future
tense (as at the end of the *Agamemnon*), undercutting its own sense
of an end. μετακοιμισθέν, 'to go to another bed' ('lulled to its rest',
Lloyd-Jones), seems almost to suggest that major cause of Ate as an
end to Ate – adultery, the misuse of beds! More ominously, the final
word of the play, ἄτη, is a presage of possible disaster to come (as
with the future tenses) – the refusal of the end they had suggested by
ἐτελέσθη.

I have argued, then, that the manipulation of the signifier–signified
relation, which constituted an essential dynamic of Clytemnestra's
trickery, also constitutes Orestes' πειθὼ δολίαν, which by a process
of ironic inversion is adopted to achieve his act of revenge. This
reversal of values is seen in a series of further paradoxes, revolving
around the assertion of the validity of the ties and boundaries of
society by an act of their transgression – which senses of liminality
and transgression are linked by Vidal-Naquet and Zeitlin to the
initiatory status of the young Orestes. This middle play of a trilogy
marks the limen that joins to disjoin, disjoins to join. The *glissement*
of signs involved in that manipulation of signifiers results in the
fearful search for definition in (beyond) the series of shifting sites of,
particularly, the vocabulary of familial and societal relationships –
φίλος/ἐχθρός, πατήρ/μήτηρ, τίκτειν, τρέφειν, φρόνημα, τόλμα,
νίκη – a search both constituted by and, ironically, undercut by the
sense of slippage. The extensive passages of projection – the many
and lengthy prayers and invocations, the discussion of the terminology
to use, the dream analysis, the passage towards recognition – mark the
attempt through the predictive qualities of language to achieve
control, order, a telos, in this narrative of reversal and inversion, a
control, order and telos that the elusive, transgressive qualities of
language seem to place at risk. The interpenetration of this language
of verbal communication and the terminology of sight works towards
the rejection of a simple object of perception: this is true particularly
in the last scene of the play, and particularly through the difficult
metaphorisation of the object of vision in language; the vocabulary

of the visual and the verbal undercut the certainty, the fixity of each other. The recognition (in the theatre) of the necessary interpretation of that which is shown, seen, is also an important step towards the development of the male discourse of paternity, which points towards Apollo's rejection of the mother in procreation, and recalls the invocation of πατρῷα κράτη in the great kommos. This rejection of the mother and attempted adoption of the role of the father in society also places Orestes in the network of initiation motifs. The focus on this conflict of Orestes and Clytemnestra (and the resultantly small role for Aegisthus) is a constitutive link in the continuing opposition of the sexes (which is also depicted as interwoven with the difficulties of communication). In particular, the intertextuality with the discourse of the *Odyssey*, (which, to a degree, constitutes that focus) sets up an important network of differences, revolving around the notions of generational continuity, initiation, the sexual and social constitution of the *oikos*; this network seems to be leading towards a defining of the subject in society, which looks towards the political discourse of the *Eumenides*, as well as recalling for us the playing of this drama before the city. This narrative of intergenerational conflict, however, is often itself depicted in terms of the problematic of generational continuity, that is, through the metaphorical use of τίκτειν, τρέφειν, μήτηρ, πατήρ, γένος – in this sense narrative tells narrative itself, a self-reflexive text.

In this extremely complex and difficult text, which is all too often under-appreciated by critics, or at any rate, under-discussed (with the exception of the much debated set pieces of the *kommos* and the recognition scene), I have tried to trace, as this conclusion may recall but scarcely can sum up, the varying interpenetrations in the discourse of the *Choephoroi*, as in the *Agamemnon*, of language, sexuality, narrative.

3

The word of the law: δίκη in the *Eumenides*

ὑμνέομεν καὶ δὶς καὶ τὸ τρίτον.

Theocritus

Protologue...

The first word of the *Eumenides* is πρῶτον: a prologue which describes the origin of the mantic authority of Apollo begins with the word 'first' – a prologue to a play which will turn on relations of origin, or parenthood. 'The apodosis to πρῶτον μέν is ἔπειτα in 29' (Paley): but also πρῶτον could be construed with θεῶν; μέν would thus be answered by δέ in 2, 4, 8. The ambiguity of the first prayer or first god (which origin?) marks the difficulties surrounding the point of origin which we noted in the *Agamemnon* and *Choephoroi*. The address continues with τὴν πρωτόμαντιν Γαῖαν: a further πρωτό- picking up and extending πρῶτον μέν an extended origin?). Between these firsts comes the verb πρεσβεύω, which is translated normally as 'I give honour, seniority' (or 'place first'), but which also implies 'to be older than'. This suggests the continuity of the generations – a continuity in tension with a fixed point of origin? There is also set in play the tension between the desired continuity of the family and the undesired continuity in crime and punishment (depicted in terms of the generation of children!) resulting in the destruction of the family of Atreus, which is to be resolved in this trilogy.

The priestess' version of the myth is described as λόγος τις (4). This places the story within the shifting world of communication, and indeed the description of Apollo's succession is markedly different from Pindar's, say, and Euripides' near-contemporary versions of the story, and also from the Homeric Hymn to Apollo, each of which accounts contains references to Apollo's violent dispossession of the incumbent of Delphi. πρῶτον, the origin, first word of the prayer and the logos, in the prayer and the logos: the origin is both in and of logos. But it is open to the sliding of logos as marked by the emphasis on the willingness of Themis' abdication, which stands in opposition to the common version of the tale, as told in the Homeric Hymn, Pindar (as quoted in the scholion on this passage) etc. The story of the priestess tells also the origin of the name Phoebus (from the grandmother instead of the grandfather) which not only emphasises the 'impression of matrilineal descent given by lines 1–7',[1] but also places the origin of a name in the terminology of generation (as we saw, though differently, with, say Διὸς κόρα at *Cho.* 949). This name is παρώνυμον, 'formed by a slight change or inflection' (L.-S.-J.): παρα marks the sense of deviation we noted with παρανικᾷ, πάρφασις, παρακοπά, but here it is deviation *in a name* – in other words, precisely the shifting of the signifier which constituted the search for the fixing of meaning, in which remains sited the search for the fixed origin.

After this implied matrilineal descent, however, (and this is a tension which constitutes the dialectic of the trial) comes the male force of Zeus the father's prophet:

τέχνης δέ νιν Ζεὺς ἔνθεον κτίσας φρένα
ἵζει τέταρτον τοῖσδε μάντιν ἐν θρόνοις·
Διὸς προφήτης δ' ἐστὶ Λοξίας πατρός   (17–19)

Zeus 'set him up', Zeus, as causal agent. He founded in him ἔνθεον...φρένα, which looks back to the hymn to Zeus, and the connection of φρεν-/σωφρονεῖν with the principle of the male: Loxias is the prophet of Zeus the father; note how the embedding of the subject phrase, emphasised by the hyperbatic δέ, between the two dissyllables Διός and πατρός, enforces the interdependent relation, as the genitive πατρός recalls Zeus' generative role, as well as the-name-of-the-father, the paternal metaphor, that we discussed in the *Choephoroi*. At this culminating point, the priestess marks the end of the first part of the prayer: τούτους ἐν εὐχαῖς φροιμιάζομαι θεούς.

She continues, however:

Παλλὰς προναία δ' ἐν λόγοις πρεσβεύεται   (21)

'Pallas is given seniority, honour', 'placed first'. This appears to be in contrast to πρεσβεύω...Γαῖαν (1–2): thus Verrall opposes ἐν λόγοις and ἐν εὐχαῖς, 'a distinction between possessors of the place, past or present, who receive "petitions" (εὐχαί), and the other divinities...who demand rather "mention" (λόγοι)'. But Zeus did not possess the place but is in the εὐχή (characterised ὡς λόγος τις) and, moreover, the opening lines are described as a preface (φροιμιάζομαι) which implies a continuation – the actual 'petition', for example (the optative), comes at 29–30, in the 'mentions'. Earth and Athene Pronaia both given priority, then? The first point of worship doubled?

She continues with an expression of honour (σέβας, as we often saw in the *Choephoroi*, forms the correct expression between men and

1 Lebeck 1971, p. 207.

gods) first for the nymphs and Dionysus, the divinities of the mountain, with the regiment of dangerous women, the Bacchants; secondly, for Pleistos the river of Delphi; and then for Poseidon; and finally for τέλειον ὕψιστον Δία, Zeus Teleios, to whom Clytemnestra had also prayed (under different circumstances, but both women pray for fulfilment through Zeus). ἔπειτα μάντις...καθιζάνω (29): she too, part of this hierarchy, is in the series of prophets (and in this she recalls Calchas, Cassandra and so on), and as now she is led by the god (33), so in her terror (61–3) she will pass authority to the figure of the god, as healer and seer (cf. pp. 79–81).

So after this solemn opening, the priestess enters the shrine of Apollo. She re-enters from the shrine terrified, δείσασα (38), unable to walk, γραῦς οὐδέν, ἀντίπαις μὲν οὖν, which recalls the old men (*Aga.* 72–8), the sense of the trigenerational structure of society (another expression of an idea not uncommon in Greek writing, which takes on a further significance in this play of origins and generation). The sight she has seen (ὀφθαλμοῖς δρακεῖν, 34; ὁρῶ, 40; εἶδον, 50; ὄπωπα, 57) is also terrible to say (λέξαι, 34; ἐρῶ, 45; λέγε, 48), recalling the interpenetration of the vocabularies of sight and speech in the *Choephoroi*. Her description of what she sees (once again the entry into markedly metaphorical language of the object of vision) is important not only for the terms it uses, which I shall discuss briefly below, but also because it acts as a build-up of suspense and expectation before the entry of the Erinues themselves – and as a dramatic shock, particularly after her opening prayer's expansiveness and ironic petition for better fortune than before in the entry to the shrine.

Moreover, the figure of the priestess, the authority of/from god, says she *sees* the Erinues. The vision of them had been the sign of Orestes' madness: soon they will become leading characters on stage. Once again the *effet du réel* of the text is challenged by the transformation of what had been seen as a fantasy, a δόξα, of Orestes' madness into what is to become a litigant in the court case. As Orestes' madness challenged 'the world to question itself...to order itself by its language, compelled by it to a task of recognition, of reparation'[2] so the realisation, verification of the visions of madness challenges that recognition, that reparation, returns to the question. The possibility of even the definition of the object of vision of the madman *as* the vision of the madman, that is to say its non-referentiality, is thrown into doubt by this gesture.[3]

---

[2] Cf. pp. 202–3.
[3] It is to avoid this, presumably, that it has been suggested that the Erinues *are* on stage at the end of the *Choephoroi*, visible to Orestes, but behind the chorus members. Whatever its merits as a staging, this points, as does the priestess' further description,

Orestes is described as ἄνδρα θεομυσῆ, 'abominated of god', which points to the ambiguity of his position both as supported of / supported by Apollo, Hermes, Zeus, and also as the enemy of the Erinues for his transgression. As he had said (*Cho.* 1034ff.), he is at the *omphalos* with his wreath, a suppliant, wreathed σωφρόνως, which seems to pick up *Cho.* 1026 ἕως...ἔτ' ἔμφρων εἰμί, and the earlier references to φρέν-/φρον- and particularly Zeus' power to teach σωφρονεῖν: as the madman, pursued by the Erinues, it is precisely to σῴζειν φρένας that he has approached the shrine.

The description of horror at the Erinues, the priestess' attempt to find a visual *likeness*, picks up several key terms from the *Choephoroi* and *Agamemnon* as well as preparing further for their appearance as speaking characters in the play: ἐκ δ' ὀμμάτων λείβουσι δυσφιλῆ λίβα (54) recalls Orestes' fearful description (*Cho.* 1058) κἀξ ὀμμάτων στάζουσιν αἷμα δυσφιλές, again drawing attention in δυσφιλῆ not only to the 'unpleasantness' of the drops from their eyes but also to the basis of their attack (the corruption, transgression of the bond of *philia*). Entrance to the temples of the gods and the houses of men is again stated (55–6) as a criterion of recognition, acceptance – banishment from which was what Orestes feared (*Cho.* 289–96). Nor can the priestess imagine the generation of such creatures – the normal Greek questions to a stranger, What land? What parents?, are seen in a different light set here within the discussion we have seen of parentage, the search for an origin. The Erinues' lack of one parent, the father, their non-participation in sexual exchange, mark their separation from human society (so, too, as we will see, for Athene).

...and protection

Following on from the priestess' final words describing Apollo as the healer-seer and cleanser, Apollo, the god himself, now speaks to Orestes, the supporter of the god to be supported by the god. Apollo's protection is assured against enemies (ἐχθροῖσι) διὰ τέλους, 'to the end' (Lloyd-Jones), 'for ever' (Sidgwick). The ambiguities of *telos* in the last play remain irrepressible. 'Death', 'initiation' etc. hover as implications and possibilities in the teleological structure of the predictive narrative.

καὶ νῦν ἁλούσας τάσδε τὰς μάργους ὁρᾷς　　　　(67)

'And now you see these mad ones overcome'[4] (Lloyd-Jones). The

---

to the difficulty of reading through the text's language to a simple, external, referentiality.

[4] There has been some discussion as to what 'overcome' signifies: does this imply agency of Apollo? ἁλούσας is picked up by πεσοῦσαι in the next line (continuing the military image): it is unclear, however, if the sleep was sent by Apollo (we may remember sleep

Erinues are here characterised as 'mad' – as we have been calling Orestes – and the verb ὁρᾷς marks the (criterion of) madness, the vision which has been instantiated around the *omphalos*. With the acceptance of the visibility of the Erinues, the verification ὁρᾷς, the basis of Orestes' madness is put at risk: indeed, Apollo concludes his advice to Orestes:

> ...μὴ φόβος σε νικάτω φρένας   (88)

As we saw (pp. 79ff.), this expresses the relation between the present and the future as 'fear', but it also seems to assume Orestes' present sanity: it echoes φέρουσιν γὰρ νικώμενον | φρένες δύσαρκτοι πρὸς δὲ καρδίᾳ φόβος (*Cho.* 1023–4), which was how Orestes' characterised his loss of mind. Again we see the criterion of judgement of the level of madness/sanity in the text seems challenged between the plays.

The description of the Erinues as γραῖαι παλαιαὶ παῖδες, as well as a 'bold and contemptuous oxymoron' (Sidgwick), is explained further by the next statement that they do not have any intercourse, particularly sexual, with any god, animal or human being (a tripartite systematisation we discussed in Ch. 2, pp. 191ff.). For sexual activity (particularly as formalised in marriage) is often the dividing-point between the status of παῖς/κόρη and γυνή (marriage as the *telos* of female experience, cf. Vernant 1973, 1980): though old in age they remain 'young' in status, by criteria of age-class. These distinctions will also be important in Athene's self-definition (738ff.).

Orestes is ordered to flee to Athens. He must become the outcast and wanderer as he had been threatened were he not to have committed the matricide. This journey is described as πόνον, which refers back to the many examples of πόνος in the *Agamemnon* and the *Choephoroi*; and, as we noted on *Aga.* 1, in its status as a technical term from the mystery rituals (so indeed is the motif of 'wandering'), this toil of Orestes develops 'the majestic comparison between the institution of his city and the eternal economy of the κόσμος which is implied in the echoes of mystic terminology'.[5] This is further emphasised by the repetition of the phrase 'release from toil', ἀπαλλάξαι πόνων (83), juxtaposed to the recapitulation of Apollo's order of the matricide (84), which seems to link the rejection of the mother, an indication, as we discussed above, of the generalised pattern of puberty rites, to the allusions to the mysteries: the entrance to adulthood (male, sexed, with authority) is linked to the institution

---

being used in such a way in the *Iliad* by divine figures). Perhaps it also refers to his description of them as mad – they are taken now as Orestes was.

[5] Tierney 1937, p. 21.

of the mysteries (under a more general heading 'initiation', *rites de passage*).

In Athens, Orestes will find δικαστάς, the mediators introduced by Electra's question (*Cho.* 120), and soon to be seen to be also the technical term 'jurors', and he will find θελκτηρίους μύθους. This looks back to Clytemnestra's πόνων θελκτηρία στρωμνή (*Cho.* 670–1), where we noted the connection of θελκτηρία with sexual blandishments and tricky language. This prediction seems ironically double-edged in its recognition of the connection between sexuality and language (which forms the basis of Athene's saving language) and its unavoidable connection with the bad connotations of, say *Il.* 14.215ff. (q.v. p. 165). Some, indeed, have seen this hope to find 'beguiling language' as an early indication of the uncertainty of the god of truth's status in the trial to come.

Apollo further exhorts Hermes to escort Orestes, pointing the suitability of the name πομπαῖος, which normally, of course, refers to the passage of life to death, another hint towards the process of initiation, the transitional nature of *rites de passage*. This is picked up (93) with εὐπόμπῳ, which hints also at the final procession of the play, as well as the possibility of good and bad escorting (the Erinues are the 'bad' escorts, cf. 205–6). Hermes is addressed as αὐτάδελφον αἷμα καὶ κοινοῦ πατρός (89), 'my very brother' (Verrall). The implication that Hermes is absolute kin with Apollo in that he has a common father (despite different mothers) looks forward to Apollo's distinction of parentage in the trial (657ff.). Zeus, too, concludes Apollo, respects the sanctity of outlaws (σέβει/σέβας, 92, once more indicates the hierarchy of respect in society). In this way, Apollo, Zeus, and Hermes are ranged on the side of Orestes.

This short scene, then, develops the basis and nature of Apollo's continuing support for Orestes, in vocabulary which once more marks the social, religious, sexual terminology in which the oppositions of the trial will be constituted.

Doxa to *doxa*

After this scene of Apollo and Orestes comes the scene of Clytemnestra's ghost and the Erinues. The motive forces of the drama, of the opposition formalised in the court-case, are seen here in these parallel scenes: as Apollo encourages Orestes, so Clytemnestra encourages the Erinues. The ghost of Clytemnestra, however, appears as a dream, in a dream: ὄναρ γὰρ ὑμᾶς νῦν Κλυταιμήστρα καλῶ, as the insubstantial vision, δόξα (of dreams, *Aga.* 275, 421) that characterised

Orestes' madness (*Cho.* 1051). But a dream that speaks to all: the confusion of a simple level of 'reality'. As the Erinues seem to be an instantiation of a δόξα, so now does Clytemnestra, who had said οὐ δόξαν ἂν λάβοιμι βριζούσης φρενός (*Aga.* 275), but who now says εὔδουσα γὰρ φρὴν ὄμμασιν λαμπρύνεται· | ἐν ἡμέρᾳ δὲ μοῖρ' ἀπρόσκοπος βροτῶν.[6] She reverses the normal standard of clarity (light) obscurity (dark) now in her encouragement of the daughters of Night: yet there remains the metaphor of sight as clarity ('the mind is bright with *eyes*') and blindness as obscurity (taking ἀπρόσκοπος as active: 'it is the fate of mortals to be blind') which seems in uneasy conjunction with the reversal of the expected relation of day and night, or emphasises such reversal. ἀπρόσκοπος is also taken as passive, 'unseen', which points again to the unclear and worrying relation between present and future, so often stated in the trilogy.

Clytemnestra's opening remarks (94–102) are 'written with an effective vehemence which is very dramatic: the broken and rough grammar being exactly imitative of strongly excited speech' (Sidgwick). Indeed, the pace of the opening of this play (after the priestess' solemn first speech) with its rapid transformations between scenes, short bursts of dialogue, is overall 'very dramatic', 'strongly excited'.

Clytemnestra's lack of honour after death is parallel to Agamemnon's as mourned in the *kommos* (ἀπητιμασμένη, 95 and ὄνειδος, 97, were important terms in the *kommos*' description of Agamemnon's death). Her dishonour is particularly because her death was at the hands of τῶν φιλτάτων (which recalls the defining problem in the *Choephoroi*). The Erinues have had her sacrifices. Now they are told Orestes has escaped 'like a deer'. The hunting imagery is reversed (Orestes now as prey). He has escaped from 'the nets' as Agamemnon had been enveloped.

The chorus begin to groan, whine (μυγμός) and Clytemnestra continues her complaint: again the expectation is tightened as the chorus move (as did Cassandra) from inarticulate noise to words – the

---

[6] This passage has been challenged by, amongst others, Lloyd-Jones, who deletes 104 and 105, as 105 makes no sense. ὄμμασιν λαμπρύνεται picks up ὁρᾶ...πληγάς, specifying the strange sort of sight. πληγάς as used of Zeus destroying Troy (*Aga.* 367), Clytemnestra killing Agamemnon (*Aga.* 1343–5), Orestes killing Clytemnestra (*Cho.* 312ff.) implies the reciprocal acts of violence. Indeed, it is used later (933) for the vicissitudes, punishments of life itself: here, then, it indicates both her wounds from Orestes (in the series of reciprocal actions) and her exhortation to the Erinues to punish: thus the continuation of the *gnome* (where βροτῶν appears as part of the generalising of the *gnome*) has a particular irony, since indeed the fate of the mortal they are to pursue is ἀπρόσκοπος *by them* (his escape). With this, then, and the plays on the reversal of the (expected) imagery of light that I will discuss, it does not seem sufficient merely to delete the lines, to remove their difficulty.

first of which, λαβὲ λαβὲ λαβὲ λαβὲ φράҙου, break through extremely dramatically – a grim echo of the hunter's cry. Clytemnestra, however, retorts:

ὄναρ διώκεις θῆρα   (131)

ὄναρ, a neuter commonly used adverbially in Attic to mean 'in a dream', could grammatically also be in apposition to either the subject or the object of the sentence: with the object, as Verrall takes it, 'you pursue the dream quarry instead of the real one' (the standard opposition of dream/reality here used by the dream, Clytemnestra!); with the subject, 'you a dream [i.e. something ineffectual] pursue your quarry', which, while a less likely sense, is paralleled by ὄναρ...καλῶ (116). In either sense, the irony of a dream deprecating the reality of a dream to characters previously called δόξαι seems to question any simple level of reality or even *effet du réel* in this scene.

Clytemnestra likens the chorus to the dog in the chase (a further implication of the likenesses to dogs I considered above, pp. 204–5), and she encourages them:

...μή σε νικάτω πόνος   (133)

This echoes μὴ φόβος σε νικάτω (88), and further makes parallel the two scenes: the motivating figures of Apollo and Clytemnestra each exhort both the hunter and the prey 'not to let *phobos/ponos* conquer' (in the struggle for victory). She encourages them also to let their hearts ache for ἐνδίκοις ὀνείδεσιν (as opposed to the ὄνειδος she receives in the Underworld). For such approaches are goads to τοῖς σώφροσιν: the adoption of the language of the Zeus hymn[7] and the *kommos* marks both the parallelism of action and also the reversal of Clytemnestra from object of revenge to revenger: her adoption here of the language of δίκη/φρήν marks the growth of the sense of reversal, the clash of δίκη with δίκη.

The awakened and emotional chorus lament their sufferings (142–6), and their prey's escape:

ἐξ ἀρκύων πέπτωκεν, οἴχεται δ' ὁ θήρ·
ὕπνῳ κρατηθεῖσ' ἄγραν ὤλεσα   (147-8)

The metaphor of the hunt has turned Orestes into (the) animal (Orestes). The chorus turn, however, to blame Apollo, and offer a first

---

[7] Clytemnestra has, as we have seen, been characterised for her φρόνημα, τόλμα. Her denying of the male principle, and in particular her desire, rashness, will, have been depicted as the crossing of the restraints of σωφρονεῖν (cf. e.g. p. 141) – is her use of σώφροσιν here another ironic reversal?

statement of their cause. The god of truth is described as a thief (ἐπίκλοπος, the legal vocabulary realised in the trial) and accused of 'riding over' (more animal imagery) the distinctions of age: νέος δὲ γραίας δαίμονας καθιππάσω. This is sited within the structure of generational conflict, a divine instantiation of the young Orestes' act, itself the instantiation of the metaphorical structure of *tiktein*. Apollo's protection, they concede, may be respect for a suppliant (ἱκέτην σέβων – as Apollo had said, 92), but that respect is also for a man (ἄνδρα marking also a sexual distinction?), a man who is ἄθεον, 'godless' (which recalls both the support of precisely the gods for his matricide and Pylades' earlier authorisation of it), and further who is τοκεῦσιν πικρόν, 'bitter to/for his parents'. The masculine plural τοκεῦσιν both ignores and emphasises the distinction between mother and father so important for the dynamics of the play. Indeed, πικρόν is a term which was placed in the structure of interfamilial conflict at *Cho.* 234, the paradox which Orestes had remarked: τοὺς φιλτάτους... πικρούς. As the chorus point out the veiling rhetoric of Apollo's claim just to be honouring a suppliant, so too they veil different implications in their own rhetoric. Significantly, then, after the further accusation of robbery by Apollo, the chorus ask τί τῶνδ' ἐρεῖ τις δικαίως ἔχειν; This is more than a rhetorical question or a question of rhetoric: it not only recalls the problematic definition of δίκη, central to the trial, but also more precisely echoes such questions as τί τῶνδ' οὐκ ἐνδίκως ἀγείρω (*Cho.* 638), where we noted the function of language in the determination of *dike*: 'Who will *say* these things are just?' It will be precisely the *saying what is just* which will constitute the resolution of the trial scene. The resolution will be in and of language.

The chorus continue with a restatement of the motivating force of Clytemnestra, the dream, a description of their emotions in strong and metaphorical terms:

> ἔτυψεν δίκαν διφρηλάτου
> μεσολαβεῖ κέντρῳ
> ὑπὸ φρένας, ὑπὸ λοβόν·
> πάρεστι μαστίκτορος δαΐου δαμίου
> βαρύ τι περίβαρυ κρύος ἔχειν   (156–61)

The repetitions, alliterations (ὑπὸ φρένας, ὑπὸ λοβόν, δαΐου/δαμίου βαρύ... περίβαρυ κρύ-) are marked here, as is the image of the charioteer of the mind, which seems to echo Orestes' description of his own rising madness. As with the description of the Erinues as 'mad', so too here the depiction of their emotions in terms recalling Orestes' loss of wits stands to confuse the definition of the level of madness and sanity in the text.

Antistrophe β returns to complaining of the younger gods (first strophe: emotional outburst; first antistrophe: complaint about Apollo; second strophe: explanation of emotional outburst; second antistrophe: complaint about the younger gods in general). The gods' excessive authority (κράτος) is completely beyond *dike* – again we see the assumption of the discourse of δίκη and the notion of excess (ὑπερ) that we noted in Agamemnon's, Clytemnestra's, Orestes' action. The argument among the divine uses the same vocabulary. Apollo, on his own responsibility, contrary to the law of the gods, is honouring a mortal. τίων echoes its many occurrences in the *Agamemnon* and *Choephoroi*, recalling also τίνω/τιμῶ, which implies the punishment they are suing for as well as the relationship beween Apollo and Orestes. Apollo's 'honouring' is destroying the old system of reciprocation (παλαιγενεῖς...μοίρας). Once again, an action is described and defined in terms of *generational* (παλαιγενεῖς) conflict.

They end their chorus (by far the shortest *parodos* in the trilogy – continuing the pace of the action) with a series of threats: as with so many earlier choruses, this song ends with a future tense, an extension from the present is characterised by its vagueness: Orestes will not escape even if he flees underground (precisely where the Erinues would presumably dispatch Orestes, were they to catch him cf. 339–40!), but rather as someone who is still without purification he will be punished – ἕτερον ἐν κάρᾳ μιάστορ' εἶσιν οὗ πάσεται. Who or what ἕτερον μιάστορ' is, is quite unclear, as is the place to which οὗ refers, and indeed the process πάσεται, 'he will get, acquire'. But the performative status of the threat itself remains frightening in its very unclearness.

The *parodos*, then, develops the tension between the Erinues as motivated by Clytemnestra and Apollo as supporter of Orestes, particularly in terms of the hunt and in terms of generational conflict and respect. These terms notably pick up earlier scenes of conflict in the trilogy, as the argument between the divine figures reflects and develops the human struggle.

Revenge and vindication

Apollo and the Erinues are now set in opposition to one another, as Apollo turns the chorus out of Delphi's precincts. It is a clash which not only serves to site their opposition in the discourse of the trilogy (after the two scenes of support), but also is a prelude to their further clash in the trial scene – where the outcome and procedure signifies in its differences and similarities to this earlier exchange. As we will see, the trial's importance may be regarded as stemming from its attempt to transcend such earlier conflicts' violent results.

Apollo returns taunt for taunt: the opposition between Apollo and the Erinues is strongly marked here, not least by the threat of direct physical violence (181–4), in language as powerful as the expressions of the Erinues:

> μὴ καὶ λαβοῦσα πτηνὸν ἀργηστὴν ὄφιν
> χρυσηλάτου θώμιγγος ἐξορμώμενον
> ἀνῇς ὑπ' ἄλγους μέλαν' ἀπ' ἀνθρώπων ἀφρόν,
> ἐμοῦσα θρόμβους οὓς ἀφείλκυσας φόνου   (181–4)

The description of his arrow as 'a winged snake' recalls the interplay of the image of the snake in the *Choephoroi*; as Orestes was turned into a snake (ἐκδρακοντωθείς) to effect the god-ordered matricide, so does the god's snake-weapon protect him against the force of the δεινῆς δρακαίνης (128), which now pursues him. The physical details of the 'black foam from men', of 'vomiting up the clots of gore which you sucked up', as with the priestess' emphasis both on her physical reaction (37ff.) and on the description (51–4) of the Erinues' physicality, mark in their vivid strength a force of reaction to the unnatural form. As Apollo concludes after his description of the frightful barbarism of the punishments of the Erinues:

> οἵας ἑορτῆς ἔστ' ἀπόπτυστοι θεοῖς
> στέργηθρ' ἔχουσαι· πᾶς δ' ὑφηγεῖται τρόπος
> μορφῆς   (191–3)

The opposition of their pleasure, love, στέργηθρ', and the hate of the gods is explained and supported, by the 'manner of their shape'. Their unnaturalness is seen in their unnaturalness of form (cf. Athene's remarks at 410ff.). As Clytemnestra perverted, corrupted the pattern of natural imagery, so the Erinues are to be depicted in their bringing of blight, their frightening physicality, as in opposition to the healthiness of natural generation. As this apparent unnaturalness may be thought to contribute to the devaluing of the feminine cause that they represent, so their final incorporation into the order of the city will be a reordering of the boundaries of naturalness to include, at least on the margins, the figures of the Erinues as protectors of the naturalness they here are opposed to (cf. e.g. 938ff.).

Their punishments (δίκαι) show this blight in the castration of children (188) and the destruction of the seed (σπέρματος...ἀπο-φθορᾷ, 187 – which picks up, for example, the description of Orestes as 'seed' at *Cho.* 236). The outcome of Clytemnestra's corruption still threatens the seed, Orestes, who is the hope of generational continuity, the seed of family. These punishments are joined to the barbarisms of eye-gougings, stonings, mutilations, impalings beneath the spine (the grammar of this sentence, as of Clytemnestra's opening words, is, as Verrall notes, more forceful than regular). Apollo concludes:

λέοντος ἄντρον αἱματορρόφου
οἰκεῖν τοιαύτας εἰκός, οὐ χρηστηρίοις
ἐν τοῖσδε πλησίοισι τρίβεσθαι μύσος.
χωρεῖτ' ἄνευ βοτῆρος αἰπολούμεναι·
ποίμνης τοιαύτης δ' οὔτις εὐφιλὴς θεῶν   (193–7)

The conjunction of οἰκεῖν, which expresses a sense of living in society (*oikos*), with 'the lion's cave'[8] marks their separation from human society, as does the continuation of the animal imagery. But they are separated too from the divine presence of the oracle (and entrance to the temple is a criterion of acceptance). Indeed, Apollo claims they will 'rub off pollution' on the shrine, as the Erinues had accused Apollo (166–70) and as the priestess had described Orestes (θεομυσῆ). The clash of the Erinues and Apollo is polarised into mutual accusations of sacrilege and pollution.

The description of the Erinues as a flock without a shepherd is interesting and implies more than the scholion's suggestion of 'wild animals'. ποιμήν, for example, is used regularly in Homer, particularly of Agamemnon to express the relation of a king to his people or of the lord of the *oikos* to his family. To be without this figure is precisely the state into which Clytemnestra thrust the *oikos* of Atreus, and the Erinues, following the mother's curse, are a chorus without a figure of authority, without a paternal figure. It picks up furthermore both 78–9, βουκολούμενος | πόνον (which makes parallel the flight of Orestes and the pursuit of the Erinues again) and also 91–2, τόνδε ποιμαίνων ἐμὸν | ἱκέτην, which further contrasts the pursuit of the Erinues without a shepherd to the flight of Orestes who is 'to be shepherded' by Hermes. εὐφιλής is not simply 'is loved by' (Lloyd-Jones) but picks up δυσφιλής at 54 (*Cho.* 1058, 624–5). It is not simply the relation of *philia*, but the relation as qualified by εὐ- (which also implies the possibility of δυσ-); it assumes the shifting status of *philia* as we saw in the *Choephoroi*, the redefinition necessary to the accommodation of matricide.

This opposition of speeches is further developed in the sticho-mythia that follows – the opposition marked by ἀντάκουσον ἐν μέρει (198):

[8] Recalling the lion in the house (οἰκεῖν), and the two-footed lioness (*Aga.* 1288), the double lion (*Cho.* 938). 'Lions', like 'dogs', are images which stretch in signification through their differing repetition in the trilogy.

αὐτὸς σὺ τούτων οὐ μεταίτιος πέλῃ
ἀλλ' εἶς τὸ πᾶν ἔπραξας ὡς παναίτιος   (199–200)

This accusation of responsibility, which refers back, for example, to
Aga. 811, θεοὺς...τοὺς ἐμοὶ μεταιτίους, and to *Aga.* 1486/1505, the
play on παναίτιος/ἀναίτιος, and to the chorus' hope of seeming
innocent, *Cho.* 873, ἀναίτιαι, indeed, to the whole system of over-
determined causality, attempts to cut through this system (as with the
chorus' remarks, *Cho.* 1044–7). It attempts further to polarise the
opposition between themselves and Apollo (with the result that
Orestes is treated merely as stake, as object of prey and defence). But
their expression of blame here seems insufficient to the complexity
of the patterns of responsibility not only in its aggressive simplicity,
which is opposed to the complex network of causality and over-
determination, but also in the specific reminiscence of Zeus as
παναιτίου (*Aga.* 1486). (Can both Zeus and Apollo be 'responsible
for all' and not 'responsible in part'?) It cannot enforce the
opposition it so strongly demands. Apollo, however, takes up the
challenge:

πῶς δή; τοσοῦτο μῆκος ἔκτεινον λόγου   (201)

He offers the debate (λόγου) – echoing Agamemnon's words to
Clytemnestra (*Aga.* 916), the earlier opposition in debate of male and
female. The Erinues begin to catechise the god:

ἔχρησας ὥστε τὸν ξένον μητροκτονεῖν;   (202)

τὸν ξένον is a further rhetorical point with μητροκτονεῖν – not only
is Orestes a matricide but also one from the sacred position of ξένος.
But the paradoxical conjunction of ξένον/μητρο- recalls the play on
ξένος/φίλος and not ξένος/φίλος (pp. 168–9): can one be / not be
ξένος in one's own house? In familial strife, the normal moral terms
shift.
     Apollo replies:

ἔχρησα ποινὰς τοῦ πατρὸς πέμψαι· τί μήν;   (203)

ποινάς marks the reciprocity we have noted before: τοῦ πατρός after
μητροκτονεῖν emphasises the opposition of mother/father, female/
male, active/passive. His order was father-revenge – the killing of
Clytemnestra certainly constitutes the revenge of the father and the
matricide, but the valuation of the father as opposed to the
undervaluing of the mother is stressed.
     The Erinues ask if he undertook to receive the 'fresh blood'
(reception, δέχομαι, or rather the lack of it, marks the outcast,
particularly non-reception at the religious rites and in the home), and
Apollo replies that he indeed ordered him to come as polluted

suppliant for purification (προστράπεσθαι) at his house, δόμους
(205). They reply, with some irony:

καὶ τὰς προπομποὺς δῆτα τάσδε λοιδορεῖς;   (206)

'Why reproach his *escorts*, then?' προπομπούς sarcastically refers
to their particular sort of less than friendly escort service (cf. 212).
Such aggressive rhetoric and manipulative language is as much a part
of the Erinues' speech as it was for their motivator, Clytemnestra.
Apollo aggressively replies, however:

οὐ γὰρ δόμοισι τοῖσδε πρόσφοροι μολεῖν   (207)

The Erinues are not 'fitting to approach these buildings'.[9] What is
fitting to a house invokes the house and what befits it as the continuing
field of conflict, despite the change of settings. It is, however, the
Erinues claim, their office, as they have been charged. Apollo asks
what is this τιμή – the term used so often in the *kommos* and by
Clytemnestra's ghost for the systematisation of respect – and what is
their γέρας, which, returning their sarcasm, he terms καλόν. *Geras*,
as it often does in Homer, indicates the physical manifestation of *time*,
'a gift of honour'. It will be the Erinues' τιμή and γέρας that are
at stake throughout the trial and its aftermath (cf. e.g. 780). Their
expression of their role, 'we drive matricides from their homes', is
questioned by Apollo, however:

τί γάρ; γυναικὸς ἥτις ἄνδρα νοσφίσῃ;   (211)

He turns the opposition of son and mother to the earlier, wider
(non-generational) distinction between male and female (γυναικός/
ἄνδρα), referring to Clytemnestra's killing of Agamemnon.

οὐκ ἂν γένοιθ' ὅμαιμος αὐθέντης φόνος   (212)

'That would not be the shedding of one's own blood with one's own
hand' (Lloyd-Jones). ὅμαιμος, which picks up the numerous
references to 'blood', in particular 'shared' or 'same' blood
('blood-relations', e.g. *Cho.* 1038, *Eum.* 89) refuses to recognise as
of equal value the bond between husband and wife, and the bond
between blood-relations, the family. It ignores the bonds of exchange
between families constituting marriage and social organisation, in
order to maintain a valuation of the bonds between generations.
Indeed, Apollo replies:

ἦ κάρτ' ἄτιμα καὶ παρ' οὐδὲν ἠργάσω
Ἥρας τελείας καὶ Διὸς πιστώματα.
Κύπρις δ' ἄτιμος τῷδ' ἀπέρριπται λόγῳ
ὅθεν βροτοῖσι γίγνεται τὰ φίλτατα.
εὐνὴ γὰρ ἀνδρὶ καὶ γυναικὶ μόρσιμος
ὅρκου 'στὶ μείζων τῇ δίκῃ φρουρουμένη   (213–18)

---

[9] Note δόμοισι of the temple: the divine 'house', linking (interpenetration of vocabulary)
the divine and human through 'house', 'home', the centrality of the *oikos*.

He focuses on the lack of respect (ἄτιμα) and the valuing at naught of precisely the pledges of Hera Teleia and Zeus. Hera Teleia is the goddess of accomplished marriage (it also recalls the prayers to Zeus Teleios), 'as marriage was a τέλος, an accomplished rite' (Sidgwick). The marriage of Zeus and Hera was the ἱερὸς γάμος, the sacred or ideal marriage (despite – because of? – the disagreements and in-fidelities of legend). It is set in opposition to the implied lack of revenge of Agamemnon – the regicide as an act of hostility by the *wife* against the *husband*. Aphrodite, too, would then be without the respect (ἄτιμος) on which the Erinues had based their argument. λόγῳ, at 215 ('by your plea', Lloyd-Jones, Verrall; 'by your word', Davies), again sets up this opposition of theirs as an opposition of logos to logos (argument/discourse/language) as the court-case will be. From the goddess of love come into being for mortals τὰ φίλτατα, which signifies not merely man's 'dearest joys' (Verrall), but within the opposition of φίλος/ἐχθρός and picking up πρὸς τῶν φιλτάτων (100), also the established bonds of the family. Marriage and its sexuality are the necessary precursors to the coming into being of precisely the ties the Erinues have emphasised: without marriage, no family, no blood-ties. εὐνή, the 'marriage-bed', or 'sexual union', is, and this is the explanation (γάρ) of the previous sentence(s), 'greater than an oath' (an exchange beyond the exchange of words); it is μόρσιμος, uniting 'the destinies of man and wife with special reference to the...meaning of μοῖρα *part* or *share*' (Verrall). It is a bond also 'guarded by *dike*', which claims *dike* for Apollo's case, as he had dismissed the δίκαι of the Erinues (187ff.). Thus, he con-cludes, they do not pursue Orestes ἐνδίκως, if they do not pursue also other offenders: it is on the demonstrable inequality of their re-quirements for punishment that he bases his attack (defence), and not on the innocence of Orestes:

τὰ μὲν γὰρ οἶδα κάρτα σ' ἐνθυμουμένην
τὰ δ' ἐμφανῶς πράσσουσαν ἡσυχαίτερα   (222–3)

πράσσουσαν, as before, has the implication of 'revenge' as well as 'treat', 'do'. For the Erinues are the figures of revenge for whom in particular doing is revenging. Apollo concludes this speech of vindication:

δίκας δὲ Παλλὰς τῶνδ' ἐποπτεύσει θεά   (224)

δίκας here, particularly after ἐνδίκως (218), δίκαι (187), marks the multivalent shifting between singular and plural of this term, the clash of *dike* and *dike* as opposed to the implied single standard of ἐνδίκως. In particular, here, Apollo seems to look forward to Athene's role in the trial (δίκη), her role of distinguishing the cases (δίκαι).

ἐποπτεύσει looks back to (e.g.) *Cho.* 1, 246, 1063, where the guardianship of the gods was expressed in visual terms, thus linking Athene to Apollo, Hermes, Zeus, Agamemnon, as overseers to the action, a prelude to her determining role in the final scenes of the trilogy.

The chorus assert their determination never to leave the man (τὸν ἄνδρα cf. 151, 211) – their certainty is to be undercut by Athene's *peitho* – and Apollo tells them to chase after him. The Erinues reassert their right to τιμή against Apollo's slurs:

$$\text{τιμὰς σὺ μὴ σύντεμνε τὰς ἐμὰς λόγῳ} \qquad (227)$$

λόγῳ, 'by speech', 'by argument', 'by a definition', is precisely how, indeed, their τιμαί will be altered by Athene.

Apollo, however, would not even accept their τιμαί (the opposition of divine forces is mutually exclusive), which, the chorus claim, is because he is accounted great beside the throne of Zeus:

$$\begin{aligned}
&\text{μέγας γὰρ ἔμπας πὰρ Διὸς θρόνοις λέγῃ.}\\
&\text{ἐγὼ δ', ἄγει γὰρ αἷμα μητρῷον, δίκας}\\
&\text{μέτειμι τόνδε φῶτα} \qquad\qquad (229\text{--}31)
\end{aligned}$$

The Erinues (ἐγὼ δέ), with no word with regard to suppliants, offer the motivation of the mother's blood (αἷμα μητρῷον), which drives them to pursue, sue for,[10] δίκας. This desire for *dikai* picks up δίκας (224), δίκαι (187), (δίκη, 218; ἐνδίκως, 221). In demanding punishment, 'revenge', they also suggest (ironically from their mouths) the 'legal proceedings' and 'Justice' to come. Apollo, however (ἐγὼ δέ), reaffirms his support for the suppliant and the role of purification among men and gods, as he too looks forward to the coming action. The shifting of δίκη continues the problem of definition from the *Choephoroi*, with both sides of the clash of language claiming δίκη (ξυμβαλεῖ δίκᾳ δίκα) and both sides claiming the justice of their view of δίκη (ἐνδίκως). *Dike* remains a term of and for appropriation.

Thus this scene of Apollo's vindication of Orestes and the Erinues' assertion of the need for revenge ends with a position of exclusion and opposition (the Erinues to chase, Apollo to protect) as the scene was structured around the forcible opposition of Apollo and Erinues (new/old, male/female, father/mother, son/mother). Orestes within the oppositions of this scene becomes the θῆρα/ἱκέτην, the object of pursuit and protection – although it had been the ambivalence of his action that constituted the opposition.

---

[10] On the difficulty of μέτειμι, cf. Sidgwick ad. loc.

Suit and pursuit

The build-up towards the trial continues as the scene shifts to Athens and Orestes offers prayer to Athene, Athens' goddess, to help him. Orestes prays for reception (δέχου) – the criterion of recognition in society and by society which was questioned by the Erinues in Orestes' case and accepted by Apollo. Orestes calls himself ἀλάστορα, 'victim of avenging spirit' (Sidgwick.). Sidgwick also notes the active meaning of the word 'avenging spirit', but does not recall the connection here with Clytemnestra's φανταζόμενος δὲ γυναικί... ἀλάστωρ (*Aga.* 1500–1) and the prediction of Orestes precisely as ἀλάστωρ (*Aga.* 1508). Here there is a continuing ambiguity: is Orestes pursued by the spirit of revenge from the house of Atreus or is he, by his matricide, the *alastor* personified? 'In this mechanism of a repetition we have the very essence of revenge.'[11] But here, even with regard to the reciprocity of action, the active/passive *oscillation* of the sense of ἀλάστωρ (as we have seen with other terms) confuses in such doubling a simple model of reversal and repetition. ἀλάστωρ is always already a repetition and reversal in oscillation, shifting between active and passive. And its 'proper' (Wecklein) sense is 'the wanderer'!

Orestes claims he has been purified (cf. 41, 205): οὐ προστρόπαιον οὐδ' ἀφοίβαντον. ἀφοίβαντον, 'uncleansed', also ('of course', Sidgwick) refers to the agent of purification, Φοῖβος: the pun suggesting an etymological connection between Apollo and purity? Orestes has worn down, blunted the impurity by ἄλλοισιν οἴκοις καὶ πορεύμασιν βροτῶν (239), that is, by his acceptance and reception in the social organisations and the 'haunts', 'passages' of men. So now (pre)serving the orders of Loxias, he comes to the house (δῶμα), the temple and statue of Athene for a further reception, and he waits for the τέλος δίκης (243). Here three extremely important constellations of meaning conjoin. ἀναμένω is sited in the problematic of the unclear projection from present to future, from *arche* to *telos*. But here it is a τέλος that with δίκη also suggests a fulfilment, initiation, a rite, as well as the threatening implications of 'death as a punishment', 'death from legal proceedings'. οὐ γὰρ οἶδ' ὅπη τελεῖ – the ambiguity is (in) τέλος itself. For *dike*, too, is what the Erinues have sought as *telos*, and how Apollo has justified the action, and it is the law-court to follow. Waiting for the *telos* consisting in, coming from, *dike* is therefore richly ambiguous. The openness of this

---

[11] Irwin 1975, p. 116: he has relevant material here on the Oedipal model and repetition (pp. 88ff.) within the family, and on the reversal fantasy of the son.

phrase stands as prelude, too, to the next lines of the Erinues which, as we will see, concentrate on their pursuit, their treatment of Orestes as passive object: after Orestes/Apollo, Clytemnestra/Erinues, Erinues/Apollo, now the conflict turns to Erinues/Orestes. The pairings of the scenes create a system of doublings, διπλῆς μαραγνῆς, a pattern of oppositions structuring the argument, as we will see, leading towards the formal oppositions of the law-court.

True supporters of Clytemnestra, the chorus follow τἀνδρὸς ἐκφανὲς τέκμαρ – as with Clytemnestra's beacons, the 'clear signal' (cf. *Aga*. 315–16) marks the signifying process (as Orestes had stated a clear signal was only possible 'man to man', *Cho*. 668). So too μηνυτῆρος ἀφθέγκτου φραδαῖς, 'the unvoiced informer', is reminiscent of ἄναυδος...σημανεῖ (*Aga*. 496–7), where we read the oppositions of language and signals without language. Thus we are once more reminded of the problematic of communication before the law-court is constituted. φραδαῖς, however, not only is from φράζω which, as we saw, with its implications of both voiced and non-voiced communication, undercut the opposition of showing and saying, but also it was precisely the term used for Orestes' divine motivation: θεόθεν εὖ φραδαῖσιν ὡρμημένος (*Cho*. 941). The signals from Apollo to Orestes are followed by the signals from Orestes to the Erinues. The repetition of this rare poetic noun, then, marks once more the repetition and reversal of action.

They are pursuing him as a dog pursues a fawn: ἐκματεύομεν echoes κυνὸς δίκην...ματεύει...φόνον (*Aga*. 1093–4, and σὲ καὶ ματεύω (*Cho*. 892), earlier preludes to bloodshed, earlier huntings – again the sense of repeated action is formed by repeated vocabulary. They are, however, exhausted by μόχθοις ἀνδροκμῆσι. Both Sidgwick and Verrall (following the scholion) relate ἀνδροκμῆσι to the generality of ἀνθρώποις: but not only does ἀνδρο- point (as before) to the sexual differential (cf. 151, 211, 225), but also, more specifically, Clytemnestra had called for an ἀνδροκμῆτα πέλεκυν before her conflict with Orestes (*Cho*. 889). The echo of Clytemnestra (drawing the Erinues and their motivator closer) helps to specify the reference to Orestes. Indeed, their pursuit over sea and land has led them now to where he is 'cowering down', καταπτακών. πτάκα was the term used by the chorus in the *parodos* of the *Agamemnon* for the sacrificed pregnant hare (*Aga*. 137) – the hare which was pursued by πτανοῖσι κυσὶ πατρός. Here we have the ἀπτέροι(ς) (250) μητρὸς κύνες (*Cho*. 1054) (and κύων, 246 etc.). The sacrifice of that hare may yet result in θυσίαν ἑτέραν (*Aga*. 150), another sacrifice of a cowering creature.

They spot Orestes and break into excited lyrics. The unpunished mother-killer (256) clings to the altar of the goddess 'awaiting *dike*' (ὑπόδικος, 'awaiting trial'). But this is declared impossible (261) because

> αἷμα μητρῷον χαμαὶ
> δυσαγκόμιστον παπαῖ
> τὸ διερὸν πέδοι χύμενον οἴχεται   (261–3)

This echoes *Cho.* 48, 66–7, 73, 520–1: will purification prove, as Orestes had said, 'a vain labour' (*Cho.* 521)? The spilling of blood calls for a return, ἀντιδοῦναι δεῖ (264), ἀντιποίνους τίνης (268): reciprocity, exclusion, opposition, payment – the continuing imagery. As the blood flowed to the ground, so the Erinues must suck a drink which is awful in the drinking, from his live limbs. As in the *Choephoroi*, there seems to be forged a sympathetic connection between the pouring of blood and libations and drinking.

Their punishment will have a preventive effect on any mortal who wishes to be ἀσεβῶν (that is, denying the correct hierarchy of respect) to either a θεόν, or a ξένον, or their τοκέας φίλους. *Xenos* is the role Orestes adopted and corrupted towards his mother; the plural 'engenderers', 'parents', qualified by φίλους, recalls the definition of *philia* with respect to parentage in the *Choephoroi*, and masks the distinction between parents in the *Choephoroi* and in the trial scene of the *Eumenides*. His matricide was, however, explicitly on the instructions of an honoured god. As often, a general statement of the chorus has implications, then, in its similarities to *and* its differences from the specificity of Orestes' case. This specificity is suggested by:

> ἔχονθ' ἕκαστον τῆς δίκης ἐπάξια   (272)

δίκης has the implications (of course?) not only of 'Justice' (Lloyd-Jones' capitalisation) but also of the punishment they seek – and of the court-case to come. This justice (etc.) is because mighty Hades holds mortals to account – the financial imagery of εὔθυνος picking up τίνης (268), ἐπάξια (272) – because he 'overlooks (ἐπωπᾷ) all with a mind that inscribes'.[12] Again with an expression of causality, we find a further over-determination: as do Zeus, Apollo, Hermes, Agamemnon, the gods, fate, so too does Hades *overlook* events.

Orestes now tries his first reply to the Erinues (after Apollo's in the previous scene – both look forward to the joint defence in the trial where the order of speakers is reversed; so that Apollo offers the final statement of their cause, as he offered the first).

Orestes 'schooled in misery knows' (276) to speak and to keep silence, ὅπου δίκη. This is not only a reminder of his own semi-religious exhortations to Electra at *Cho.* 581 (recalling the dangerous

---

[12] On images of writing cf. Pfeiffer 1968.

properties of language), but it also looks forward both to his speeches in the trial (ὅπου δίκη), and his often remarked-on[13] silence after the moment of decision and his speech of thanks. For the present he claims a σοφοῦ διδασκάλου[14] and continues to argue for his unpolluted state, as he has been purified through the ministrations of Apollo.[15] This argument, marked as *logos* (284: from the σοφοῦ διδασκάλου?), is based on his intercourse in society without damage: he has been no outsider. Thus he can call on Athene, the goddess (that is, he can take part in religious invocation), ἀφ' ἁγνοῦ στόματος εὐφήμως. His respectful prelude to invocation marks the purity and danger of speech in the predictive language of prayer.

His prayer offers himself and his people and land as an ally,[16] πιστὸν δικαίως ἐς τὸ πᾶν τε σύμμαχον. δικαίως here, the appropriation of the term *dike* to Orestes' cause (and to the political discourse of the alliance promised), also seems to hint towards the process by which this faith will come about, namely, by δίκη, by the court. His prayer continues in a traditional form, 'If you are *a*, if you are *b*, then come...', the prayer for epiphany strikingly realised in this play by the appearance of Athene as a speaking character. It is to help φίλοις (φιλία may determine a relationship between men and gods according to Benveniste, and it was so seen in Pylades' authorisation of the matricide) that she is to come from where she πλάκα θρασὺς ταγοῦχος ὡς ἀνὴρ ἐπισκοπεῖ. ἐπισκοπεῖ links Athene again (cf. 224) to the other figures of authority, motivating agents, who 'overlook', but her description as 'brave captain of war like a man', particularly with the specific noun ἀνήρ, draws attention to the military, masculine attributes of Athene which will be important. For she is to be τῶνδ'...λυτήριος (298). She is prayed to as the force of resolution.

The chorus respond with threats in direct and exclusive opposition to the support of Apollo and Athene. Orestes is now depicted as a fattened sacrifice (304) who will be slaughtered (305) without altar – the threatened θυσίαν ἑτέραν. The vocabulary of Clytemnestra's killing of Agamemnon, Agamemnon's killing of Iphigeneia, returns, marking the repetition of action. And round Orestes at the image of Athene, they begin their 'binding-song'.

---

[13] Cf. e.g. Taplin 1977, pp. 402–10.

[14] Does this phrase suggest something of the nascent Sophist movement, or of the Presocratic writers? Apollo's apparent indebtedness to scientific discourse in the trial scene is often remarked on.

[15] On the significance of the pig cf. Zeitlin 1978.

[16] This is often taken as a reference to the Argive alliance, recently concluded for Athens. Is this another example of the search for an origin, a sort of 'etymon' for the treaty? On the treaty, see now Macleod 1982.

Binding promises

After the importance of language and communication that we have read throughout the trilogy, and here specifically before the speeches leading to the oppositions of the trial and before the trial scene itself with its set debates which will be followed by the final scenes of *peitho* and blessing, we see an extended instantiation of what we have described as the predictive/predicative force of language, in the form of a 'binding-song', that is, a spell, an incantation (the religiosity of language again) to control events, and in particular to control and bind Orestes. Before the 'new', 'secular' power of the word, that is, the word of the judge deciding between the words of the litigants, we see the 'old', 'religious' force of the magic of language.

Their song will be of the relation of themselves and the human race, their λάχη (cf. 334, 340, 349, 385). It will be the description of themselves and their rights. The song will recall, however, many key terms of the trilogy thus siting the chorus within the discourse.

They describe themselves as εὐθυδίκαιοι – that is, not merely δίκαιοι, but 'straight', 'immediate' in δίκη – a *hapax legomenon* which expresses an unmediated *dike*, but which by its prefix εὐθυ- also suggests the possibility of an opposite predication. Their wrath (μῆνις) recalls the waiting anger spoken of by Calchas: μίμνει... μῆνις τεκνόποινος (*Aga.* 154-5). This ire visits itself not on those with 'pure hands' but on those with 'bloody hands', which recalls Electra's prayer for 'pious hands' (*Cho.* 141), as well as the problems of purification and the staining of blood. They are straight witnesses to the dead, μάρτυρες ὀρθαί, which also looks forward to the trial, as ὀρθαί picks up εὐθυ- in its sense of direct linearity.

πράκτορες αἵματος
αὐτῷ τελέως ἐφάνημεν   (319–20)

πράκτορες means not only 'doers' and 'avengers', pointing to the reciprocity inherent in action (πράσσω), but also in Athens it was a technical term for tax-collectors,[17] a further image within the economic images of exchange and payment. This perhaps finds an echo in τελέως – not only 'finally', but also with the implications of τέλος, 'a tax' (sacrifice, death). τέλος, inscribed at various points of the narrative, linking various constellations of terms and ideas, in this way both expresses the point of completion, fulfilling the teleological

---

[17] Cf. Demosthenes 778.18, Antiphon 147.14.

implications of the narrative, and in the same gesture, sited by its polysemy in the play of differences, challenges that fixed point.[18] The first strophe opens with an address and a genealogy, μᾶτερ ἅ μ' ἔτικτες ὦ μᾶτερ Νύξ, which, as the scholion notes, is suitable since the debate is concerned with Orestes and his mother. So this stanza will end with the reiteration of their cause in the description of Orestes as ματρῷον ἅγνισμα κύριον φόνου. The boldly transferred epithet ματρῷον, however, 'atonement for a mother's slaughter', suggests also 'a mother's atonement for slaughter', which is precisely Orestes' defence of the matricide! Once again the complex polysemy of the lyrical expression suggests precisely and significantly the reversal and repetition of action. So too κύριον ('the proper', 'my own' atonement etc.) evokes the term κύριος, the 'lord and master' of the *oikos* (in the normal system of hierarchical authority) with particularly the sole right and power to give and take the women in marriage; again, the chorus' expression recalls both Clytemnestra's crime *and* Orestes' desire for reinstatement in the act of invoking the need for punishment. This allusive doubleness continues: 'punishment for the blind and the sighted' (323–4) recalls the shifting criterion of visibility we have been tracing in particular in the *Choephoroi* (so now Orestes' δόξαι dance for us!). ὁ Λατοῦς...ἷνις, particularly in conjunction with ἅτιμον τίθησιν, recalls the prologue's genealogy of authority: the origin of authority is conceived as the origin of birth, as we have seen the origin of narrative depicted in terms of childbirth and descent. γένεσις continues as focus. Indeed, here at the beginning of the hymn of binding, the opposition of Apollo and the Erinues is expressed in terms of the opposition of their descents, which are significantly matrilinear. And furthermore, πτᾶκα (326) (πτῶκα Sophianus and Page) recalls καταπτακών (252), and the hare of the *parodos* of the *Agamemnon*, as ἐπὶ...τῷ τεθυμένῳ (328) recalls the κυσὶ...θυομένοισιν at *Aga.* 136–7, and the θυσίαν ἑτέραν at *Aga.* 150. So the complex reiterations of Aeschylean lyric twist and reverberate.

The binding-song describes itself as παρακοπά (the term used to describe Agamemnon's sacrifice of Iphigeneia). The force of *para* as deviation, transgression, is picked up in παραφορά, 'a carrying *para*', 'distraction', which is φρενοδαλής, 'mind-spoiling'. As with the force of desire (τόλμα/φρόνημα) which παρανικᾷ, as with the series of tragic acts of transgression in the house of Atreus, as with the power of Zeus, so here the focus is on the effect/affect of φρένες.

---

[18] The most extensive work on *Telosgedanke* is Fischer 1965. While recognising much polysemy in the *telos* terminology, he fails to follow his argument through sufficiently. See Goldhill 1984.

As Orestes had hoped to stay ἔμφρων, as σωφρονεῖν was particularly valued, so now there is another assault on the φρένες of Orestes. Their song[19] both binds and spoils the mind; yet it was the very appearance of the Erinues which constituted Orestes' 'madness'. Now the Erinues constitute the acceptable levels of 'reality' of the text. They talk of driving mortals mad through song, as their song spoils the possibility of defining a coherent, consistent criterion of madness/sanity, referentiality/reality for the text? 'Maxima pars hominum morbo iactatur eodem?'

Their appointed lot is pursuit of αὐτουργίαι unto death: but

θανὼν δ'
οὐκ ἄγαν ἐλεύθερος   (339–40)

The sense of death as an end which was ignored by the *kommos* and Clytemnestra's ghost, is now turned to a sense of death as an obscure continuation of the fears and threats of life (as indeed Clytemnestra had expressed her torments among the shades). The lack of a main verb for this sentence once more leaves without precision narrative's fearful passage.

They repeat the *ephymnion*: the perfect tense τεθυμένῳ, 'having been and being sacrificed', 'victim', after the expression of the continuation across the boundary of death of the punishment of the Erinues, takes on a further implication; it will indeed be a continuing sacrifice (τέλος?).

This lot has been accorded them since birth, a further genealogy; but they and the immortals do not come into contact. After βροτοῖς (333), θνατῶν (336), the chorus seem also to be invoking the tripartite systematisation we have noted, as indeed the separation is again expressed by (non-)presence at feasts and sacrifices, which was the criterion of acceptance and recognition for mortals. Rather their sphere of action is the destruction of houses and blinding: the female is aligned with the dark side of things (cf. the strangely negative expression of 'lacking white robes', 352). They operate when domestic warfare assaults a *philon* (which recalls precisely the difficult definition of *philia* in the house of Atreus). In these duties, however, they desire separation from the gods, and not εἰς ἄγκρισιν ἐλθεῖν. They desire to avoid the process of judgement. But this looks forward to Athene's questioning and to the subsequent acceptance of the judicial procedure, a procedure similar to what the Athenian courts called precisely ἀνάκρισις. Again, the allusion undercuts the possible simplicity of the expression. Indeed, the proclaimed difference

---

[19] Described as ἀφόρμικτος: cf. *Aga*. 990ff. τὸν δ' ἄνευ λύρας ὅμως ὑμνῳδεῖ θρῆνον Ἐρινύος αὐτοδίδακτος ἔσωθεν θυμός – again a realisation of a metaphorical level.

between gods, mortals and Erinues, as the court-case will demonstrate, creates a systematisation and not just a separation.

From their separation from the Olympians, the chorus turn to humans: ἀνδρῶν (367). Underground, even proud reputations (δόξαι... σεμναί) fade and waste away unhonoured, ἄτιμοι (normally σέβας and τιμή imply each other). Such fading and wasting is the effect or accompaniment of their black-robed approach (as the sight of the Erinues had maddened Orestes) and of their ὀρχησμοῖς...ἐπι-φθόνοις ποδός: ἐπίφθονος (*Aga.* 134) was how Artemis described the act of walking on the tapestries (*Aga.* 921): now it indicates the act of pursuing Orestes; ὀρχησμοῖς, too, implies not only the general method of approach but also the particular instantiation of this χόρος. Interestingly, δόξαι was how the chorus described Orestes' vision of the Erinues; σεμναί is how they describe themselves (384), and how they are finally termed (1041) – indeed, it is how the Erinues were known in Athens (σεμναὶ θεαί, cf. e.g. Soph. *O.C.* 90, 459). κατὰ γᾶς is where the Erinues are eventually sited: ἴτε καὶ σφαγίων τῶνδ' ὑπὸ σεμνῶν κατὰ γῆς (1007–8): and there they will be without their τιμαί, as now defined. These lines describing their present actions seem also (paradoxically) to contain (the reversal of) the future: predication as prediction. Always already reversal.

The third *ephymnion* comes after the third strophe rather than the second antistrophe; nor is there a fourth *ephymnion* between the third antistrophe and fourth strophe. Both these 'omissions' have been 'rectified' by textual critics, though Page maintains the manuscript order. In this 'perfectly complete and regular movement' (Verrall – he supplies the missing stanzas!), then, the structure implied by the first six stanzas is broken, marked by absences: is this 'ill-ordered' responsion like the *parodos*' irregular pattern of iambics and dochmiacs,[20] like the chorus 254–75, a mark of the implied disorder of nature of Orestes' sin and the Erinues' punishment?

In his fall, the pursued sinner

$$...\text{οὐκ οἶδεν τόδ' ὑπ' ἄφρονι λύμᾳ} \qquad (377)$$

He experiences a lack of knowledge (as did Orestes?) because of mindless derangement. λύμᾳ, as does the remainder of this antistro-phe, seems reminiscent of *Cho.* 286–90 (λυμανθὲν δέμας), that description of Orestes' fear from the darkness, the confusion and madness. His fears had been for what would happen, however, if he did *not* avenge Agamemnon: this instantiation, then, stresses the ineluctable logic of the double-bind. The vagueness of the rumour

---

[20] The responsion of the *parodos* is as expected, of course.

talking of a certain, dark, mist (that is, not just the vague nature of
this threatening 'dark mist' but its siting as the (vague) *speech* of
rumour) is further confused by the subject of πεπόταται being
μύσος/κνέφας (which is in apposition to which?) when one might
have expected the word of speech as at *Suppl.* 657, *Sept.* 84. As so
often in this play, both grammar and sense lead to the confusing,
unspecific expression of punishment to come (cf. 176, 340).

They further describe themselves as εὐμήχανοί τε καὶ τέλειοι.
Beyond its significance of 'good at devising and fulfilling', this
phrase also recalls Clytemnestra's prayer to Zeus Teleios, and
Apollo's appeal to Hera Teleia, as well as the multiple associations
of τελ-. Here, in particular, this echoing is of importance: the Erinues
are sacrificers, fulfillers – is it for Orestes' death or his initiation? The
choices of the narrative rest within the implications of the term: which
τέλος? The problem of definition is also the problem of narrative.

The Erinues are also κακῶν...μνήμονες – recalling *Aga.* 154–5,
the sense of deferred retribution – σεμναί (cf. pp. 198, 231 above),
and δυσπαρήγοροι βροτοῖς – as will be proved by the trial scene and
the divine *peitho*. They pursue their duties 'separate, sited apart from
the gods' (the systematisation of gods, mortals, Erinues) in 'sunless
filth/damp', which again opposes implicitly dark/filth, and light/
purity. And (in this stanza of description) their tasks are

> δυσοδοπαίπαλα δερκομένοισι
> καὶ δυσομμάτοις ὁμῶς   (387–8)

Unlike the phrase ἀλαοῖσι καὶ δεδορκόσιν (323) with which they
opened their lyric song, here the opposition of light/dark, seeing/blind
seems something less of a binary opposition in the term δυσομμάτοις –
'scarce seeing', 'difficult in eyes'. It echoes not so much the
'blinding' of ἀμαυροῦμεν (358–9), as the confusion of sight, the mists
of 379–80. Not only do they exert power over living and dead, but
also 'the living sinner walks already overcast with the same shades
into which he finally passes' (Verrall). The extension across the
boundary of the opposition of life and death is paralleled here in the
change from the normal opposition of sight (alive) / no sight (dead)
to a single shifting standard of seeing.

They conclude with a question (which will be restressed in the
second stasimon) as to which mortal would not feel respect and fear
for them when he/she heard of the θεσμόν, τὸν μοιρόκραντον ἐκ
θεῶν δοθέντα τέλεον. μοιρόκραντον, particularly with δοθέντα, points
to its own etymology, and recalls 335, the gift of their authority from
their sister Moira; and τέλεον echoes τέλειοι (382), and also implies
bringing about the *telos*. In this way, the binding-song concludes with
the expression of a *telos* authorised by its origin.

The binding-song, then, even when it stresses the lot and authority of the Erinues as separate from the Olympians and mortals, is bound and woven into the network of reverberating vocabulary and images of the *Oresteia*. The boundaries between characters and scenes are echoed across within the discourse of the trilogy, as the lyric language repeats, recalls, reverses in its ironic doublings. Again the plurality of the text resists a simple reading of the words of the ὀρθαὶ μάρτυρες.

Just-ification?

The arrival of Athene in answer to Orestes' prayer heralds a scene in which the possibility of a law-court trial is opened by Athene's questioning of the Erinues and Orestes – a questioning which not only places the goddess in the position and role of arbitrator, but also marks the terms in which the trial will be conducted.

Her first statements significantly recall not only her military prowess in the Trojan War, but also her support for the Greeks under Agamemnon, and, finally, for her own citizens, Θησέως τόκοις (402). Each of these ideas will prove important to her position in the play. Like the Erinues, she crosses the sea without wings 'in pursuit', διώκουσ' (403). But this and other verbal echoes mark the differences between the two immortal figures: indeed, she expresses her wonderment (not fear) at the sight before her, both Orestes and Erinues. She addresses first the chorus:

> ὁμοῖαι δ' οὐδενὶ σπαρτῶν γένει
> οὔτ' ἐν θεαῖσι πρὸς θεῶν ὁρώμεναι
> οὔτ' οὖν βροτείοις ἐμφερεῖς μορφώμασιν   (410–12)

The systematisation of neither mortal (human) nor goddesses differentiates the Erinues in their appearance (though their sex – ὁμοῖαι – is not in doubt). The chorus offer an immediate answer: πεύσῃ τὰ πάντα συντόμως, Διὸς κόρη. Like the messenger of the *Agamemnon*, like the simplicity of the chorus of the *Choephoroi*, the Erinues offer a full reparation of speech, the clean cut (συντόμως)[21] of distinctions. But the naming of Athene as Διὸς κόρη particularly after δικαίων in the previous line, recalls the etymology of δίκη as Διὸς κόρη (*Cho.* 948ff.). Does this link Athene and *dike* together, authorising her authority in the trial? This suggestive echo immediately challenges τὰ πάντα συντόμως.

The chorus tell Athene their parentage (only mother) and name, which Athene recognises. With a certain emphasis (γε μὲν δή), the

---

[21] Remembering, however, 227: τιμὰς σὺ μὴ σύντεμνε...λόγῳ: here precisely they abridge their honours in a speech, by speaking συντόμως!

chorus proceed to offer to speak of their τιμάς (as they have often done before). Athene, somewhat ironically after their emphasis, replies: μάθοιμ' ἂν εἰ λέγοι τις ἐμφανῆ λόγον: if the daughters of Night would speak a clear logos, she would learn: the goddess of wisdom marks the heuristic gap and the problem of hermeneutics. The chorus offer: βροτοκτονοῦντας ἐκ δόμων ἐλαύνομεν. But they had in their argument with Apollo stressed that their actions were precisely towards *only kin-murder*: this inconsistency or confusion is, then, significantly preceded by ἐμφανῆ λόγον and the optative mood. Once again, we find the juxtaposition of an assumption of clear speech with a statement of uncertain implication.

They explain their duties further (the vagueness of the threat of 423 is marked) and tell of Orestes' crime (425). Athene questions, however, the *motivations* of Orestes' crime:

$$\text{ἀλλ' ἢ 'ξ ἀνάγκης ἢ τινος τρέων κότον} \qquad (426)$$

These alternative motivations of necessity and fear of someone's wrath have already been seen in Orestes' description of his impulse to matricide (*Cho.* 275). But the chorus reject the value of motivation itself in the case – ποῦ γὰρ τοσοῦτο κέντρον ὡς μητροκτονεῖν; They ignore their own earlier accusation (200) that the responsibility was totally Apollo's – which had ignored the role of Orestes! Indeed, in handing the role of judge to Athene, they say (433): κρῖνε δ' εὐθεῖαν δίκην (picking up their claim to be εὐθυδίκαιοι/ὀρθαί), 'judge a direct, absolute *dike*'. As opposed to Orestes' possible justification through motivation, they require an immediate, straight, penalty. As we will see, however, it is their very desire for δίκη which also opens the possibility of the trial (δίκη).

Athene indeed turns to hear the other side's argument (λόγου). For there are two sides present (δυοῖν παρόντοιν) – the doubling of opposition. But the chorus interrupt the goddess with ἀλλ' ὅρκον οὐ δέξαιτ' ἄν. οὐ δοῦναι θέλει. The change from optative to indicative and the lack of connective between sentences and the irregularity of grammar again seem to mark a certain force in the Erinues' outburst.

This reference to oaths seems to make Athene's questioning parallel to the ἀνάκρισις of Athenian legal procedure,[22] the primary questioning and presentation of evidence before referring the case to court – the ἀνάκρισις that the chorus rejected strongly at 362. For Orestes cannot claim, as he would be required in an *anakrisis*, that he did not commit a crime. Athene, however, retorts to the chorus:

$$\text{κλύειν δίκαιος μᾶλλον ἢ πρᾶξαι θέλεις} \qquad (430)$$

[22] Sidgwick and Verrall provide material on this.

The distinction between being called δίκαιος and doing δίκαια, as well as pointing out the limitation of asking for an oath[23] against a plea of justification, also points to δίκαιος (possessing, following, δίκη) as a (predicable) signifier; that is, 'being just' is sited as a function of language as well as of action, as, indeed, the outcome of the trial and the constitution of the trial are in/through language. The chorus request further information (as so often in the stichomythia of this trilogy), and the concession of respect (σοφῶν) by the chorus at this early stage is noteworthy. Athene explains:

ὅρκοις τὰ μὴ δίκαια μὴ νικᾶν λέγω (432)

'I mean [give the logos] that things which are not δίκαια should not have victory by oaths.' This recalls the play between νίκη and δίκη that we read in the *Choephoroi*, the earlier prayers for victory and the shifting senses of *dike*. Now there is to be no victory without also *dike*: the implications of Electra's doubting word play are being drawn forth.

The chorus cede, κρῖνε...εὐθεῖαν δίκην. The shifting of δίκη makes this remark ironic in an important way, as it makes possible the concession of the Erinues to the process of the trial. For their desire for the *dike* of punishment is turned to the acceptance of the *dike*...of the law-court. And between their desire for swift, direct punishment, and the court-case to come stands the concern for the multivalent 'Justice'. Athene asks surprisedly if they would entrust her with the αἰτίας τέλος – 'the outcome of the charge'; but the ironic implications of *telos* remain – 'death', 'initiation', 'fulfilment', which are the doubtful outcome of the narrative. αἰτία, as before, means not only charge but also 'ground', 'cause', 'origin'. This picks up παν-/μεταίτιος, the problematic of causality, responsibility in which the trial is constituted. The court-case, then, will decide in language between the choices constituted in the terms δίκη, αἰτίας τέλος: it will be a decision in language of definition of language.

Athene turns to Orestes and requests his parentage, race, country, and συμφοράς, 'circumstances' – which was the word used to describe the arrival of the beacon-light (*Aga.* 24), the destruction of Troy (*Aga.* 572), the misery of the chorus of the *Choephoroi*, the death of Clytemnestra at the hands of her son (*Cho.* 931), indeed, the woes of the house in general (*Aga.* 18). These echoes, and the διπλῆ qualities of συμφορά, recall the narrative of reversal and repetition that the trial is to end, here at the opening of the legal proceedings. If, she continues, it is relying on *dike* (the multivalency and irony of which is marked) that he sits guarding (as he is guarded by) the *bretas*,

---

[23] As Sidgwick, Verrall, Lloyd-Jones point out.

a σεμνός suppliant, like Ixion[24] the first suppliant, then let him answer something εὐμαθές (from the σοφοῦ διδασκάλου?) to all these things. And so Orestes, in a coherent and well-turned speech, defends himself: after the introductory questioning to define the charge, there comes the speech of defence.

First (πρῶτον) he removes the worry of her last words (note the rhetorical antitheses πρῶτον/ὑστάτων, μέλημα μέγα/τεκμήριον μέγα, πόλιν/ἄπολιν). He is not προστρόπαιος but has been purified: he describes again (cf. 28off.) the process of sacrifice, the blood flowing for blood spilt, of cleansing in blood and water. This process is described as a 'great proof' (447), which sites it not only within the legal vocabulary of the trilogy, but also as referring back to the recognition scene and the beacon-speeches scene, those earlier processes of recognition and hermeneutics. Once again 'proof' is called into play; once again (ἐπῶν, 444; λέξω, 447; λέγω, 453) it is proof in and by language.

He states his race and father – whom Athene knows well[25] (a touch of special pleading?). Agamemnon is named with his status in the international expedition, as leader of the men (ἀνδρῶν) of the expedition to Troy, with whom Athene destroyed the city of Ilion – again the link between Agamemnon and the judge of his son, here in military action, which looks back to her opening speech, her possession of Scamander's lands.

Opposed to this description of the Trojan war (which ignores its 'sinful' implications in the *Agamemnon*) is the king's death at home (459). Orestes does not name his mother, however, but calls her κελαινόφρων – 'black' (like the daughters of Night) 'in her φρήν', which recalls the excesses of φρόνημα, the disturbances of φρένες (which has been the description of the series of tragic acts of *ate*), and also the desire and power for the control of φρένες in the σωφρονεῖν of Zeus.

> ποικίλοις ἀγρεύμασιν
> κρύψασ', ἅ λούτρων ἐξεμαρτύρει φόνον.   (460–1)

This is not only reminiscent of the ὀνείδη of the *kommos*, but also evokes Orestes' attempted proof of the circumstances of murder (*Cho.* 1010, cf. pp. 198–9) and the problem of definition there, as we approach the trial, its witnessing, its institutionalised defining.

He returned (κατελθών, cf. *Cho.* 3 κατέρχομαι) and

---

[24] προσίκτωρ/'Ιξίονος suggests, for Sidgwick, an etymological connection, 'possibly even the origin of the story'. Again the origin of a word and the origin of a narrative or a practice are brought together.

[25] Verrall questions this sense of 'know' (although he accepts the sense 'be informed', 'learn') and suggests 'to whom thy question aptly leads': a different special pleading of flattery.

ἔκτεινα τὴν τεκοῦσαν, οὐκ ἀρνήσομαι,
ἀντικτόνοις ποιναῖσι φιλτάτου πατρός   (463–4)

τὴν τεκοῦσαν looks back to *Cho.* 913, 928 etc. and forward to its
denial at 659ff. His admission of this fact (οὐκ ἀρνήσομαι) stands in
opposition to the logic of the oath. And his excuse recalls many of
the terms we have discussed above: ἀντικτόνοις expresses the sense
of exclusion and opposition but also it is a term which was undercut
at *Cho.* 121/144, 275, where in Electra's questioning of the language
of prayer the supposed simplicity of opposition and exclusion was
seen as uncertain. ποιναῖσι expresses the sense of exchange, of
punishment as a reciprocity; φιλτάτου πατρός restates the motivation
of the *Choephoroi*: the hierarchisation of φιλία towards the Father.
Furthermore, Orestes offers Loxias as κοινῇ...ἐπαίτιος, 'in common
cause/responsibility' – after μεταίτιος/παναίτιος/αἰτίας now an
agent is κοινῇ...ἐπαίτιος, 'responsible' but 'in common'. Apollo's
agency, his threats of agony were a spur, <u>ἀντί</u>κεντρα (after τοσοῦτο
κέντρον, 427), to act against τοὺς ἐπαιτίους: the repetition of ἐπαίτι-
places Apollo (and his agent in common) in opposition (ἀντὶ...ἀντί)
to Clytemnestra/Aegisthus, which as with e.g. *Cho.* 836–7 organises
the problematic of causality in a binary opposition.
        Orestes concludes his first defence, picking up 430–5:

σὺ δ' εἰ δικαίως εἴτε μὴ κρῖνον δίκην.
πράξας γὰρ ἐν σοὶ πανταχῇ τάδ' αἰνέσω   (468–9)

δικαίως...δίκην points precisely to the ambiguities which constitute
the drama here: can one judge a δίκην to be not δικαίως – that is, not
according to δίκη? Only by the shifting of sense between 'case',
'court', 'punishment' and 'absolute Justice', 'Right': that is, by
resisting the defining implied by κρῖνον, the word of the Judge. Or
is it perhaps a further example of prejudicial rhetoric, trying to
restrain the possibility of declaring his case (δίκη) to be not just
(without δίκη, not δικαίως)?
        Athene responds:

τὸ πρᾶγμα μεῖζον εἴ τις οἴεται τόδε
βροτὸς δικάζειν   (470–1)

'Not any mortal can decide', 'determine'[26] the affair. Nor, however,
can she by her own authority:

οὐδὲ μὴν ἐμοὶ θέμις
φόνου διαιρεῖν ὀξυμηνίτου δίκας   (471–2)

Here, however, her rejection of a divine right to 'distinguish',

---

[26] δικάζειν often has δίκας as its object. Cf. e.g. Hes. *Op.* 39 (for an earlier important text
concerned with δίκη, and its definition).

'separate', δίκας in the plural, suggests the opposition of cases – which picks up the sense of δικάζειν. But how does this relate to Orestes' εἰ δικαίως εἴτε μή, with its assumption of an absolute *dike*? She expresses this opposition of cases in a series of broken sentences 'to mark the agitation of her thoughts' (Verrall): on the one hand, 'Orestes has arrived having completed the rites satisfactorily, bringing no harm to δόμοις'; on the other hand, 'the Erinues have a portion (μοῖραν) which is οὐκ εὐπέμπελον'. This implies both 'not easily placatable', and 'not easily sent away' – perhaps looking forward to the difficulty in persuading the Erinues before the final procession (πομπή).

καὶ μὴ τυχοῦσαι πράγματος νικηφόρου   (477)

The Erinues' expectation of πράγματος νικηφόρου, particularly after πρᾶγμα...δικάζειν recalls the play δικηφόρος/νικηφόρος and also Athene's remark (430) separating δίκη and νίκη as predications. Indeed, the Erinues' pursuit of punishment, their pursuit of destruction of a victim, allows a closeness of sense between *dike* and *nike* – an exclusive opposition of result of an exclusive opposition (battle). They demonstrate the concern for δίκη as νίκη. There remains for the land of Attica the threat of the Erinues' sickness and poison, which is ἐκ φρονημάτων. The term φρόνημα, which Zuntz[27] takes as an 'archaic meaning (a *hapax* to us) of "breast",' was used to depict the will to transgress of Clytemnestra, and Agamemnon (cf. e.g. pp. 141, 160). Here it marks precisely the threat of the continuing reversal and transgression through the excess of action. In the face of this opposition (ἀμφότερα μένειν πέμπειν τε – the double-bind) she chooses δικαστάς, mediators, jurors, to make the decision: instead of διαιρεῖν, she proposes δικαστὰς αἱρεῖν. Not choosing between, but choosing people who stand between. These people are to be bound under oath, an ordinance for all time (the foundation of the Areopagus). Both sides (plural ὑμεῖς) are to call μαρτύρια and τεκμήρια, 'witnesses' and 'proofs' – referring back to the witnesses called by Orestes to the murder, to the proofs of the beacon-speeches scene, and the recognition scene and elsewhere. Athene instigates the institutionalisation of these hermeneutic processes towards the word of law. These proofs and witnesses are ἀρωγὰ τῆς δίκης ὀρκώματα: 'helpful for, assistance to, *dike*'. And once again the sliding of *dike*, the openness of its meaning, defies the limits that ὀρκώματα are meant to define: the promise of the delimited truth of ὀρκώματα is undercut by the shiftings of the term, *dike*, which the ὀρκώματα are meant to serve. Indeed, Athene concludes, after saying she will choose the best of her citizens:

[27] 1981, p. 85.

ἥξω διαιρεῖν τοῦτο πρᾶγμ' ἐτητύμως   (488)

The 'affair' (which term recalls 470, 476 where we saw the possibility or either/or both/and *dike/nike*) is to be distinguished, defined, divided ἐτητύμως. ἐτητύμως is not only 'accurately' but, as Verrall notes, 'pressed to its full and literal force': that is, as we saw pp. 6off., it expresses (the desire for) the control of (the *glissement* of) language by the etymon, by the 'true' and 'literal' *origin* of sense. Thus after these plays made possible by the shifting of the term *dike*, the court (itself termed *dike*) through its jurors (δικαστάς) will make an accurate decision (δικάζειν) between the two cases (δίκας) either for punishment, revenge (δίκη) or through an appeal to a wider Justice (δίκη) for freedom. In the decision which is the aimed for closure of narrative, it is also deciding on the significance of the single word. It is defining, dividing ἐτητύμως. The drawn votes, however, will leave this opposition between *dike* as 'punishment'/'revenge' and 'Justice'/'case' in play – to be decided by the vote of Athene. ἥξω, then, placed between what Verrall and Sidgwick take as the subject of the epexegetic infinitive διαιρεῖν, and the infinitive itself, introduces a grammatical possibility[28] that it is indeed Athene on whom the act of division, definition, will rest: 'having chosen...I will come to decide'. And it is this grammatical shifting, with the difficulty of δίκης (486), which both constitutes the desire for, and undercuts the certainty of ἐτητύμως.

'The end and the beginning were always there'

The chorus now sing the second stasimon: like the binding-song, this constitutes the linking fissure between scenes, commenting on the action, but from a leading agent in the action it is also placed within the series of oppositions and of doublings that we have been discussing: in opposition to Athene's speech opening the possibility of the trial, it offers a further statement of the implications of the avoidability of a punishment that is reciprocal to the crime and direct. Direct punishment is set against the possibility of doubt, discussion of motivation opened by the institution of the law-court. Thus in this dual status the discussion of δίκη (which we have seen also in other choruses) is particularly charged.

νῦν καταστροφαὶ νέων
θεσμίων, εἰ κρατήσει δίκα τε καὶ βλάβα
τοῦδε μητροκτόνου   490–2

[28] Reading Page's text. (Note the ambiguity captured in Lloyd-Jones' translation). If 489 is kept, and in that place, and if περῶντας is read, then it would be much more difficult to make ἐγώ a subject of διαιρεῖν. However, ἐκδίκοις φρεσίν has a further vertiginous effect with its assumption of δίκη in the sense of 'absolute rule', 'law', 'right'.

This genitive νέων θεσμίων has been discussed at length by critics. Is it to be read as an objective genitive, 'overthrow of new laws', which is Dover's reading: '*Now* there will be an overthrowing of new laws, if the δίκη of this matricide prevails'? If the matricide goes unpunished (and note δίκα ⟨τε⟩ καὶ βλάβα, where βλάβα colours their use of δίκα), then this new institution will have no authority in the future. Or is it a sort of qualitative genitive, 'overthrow consisting in new laws'. 'Now comes final ruin, now with the new law' (Verrall)? καταστροφαί, too, implies both a 'subversion' and a 'sudden end'. Some have argued that this is an important distinction which will/can lead to an understanding of Aeschylus' own political views. But the ambiguity is inherent in the genitive and despite the opposing attempts to read this genitive in a single way, the inherent potentiality of opposite reading cannot be totally repressed. Moreover, this ambiguity itself may be significant. For it marks the interplay between the chorus' acceptance of the process of law, their submission to the trial, and their refusal to accept the decision of the court (unless they win!), an interplay which constitutes the dynamics of the latter part of the play, namely, their threats to Athens *after* the decision in law. And this dynamic, as we will see, is of great importance to the trilogy. The ambiguity of their position is seen in the unresolved ambiguity of the genitive phrase: is it the destruction *of* the new laws or destruction *from* the new laws that they proclaim?

The continuation of the stasimon, however, is with the implications of the non-punishment of Orestes – the deterrence argument. It is expressed in language which recalls the *ainos* of the lion in the house, and the other connections of terms of genesis and narrative. ἔτυμα παιδότρωτα thus also implies 'wounds from real children' (children of their parents) as well as 'real wounds from children'. ἔτυμα implies (again) the 'literal', 'whole' sense, that is, of all its parts: in other words, a splitting of the signifier παιδότρωτα, which stands against the certainty of accurate delineation of the term. The possibility of active/passive sense for -τρωτος is to be noted, the sense of reversal and repetition.[29] But not only is it a splitting of the signifier: in its joining together (*compound* adjective), it represses, plugs the gaps between signifiers, 'thus dramatising the splitting/doubling force of significations'.[30] With its shifting, echoing plays of compounding and dividing, such as we have been reading with δίκη, δίκας, ὑπόδικος, δικηφόρος, ἔκδικος, ἔνδικος, δικάζειν, δικαστάς, Διὸς κόρη, διαιρεῖν,

---

[29] Verrall notes from Hesychius παιδός· ἀκμή and suggests 'point-wounding' with a pun on παιδός, 'of a child'.

[30] J. G. W. Henderson's phrase. Headlam's ἐτυμοπαιδότρωτα would also emphasise this strongly, with the assumption of the mark of the etymon into the word itself.

διά, νίκη, νικηφόρος, νικεῖν (and so one could go on), the Greek language in particular sets its flighty signifiers in riotous reverberation.

The Erinues, who *watch* mortals, βροτοσκόπων, threaten that they will release 'every kind of fate', πάντ'...μόρον. They will collapse distinctions between crimes, between punishments to fit the crimes, and will release 'toils', which result in prayers and attempts at speaking to assuage. But these talking cures are 'uncertain', 'unfixed', οὐ βέβαια, and sought by a person τλάμων, 'wretched'/'bold' (cf. p. 160) in the search.

They continue with the failure of this language (μηδέ τις κικλησκέτω ...τοῦτ' ἔπος θροούμενος) in the face of misfortune (τετυμμένος picks up the reciprocity of τύμμα τύμματι τεῖσαι at *Aga.* 1430; συμφορά is reminiscent of the doubling of action, cf. e.g. *Cho.* 931.). The ἔπος is ὦ Δίκα ὦ θρόνοι τ' Ἐρινύων. Δίκα is precisely the ἔπος the definition of which is being sought ἐτητύμως, and it is the θρόνοι Ἐρινύων, the authority of the Erinues, which is placed at risk by the process of going to law. Such words are the lament of a father (πατήρ) or ἡ τεκοῦσα – note the term is not μήτηρ, the 'normal' parallel for πατήρ, but 'she who gave birth', which is almost a reversal of the distinction of Apollo (658–61), from the Erinues, his opponents. The parents lament because the house of *Dike* is falling. The appeal to *Dike* is because or as the house of *Dike* falls: the appeal to a slipping criterion...

The chorus continue with an expression of the role of Δίκη in society. It is translated normally in these passages as 'Justice', which scarcely suggests (does justice to?) its multivalency, its implication of reciprocal punishment as instantiation of moral justice, as well as its position as introduction to the law-court (δίκη) to hear the cases (δίκας) before the δικαστάς. Interestingly, though, these passages echo many of the earlier moral statements: τὸ δεινὸν εὖ καὶ φρενῶν ἐπίσκοπον δεῖ μένειν. τὸ δεινόν, 'awe', 'terror', 'wonder' – almost an oxymoron with εὖ – is as an 'overseer' of φρενῶν – which looks back to the hymn to Zeus, the first stasimon of the *Choephoroi* and many other places. The attitudes of men may be perverted to the overweening φρόνημα, but may also be restrained in σωφροσύνη: like Zeus' καὶ παρ' ἄκοντας...χάρις βίαιος (*Aga.* 181–2), σωφρονεῖν here comes ὑπὸ στένει – under duress. For both cities and mortals need *dike*. This reference to individual and group, like the widening of action to divine protagonists and elders of the whole city as judges, is a continuation of the generalising principle which may be seen not only in the generalising function of many of the chorus' comments on the action, but also in the tendency to express conflict in the more general oppositional structures of male/female, child/parent. Nor should one forget the performance of the text before the *polis*. So the chorus stress the need for reverence (σέβοι indicates, as before, the maintaining of the hierarchical bonds of respect), reverence for δίκη, which as with Strophe β is the emphatic last word of the stanza.

Developing the sense of σωφρονεῖν, the chorus praise τὸ μέσον, and living neither 'without law, restraint' – the ignoring of ties – nor 'governed by a despot'. So, they conclude, 'the middle ground' is that to which god gives κράτος (around which we have seen members of the house of Atreus struggling) but with regard to other things, he 'oversees' (ἐφορεύει) 'in other ways'.

ξύμμετρον δ' ἔπος λέγω   (533)

This ἔπος, in contrast to the ἔπος at 510, is ξύμμετρον, 'of like measure':[31] this either refers back (μέτρον echoing μέσον) to the praise of the middle path of control, and regards their argument as an example of the moderate; and/or it looks forward to the argument to come: 'I utter a word to fit the case' (Lloyd-Jones). What does follow, refers back strikingly to the second stasimon of the *Agamemnon*, the connection of the passage of sin and the passage of the generations: ὕβρις is the 'child', τέκος, of δυσσεβείας (τίκτειν the common term, as we saw in the *Choephoroi* also for narrative/childbirth); δυσσεβείας expresses the corruption of the relation of σέβας (picking up 525). Opposed to this is the health of mind (φρενῶν, 536 picking up φρενῶν, 518) which leads to the desirable blessing of ὄλβος (as opposed to the often deprecated corruption of φρένες, which leads to disaster). ὡς ἐτύμως, by which τέκος is qualified, 'the very "child"' (Verrall) seems to point to a precision in the terminology (cf. 496, 488) or rather draws attention to some significant verbal play: Verrall suggests that it is not simply that the metaphorical use of τίκτειν/τέκος is marked here also as a literal usage with regard to Orestes, (the significant interpenetration we have noted before) but that there is also a play on a missing term (for which he also refers to *Suppl.* 81–5) namely, κόρος, which means both 'insolence' and 'boy' – a double meaning which 'was especially famous...noted...as well by other poets'. Indeed κόρος is often called the 'child' of ὕβρις, or, sometimes, the producer of ὕβρις – cf. Theog. 153. Pind. *Ol.* 13.12, Her. 8.77: indeed, these stanzas are reminiscent in their general moral tone of Hesiod, Theognis, Solon – particularly in the stated need for δίκη as opposed to κόρος/ὕβρις in the city, a need which forms the

---

31 ἔπος also 'verse', μέτρον, 'metre': πάντι μέσῳ κτλ. / δυσσεβείας μέν κτλ. are indeed metrically equal: ξύμμετρον, self-reflexive, verse-text as verse-text. λέγω: the recognition of speech. Cf. Verrall.

expression of the conservative virtues also cited by 'political' critics
of this passage in their attempt to draw conclusions about Aeschylus'
political beliefs. But even without Verrall's reading, we see a search
for the origin of a word to define its accurate meaning (ἐτύμως) in
a play on a term of origination: the control for the explanation of
events is in the metaphor of childbirth, as the narrative is of the child
and parent, origination. And this play comes before the law-court's
search to διαιρεῖν...ἐτητύμως, a decision which will turn on the
relations of parents and children, the nature of the origin of
childbirth.

Thus again they exhort reverence for *dike*:

> βωμὸν αἴδεσαι Δίκας
> μηδέ νιν κέρδος ἰδὼν ἀθέῳ ποδὶ
> λὰξ ἀτίσῃς   (539–41)

This echoes *Aga.* 380ff., λακτίσαντι...Δίκας βωμόν – where also
κόρος is expressed as a motivating principle, πρὸς κόρον (*Aga.*
382) – which may strengthen Verrall's reading to 534ff. This seems
to link the chorus of Erinues with the chorus of old men, the second
stasimon of the *Agamemnon* with the second stasimon here. As we will
see, the remainder of this antistrophe also picks up many key terms,
not only in that chorus but also from the trilogy in general. The
position of the chorus here seems much closer, then, to the earlier
choruses, and less radically set in an opposition around the term
δίκη. Yet the repetition of terms, after the chorus' reluctance and
then willingness to accept the law-court, after the different readings
of δίκη, serves to mark also the possible difference in meaning here:
for *both* the similarity to *and* the difference from the reciprocity and
revenge of the *Agamemnon* and the qualification of δίκη by Athene
result in a significant tension in such terms of the chorus as
ποινά/τέλος/σέβας/τοκέων/προτίων/ξενο-τίμους/αἰδόμενος; so we
may say that ποινὰ γὰρ ἐπέσται points not only to the reciprocity
of revenge, the economic imagery of exchange, but also recalls the
were-gild, here before the trial for murder which will *not* enforce the
murderer's death. κύριον μένει τέλος: τέλος has the ambiguities we
have discussed; here in particular the chorus imply 'death', 'end'.
But it also recalls τέλος δίκης (243), the result of the trial, which is
precisely not 'death', nor, as we will see, the 'end', but an initiation
of Orestes into his role in society as leader of the *oikos*. κύριον not
only implies 'fixed', 'appointed' but also with reference to ὁ κύριος,
it suggests an end which is the beginning of the authority of the
κύριος – an ambiguity brought out by Lloyd-Jones' translation, 'a
sovereign power awaits'. πρὸς τάδε τις τοκέων σέβας εὖ προτίων:

σέβας, which is, as we have seen, the correct hierarchisation, system-atisation of relations, requires εὖ προτίων, 'honouring before in a good manner'. But the plural τοκέων masks and emphasises the problems of the *Choephoroi* concerning the respective valuation of mother/father, male/female, society/*oikos*, etc. Similarly ξενοτίμους ἐπιστροφὰς δωμάτων αἰδόμενός τις ἔστω, while appearing to stress the normal relation between *xenia, aidos*,[32] may imply in the *hapax legomenon* ξενοτίμους both 'honouring *xenoi*', and 'valuing, estima-ting *xenoi*' which thereby points also to the transgression of the relation of *xenia*, the sense of both *xenos* and not-*xenos* which we saw in the *Choephoroi*. Indeed, ἐπιστροφὰς δωμάτων also recalls Clytemnestra's ominous words at *Aga.* 972, ἀνδρὸς τελείου δῶμ' ἐπιστρωφωμένου. Again, significantly, the moral phrase recalls its corruption.

The *dikaios* man who will be οὐκ ἄνολβος (double negative), and never completely destroyed (cautious promises!), is opposed to the man who is ἀντίτολμος (a *hapax legomenon*). ἀντι- expresses the sense of opposition we have been tracing, as -τολμ- refers back to the house of Atreus' reciprocal, repetitious acts of transgression (cf. *Cho.* 996). Indeed, ἀντίτολμος could be applied to several of the main figures of the play. The chorus here, although they are themselves the very instantiations of revenge, seem to reject the excessive force of violent opposition by which members of the house of Atreus have effected their revenges.

This sense of transgressive deviation is picked up in παρβάδαν, and *dikaios* is followed with ἄνευ δίκας. The image of the shipwreck also recalls *Aga.* 1008ff., another passage concerned with the nature of sin and punishment, as ξὺν χρόνῳ recalls the lion in the house, χρονισθείς. Punishment is deferred, but necessarily comes in the form of πόνος (556), which reminds us of the trilogy's opening prayer. In this stanza in particular, as so often in tragic choruses, the general and the specific are mutually implicative.

The final stanza of the stasimon is a vivid image of the fate of the sinner, calling in vain in the midst of the storm to those who hear nothing (intentionally?) as

> γελᾷ δὲ δαίμων ἐπ' ἀνδρὶ θερμῷ
> τὸν οὔποτ' αὐχοῦντ' ἰδὼν ἀμηχάνοις
> δύαις λαπαδνὸν οὐδ' ὑπερθέοντ' ἄκραν   (560–2)

The daimon laughing ἐπ' ἀνδρί recalls also the possessed Clytem-nestra, as daimon, exulting over her husband's body. So, too, ἐπ' ἀνδρί, particularly with ἰδών following, recalls the prayers to divine

---

[32] Cf. Benveniste 1969, Vol. I, 335ff.

overwatchers; but it is now no longer 'looking over' but 'laughing over'. In the sinful world of the Erinues, the controlling deities are seen as the malicious spirit, laughing over his enemy's downfall. This victim is the one who 'boasts "never"', despite the ineluctable woes surrounding him. His foolish rashness is the foolishness he expresses in a hope for certainty: the failure of a human's predictive language once more. And so he perishes unwept, unseen, 'shipwrecked on the reef of *dike*'. He who kicked the altar, founders on the ἕρματι (cf. *Aga.* 1007).

So, before the trial scene, the *dike* to define *dike*, and after the initial questioning (ἀνάκρισις), in which they rejected and then accepted the trial, because of a distinction made by Athene between the name and the action of δίκαιος, the chorus sing of the need for respect of *dike*. In terms recalling the tragic transgressions of the Atreid house, they sing of the results of possible acquittal, the results both of accepting *dike* as a principle and, conversely, of ignoring the hierarchies of authority and respect. The shifting senses of *dike* in these oppositions mark (the need for) the search for definition which is necessitated by the play of differences as it is undercut by it. The translation of δίκη as 'Justice' or 'justice', or the attempt to construct a simple transitional model from old vengeance to new justice, seem particularly insufficient, in the face of such complexity.

The decisive theological sign

And so we reach the trial scene itself. Athene summons the trial: when the council-place is full, there is to be silence to learn her ordinances 'for the whole city for everlasting time'. Here, before the whole city, the city's goddess proclaims the origins of the Areopagus, the rights of which institution were debated in Athens shortly before the production of the *Oresteia*. These ordinances are to be heard and learnt

$$...\text{ὅπως ἂν εὖ καταγνωσθῇ δίκη} \qquad (573)$$

'So that *dike* may be judged, charged, sentenced well': again *dike* implies the case/punishment, and also the wider notions of Justice, what is right. The manuscripts read δίκη, however, which with τόνδ' is read by Verrall – 'that he (Apollo? Orestes?) may be judged δίκη' – both 'rightly' etc., and 'by process of law' – the purpose for which (ὅπως ἂν) they have gathered. The ambiguities of δίκη continue. It must be judged well.

The chorus begin their cross-examination with a question designed to specify the role of Apollo in the event:

ἄναξ Ἄπολλον, ὧν ἔχεις αὐτὸς κράτει.
τί τοῦδε σοὶ μέτεστι πράγματος λέγε   (574–5)

κράτει, 'exercise κράτος over what is yours', recalls the dispute of κράτος in the *oikos*. τί...μέτεστι, 'what part, share?' evokes the play between μεταίτιος/παναίτιος/ἐπαίτιος. Now to clarify the causality? πράγματα is a common term in particular for legal business and it picks up specifically 470, 488, Athene's description of the business at hand. Juxtaposed to λέγε, however, it recalls the common opposition between πρᾶγμα and λόγος, and points to the clash of λόγοι (to decide the πρᾶγμα): the πράγματα to come are λόγοι.

Apollo claims that he comes μαρτυρήσων – to be a witness that Orestes has been purified and cleansed of the slaughter – and ξυνδικήσων: in Athens, particularly, to be a ξύνδικος is to be 'a public advocate', 'to defend the interest of someone publicly', but also, with αὐτός it suggests 'to go through the δίκη together', 'to be a co-defendant'. The reason is αἰτίαν...ἔχω...τοῦ φόνου. αἰτίαν once more relevantly signifies both 'charge' and 'responsibility', 'cause'.

So with terms that are the technical terms of the Athenian court, he turns to Athene to bring in the proceedings and she gives the floor to ὁ διώκων. The 'prosecutor' in Attic legal vocabulary here has its 'literal' sense as 'pursuer', 'hunter'. The turning to law of the pursuit of vengeance is marked by the shift in sense of the repeated word.

The chorus begin their prosecution, marked (586) as the exchange (ἀμείβου) of words, ἔπος...πρὸς ἔπος ἐν μέρει, with the question of 'fact': τὴν μητέρ'...εἰ κατέκτονας (587). This Orestes accepts (588). The chorus reply: ἓν μὲν τόδ' ἤδη τῶν τριῶν παλαισμάτων. This recalls not only the significance of third as last (in this third play of the trilogy), but also the specific reference to Zeus' generational conflict (the third generation) at *Aga.* 171, and also οὐκ ἀτρίακτος ἄτα (*Cho.* 339): the continuing force of ἄτη is threatening Orestes (here as there). Orestes notes, however, that he is not yet defeated. He will, nevertheless, soon have to turn to Apollo. The chorus ask ὅπως he killed her: this could be taken as both 'how he came to kill' and 'in what manner he killed her'. Orestes willingly tells (λέγω picking up λόγον, 590), but relates the answer directly to 'in what manner', which 'is...plainly immaterial' (Verrall): 'His reply...is an ignoratio elenchi.' Once more, in this word exchange of cross-examination, the gap between speakers[33] is pointed. The chorus (specifying ὅπως?)

---

[33] That is, he specifies the ambiguity in one way, but not the way we read the chorus to mean – our specifying in another way marks the heuristic of *our* reading.

ask: πρὸς τοῦ δ' ἐπείσθης καὶ τίνος βουλεύμασιν; They now willingly question for his motivation. Orestes appeals to the oracles of Apollo. To which the chorus reply with some surprised irony:

ὁ μάντις ἐξηγεῖτό σοι μητροκτονεῖν;   (595)

The 'seer instructed you to kill your mother?' ('The oracle should ...have foreseen the consequences of such an act' (Verrall)). The term for instruction is that of instruction in the forms of religious rites, which seems somewhat ironic in its juxtaposition to the most irreligious act of matricide. Orestes claims, however, to find no blame up to this point with τὴν τύχην, his fortune, but the chorus picking up the limitative δεῦρό γ', point to the possibility of reversing his statement in the future (note that change of fortune is again expressed as change of speech, cf. *Aga.* 705–16): Orestes (taking a more offensive role in his defence) now restates his trust in Apollo, and also mentions the help πατήρ sends from the tomb, which, as the scholion points out, also recalls the fact that it is his mother from the netherworlds who motivates the Erinues themselves. Indeed, the chorus reply with bitter irony (returning the offensive):

νεκροῖσί νυν πέπισθι μητέρα κτανών   (599)

'Trust then in corpses since/after having killed your mother.' Particularly after the appearance of Clytemnestra's ghost, trust in the dead is double-edged support.

Orestes returns the attack with a reason for the matricide: δυοῖν γὰρ εἶχε προσβολὰς μιασμάτοιν (600). This riddle of two, double pollutions recalls the ambiguities of δυοῖν μιαστόροιν (*Cho.* 944), where we saw the unavoidable implications of Orestes/Pylades as well as Clytemnestra/Aegisthus (the logic of the doubling narrative, the διπλῆ συμφορά). Here, too, particularly with προσβολάς, which was the word used (*Cho.* 283) of Apollo's threat of attack (by Erinues!) if Orestes failed to achieve the revenge, the 'dual pollutions' seems to suggest not only the sin but also the punishment of Clytemnestra: the logic of the double; of reversal and repetition.

Orestes explains what he means by δυοῖν:

ἀνδροκτονοῦσα πατέρ' ἐμὸν κατέκτανε   (602)

The dual status of her pollution is through the predication of a double status to Agamemnon as the husband of Clytemnestra and the father of Orestes. A person is not named, but classed: Clytemnestra in killing a person has transgressed relations, classifications. This distinction of the category of a person is essential also to the Erinues' remark that they chase only blood-relations; and it will be the definition of this boundary which will decide the trial. But essential to this process of (re-)naming (categorising) is the separability of the signifier from a signified, which constitutes predicability. The separation of signifier and signified, which constituted the possibility of Clytemnestra's crime, the ambiguity of Orestes' revenge, will also therefore constitute the power of the law to define by the word of the Judge, the power to define the categorisation of relations, that is, their naming.

The chorus draw the obvious conclusion of the logic of revenge: it is expressed in a highly rhetorical way, however:

τί γάρ; σὺ μὲν ʒῆς ἡ δ' ἐλευθέρα φόνῳ   (603)

This leaves the implications of (the continuing retribution of) φόνῳ for Orestes unspecified, but strongly hinted at. Orestes turns (defensively?) to Apollo's earlier point that the Erinues did not (however) pursue Clytemnestra. As before, the chorus state the distinction of blood-relations: Clytemnestra and Agamemnon were not ὅμαιμος, 'of/with the same blood'. Orestes asks: ἐγὼ δὲ μητρὸς τῆς ἐμῆς ἐν αἵματι; 'Am I of the blood of my mother?' But the Erinues' dismissal of such a question[34] is forcibly stated:

πῶς γάρ σ' ἔθρεψεν ἐντός, ὦ μιαιφόνε,
ʒώνης; ἀπεύχῃ μητρὸς αἷμα φίλτατον;   (607–8)

ἔθρεψεν, we have seen, is an important term: it is both a normal role for parents and yet to be distinguished from the role of the 'mother' (as we saw in the speech of the τροφός in the *Choephoroi*). Indeed, Apollo will claim the 'mother' to be (merely) τροφὸς...κύματος (659). Their use of the term contains the seed of Apollo's argument also; so, too, their second question recalls the paradox of φιλτάτους ...πικρούς. The mother's blood, they claim, is surely the most φίλος, closest of kin – yet the definition of the mother as precisely φίλτατον and not φίλτατον was the struggle of the *Choephoroi*. Orestes, however, cannot simply reject his mother's blood as not φίλτατον: he has no further argument, but turns (defeated? at a loss?) to his divine protector to bear him witness: ἐξηγοῦ δέ μοι (ironically picking up the chorus at 595 – 'religious instruction') ...εἴ σφε σὺν δίκῃ κατέκτανον. | δρᾶσαι γάρ, ὥσπερ ἔστιν, οὐκ ἀρνούμεθα. The adverbial qualification σὺν δίκῃ recalls, amongst others, particularly the play at *Cho.* 144 where the possibility of the non-simplicity of the reciprocity of revenge was opened by the qualification σὺν δίκῃ. Such qualifying of action is now required for Orestes' defence since (γάρ)

---

[34] Verrall finds Orestes' argument 'superfluous and embarrassing', and thus suggests that it is a rhetorical metaphor: Clytemnestra, in other words, dissolved the bonds of family by her actions, and Orestes is thus not the 'same sort' as his mother. That Apollo uses the argument in a way Verrall does regard as literal, is a further example of what Verrall sees as the god of truth's untrustworthiness.

there is no way he can deny that he *did* the deed. It is the (possibility of) predication σὺν δίκῃ that is the condition of possibility of Orestes' acquittal.

> ἀλλ' εἰ δικαίως εἴτε μὴ τῇ σῇ φρενὶ
> δοκεῖ, τόδε αἷμα κρῖνον, ὡς τούτοις φράσω   (612–13)

εἰ... εἴτε μὴ marks the possibility of opposite predications of δικαίως – which is the condition of possibility of the court. Furthermore, Apollo is asked αἷμα κρῖνον: 'Judge this blood.' Indeed, the debate will turn on the definition of αἷμα: Orestes, then, handing his case to his co-defendant, refers back to the development of the constitution of the trial as well as looking forward to its conclusion.

Apollo promises he will speak (λέξω: first word; his logos) δικαίως. This appropriates for his speech both the status of established truth as the word of the father (621: the word of law is spoken δικαίως), and yet, after εἰ δικαίως εἴτε μὴ..., it is also sited in opposition to the Erinues as non-absolute. As we argued on pp. 139–40, the very capability of citation of the father's words as authorisation (from the origin) marks in their repetition the trace of difference. Here, we see the paradox of asserting δίκη as a moral absolute in the instantiation of δίκη as opposition; that is, in the court-case with its paired δίκαι. Indeed, Apollo says τὸ μὲν δίκαιον τοῦθ' ὅσον σθένει μάθε. | βουλῇ πιφαύσκω δ' ὕμμ' ἐπισπέσθαι πατρός (619–20). In the claim of right for his case through the authorisation of the father (πατρός emphatically picking up πατήρ, 618), an opposite authorisation is also suggested, namely, the role of the mother which has been constantly cited in opposition to the father, and which, indeed, the chorus pick up in τὸν <u>πατρὸς</u> φόνον | πράξαντα <u>μητρὸς</u> μηδαμοῦ τιμὰς νέμειν; The constitution of the debate in the opposition of mother/father, female/male, then, further challenges the simple authority of Apollo as word-of-the-father as truth.

Indeed, the chorus strongly mark the word of Zeus as a recession of citations:

> Ζεύς, ὡς <u>λέγεις</u> σύ, τόνδε <u>χρησμὸν</u> ὤπασε
> <u>φράζειν</u> Ὀρέστῃ τῷδε   (622–3)

'Zeus, as you say, gave you this oracle to indicate to this man Orestes' – 'you say that he said for you to say...', which (sited in the problematic of the exchange of words) points also to the continuing exchange of *our* reading ('we may say...'). This reply of the chorus neatly points the illogicality of simply authorising the murder[35] as

---

35 Thomson, *Oresteia* Vol. I, p. 64 (new ed.): 'Appeals to authority are useless when there is a conflict of authority.'

defence against Orestes' punishment. The reciprocity of action implied (as we have seen) by πράξαντα / τιμὰς νέμειν calls for reciprocal punishment. Apollo, however, asserts the asymmetry of the opposition: τιμάς are what is paid for compensation; and they are also the honours, marks of respect, marking the reciprocal (but not necessarily equal) bonds of society.[36] Apollo asserts the different 'honour' of a man and husband (ἄνδρα, 625; ἄνδρα, 635; ἀνδρός, 636); the male is 'noble', γενναῖον, 'honoured', τιμαλφούμενον, 'by the Zeus-given sceptre' (authorising authority in the generative function of the genitive 'of/from Zeus'). More than this, however (he continues), is the fact that the man's death was at the hands of a woman,[37] and Apollo proceeds to describe Agamemnon's death, drawing out many of the implications of the *kommos* into an extended statement of the shame of the man of the army who was killed by trickery in his bath:

> ἀνδρὸς μὲν ὑμῖν οὗτος εἴρηται μόρος
> τοῦ παντοσέμνου, τοῦ στρατηλάτου νεῶν.
> τὴν δ᾿ αὖ τοιαύτην εἶπον ὡς δηχθῇ λεώς,
> ὅσπερ τέτακται τήνδε κυρῶσαι δίκην   (636–9)

The man is παντοσέμνου – 'deserving of *all* respect', 'deserving of respect *in every way*'. The argument is once more inflated to a position of binary opposition and exclusion. Agamemnon was 'emperor of the fleet' (Verrall).[38] But the woman...(and here the opposition is in fact a rhetorical refusal to describe, a sort of paraleipsis) 'is such', a description which, he says, is spoken 'to sting the people of the court to anger'.

The chorus have a return argument, though:

> πατρὸς προτιμᾷ Ζεὺς μόρον τῷ σῷ λόγῳ,
> αὐτὸς δ᾿ ἔδησε πατέρα πρεσβύτην Κρόνον.
> πῶς ταῦτα τούτοις οὐκ ἐναντίως λέγεις;
> ὑμᾶς δ᾿ ἀκούειν ταῦτ᾿ ἐγὼ μαρτύρομαι   (640–3)

πατρός, the father, emphatic first word, is the one whose fate Zeus honours: προτιμᾷ, as with προτίων (545), indicates the hierarchisation of respect. But this argument of Apollo is marked by the Erinues as such (merely an argument) by τῷ σῷ λόγῳ. The Erinues do not allow his logos the self-evident status of truth. They then proceed to turn honour of the father against the patriarchs. For Zeus himself

---

[36] See now on τιμή Macleod 1982, pp. 138ff.

[37] Not even an Amazon: the allowable female opposition in war – but cf. Merck 1978 for the interplay (from one point of view) of the Amazonomachy and this trilogy.

[38] Winnington-Ingram (1949, p. 142) notes the destruction of the Argive fleet, and Agamemnon's humiliation in the carpet scene. εἴρηται marks this description as logos, speech.

bound his father, old man Kronos. To this inconsistent respect for the father (ἐναντίως λέγεις) they beg the jurors to attend as witnesses. Apollo's reply, however, begins with an insult:

ὦ παντομισῆ κνώδαλα, στύγη θεῶν   (644)

κνώδαλα seems to be a term within the tripartite systematisation we have considered, neither a god (στύγη θεῶν), nor human. μισῆ and στύγη (and by implication φίλος), as the expressions of bonds between men and gods, here too are used of the expression of the separateness of the κνώδαλα: they are παντομισῆ as Agamemnon was παντοσέμνου. Apollo's defence is that bonds may be undone, but the spilling of blood (of a dead man) is irrevocable – which recalls *Cho.* 48, 66, 520ff. etc. This argument is also sited/cited as the dictum of the father: οὐκ ἐποίησεν πατὴρ οὑμός – οὑμός linking Apollo to Zeus (Orestes/Agamemnon, Apollo/Zeus). This defence against filial impiety may seem 'grotesque' (Sidgwick) for a modern reader – but within the argument of absolute reciprocities of revenge, reversibility in the sense of undoing may be an important distinction. But again Apollo's defence of the *ad hominem* argument concerning Zeus the father leaves him open to a further attack with regard to Orestes' punishment: this process of argumentation highlights once more the process of exchange of logoi, and the manipulation of this process of exchange in the development of logos:

πῶς γὰρ τὸ φεύγειν τοῦδ' ὑπερδικεῖς ὅρα·
τὸ μητρὸς αἷμ' ὅμαιμον ἐκχέας πέδοι
ἔπειτ' ἐν Ἄργει δώματ' οἰκήσει πατρός;   (652–4)

How can Orestes, then, seek acquittal having spilt his mother's αἷμ' ὅμαιμον – 'blood which is the same blood' (cf. 605–13)? ἐκχέας πέδοι recalls *Cho.* 48 and images of flow in that play, as δώματ' οἰκήσει recalls the fact that the house and not merely Orestes' life is at stake, or rather that it is Orestes' initiation into his role (as πατήρ) in the *oikos* of his father, the generational continuity of the *oikos*, that is at risk. ὑπερδικεῖς, 'advocate', recalls also *Aga.* 1396, where ὑπερδίκως, 'excessively just' was a correction (μὲν οὖν) for δικαίως, describing the transgression of Clytemnestra's murder: is there an implication here that Apollo's position is not, as he had suggested, simply δικαίως?

Apollo now challenges αἷμ' ὅμαιμον: as Orestes' exchange with the chorus stopped precisely at the point of the closeness of his mother's blood, now Apollo, too, has been forced by the turn of discussion to question that link of son and mother in blood. It is, within the development of the arguments, the step that has to be taken: it is (only) the mother's connection with the son which can and must be

challenged to achieve Orestes' defence. And after his speech asserting
that there is *no link*, Athene will mark the end of the exchange of views
with ἅλις λελέγμενων, 'enough has been said'. It is enough to
challenge the connection between mother and son.

Apollo's position is marked as logos in his opening words:

καὶ τοῦτο λέξω καὶ μάθ' ὡς ὀρθῶς ἐρῶ.
οὐκ ἔστι μήτηρ ἡ κεκλημένη τέκνου
τοκεύς, τροφὸς δὲ κύματος νεοσπόρου.
τίκτει δ' ὁ θρῴσκων ἡ δ' ἅπερ ξένῳ ξένη
ἔσωσεν ἔρνος, οἷσι μὴ βλάψῃ θεός[39]   (657–61)

His position is also marked as a question of definition, ἡ κεκλημένη –
and hence he claims (657) ὀρθότης for his language. It is the naming
of the 'mother'; it is to distinguish between τοκεύς and τροφός
(harking back to the nurse of the *Choephoroi*) denying the applicability
of τοκεύς to the μήτηρ. The etymological link τοκεύς–τέκνου is
suggested here in the moment of search for the origin of the child:
the 'mother', he claims, is a 'nurse' – conflating the distinction we
had seen in the *Choephoroi* – whereas the 'one who mounts', 'sire'
is the begetter, τίκτει. This assertion of paternity, the function of
generation *solely* with *the male*, seems also the gesture which allows
Apollo to claim his authority solely from Zeus, to assert the word-
of-the-father. We see a development of the connection between
paternity and the male discourse of authority we have discussed
before; but further, with regard to τίκτειν as a metaphor for logos,
with regard to the search for a simple origin for words (to constitute
truth), we see the necessary rejection of the normally assumed *duality*
(διπλοῖ/ἀμφιθαλής) of parentage by/in the *singleness* of the *father*.
Indeed, the proof (τεκμήριον) of Apollo is the presence of Athene,
as witness to the fact that a father can give birth without a mother:
she is παῖς Διός, child of the father, Zeus. Yet the story of Athene's
birth, variously told, includes the contest between Hera and Zeus (the
holy marriage) to produce children individually, and Hera produced
the giant Typhaon (cf. *Hom. Hymn to Apollo* 305–55) (or according
to a version quoted by Lloyd-Jones, Hephaestus). Can the logos of
Apollo in its claim for the singleness, linearity of the relation
father–child exclude the further linearity of the relation mother–
child? Can the establishment of the discourse of paternity (the word-
of-the-father) as the word of truth by its derivation from a fixed and
single origin avoid in this proof the suggestion of its own
unstableness?

[39] ἔρνος, as Clytemnestra described Iphigeneia (*Aga.* 1525). Why the qualification (εἰ
μή...)? Winnington-Ingram (1949) suggests it is to remind us of the pregnant hare's
death, *Aga.* 120 – a failure of generational continuity.

Apollo continues with a 'bribe' (Verrall) to Athene and Athens, promising eternal support for the city and goddess (echoing 289ff.), but has no further argument to offer, and when Athene concludes the debate (ἅλις λελεγμένων – enough logoi) with an instruction to the jurors to cast a δίκαιον vote,[40] both Apollo and the Erinues readily concede they have ended their argument. Athene turns to address Ἀττικὸς λεώς – which refers to the jurors, who were called λεώς (638) – but is there also a reference to the πόλις gathered in the theatre? Indeed many critics have taken this passage to refer to the political situation in Athens at the time – though as Dover has noted, the political vocabulary of this speech in its moral generalities is applicable to most political positions, and thus puts at risk attempts to specify a political content. Macleod, indeed, in a good article, has argued that 'in those places in the *Eumenides* where topical allusions have been detected, there are rather – or at least also – links with the rest of the trilogy. So, if we speak of "politics" in the *Oresteia*, it may be helpful to give the word a different sense, "a concern with human beings as part of a community".'[41] In the course of my discussion, I will take the opportunity to add and specify some further ways and occasions that these political concerns and vocabularies are woven into the text. For example, let us consider the 'firsts' of this speech.

The jurors are deciding the first trial for homicide, πρώτας δίκας... αἵματος χυτοῦ. This procedure will be an establishment for ever on the Areopagus for the people of Aegeus. Athene then offers an etymology of the name 'Areopagus': here the Amazons[42] pursuing Theseus (the son of Aegeus) raised a camp and sacrificed to Ares: ἔνθεν ἔστ' ἐπώνυμος | πέτρα πάγος τ' Ἄρειος. This etymology of the name comes at the same time as the moment of the expression of the origin of the establishment on the hill, the foundation myth of the Areopagus (as Macleod and others have termed it). As an origin, it is sited within the series of always already questioned origins (childbirth, words, narrative), that we have been tracing throughout the trilogy (and especially in Apollo's immediately preceding argument). Even the status of πρώτας δίκας has been challenged![43] As another story of origination, the 'political' implications of this passage are closely woven into the discourse of the play.

Moreover, as the etymological origin of the word cannot control

---

[40] As before, the 'δίκαιον vote' implies a vote about δίκη as punishment, δίκη as justice, δίκη as law-court, case.   [41] 1982, p. 132.

[42] Cf. Merck 1978. The wild women defeated by the civilising king Theseus are depicted often on temples. Cf. also the lapiths/centaurs and the fight for civilisation against the wildness of the uncivilised.   [43] See Verrall on 688–93.

its sense within the play of signifiers, as the origin of the Areopagus, the θεσμός, stands challenged in its constant and fixed status, so too the search for the origin of this speech of Athene in the political views of Aeschylus is insufficient to control the play of signifiers within the discourse of the work. For Athene's language picks up and develops many of the terms of the discourse we have been discussing, and in particular, as Lloyd-Jones notes, the second stasimon of the *Eumenides*: σέβας (690) is linked to φόβος, described as ξυγγενής (kinsman, related). Respect and fear will restrain wrongdoing: fear, which we have seen as a reaction to an ability to predict narrative or to control language, now works with respect, the definition of boundaries, of relations, to help to prevent transgression (ἀδικεῖν), which in this work has involved precisely the lack of restraint with regard to the controls of language and respect. τό τ' ἦμαρ καὶ κατ' εὐφρόνην (692) in the imagery of light and dark not only recalls the often difficult vocabulary of day/night/clarity (before the decision of the court), but also εὐφρόνην specifically evokes Clytemnestra's opening pun in the *Agamemnon*, precisely her lack of φόβος/σέβας with regard to the boundaries of language.

> κακαῖς ἐπιρροαῖσι βορβόρῳ θ' ὕδωρ
> λαμπρὸν μιαίνων οὔποθ' εὑρήσεις ποτόν   (694–5)

μιαίνω, 'pollute', was used by the messenger in the *Agamemnon* for the pollution by (the misuse of) language. Here the appeal for clarity, λαμπρόν, (as of Cassandra's prophecy at *Aga.* 1180) is opposed to such evil admixtures. Like Cassandra's language, however, does the very openness of the metaphors stand awkwardly with the sought-for clarity?

The goddess' subsequent words on the place of *dike* in society (696–9) follow the words of the chorus (517ff.) so closely that Dindorf presumed them spurious. Athene, however, despite her acceptance of the chorus' terms will not (as 734ff. will show) accept their definition of *dike*. Her repetition of the need for restraint with regard to *dike* serves to mark the difference in the sense of *dike*, despite their apparent agreement in and authorisation of the place of *dike* with regard to society. As the Erinues spoke of *dike* in general in its implications for the *kosmos* so this new βουλευτήριον is to have such a role for the city:

> κερδῶν ἄθικτον τοῦτο βουλευτήριον
> αἰδοῖον, ὀξύθυμον εὑδόντων ὕπερ
> ἐγρηγορὸς φρούρημα γῆς καθίσταμαι   (704–6)

As Macleod has shown, these terms refer back significantly through the trilogy. For example, the permanent watchfulness of the court may be opposed to the sleeping Erinues, the different guardians of *dike*; the respect for the council (αἰδοῖον) may be opposed to the transgressions of *aidos* by Clytemnestra, Agamemnon, Orestes.

Athene declares this ordinance an exhortation for the rest of time and calls on the citizens to be straight, upright (ὀρθοῦσθαι), which echoes both the Erinues' claim to be ὀρθαὶ μάρτυρες and Apollo's ὀρθῶς ἐρῶ. The term which indicates correctness in speech, defining, action, is itself an object of appropriation in this trial of law.

καὶ ψῆφον αἴρειν καὶ διαγνῶναι δίκην   (709)

Athene had talked of διαιρεῖν τοῦτο πρᾶγμα (488) as the aim of the trial, now the jurors are to ψῆφον αἴρειν καὶ <u>διαγνῶναι</u> δίκην: the splitting into different parts of the function of splitting points to the process of separation involved in the act of decision (διαγνῶναι), the decision of δίκην (δίκας), which is precisely the term whose meanings are to be separated. So she finishes: εἴρηται λόγος. Her speech, too, is marked as logos.

As the voting (presumably) takes place, the chorus and Apollo in turn exhort, threaten and promise the voters.

The chorus begin with a threat to Athens (as Apollo had promised good things) if the jurors 'slight' (ἀτιμάσαι) them – Apollo retorts with an appeal to the authority of his and Zeus' oracles (recalling the punning necessity χρησμοῖς…χρή at *Cho.* 297). The chorus retort that if there is respect (σέβας) for αἱματηρὰ πράγματα (the deeds of *blood*), his oracles will be polluted (recalling e.g. 162ff.).[44] Against which Apollo recalls his father's treatment of Ixion, the first killer, first suppliant. But his sarcastic question ἦ καὶ πατήρ τι σφάλλεται βουλευμάτων; 'Is (my) father in any way tripped up in his wisdom?', is accepted by the chorus as a *statement* of fact, a sort of cledonomantic turning of the grammar: λέγεις (pointing to the exchange of logos again). And they repeat their threat to the land, dependent on whether they τυχοῦσα τῆς δίκης: 'hit on, reach *dike*' ('decision', 'punishment' etc.) – but it must be reaching a *dike as they wish*. Apollo retorts that the Erinues are without honour (ἄτιμος – their threat had been dependent on their loss of honour, τιμή, as at 227 etc.) and that he will win, νικήσω. Again we see the play, constituted by the opposition of the Erinues and Apollo (as seen in these paired couplets) between δίκη (τυχοῦσα τῆς δίκης, 719) and νίκη. The equivalence of these terms for Apollo and the Erinues (resisting the mediating point) is seen precisely in the paired boasts/threats for δίκη (Erinues) and νίκη (Apollo). However, the Erinues turn even this to a taunt:

---

44 Winnington-Ingram notes with regard to the sanctity of the Delphic oracle that the oracle had medised (1949, p. 142).

τοιαῦτ' ἔδρασας καὶ Φέρητος ἐν δόμοις·
Μοίρας ἔπεισας ἀφθίτους θεῖναι βροτούς   (723-4)

His victory would be the second example of his interference in the
fate of a mortal with regard to the moment of death. This reversal
of the natural order (described as *persuasion* of the Fates) refers to
the story of Admetus, who was allowed not to die young, provided
someone else would die in his place. The reason for Apollo's kindness
(to one who reveres, σέβοντ') was his period of slavery enforced by
Zeus 'for a previous interference with the course of divine law'
(Verrall). The chorus hint therefore at an indication of a split between
Zeus and Apollo, father–son rivalry. The Erinues further taunt his
justification with:

σύ τοι παλαιὰς διανομὰς καταφθίσας
οἴνῳ παρηπάφησας ἀρχαίας θεάς   (727-8)

καταφθίσας picks up ἀφθίτους. The taunt is not merely of making
mortals non-destroyable, but of actively destroying the ancient
categorisations: διανομάς. The reminder of his disgraceful deception
brings forth the rage of Apollo (cf. 640-5, his earlier reaction to the
Erinues' clever argumentation):

σύ τοι τάχ' οὐκ ἔχουσα τῆς δίκης τέλος
ἐμῇ τὸν ἰὸν οὐδὲν ἐχθροῖσιν βαρύν   (729-30)

Apollo's ἔχουσα τῆς δίκης τέλος marks the law's apparent teleology,
the moment of decision that they await. But this phrase also echoes
paragrammatically the chorus' τυχοῦσα τῆς δίκης, and thus re-marks
in its similarity of sound and difference of sense the tensions in the
term *dike*. Indeed, the difference and similarity between δίκης and
τέλος δίκης is significant: it will be the way that the τέλος δίκης which
Apollo awaits is neither the final *telos* of the process of the reordering
of things, nor the Erinues' hoped-for end of the judicial process, that
constitutes the dynamics of the play after the decision of the court.
Indeed, the chorus wait (μένω recalls Orestes' wait at 243, ἀναμένω
τέλος δίκης) to hear what is δίκης...τῆσδε 'this *dike*', ἀμφίβουλος
οὖσα θυμοῦσθαι πόλει (733). 'With double intention', 'uncertain', a
hapax legomenon, points not only to the doubling of arguments, not
only to the double-bind of threats to the city that Athene had noted
(480), but also to the doubleness in the term *dike* itself.

So these short speeches (711-33) recall many of the major referents
which constitute the debate, polarised in forms of opposed couplets,
marking the opposition to be instantiated in the tied vote.

The voting is assumed to take place during these speeches
(711-33) – but the asymmetry of the chorus' last short speech (731-3)

which is three lines, after the couplets of the preceding ten speeches, removes the possibility, should one so seek it, of any neat and simple linking of stage-action to words (such as Kitto so forcibly demands). The critical debate here, however, is not so much concerned with the staging of the scene (though, as we will see, it returns to this often), as with whether Athene's vote makes the number of votes equal to achieve Orestes' acquittal, or the divine deciding vote is between votes already equally matched on the human level.

Müller, Sidgwick, Verrall, Thomson, Lloyd-Jones, Davies, Podlecki and others agree on the 'impressive symbolism'[45] (Sidgwick) of the scene of Athene's symbolic vote being held up after the voting has finished, and Thomson has an extended consideration of the literature (*Oresteia* Vol. II, pp. 220–1), noting this vote as the origin of the Vote of Athene, which was used in Athens to separate a tied vote in favour of the defendant. Against this, however, are the Germans, Hermann and Wilamowitz, most recently championed by Gagarin, who claims he hopes he will 'finally lay Müller's interpretation to rest'. He begins with the number of speeches, which, he says, suggests 'precisely eleven' jurors, but then because of the asymmetry he also concludes (1975, p. 122) that 'other scenarios are possible' (less 'precisely'?). He proceeds to the deictic 735: 'She must either be pointing to it, or more likely , holding the pebble in her hand.' Does 'must' mean there are only two possibilities? Only 'either...pointing' 'or...holding'? How is this argued for? Is it just by the assumption of the simple referential presence of the deictic (despite 'either...or'), which, as we saw in the recognition scene and elsewhere, is not always a safe assumption? 'Holding the pebble...' Hold it! 'Holding' what? Is τήνδε ψῆφον the same as the votes the jurors are instructed to use? How can one tell? Verrall suggests, for example, that 'this vote' is the outstretched, protective arm of Athene, that it is a metaphorical pebble – marking Athene's position as part of the trial but apart from the opposition of Apollo and Erinues, apart from the vote of binary opposition. How can Gagarin, particularly after the complex interplay of metaphorisation in this highly complex poetical text, assume a simple, clear referentiality for ψῆφον? How can he 'precisely', 'finally', separate metaphor from *effet du réel* here? Even if we were to allow the simple presence of a simple pebble (repressing the doubt of his interpretation as he hopes to 'lay Müller's interpretation to rest'), how does he continue? 'She

---

[45] There is, of course, 'impressive symbolism' for both stagings: with Gagarin, the vote is as close as it possibly could be, that is, with both divine and human wisdom the votes are equal and are separated only by the proviso κἂν ἰσόψηφος; with Sidgwick *et al.*, the equality of the votes is decided by the significant act of mediation.

does not indicate when she will cast her vote.' Indeed: προσθήσομαι 'I will add' – but no indication of when/how. Will his argument depend then merely on an interpretation of staging? But first, from 'unconditionally her intention to vote', he concludes: 'throughout the scene the language consistently implies that Athene physically casts her vote'. The intention may well imply the fact that a vote of Athene is to be registered, but it implies nothing about the nature of the vote. So wherefore '*physically* casts'? Is that adverb just (necessary) backing for his view of the physical staging as providing an answer? So his next argument indeed is concerned with staging: despite the possibility of other stagings, he suggests that Athene moves forward at 733 to cast the twelfth vote: 'such staging is by far the simplest and would easily clarify any possible ambiguity in the spoken text'. This argument shows the favoured stagecraft circularity of discovering action from the ambiguities of the text to limit the ambiguities of the text – interpretation to efface the work of interpretation in a supposed easy clarity. Thus despite these 'possible ambiguities' and the need to clarify, he claims 'virtually all the evidence supports this one view' – which, as with Fraenkel on the carpet scene, raises questions of 'evidence of what?' 'is evidence really separate from the work of reading, interpretation?', 'isn't the evidence constitutive of the one view rather than the proof of it?'. And notice how 'virtually all' opens even in Gagarin's conclusion the requestioning. If not 'all', then how would it 'easily clarify *any possible* ambiguity'? Is the 'evidence' which does not 'support this one view' in opposition to it? Or is there 'evidence' which neither 'supports' nor opposes? 'Evidence' which proves nothing? 'Evidence' of what then? Does the polite restraint of 'virtually' point in fact precisely to the teleology of (the search for) 'evidence'?

Once again we have seen in a crux of dramatic representation the difficulty of reading a dramatic text as specifying its performance. Again the ambiguities and doublings of the plural text constitute the text's necessary performance as necessary violence.

In some senses, however, it is far more important to consider the reasons Athene gives for her vote. For all agree that it is through the vote of Athene that the acquittal is attained, and like the litigants she gives her reasons for voting one way:

> μήτηρ γὰρ οὔτις ἐστὶν ἥ μ' ἐγείνατο
> τὸ δ' ἄρσεν αἰνῶ πάντα, πλὴν γάμου τυχεῖν
> ἅπαντι θυμῷ, κάρτα δ' εἰμὶ τοῦ πατρός.
> οὕτω γυναικὸς οὐ προτιμήσω μόρον
> ἄνδρα κτανούσης δωμάτων ἐπίσκοπον   (736–40)

Athene has no mother. This separates her from the norm of society (even of the gods). Moreover, she praises the *male* in all things, that is, in terms of the opposition of male and female we have seen, she votes for Orestes as the male (note τὸ ἄρσεν, the generic, scientific term); without a mother, she has been separated from the genealogy of birth from the female, which would tie her to the female. But she has no part in marriage: despite (πάντα, πλήν) her otherwise complete praise for the male, she does not enter into the system of exchange between men: she rejects the role of a woman in male society, marriage. Indeed, she is, as we have seen at 292–7, 396–402, the warrior-goddess, taking part in battle, precisely the male domain. As Vernant notes, warfare is the initiation into the society of men as marriage is of women. She is with all her spirit τοῦ πατρός – the genitive phrase connotes of, from, consisting in, part of, supporting the father. This is what Orestes claimed, as did Apollo, as authorisation and aim – the paternal metaphor, the word 'of-the-father', πατρός. For this reason, she will not put before in honour (προτιμήσω, cf. 640 etc.) the fate (μόρον, cf. 640) of a woman who has killed her husband/man. ἄνδρα is both the sexual determinant and the male role in society – in as much as they can be separated – as is further clarified by δωμάτων ἐπίσκοπον: 'the man', like the gods, Erinues etc., is an 'overseer' of the houses: the position of the husband (man) is as master of the *oikos*. Athene is a female who transgresses the opposition of male/female in her support of the male, and in her rejection of the female role in favour of the male; Athene represents the vote which allows the acquittal of Orestes – that is, the escape from the pattern of reciprocal revenge which has been depicted in terms of an opposition of the sexes, precisely because she stands between and against the opposition. Her vote is achieved because of, through, her confusion, transgression, mediation of boundaries – both male and female. The goddess expresses her androgyny. Thus even if the votes are equal (for the male and the female) Orestes will be freed, because of the position which transcends (as it emphasises[46]) the opposition of the sexes.

So, after her speech for Orestes, which is expressed in such markedly sexual terms, Athene tells the jurors, the elders of the city, to count the votes. Orestes and the Erinues both express their concern, Orestes for either death or life, expressed as φάος βλέπειν (746), which contrasts with the Erinues' appeal to Νὺξ μέλαινα μῆτερ (745); for them, it is destruction or maintenance of their honours.

---

[46] In marking Athene as separate, it delineates the poles from which she is separated – by her manifestation of both male/not-male, female/not-female. Athene is seen as a part of, as she is apart from, both sexes. Winnington-Ingram 1949 is extremely good on this.

These paired oppositions stand against the mediation of Athene. Apollo exhorts the jurors to count, showing reverence for not-doing-wrong (τὸ μὴ ἀδικεῖν σέβοντες), which picks up Athene's and the Erinues' moral vocabulary (e.g. 698ff., 545–9). For a single vote (as will be the case – one as opposed to two) could set upright an *oikos* (the emphasis remains on the *oikos*, not merely on Orestes). ὤρθωσεν picks up ὀρθῶς (748), once more stressing ὀρθότης as a standard of correctness, precision.

And Athene announces the result:

> ἀνὴρ ὅδ᾿ ἐκπέφευγεν αἵματος δίκην
> ἴσον γάρ ἐστι τἀρίθμημα τῶν πάλων   (752–3)

The sexual determinant, ἀνήρ, comes first word; 'the man' has escaped αἵματος δίκην.

Orestes replies in a long speech of thanks for his deliverance, which picks up many of the major terms of the discourse that have constituted the trial and this, its decision: Athene (ὦ Παλλάς) is clearly marked as the saviour, ὦ σώσασα, the saviour of the *house*, δόμους, in her re-establishment of Orestes in the *oikos*, κατῴκισάς με; Orestes, who has been deprived of the country *of his fathers*, πατρῴας, will now be recognised ('one of the Greeks will *say*' – that is, call, define, in language) in his full role in society:

> ''Αργεῖος ἀνὴρ αὖθις, ἔν τε χρήμασιν
> οἰκεῖ πατρῴοις, Παλλάδος καὶ Λοξίου
> ἕκατι καὶ τοῦ πάντα κραίνοντος τρίτου
> Σωτῆρος᾿   (757–60)

The man (ἀνήρ again) is no longer wandering (cf. e.g. *Cho.* 1042) but placed in his own territory ('Αργεῖος – his international status as well as the society of which he is a member, cf. p. 189); he inhabits an *oikos* (οἰκεῖ); his role in the *oikos* is maintained among the possessions[47] of his father(s) (and we have commented before with regard to his economic vocabulary on connections between property and the male discourse of paternity). The generational continuity of the *oikos* has been assured thanks to Pallas and Loxias and τοῦ πάντα κραίνοντος τρίτου | Σωτῆρος. This description refers back to the imagery of 'the third' as final (cf., most recently, 589), and, in particular, is a reversal (back to the norm) of Clytemnestra's blasphemous prayer (*Aga.* 1384ff.). It also recalls, however, ἔπραξεν ὡς ἔκρανεν at *Aga.* 369 (also expressed of Zeus), and Διὸς παναιτίου πανεργέτα (*Aga.* 1485–6); and thus it stresses the motive power of Zeus, here in the victory of his agents. But the reminiscences of the over-determination of motivation, those many supplements to the *all*-completing, *all*-

---

[47] Cf. *Cho.* 275. The economic motivation returns.

responsible Zeus, and the reminiscence of, for example, the tautology of ἔπραξεν ὡς ἔκρανεν, lead also to the reminiscence of the doubtful questioning of the chorus of the *Choephoroi* (*Cho.* 1073) as to whether the third saviour has really come. Indeed as we will see, the play is not at an end. σωτῆρος of Zeus picks up σώσασα (754), multiplying (doubling) the role of saviour: it will be in the interplay of two and three, the double and the third, that the dynamics of the end are formed.

Orestes states again the priority of father over mother – the distinction of the trial:

ὃς πατρῷον αἰδεσθεὶς μόρον
σώζει με, μητρὸς τάσδε συνδίκους ὁρῶν   (760–1)

Respect for the parental has been often expressed, and was Orestes' compunction before his mother's breast. But it is the father of the gods' respect for πατρῷον...μόρον which links now Orestes, Apollo, Zeus under the generality of the 'paternal' (πατρῷα κράτη) – and as opposed to the sight of his mother's advocates.

Thus Orestes says he will return home, promising again the support of the Argives for ever, and thus he leaves (χαῖρε) wishing them success against opposition (ἐναντίοις – recalling the trial's oppositions, the latest of a series of exclusive oppositions characterised by -ἀντι-). So too the depiction of this success as σωτήριον recalls ὦ σώσασα, as it echoes the prayer for a saviour (cf. e.g. *Cho.* 236, 1073) particularly of the household. So also δορὸς νικηφόρον not only implies war successes, but also recalls the prayer for δίκη νικηφόρῳ, the search for δικαστής/δικηφόρος; it evokes also νικήσω (722), which picked up τῆς δίκης (719). He has won in the trial a victory against opposition (cf. *Cho.* 890): Orestes has won a *nike* in the *dike*.

As the institution of the new civic power of the word, the trial turned on claims concerning the relations of the sexes, child and parent, and the strange mediating position of the institutor of the legal process, Athene, who also expressed her reasons in explicitly sexual terms. The trial, as (formal) culmination of the oppositions of the narrative, interweaves the discourses of language exchange and sexuality in the new civic establishment, as Clytemnestra and Orestes were depicted as transgressing in their sexual and linguistic relations. A culmination...but not *telos*, however, as the Erinues threaten to set the process of reciprocal revenge moving again by wrecking the land whose elders have been a cause of their rejection in the trial.

The end justifies...?

The chorus indeed regard the outcome of the trial as a defeat for themselves. Orestes himself is almost forgotten as they break into the third stasimon with outrage at the action of the younger gods, who have trampled on the ancient laws, taking the rights of punishment from their hands (which picks up 731, 490ff., 227, 162, 150–1). Now without honour, status (ἄτιμος), without the respect paid to them, they recall their threats:

> βαρύκοτος
> ἐν γᾷ τᾷδε φεῦ
> ἰὸν ἰὸν ἀντιπενθῆ μεθεῖσα καρδίας
> σταλαγμὸν †χθονὶ
> ἄφορον   (810–14)

As ἀντιπενθῆ suggests, the poison will be 'in revenge for grief'. The word of the law, the acquittal (as victory) rather than settling the series of oppositions, has transferred the conflict to one between Athene as protector of Athens and the Erinues as the outraged persecutors of the city of the acquitters.[48] The word of the law, rather than extinguishing the force of opposition (any more than the decision of Agamemnon to respect Zeus and kill Iphigeneia resolved the κακῶν of his situation), is, like Agamemnon's action, the cause of further opposition in its very act of decision: such is the logic of the double-bind, where each act, the decision between a polarity of forces, results in a further polarity of forces. This continuing doubling of repetition and reversal threatens the singleness of the word of the law, the moment of decision, with a remultiplication into the doubleness of opposition. The τέλος δίκης is thus placed at risk as an end (τέλος), or rather the τέλος as end is resited in the future: indeed, the chorus cry ἐκ δὲ τοῦ λειχὴν ἄφυλλος ἄτεκνος, ὦ δίκα δίκα, πέδον ἐπισύμενος (784–6). The description of the scurvy which will destroy the fertility not only of plants but also of parents/children (the denial of the work of generational continuity, which is the victory of Orestes) is interrupted by an appeal to δίκα, precisely the term whose sense was to be defined by the trial – but now the term in which the chorus couch their opposition to the result of the trial.

They have suffered things hard to bear among the citizens and so they threaten to cause the city troubles: the reversal/repetition so often marked by such active/passive play. ἰὼ μεγάλατοι κόραι δυστυχεῖς Νυκτὸς ἀτιμοπενθεῖς: as daughters of Night (as opposed to the male genealogies of Orestes, Athene, Apollo, Hermes), they are unfortunate and grief-stricken in their loss of τιμή.

---

[48] Cf. Taplin 1977, pp. 407ff., especially p. 409.

Athene, however, in iambic trimeters, replies to their outraged lyric expressions:

ἐμοὶ πίθεσθε μὴ βαρυστόνως φέρειν·
οὐ γὰρ νενίκησθ᾽ ἀλλ᾽ ἰσόψηφος δίκη
ἐξῆλθ᾽ ἀληθῶς οὐκ ἀτιμίᾳ σέθεν   (794–6)

ἐμοὶ πίθεσθε, her opening words, stress the term which will be extremely important to the following passages – Athene's πειθώ, persuasion. After the importance of *peitho* for Clytemnestra with regard to Agamemnon (cf. *Aga.* 943) and for Orestes with regard to Clytemnestra (cf. e.g. pp. 169ff.), the text further focuses on the exchange of words. Remembering, however, both Orestes' comments on the difficulty of communication between male and female, and also the use of language for victory in the opposition between the sexes (indeed, in the trial), we may note that Athene's use of *peitho*, her language, is not set up in terms of male in opposition to female (since she is neither wholly male nor female) nor aimed at victory in the sense of the destruction of her opponent, but at the relocating of the τιμάς of the Erinues (rather than συντέμνειν λόγῳ). She aims to manipulate the shifting of the signifiers τιμάς/δίκη/νίκη but towards a position of agreement rather than a position of opposition, towards a position from which opposition is not a result, and from which further conflict does not arise. Thus Athene's use of πίθεσθε, as well as marking the continuing emphasis on the exchange of language, the floating of signifiers, also registers the difference of the exchange of words to come from the *peitho* of Clytemnestra and Orestes, a difference based on the varying constitution of the opposition addresser/addressee, the difference of the sexual opposition.

μὴ βαρυστόνως φέρειν echoes the chorus' βαρύκοτος/στενάζω/δύσοιστ᾽ but shifts the emphasis to 'heavy grief' rather than 'heavy in wrath...grieve'; similarly, δύσοιστ᾽ becomes μὴ...φέρειν – implying the possibility of different predication, suggesting in these reworkings of the expression of the chorus' rage and grief the move towards agreement, the lessening of their anger. For they have not been defeated (νενίκησθ᾽) but the trial (δίκη) was of equal votes. There is a 'justice', δίκη, beyond the simple battle metaphor νίκη (the importance of the play between δίκη and νίκη to the dynamics of these later passages is here evident). But the reason for this is stated again to be the 'clear testimonies' ἐκ Διός, which implies both 'from Zeus' in a causal sense, and 'from Zeus' in a derivative sense (birth – as she is ἐκ Διός). These proofs were given by his son (ἐκ Διός), Apollo. λαμπρὰ μαρτύρια, 'clear, shining testimonies', marks the connection between the witness (μαρτυρῶν, 798) as one who sees and that which is both 'clear to sight' and 'gives light', 'shines' as a value in discourse. Thus importantly, here after the attestation of paternity by the son of god as a proof in the authorised legal process, the importance of vision to proof and recognition is recalled by the daughter of god, who is κάρτα...τοῦ πατρός.

She continues to beg restraint from the blight of crops and σπερμάτων (in contrast to the σπέρματος σωτηρίου of the child in a system of generational continuity, cf. *Cho.* 236):

> ἐγὼ γὰρ ὑμῖν πανδίκως ὑπίσχομαι
> ἕδρας τε καὶ κευθμῶνας ἐνδίκου χθονὸς
> λιπαροθρόνοισιν ἡμένας ἐπ' ἐσχάραις
> ἕξειν ὑπ' ἀστῶν τῶνδε τιμαλφουμένας   (804–7)

The reason for their restraint is to be a promise of Athene: as with the threats of the Erinues, Athene's promise (and *peitho*) mark the crossing of the gap between present and future, signifier and signified, addresser and addressee. Her promise, which is given πανδίκως, 'with all δίκη', 'in every sense of δίκη', is that they will have an established seat and cavern in an ἐνδίκου land, the land which possesses, is constituted in δίκη.[49] Their reproach of the loss of δίκα, at e.g. 785 (the punishment of Orestes which constitutes Justice), is approached by Athene with a promise 'with all δίκη' that they will have in a land which is ἔνδικον an honoured position (τιμαλφουμένας picking up 626 and the references to loss of honour, e.g. 792, 796 etc.). They will be part of the system of δίκη/τιμή rather than defeated by and outside the system: she proffers the incorporation of the Erinues in the institutionalisation of justice.

The chorus, however, repeat their stanzas 777–92. After the promise of Athene, the repetition marks the failure to bridge the gap, the unwillingness of the chorus to amend their discourse to Athene's terms.

She returns with further arguments to these same words:

> οὐκ ἔστ' ἄτιμοι μηδ' ὑπερθύμως ἄγαν
> θεαὶ βροτῶν κτίσητε δύσκηλον χθόνα   (824–5)

She asserts their possession of τιμή (picking up ἀτιμοπενθεῖς, last word of the chorus). Nor, as goddesses, should they blight the land of mortals ὑπερθύμως – 'with excessive wrath', which excess we have noted in all the action of reversal and revenge. This is also the first time another character in the play has called the Erinues θεαί (marked in its juxtaposition to βροτῶν): indeed, in the tripartite systematisation that appeared to be being developed, they were

---

[49] This is not merely flattery of Athens, but a positive argument too – that the Athenians cannot be punished justly if they are ἐνδίκου.

opposed (in the discourse of Apollo, Orestes, Athene) to the gods and
to mortals – and had been described in imagery suited to hunting
animals or subterranean creatures. Now Athene (flattery? a suggestion
of future status?) calls them θεαί.

Her faith and trust (πέποιθα picking up πίθεσθε) is in Zeus, and
she outlines her knowledge of Zeus' thunderbolt, which she
rhetorically questions the need of (paraleipsis), since

σὺ δ᾽ εὐπιθὴς ἐμοὶ
γλώσσης ματαίας μὴ ᾽κβάλῃς ἔπη χθονί,
καρπὸν φέροντα πάντα μὴ πράσσειν καλῶς   (829–31)

Peitho will be easy with them, as opposed to the words 'of a
vain/rash tongue which bears a fruit of evil in everything' – the
power of the curse. It is the exchange of language (giving and
receiving) which the end of the play is to regulate. Through the means
of Athene's *peitho*, the end of the just(ified) city is being approached.

The Erinues are (832) to restrain the 'bitter force of that black
swelling',[50] so they may be σεμνότιμος καὶ ξυνοικήτωρ ἐμοί. σεμνότιμος, as Agamemnon was described at *Cho.* 356, indicates together
in the compound adjective the honour (τιμή) and respect (σέβας) that
they seek (the reciprocal marks of status in the hierarchy of the
system). ξυνοικήτωρ, fellow-dweller in an *oikos*, as before (cf. e.g.
654–6, *Cho.* 291ff.), expresses the mark of acceptance in society (is
the city being depicted as Athene's *oikos*?). Thus they will receive
the land's prime offerings 'for children and the τέλη of marriage',
that is, for fertility as opposed to blight, and for generational
continuity as opposed to the destruction of the *oikos*, both with regard
to the rites and sacrifices of marriage (which were the bonds Apollo
had accused them of ignoring, 213ff.). As now they threaten to
destroy society, so they will be the guardians of its preservation. This
'offer' (Verrall) is termed λόγον (836), marking once more the
exchange of language (ἐπαινέσεις, 'you will praise').

The chorus, however, continue to bewail their suffering, but they
at least refer to Athene's promise, marking some acceptance of the
exchange of words (as their previous repetition of their own words
had not). Living κατὰ γᾶν is a 'defilement without honour' (like
παθεῖν, 837, this seems to echo the *parodos* again – their earlier
accusations of impurity and dishonouring). They will continue in
their rage (μένος, 840, echoes μένος, 832; κότον, 840; κότον, 800)
and bewail their misery to their mother, which points again to the
sexual determination of the trial, and the different sexual constitution
of this exchange of words. For the tricks of the gods have deprived

<hr/>

[50] The alliteration of kappas is marked.

them of their age-old honour: δόλοι recalls the god-ordered πειθώ δολία of Orestes – is Athene's *peitho* to be different? Or another god-trick?

Athene: ὀργὰς ξυνοίσω σοι. ὀργή, like φρόνημα, τόλμα as we saw (p. 141), was used to describe the force of will going beyond the boundaries and restraints of society and σωφρονεῖν: it is the expression of transgression leading to the act of reciprocal violence that constituted the pattern of revenge. Here, however, Athene (as antagonist) will 'bear with' the ὀργάς of the Erinues: it is ξύν rather than ἀντί, 'together' rather than 'against'. Indeed, she concedes the wisdom (of age) to the Erinues, but also claims for herself the power of right thinking, φρονεῖν...οὐ κακῶς, which quality, like σωφρονεῖν, we have seen opposed to ὀργάς, τόλμα. Also like σωφρονεῖν, as at *Aga.* 174ff., this quality of thought stems from Zeus: κἀμοὶ Ζεὺς ἔδωκεν.

The goddess turns to predict the future, when, she claims, the chorus will feel love and regrets for the land of Attica. προυννέπω τάδε: she proclaims, foretells these things. As with her persuasion, threat and promise, now prophecy too, is the bridge. Each generation of Athenians will increase in its τιμή (that which the chorus feared lost) and the Erinues will have an 'honoured seat', τιμίαν ἕδραν – the honour of the city and the Erinues are brought parallel, rather than opposed (as the Erinues would have it). The Erinues will receive such honour 'from men and processions of women'. The sexes join in worship, as opposed to their opposition in battle. The focus on citizens, πολιταῖς, made up of both men and women, points to the widening emphasis of these later passages, to the reconciliation of the force of the Erinues (from the mother, blood ties, etc.) with the constitution of the city. Their threat is to Attica and Athens, not merely to the *oikos* of Orestes. As we discussed, pp. 193–5, there develops, in these later scenes particularly, not merely a relation between individual and *oikos* (the constitution of that relation) but also the dis-covering of the relations of those internal ties of the *oikos* to the wider society of the *polis*. The standing back of Orestes after the moment of decision[51] and his thanks, the threats of the Erinues for the city of Athens, the description of the future glory of the city of Athens, the desire to reconcile the Erinues πρὸς δόμοις Ἐρεχθέως, γῆς τῆσδε etc., which leads towards, as we will see, the acceptance of the *polis* by the Erinues, all point to this wider relationship: it expresses a genealogy of the structure of the constitution of the *polis*. As we saw (pp. 194–5), the establishment of a sign system

---

[51] This was a decision by the elders of the court: law as the institutionalisation of the constitution of the relations of the *polis*, enacted by the men of the *polis*.

(the transformation of the Odyssean discourse, cf. pp. 183–95) requires and is marked by a new articulation of the enunciative position, a new positioning, construction of the subject, here expressly 'the identity of a speaking subject *within a social framework*'.[52] This framework is specifically of the society of the *polis*. The ending of this play is resiting the discourse of the telling of the Orestes story within the framework of the fifth-century Athenian *polis*. This conflict between Athene and the Erinues concerning the city is not, then, 'a loosely connected episode stitched to the outside'[53] of the trilogy, nor merely a patriotic ending, but is constituted in its difference from the constant and fateful oppositions of male and female which we saw as an essential dynamic of the narrative developing this new articulation of the enunciative position. It aims at an ending both in its reduction of that sexual opposition, and in its reconciliation of the Erinues *to the city*, precisely the social framework we have seen 'called for' by this new articulation. The transformation of the Odyssean discourse (as we discussed pp. 183–95, with the opposition of the sexes and with all the implications of this opposition) implies and is constituted by[54] this 'new' ending to the Orestes narrative, the relation to the *polis*.

It is not the case, then, simply that there are, as Macleod asserts, some 'important touches in the *Oresteia* which are the work of a citizen of a democracy' (1982, p. 144). As we saw earlier in a different way with the shifting vocabulary of social relations, the widest structurings of the discourse and narrative mark the trilogy's generation in the discourse of the *polis*.

So Athene calls on the chorus in their new role not to create harm ἐν τόποισι τοῖς ἐμοῖσι; to restrain war ἐμφύλιόν τε καὶ πρὸς ἀλλήλους. They are to keep war θυραῖος – 'beyond the boundaries' of the city, 'foreign'. Internal antagonisms are to be restrained:

ἐνοικίου δ' ὄρνιθος οὐ λέγω μάχην[55]   (866)

She does not advise (λέγω) the fight of the bird ἐνοικίου: a homely image this, but ἐνοικίου, 'within the *oikos*', recalls the bitter and violent action in the house of Atreus, and moreover, by implying in this context 'within the state', it points to the complex connections between *oikos* and *polis* in the language of the trilogy.

---

[52] Kristeva, as translated and quoted by Roudiez 1980, p. 18 (my emphasis). Cf. pp. 194–5 and n. 177 there.

[53] Livingstone 1925, pp. 123–4, an extreme view, perhaps. But Taplin, for example, believes that scenes from the end of the *Eumenides* may be lost, so strange an emphasis it seems to him. Cf. n. 48 above.

[54] Kristeva's phrase for this connection is 'call for' – as in the previous sentence of this paragraph.

[55] 858–66 have recently been suspected as not genuine by Dodds 1960, p. 51 and by Macleod 1982, p. 130.

Thus she offers her choice of the Erinues:

> εὖ δρῶσαν εὖ πάσχουσαν εὖ τιμωμένην
> χώρας μετασχεῖν τῆσδε θεοφιλεστάτης   (868–9)

She offers 'doing well' (active), 'experiencing well' (passive), 'being honoured, honouring, well' (reciprocal) – the voices of the play we have been considering so often in the structure of reversal and repetition. They are to have a share in this land (incorporation), which is θεοφιλεστάτης. *Philia* towards the gods recalls the hierarchisation of the bonds of φιλία with particular reference to the relations between men and gods that formed Pylades' motivating injunction. Such, too, will be the basis of their incorporation.

The chorus, however, once more repeat their cry of 837–46; but Athene once more opens the process of persuasion:

> οὔτοι καμοῦμαί σοι λέγουσα τἀγαθά,
> ὡς μήποτ' εἴπῃς πρὸς νεωτέρας ἐμοῦ
> θεὸς παλαιὰ καὶ πολισσούχων βροτῶν
> ἄτιμος ἔρρειν τοῦδ' ἀπόξενος πέδου   (881–84)

She will not tire of 'speaking good things'. This is in order that they may never say (and λέγουσα/εἴπῃς again marks the exchange of logos) that they have been 'destroyed without honour' (ἄτιμος ἔρρειν was their worry, 747) by the younger goddess (the generational conflict) and by the city-dwelling mortals (the framework of the *polis*). That is, Athene defines their refusal to accept her speech as the cause of their lack of honour, redefining their lack of honour in terms not of the trial but of their unwillingness to be received in Athens (τοῦδ' ἀπόξενος πέδου):

> ἀλλ' εἰ μὲν ἁγνόν ἐστί σοι Πειθοῦς σέβας
> γλώσσης ἐμῆς μείλιγμα καὶ θελκτήριον
> σὺ δ' οὖν μένοις ἄν   (885–7)

They would stay if respect (σέβας again) for *peitho* is holy, that is, if the relation of exchange implied by *peitho* is treated as a reciprocal tie deserving the honour paid in the hierarchisation of reciprocal respect, rather than as a force of aggressive manipulation. In apposition to Πειθοῦς σέβας is γλώσσης ἐμῆς μείλιγμα καὶ θελκτήριον, 'the coaxing and blandishment of my tongue'. Both μείλιγμα and θελκτήριον can, like *peitho*, imply a sexual context – indeed, Agamemnon was called Χρυσηίδων μείλιγμα (*Aga.* 1439), 'the fondling of Chryseis-girls', and θελκτηρία was used in a highly ambiguous way at *Cho.* 670. But these terms, while referring to their ambiguous use between the sexes (particularly in the passages above) also serve to point to the different constitution of sexuality of this exchange of words. Since this seduction of words is between Athene, the goddess who has no part in marriage and is in some ways neither male nor female, and the Erinues, who sleep with no creature, the possibility of conflict in sexual terms, which constituted the ambiguity of the terms μείλιγμα/θελκτήριον in their previous contexts, is removed: the *peitho* of Athene can be both a μείλιγμα and a θελκτήριον without the aggressive, dangerous implications of these terms because of the resiting of the sexual determinants in the exchange of language.

If they do not stay, however, they cannot, she continues, damage or be wrathful with the city δικαίως, with *dike*: for they have been offered a share in the land and in the system of honour/respect, τιμωμένη. The opposition that the Erinues are expressing is not δικαίως, because they will be part of the city 'with all δίκη' (δικαίως ἐς τὸ πᾶν τιμωμένη): if their honouring is δικαίως ἐς τὸ πᾶν, how can their opposition to it, it is implied, also be δικαίως?

The chorus at this point[56] relent, in the form of a question (in iambic metre):

> ... τίνα με φὴς ἔχειν ἕδραν;   (892)

With a question as to what she had said, the chorus also accept Athene's words: ἕδραν picks up ἕδρας (805), ἕδραν (855). Athene's reply describes their future habitation: πάσης ἀπήμον' οἰζύος (like Olympus), and tells them to 'accept it', δέχου (δέχομαι expresses the recognition by/in society, as well as the acceptance of words, cf. *Aga.* 1060, *Aga.* 1653). They allow the possibility of acceptance to investigate its nature further; καὶ δὴ δέδεγμαι, 'suppose I accept'; as with the exchange of language, Athene's offer (in language) has been received; the Erinues have entered the process of exchange. They want to know their future honour (τιμή), and Athene informs them that no *oikos* will 'flourish' without them: their sphere of action remains the *oikos* and εὐθενεῖν is especially connected with fertility, growth, not only of animals and crops, but also of men and countries: as opposed to the threatened infertility and the destruction of the *oikos*, they will ensure its health and growth.

> τῷ γὰρ σέβοντι συμφορὰς ὀρθώσομεν   (897)

---

[56] 'Why now?' asks Verrall (and others). He suggests there is a mysterious hiatus obliterating the words of the Eternal and the wisdom of the Most High (he quotes here Dante, *Purg.* 32.61). Other critics have noted this as a beginning of the exchange of language (as opposed to the chorus' refusal in the lyrics) but have offered no reason for the beginning at this point. Its arbitrariness is seen as a fault by some. Certainly the lack of explicit motivation is noticeable. Is οὔτοι καμοῦμαι a factor? The explicit appeal to *peitho*? Perhaps it marks the arbitrariness of the point of the acceptance of language, the arbitrary control on the play of signifiers to give an 'accepted reading'. Agamemnon's point of acceptance of Clytemnestra's *peitho* in the carpet scene shows a similar problem of motivation/arbitrariness, (although perhaps it is significant that he too yields after an explicit appeal to *peitho*).

For the one who shows reverence (again σέβας expresses the correct ordering of respect) 'we will straighten' events. The standard of ὀρθότης is again the term of authorisation and control. συμφοράς, too, has expressed in the trilogy the duality of good/bad fortune, the disasters of the Atreid house (cf. e.g. *Cho.* 931, *Aga.* 18). It is the straight ordering of such double events that Athene offers.

The chorus ask if this is a surety for all time, and Athene replies:

ἔξεστι γάρ μοι μὴ λέγειν ἃ μὴ τελῶ   (899)

Athene 'with a kind of dry humour' (Lloyd-Jones) says it is possible for her 'not to say what she will not fulfil'. The negative statement both opens the possibility of saying what will not happen – which points back to the numerous occasions of the different sorts of fulfilled and unfulfilled prophecy in the trilogy; but also the double negative of Athene's expression does not prove the positive statement that the chorus seeks (and seems to accept: θέλξειν[57] μ' ἔοικας καὶ μεθίσταμαι κότου). So, Athene concludes, in/under the earth they will obtain φίλους. The Erinues will enter into that relation of reciprocal honour/respect between men and gods that was seen as problematical in the *Choephoroi*: as the murder of Clytemnestra involved the redefinition of φίλος as exclusive of the mother, so the reconciliation of the Erinues is achieved by changing their hostile status to one of φιλία with the city.

So, the reconciled chorus ask for what they are to sing for the land (again the role of language as predictive, predicative), and Athene suggests:

ὁποῖα νίκης μὴ κακῆς ἐπίσκοπα   (903)

'The proverbial νίκη κακή was a victory which involved the victor in the disaster of dishonour' (Thomson); which, indeed, could be a description of the many νῖκαι we have seen (e.g. Clytemnestra over Agamemnon; Orestes over Clytemnestra). Moreover, considering the relation between νίκη and δίκη, and the depiction of success in δίκη as νίκη, this phrase, echoing Athene's denial of defeat for the Erinues at 795, marks also the change in such a relation. The δίκη which is not synonymous with the destruction of the foe (cf. 795) is here paralleled in this implication of a victory which is not necessarily good. ἐπίσκοπα, which was how the Erinues described τὸ δεινόν in society (518), are not only things 'suitable', 'hitting the mark' but also things which 'overlook' linking the blessings of the Erinues with

---

[57] θέλξειν often has the dubious connotations of θελκτήριον (cf. Kahn 1978, pp. 139ff.) which points to the gap here apparently bridged by Athene's *peitho*, and the different sexual constitution of the exchange of language.

the gods (severally and *en masse*) and fate, as the overseeing controls of the sublunary world.

These blessings are now enumerated, and, as one might expect, these expressions of harmony and goodness pick up many of the terms we have read as important in the trilogy: ἐκ... ποντίας δρόσου recalls the φοινίας δρόσου of Agamemnon's death (*Aga.* 1390), a reversal of that overturning of natural imagery (cf. Moles 1979; Peradotto 1964). The winds which εὐηλίως πνέοντ', 'blow in beautiful sunlight', contrast with the χειμὼν πνεύσας γονίας (*Cho.* 1066–7), the 'storms of fate', which were instantiated in the description of the storm destroying the Argive fleet and in the lack of winds at Aulis. So it picks up, too, the change of heart of Agamemnon: πνέων... τροπαίαν (*Aga.* 219). In the same way, καρπόν τε γαίας καὶ βοτῶν recalls the threats of the Erinues and the deprecations of Athene (cf. μηδ' ἀκαρπίαν, 801) as ἐπίρρυτον picks up οὐπιρρέων τιμιώτερος χρόνος, linking the flow of time and honour and the influx of the wealth of the land for the citizens (ἀστοῖσιν). So μὴ κάμνειν χρόνῳ recalls χρόνος from that passage, expressing a continuity of growth through time, as opposed to the repetition and reversal we have often seen associated with χρόνος in the play; cf. e.g. σὺν χρόνῳ γε μήν (*Aga.* 1378), χρονισθείς (*Aga.* 727), παντελῆς χρόνος ἀμείψεται (*Cho.* 965). The feelings of doubt and foreboding associated with the passage of time now with the blessings of the Erinues turn to hope for the future as growth rather than reversal. This sense of continuity (of growth) is developed with τῶν βροτείων σπερμάτων σωτηρίαν which recalls both the Erinues' threats to the seeds of man (ἄτεκνος... βροτοφθόρους 785ff., etc.) as deprecated by Athene (μηδ'... τεύξητ'... βρωτῆρας αἰχμὰς σπερμάτων, 801–3), and, in particular, the prayers for Orestes as the hope of generational continuity for the *oikos* (cf. e.g. σπέρματος σωτηρίου, *Cho.* 236). Once more, we see links between the saving/constitution of the *oikos* and the saving/constitution of the *polis*. Against the δυσσεβοῦντες, however, the Erinues are to come more as a destroyer – but this threat receives one line only, before a return to the 'griefless / causing no grief race of the δικαίων', those with δίκη. Such tasks, she concludes, are for the Erinues. Athene herself will ensure success in war and honour among mortals especially for τήνδ' ἀστύνικον... πόλιν. ἀστύ is often the term for the city of Athens (specifying τήνδ' further), and thus the predication of 'victorious town', 'victorious in its *astu*', is significantly a proleptic use. For prolepsis, the predicative/predictive force of speech, is the essence of 'blessing'.

The chorus pick up τιμᾶν πόλιν, the last words of Athene's speech, as they finally accept Athene's offer:

δέξομαι Παλλάδος ξυνοικίαν
οὐδ' ἀτιμάσω πόλιν   (916–17)

δέχομαι marks the acceptance/non-opposition of the offer of/in
language. ξυνοικίαν accepts Athene's offer to be ξυνοικήτωρ (833).
The city is to be dwelt in together like an *oikos*: it is not merely the
saving of Orestes' *oikos*, or of Athens, or simply the depiction of
Athens as an *oikos*, but the interpenetration of vocabulary. The *polis*
as *oikos* is also the relation of *oikos* to *polis*. For the maintenance of
patriarchy, τοῦ πατρός, in the *oikos* is placed parallel to the assertion
of society over the *oikos*, through the association of the male with
society (see pp. 193–5) and the explicit focus on the *polis*. Nor will
the Erinues refuse the relation of reciprocity in the city outlined by
Athene.

ἅ τ' ἐγὼ κατεύχομαι
θεσπίσασα πρευμενῶς   (921–2)

Now, after the trial scene, its clash of logoi, and the *peitho* of Athene,
the chorus 'make a kind prophecy and pray...': the projection of
language, but in contrast to their threats, this is a 'kindly' (πρευμενῶς)
prediction, towards the fertility of the soil – the reversal of their
earlier threat in this prayer and prediction.

Between the verses of their song of blessings, Athene sings passages
of marching anapaests: her motivation in bringing the Erinues to
Athens is kindliness towards her/its citizens (προφρόνως recalling
Aga. 174, the hymn to Zeus):

ὅ γε μὴν κύρσας βαρεῶν τούτων
οὐκ οἶδεν ὅθεν πληγαὶ βιότου·
τὰ γὰρ ἐκ προτέρων ἀπλακήματά νιν
πρὸς τάσδ' ἀπάγει, σιγῶν ⟨δ'⟩ ὄλεθρος
καὶ μέγα φωνοῦντ'
ἐχθραῖς ὀργαῖς ἀμαθύνει   (932–7)

These powerful lines echo the Erinues' description of the punishment
of the unjust (588ff.). Here, however, it is men's lack of knowledge
of the origin or cause (ὅθεν) of the 'blows of life' that restresses the
complexity and obscurity of causal relations, particularly of sin and
punishment, which we have traced through the narrative; and this
origin or cause is here placed literally in the actions of the ancestors[58] –
as we have seen the metaphor of procreation/descent function as an
attempted control or explanation (through origins) of narrative. Such
lack of clear knowledge has here the authorisation of the divine
overseer, and the powerful image of the man shouting however loudly

---

[58] As in Athens the oath taken before the Areopagus against perjury invoked destruction
of the family and descendants of the swearer by the Erinues.

at this silent doom recalls not only the drowning sinner punished by the Erinues (καλεῖ δ' ἀκούοντας οὐδέν, 558) but also the process of the exchange of language itself and, in particular, the many prayers (unanswered), promises, hopes (unfulfilled) of the human characters of the trilogy: indeed, ἐχθραῖς ὀργαῖς, a dative loosely attached to the sentence, implies the actions of repetition and reversal and hostility characterising the human exchanges of the trilogy, as well as the punishment of the Erinues; moreover, πληγή was precisely the word used of Zeus' destruction of Troy (and used in contrast to the unclear pattern of narrative leading to the destruction, *Aga.* 367–8), and it was the word expressing the reversing and repetition of action of Orestes' matricide (*Cho.* 312–13), picking up *Aga.* 1343–4 of Agamemnon's death. Here, then, rather than the move to clarity assumed by Lebeck,[59] we see an authorisation of the lack of knowledge of the human world in terms specifically recalling the action in the house of Atreus.

The chorus sing of their blessings, which consist of fertility, health of trees, crops, animals, echoing (in reverse) their previous threats (and Athene's deprecations). Pan is asked to bless (εὐθενοῦντα, cf. 895) the lambs with double fruit of the womb – which after Athene's last speech in particular recalls the doubling of repetition and reversal, the confusion of causality. They further invoke the wealth of the soil,[60] a gift of the gods (ἑρμαίαν recalls the prayers to Hermes,[61] which were attempts to control narrative, as the 'god-send', 'unexpected piece of luck' points to the apparent randomness, and lack of control of narrative for human beings). Such prayers seem to echo a Golden Age narrative – the soil giving its wealth without labour. Such is the possibility for this newly constituted *polis*.

Athene describes the extent of such power in terms of the systematised ordering of divinities and mortals: παρά τ' ἀθανάτοις τοῖς θ' ὑπὸ γαῖαν, περί τ' ἀνθρώπων (951–2), and goes on to express the controlling force of the Erinues:

φανέρ' ὡς τελέως
διαπράσσουσιν, τοῖς μὲν ἀοιδάς,
τοῖς δ' αὖ δακρύων
βίον ἀμβλωπὸν παρέχουσαι   (952–5)

φανέρ', 'clearly', stands in opposition to οὐκ οἶδεν ὅθεν or rather the clarity of the authorised punishment stands in opposition to the obscurity of the generation of cause, responsibility. As at *Aga.* 367–9

---

[59] 1971, p. 2. Cf. Ch. I, p. 20 n. 31.
[60] Which term Verrall refers to 'mines'.
[61] Davies in his edition of *Eumenides* (1885) points out that Pausanias (1.28.6) found statues of Hermes, Ploutos and Earth in the sanctuary of the σεμναὶ θεαί.

with the πληγή of Zeus, the punishment at least is observable, if not the passage of cause and effect, which uncertainty led to the tautology of ἔπραξεν ὡς ἔκρανεν (*Aga.* 369), echoed here ἐπικραίνει...τελέως διαπράσσουσιν. τελέως, 'finally' (but with the implications of 'death'/'initiation' we saw with τέλος δίκης?), particularly with διαπράσσουσιν points to the moment of punishment as an end (repressing the passage towards that end). But the ends expressed are *double* (μέν...δέ), 'some for song' (and we may recall the changing songs of woe, songs of marriage, the *kommos* etc., a series of songs which doubles into ambiguity one part of the possibility μέν...δέ!); 'some for the dimmed life of tears'. ἀμβλωπόν recalls the imagery of sight throughout the play, particularly δερκομένοισι καὶ δυσομμάτοις ὁμῶς (387–8): the evocative phrase 'eye-dimmed life' thus points to the lack of clarity in the sublunary world and also is almost an oxymoron with regard to an association of light / sight and life, and bad-sight / dark and death. Despite φανέρ' ὡς τελέως διαπράσσουσιν we see here indeed ἐπαργέμους λόγους! Even the promised ends are only the dimmed vision of life or the ambiguities of song! Once more in this theatrical text the imagery of language and vision, significantly intertwined, returns to question a proclaimed clarity of the end, here at the ending of the play.

The chorus disclaim ἀνδροκμῆτας...τύχας for young men, which refers back to their previous tasks – μόχθοις ἀνδροκμῆσι (248; cf. also *Cho.* 889); and they request ἀνδροτυχεῖς βιότους for young girls, that is, marriage, the foundation of society, the structure for human fertility, the initiation into society for women. (But is it undercut by a reminiscence of Clytemnestra's φιλάνορας τρόπους *Aga.* 856? Does the hope for marriage recall its transgression in adultery?) They ask their sisters, the Moirai, who have such authority, to effect their prayer. For they too have a share in every home and are most honoured of goddesses in ἐνδίκοις ὁμιλίαις: ὁμιλία, an expression of the widest form of societal intercourse, here formed with and in δίκη, is the sphere of action. Marriage, generational continuity, the reciprocity of society, now fall under the jurisdiction of the Erinues and their sisters.

Athene rejoices in their fulfilling these things: as so often with the predictive force of language – 'gesagt, getan'. Indeed, Athene turns to Peitho (στέργω δ' ὄμματα Πειθοῦς), and a recognition of the power of speech in the act of persuasion:

> ὅτι μοι γλῶσσαν καὶ στόμ' ἐπωπᾷ
> πρὸς τάσδ' ἀγρίως ἀπανηναμένας
> ἀλλ' ἐκράτησε Ζεὺς Ἀγοραῖος   (971–3)

The overseeing of Peitho's eyes (a further over-determination of the narrative) over Athene's tongue and mouth worked against the Erinues, who were ἀγρίως ἀπανηναμένας, 'rudely refusing' – the breakdown of communication. That was the gap bridged by Peitho. But the possession of κράτος in this was with Zeus Agoraios. The authority and force (of Peitho) was from and with Zeus as the father's authority was appealed to, and as a threat, by Athene (826ff.). Agoraios was a name given to many gods as 'protectors of city life' (Sidgwick) – city life as the exchanges of the market-place (*agora*), the privileged site of the interconnections of economic, verbal, social exchanges. 'Αγοραῖος, as the civil function, stands also in opposition to the savagery of their refusal of the exchange of speech – 'Αγοραῖος/ἀγρίως. The pun emphasises the power of language's naming, categorisation, in the development of social exchange (ἀγορεύω/ἀγοραῖος), as it marks in the shifting of the signifier the difficulty of controlling that power, the slippage in exchange and meaning.

Their strife, she concludes, which is now 'in good things' (as opposed to the νίκης κακῆς), constitutes the victory, νικᾷ – which is picked up antithetically by the chorus with τὰν δ' ἄπληστον κακῶν μήποτ' ἐν πόλει Στάσιν τᾷδ' ἐπεύχομαι βρέμειν (976–8). The striving for good things is opposed to the strife which is insatiable for bad things. And they pray (ἐπεύχομαι picks up κατεύχομαι, 922) that this strife never roars 'in the city'; and that the dust drinking the blood of 'citizens' may not exact greedy vengeance.

> δι' ὀργὰν ποινὰς
> ἀντιφόνους Ἄτας
> ἁρπαλίσαι πόλεως   (981–3)

ὀργάν (as we saw above on 848) expressed the wrath, violent emotion that led to the excess, transgression resulting in the punishment: ποινάς, as so often before, proclaims the reciprocal exchange of punishment which is here ἀντιφόνους – not a 'were-gild' so much as paying death with death – the exclusive, binary opposition of ἀντι. Such passage of transgression and reversal into punishment of further transgression is Ἄτας – made up, consisting of, from Ἄτη.[62] These terms echo the passage of the house of Atreus; indeed, they almost seem a summing-up of the narrative of the difficulties of the house. But ἁρπαλίσαι πόλεως places what might have been a general

---

[62] Triclinius ποινᾶς. Thus he presumably construes ἄτας as an accusative plural, rather than the genitive it is normally taken to be. Any ambiguity of which genitive, however, points to the interpenetration of ἀντιφόνους/ποινάς/ἄτας, the interweaving of cause and effect.

statement about the πόνοι of the *oikos* as a fear for the city and its citizens: the narrative of Orestes is an indication of what could happen in/to the city.

But opposition itself is not so much questioned as emphasised:

> χάρματα δ' ἀντιδιδοῖεν
> κοινοφιλεῖ διανοίᾳ
> καὶ στυγεῖν μιᾷ φρενί   (984–6)

ἀντιδιδοῖεν recalls ἀντιδοῦναι at 264 (of the inevitability of Orestes' punishment) but now 'joys' are given in return. κοινοφιλεῖ / στυγεῖν μιᾷ φρενί expresses the hope for a simple opposition of φίλος/ἐχθρός based on common agreement: to hate and love as one. But it also recalls the problematic shifting of these terms which took place in the familial war of the Atreids – the internecine, internal conflict so deprecated. Is it the implication that by avoiding the *stasis* in the *polis* the possibility of the simple opposition of φίλος/ἐχθρός is opened? That the force of opposition will become thus externalised?

Their conclusion that this is a cure for many things for mortals prompts Athene's question ἆρα φρονοῦσιν γλώσσης ἀγαθῆς ὁδὸν εὑρίσκει; which, as Verrall notes, is construed 'has [the chorus] found the way, then, of γλώσσης ἀγαθῆς, good speech for those who are wise?' φρονοῦσιν (for τοῖς φρονοῦσιν), would refer back to the need for (control of) φρένες, often referred to in the play, particularly here to μιᾷ φρενί (986, cf. also 1000). This need for a correct attitude of mind we have seen indeed linked to the need for correct language – that is, the control of language as the exchange of signs (cf. in particular pp. 45ff.) Her question, marked by ἆρα (which, as Verrall notes, often indicates irony or bitterness), would also point to a question of their definition of the possible opposition of φίλος/ἐχθρός, a question of the possibility of γλώσσης ἀγαθῆς. This manuscript reading is described as 'no sense' (Sidgwick), 'worse than pointless' (Verrall): and various emendations are suggested. Pauw's εὑρίσκειν seems the simplest, and is adopted by Page: 'Do they [i.e. mortals, 987] have the wisdom to find the path of a good tongue?' This would also point to the connection between φρονεῖν and the control of language. It again questions mortals' ability to find 'the road' – as, indeed, we have repeatedly seen in the trilogy, not least in the problematic definition of φίλος/ἐχθρός (985–7). Hermann, Weil, and Sidgwick read φρονοῦσα...εὑρίσκεις; 'Do you find...in your wisdom?', which maintains the connection between φρονεῖν and language and also the questioning of the Erinues γλώσσης ἀγαθῆς ὁδόν. Verrall strangely introduces two supernumerary characters, one to question ἆρα φρονοῦσιν (bitterly questioning the new-found wisdom), the other to confirm 'it⁶³ has found the road of γλώσσης ἀγαθῆς'. It is an amusing self-reflexiveness that the search for a γλώσσης ἀγαθῆς – I mean, the textual critics' attempts here to find the right word through emendation – should be at work on a phrase which itself questions with 'irony or bitterness' the capability (despite 'wisdom') of finding that γλώσσης ἀγαθῆς.⁶⁴

From the fearful masks⁶⁵ of the Erinues Athene sees great gain for 'these citizens' (the deictic τοῖσδε seems to extend its reference from the theatrical Athenian jurors to the Athenians in the theatre):

> τάσδε γὰρ εὔφρονας εὔφρονες ἀεὶ
> μέγα τιμῶντες καὶ γῆν καὶ πόλιν
> ὀρθοδίκαιον
> πρέψετε πάντας διάγοντες   (992–5)

εὔφρονας εὔφρονες...τιμῶντες marks strongly the mutual *reciprocity* of honouring (as does φίλας φίλοι, 999): if the citizens maintain the marks of respect, then the city and the land (which are not merely, as Verrall notes, synonymous terms for Athens, but indicate a possible source of the deprecated *stasis*, as well as referring to the joint blessings of crop fertility and civil accord) will be kept ὀρθοδίκαιον. The search for ὀρθότης in language and for the definition of δίκη has become the prayer for a city which is ὀρθοδίκαιον!

So the Erinues begin to take their leave, ⟨χαίρετε⟩ χαίρετ'..., from the Athenians, who are σωφρονοῦντες ἐν χρόνῳ, 'becoming σώφρων in time'. This has been thought an odd phrase: since it is the chorus who have been persuaded to desist from wrath; Sidgwick suggests 'having made your peace with us'. Verrall refers it to 989–90 (certainly it seems to pick up εὔφρονες / φρονοῦσιν/ μιᾷ φρενί) and notes the implications for Aeschylus' time and the avoidance of civil war. So Dodds finds a reference here generally to 'economic conflicts' (52–3). Thomson glosses 'by their acceptance of the deterrent influence of law' – and he refers also to 516–25 and 690–1. It does indeed seem to me that, as well as any particular reference to the reconciliation at this point in the play, it functions as a general statement referring to the role of σώφρων (which looks back to the

---

⁶³ The change of number is awkward, for sure.

⁶⁴ The question ἆρα... is normally read as a question implying the strong answer 'yes'. The analysis offered, however, shows how this question is also a warning or worry for the citizens' capabilities. Indeed, there is even something of an ironic tinge to the goddess' expression, although she does go on to outline the great gain she expects. Athene as the ironic goddess of wisdom is a not uncommon formulation, such as her relation to Odysseus in, say, *Odyssey* 13; or, in this play, at 420.

⁶⁵ πρόσωπον indicates not only 'appearance' but also 'mask', 'character in a play'; thus pointing once more to the textuality of the text, to the play as performance?

hymn to Zeus – indeed, σωφρονοῦντες is placed here between Διός, 998 and πατήρ, 1002). In other words, in being εὔφρονες, acting with μιᾷ φρενί, the citizens are showing the quality of σωφροσύνη that has been required in the passages cited above. Indeed, the next sentence indicates the respect of the father (Zeus? Or does this also imply the generality of πατρῷα κράτη?) for those 'under the wings of Pallas'. ἅζομαι is commonly used of respect for a father or a god: here the respect is from the father of the gods, marking once more the reciprocity of the relation between men and gods: Zeus supports, or is in awe of, those who in their σωφροσύνη follow the implications of the hymn to Zeus: ἦλθε σωφρονεῖν (*Aga.* 181).

Athene bids them farewell and say she will go before to show them their chamber by the φῶς ἱερόν of escorts. As the Erinues had 'escorted' Orestes (προπομπούς, 206), now they are escorted: a reversal and repetition which has not involved the necessary destruction of the opponent but the development of a new relation of reciprocity. The 'holy light' of the procession, as many critics have noted, instantiates the imagery of light and dark, and particularly echoes that of the earlier lights, the torch-beacons: the wait for ἀπαλλαγή πόνων as imaged by light is in some ways fulfilled. Athene encourages them to go to the accompaniment of σφαγίων... σεμνῶν (pointing to their name σεμναὶ θεαί, and to the new relation of respect) and to keep the ruinous from the land, as they send profit for the victory of the city. νίκη here in its instantiation recalls the developed sense of νίκη from opposition to mediation through the trial's ἰσόψηφος result, and following *peitho*. So she encourages the citizens (πολισσοῦχοι) to lead on the metics, μετοίκοις, 'resident aliens': the new constitution of the city is expressed in a term implying its basis in the *oikos*.[66]

The chorus repeat their farewells, χαίρετε χαίρετε δ' αὖθις ἐπανδιπλοίζω: ἐπανδιπλοίζω, 'to double again' (two pairs of χαίρετε), a *hapax legomenon*, recalls not only the process of repetition and reversal we have read as an essential dynamic of the narrative – that is, the logic of the double, and indeed the doubling of doubling – but also, in particular, it points towards the pairings of opposition and support in the *Eumenides* (Apollo/Orestes, Clytemnestra/Erinues, Apollo/Erinues, Orestes/Erinues, Erinues/Athene), the development towards the oppositions of the trial and the continuation of opposition between Athene and the Erinues. Those doublings have led to the reciprocity of a different sort of doubling, the doubling of exchange which forges the bonds of systematisation, order:

---

[66] So the Erinues have a status as a part of the city but distinguished from it.

πάντες οἱ κατὰ πτόλιν
δαίμονές τε καὶ βροτοὶ
Παλλάδος πόλιν νέμον-
τες μετοικίαν δ' ἐμὴν
εὐσεβοῦντες οὔτι μέμ-
ψεσθε συμφορὰς βίου   (1015–20)

The systematisation of the whole city (gods and men): νέμοντες indicates not only 'living', 'inhabiting', but also has its sense 'distribute
in order' from which comes νόμος, the law; and εὐσεβοῦντες, as we
have seen, is the expression of the correct reciprocal ties of respect
(σέβας). Maintaining law and respect, they will not find cause to
blame the συμφορὰς βίου: συμφορά was the word which expressed
particularly the sense of repetition and reversal through its double use
as 'good fortune' and 'bad fortune', its διπλῆ nature (cf. *Cho.* 931,
Aga. 18, 24). Will it be that they will not have cause to blame 'bad
fortune'? Or is the phrase a sort of litotes, 'will not have cause to
blame [i.e. will praise] their fortune'? Or is it the oscillation between
the two senses that is relevant? For it is the oscillation of doubling
which constitutes the ambiguity of the repetition in narrative (life) –
the doubling both of the repetition and reversal of revenge, and of
the reciprocity of exchange.

Athene expresses her praise for their prayers: αἰνῶ τε μύθους τῶνδε
τῶν κατευγμάτων. So she sends them below ground (a tripartite
systematisation of Olympians, ἐπιχθόνιοι, chthonians) with the
torch-bearers who guard her statue δικαίως. So the procession is to
form, made up of παίδων, γυναικῶν...στόλος πρεσβυτίδων – a
further tripartite systematisation of the generations (as we have seen
before). But here it is a procession of women (παίδων is neutral,
'children', as one might expect for those below the age of recognised
sexuality). Although most critics have posited a lacuna after 1027, the
procession of women is particularly suitable accompaniment for the
Erinues: for the Erinues as supporters of Clytemnestra (and within
the system of male/female oppositions) have represented the female
(mother) in the debate (settled by an appeal to sexual criteria) and
their harmonisation within the wider context of the city has been read
(in conjunction with the harmonisation and hierarchisation of the
relations of the *oikos* to the *polis*) as the recognition of the control of
women within the city.

Thus some critics[67] have set against the commonplace of Aeschyl-

---

[67] Cf. Zeitlin 1978 for the most recent and best development of this view. Bachofen,
Engels, Thomson, Millett, Ramnoux, Merck form something of a tradition on this. For
the feminist and the marxist in particular, this trilogy has been taken as a text of the
fall, rather than as an opportunity to join in with the glorification of progress. Millett

ean criticism (that the *Oresteia* indicates a move from ancient vendetta to modern legal justice, and that thus Aeschylus is to be read as a progressive humanist) the recognition of the myth of matriarchy, that is, that the genealogical myth of the *polis* is the justification of the structure of the *polis*, and that thus Aeschylus is to be read in this justification of things as they are, if not conservative, at least as not progressing against the status quo. There remains, however, a profound ambiguity in the reconciliation effected by Athene: for not only is this reconciliation achieved through language, *peitho*, and thus open to the slidings and ambiguities that we have seen characterising the exchange of words in this trilogy, but also if the basis of the reconciliation is the change in the sexual constitution of the opposition (of Athene and the Erinues) – that is, Athene's liminal position of both male/not-male, female/not-female – in what sense is this a reconciliation for the city made up of male and female? For the naming/categorising of society (necessary for the definitions of self/other, inside/outside, φίλος/ἐχθρός etc., the constitutive discourse of the *polis*) in its aim at univocality attempts to remove the ambiguity/liminality of predication, and indeed attempts to control the dangerous slidings of such 'special cases' as puns by designating them – a further categorisation – precisely *as* 'special cases', and thus capable of relegation to the area of comedy, obscenity, bad taste, literature etc.[68] Furthermore, we saw Clytemnestra particularly marked as dangerous partly because of her corruption of language, and we have seen the need for the control of language often voiced. The reconciliation both by means of the sexual ambiguity (of admittedly a goddess) – that is, to reassert the constitution of the *polis* with its necessary boundaries by their transgressor – and by means of *peitho* – that is, to reassert the language-defined boundaries by the manipulation of words – is, therefore, itself a paradox of reversal and transgression: for the *sexual and verbal ambiguity* of Athene *stands against* the society of the *polis* which attempts to designate itself through such polarities as male/female, inside/outside. The reconciliation through Athene itself marks the transgressed boundary in the act of asserting, constituting the boundary: the discourse is not sufficient to, or marks the paradox of, both the need for delineation/opposition and the need for reconciliation, which is the transgression

1971, for example, describes the end of the *Oresteia* as 'five pages of local chamber of commerce rhapsody' and roundly upbraids Athene for the 'sort of corroboration [which] can be fatal'. I hope my analysis shows the difficulties of both the 'progressive' and the 'reactionary' label.

[68] Also an argument essential to Austin's and Searle's speech-act theories, and to many 'ordinary-language' discussions. Derrida 1977 writes amusingly on this. So, too, from a different perspective, does Leach 1964.

of opposition and delineation. Thus it is not simply a case of defining a liminal status of Athene, and concluding that the reconciliation is thus only on the divine level, since humans are either male or female; rather there comes the recognition that through Athene the boundaries of society and language are always already transgressed. Does this add, then, a further implication to Athene's question about γλώσσης ἀγαθῆς ὁδὸν εὑρίσκει(ν)? Does it mark the impossibility of the definition in language of boundaries, and thus oppositions, without transgression? Does this imply, then, in this joining and separation, in these transgressed boundaries (the Erinues as a part of and apart from the city, as Athene is a part of and apart from the definition of the female), the continuing logic of the double? Does it in the doubling of Athene and the Erinues, the Erinues and Athens, the oscillation of sexual determination, resist the development of the third term, the term of mediation? Does this thereby resist the sought-for 'third', the culminating point that we have seen inscribed in the imagery and narrative of the play? Does it furthermore resist even the third play itself *as the culminating point*, turning the teleology of the trilogy into the oscillation of doubles? Is Athene in the *Eumenides* in opposition to Clytemnestra in the *Agamemnon*[69] (*peitho*, transgressed sexual boundaries) as much as she is the mediation between the Erinues and Apollo? As we have seen a *telos* both sought-for and unachieved in the text, postulated and challenged, so the endless divisibility of these continuing doublings is opposed to the trilogy form itself. Their joinings and separations resist the closure of reading in the moment of mediation, resist the summing of the trilogy in a fixed point of end, resist the teleology of thesis, antithesis, synthesis in the continuing parallelisms and repetitions of the double. Thus in this play of two and three, the double and the third, we find an essential (de)structuring of the dynamics of the trilogy.

The escorts' words as the procession leaves recall many of the terms of the play, resisting also the moment of final significance in repetition, citation. In their first description of the Erinues, φιλότιμοι, two key words of reciprocal action, φίλος/τιμεῖν, are jammed together in the compound adjective at this moment of harmonisation, repressing and emphasising the gaps between signifiers. Νυκτὸς παῖδες ἄπαιδες, 'childless children of Night', points to their exclusion from marriage, and the threatened destruction of generational continuity, which was a continuous concern of the play. Perhaps it means also 'children who

---

[69] Winnington-Ingram 1949, p. 144 writes of Athene's decisive role: 'We may fall into error if we attempt to answer this question without reference to Clytemnestra.'

are no children', recalling γραῖαι παλαιαὶ παῖδες (69). ὑπ' εὔφρονι πομπᾷ recalls εὔφρων (1030 etc.) and the earlier escorting of the Erinues, but also, after Νυκτός, perhaps recalls Clytemnestra's opening pun (*Aga.* 265) – they continue εὐφαμεῖτε: the focus on language, its control, especially in religious invocation. So, the Erinues are sent below the earth τιμαῖς καὶ θυσίαις περίσεπτα: they are honoured extremely (-σεπτ- from σέβας) with marks of respect (τιμαῖς – what they had been afraid to lose) and sacrifices – remembering the motif of the corrupted sacrifice as well as sacrifice as expression of relation between gods and men. εὐθύφρονες (more than εὔ-φρονες), 'straight-minded', suggests their earlier descriptions εὐθυδίκαιοι, ὀρθαί. σεμναί picks up περίσεπτα as well as the many references to σέβας/σεμνός we have commented upon. So they demand ὀλολύξατε νῦν ἐπὶ μολπαῖς, 'Cheer now to the song' (ὀλολυγμός, the cry of women), and this exhortation for further noise is repeated at 1047: 'the ὀλολυγμός...no doubt here followed' (Verrall). The last line of the play looks forward, then, marking the text's arbitrary end: νῦν ἐπί..., 'now in addition' – an *addition* to the *end*.[70] So Zeus 'who overlooks all' – which refers back to the interplay of authority, responsibility and over-determination as well as the important imagery of 'over-seeing' – is in agreement with Moira, the sister of the Erinues. Was he in opposition to her before? Thomson lists examples from other works. As female to male? In these stirring final words of the trilogy, then, the suggestion of a supplementary force or authority to Zeus 'who sees *all*', παντόπτας, recalls the tension in the power and authority of the father of the gods as it asserts such omnipotence.

Thus we have seen in the *Eumenides* a move through oppositions of pairings of support and opposition towards the clash of logoi which make up the trial. These logoi (the focus on language) pick up and develop the oppositions, problematics of definition and boundaries we saw in the *Agamemnon* and *Choephoroi* (as they echo many of the images from the earlier plays). The decision of the trial, the fixing of meaning, however, remains in its equal votes an opposition, separated by the vote of Athene, which is given on sexual criteria (of the opposition of male and female) with regard to herself as well as to the opposition of Erinues and Apollo/Orestes. The aggession of the Erinues towards the city of Athens, and their eventual incorporation in the city (through the persuasive language of Athene) develops the civic discourse we saw in the institutionalisation of δίκη in the

---

[70] 'At the words ὀλολύξατε νῦν ἐπὶ μολπαῖς the Eumenides *will* join in' (Thomson, *Oresteia*, my emphasis).

law-court, the role of 'the best of the city' etc. This civic discourse marking the new articulation of the enunciative position of the speaking subject, the development (as in the *Choephoroi* and *Agamemnon*) of the discourse of the *Odyssey*, points to the construction of the subject and the constitution of the city, the subject in the city, The organising of the relation of the internal ties of the *oikos* to the city constitutes the teleology of the genealogical myth (and we saw many plays on origins as explanations, linking narrative and language to sexuality through the metaphors of birth and descent – as the logoi of the trial itself turn on the sexual distinction of the origin of parentage). But this is a teleology which, as the search for and postulation of a single parent could not avoid the doubleness of parentage within the sexual opposition, cannot avoid, despite the weighty teleology of the *trilogy* itself, a continuing doubling and opposition. The telos of closure is resisted in the continuing play of difference. The final meaning remains undetermined.

And so (however) I have reached the ending of my reading, in which in trying to trace the interweavings, the interpenetrations of the play's and my concerns with language, sexuality and narrative, I have tried to investigate some of the parameters of the reading of this dramatic text; I have tried to investigate the boundaries, blocks, and difficulties in reading the complexities of this plural, poetic text. I have tried to open the text to its reverberating strains and skeins of meaning, and question the controls and limits of sense. In such work, I have been investigating the difficulty of reading and writing about Aeschylus' *Oresteia*.

Bibliography

As well as works cited in the text, this bibliography includes works on Aeschylus and other material which have proved instrumental in my reading.

Aarslef, H. (1982) *From Locke to Saussure*. London.

Abel, D. H. (1943) 'Genealogies of ethical concepts from Hesiod to Bacchylides', *TAPA* 74: 92–101.

Abraham, N. (1979) 'The shell and the kernel', *Diacritics* 9.1: 16–28.

Abrams, M. M. (1977) 'The limits of pluralism: the deconstructive angel', *Critical Inquiry* 3.3: 425–38.

Agard, W. (1935) 'Fate and freedom in Greek tragedy', *CJ* 29: 117–26.

Alexanderson, B. (1969) 'Forebodings in the *Agamemnon*', *Eranos* 67: 1–23.

Alexiou, M. (1974) *The Ritual Lament in Greek Tradition*. Cambridge.

Altieri, C. (1979) 'Presence and reference in a literary text: the example of Williams' "This is just to say"', *Critical Inquiry* 5: 489–510.

Anderson, F. M. B. (1929) 'The character of Clytemnestra in the *Agamemnon* of Aeschylus', *TAPA* 63: 136–54.

(1932) 'The character of Clytemnestra in the *Choephoroi* and *Eumenides* of Aeschylus', *AJP* 53: 301–19.

Angel, J. L. (1939) 'Geometric Athenians', an appendix to Young, R. S., *Hesperia*, Supplement 2, Athens.

(1972) 'Ecology and population in the Eastern Mediterranean', *World Archaeology* 4: 88–105.

Apthorp, J. (1980) 'The obstacles to Telemachus' return', *CQ* 30: 1–22.

Ardener, E. (1975a) 'Belief and the problem of women', in Ardener, S. (1975).

(1975b). 'The "problem" revisited', in Ardener, S. (1975).

Ardener, S. (1975) ed. *Perceiving Women*. London.

Aries, P. (1962). *Centuries of Childhood: a Social History of Family Life*. London (Paris 1960).

Arnott, W. G. (1979) 'The eagle portent in the *Agamemnon*: an ornithological footnote', *CQ* 29: 6–7.

Artelt, W. (1937) *Studien zur Geschichte der Begriffe 'Heilmittel' und 'Gift'*. Leipzig.

Arthur, M. B. (1973) 'Early Greece: the origins of Western attitudes towards women', *Arethusa* 6.1: 7–58.

(1976). Review essay: 'Classics'. *Signs* 2.2: 382–403.

(1981) 'The divided world of *Iliad* 6', *Women's Studies* 8.1, 2: 21–46.

(1982) 'Cultural strategies in Hesiod's *Theogony*: law, family society', *Arethusa* 15: 63–82.

(1983) 'The dream of a world without women: poetics and the circles of order in the *Theogony* prooemium', *Arethusa* 16.1, 2: 97–116.

Austin, M. and Vidal-Naquet, P. (1972) *Économies et sociétés en Grèce ancienne*. Paris.

Austin, N. (1972) 'Name magic in the *Odyssey*', *California Studies in Classical Antiquity* 5: 1–19.

Bachofen, J. J. (1967) *Myth Religion and Mother-Right: Selected Writings*. Trans. by R. Manheim, Bollingen series 84. Princeton.

Bacon, H. H. (1964) 'The shield of Eteocles', *Arion* 3.3: 27–38.

Bal, M. (1983) 'Sexuality, semiosis and binarism: a narratological comment on Bergren and Arthur', *Arethusa* 16.1, 2: 117–35.

Baldry, H. C. (1955). 'The house of the Atridae', *CR* 5: 16–17.

Bamberger, J. (1975) 'The myth of matriarchy: why men rule in primitive society', in Rosaldo and Lamphere 1975.

Barnes, J. A. (1973) 'Genetrix: genitor:: nature: culture', in Goody 1973.

Barnes, J. J., Brunschwig, J., Burnyeat, M. and Schofield, M. (1982) eds *Science and Speculation: Studies in Hellenistic Theory and Practice*. Cambridge.

Barry, H., Bacon, M. K. and Child, I. L. (1957) 'A cross-cultural survey of some sex differences in socialization', *Journal of Abnormal and Social Psychology* 55: 327–32.

Barthes, R. (1967a) *Elements of Semiology*. London. Trans. by A. Lavers and Smith of *Elements de sémiologie*, Paris, 1964.

(1967b) *Writing Degree Zero*. London. Trans. by A. Lavers and Smith of *Le Degré Zéro de l'écriture*. Paris, 1964.

(1972) *Mythologies*. London. Trans. by A. Lavers of *Mythologies*. Paris, 1957.

(1974) 'An introduction to the structural analysis of narrative', *New Literary History* 6.2: 237–72.

(1975a) *S/Z*. London. Trans. by A. Miller of *S/Z*. Paris, 1970.

(1975b) 'Rasch', in *Mélanges pour E. Benveniste*. Paris.

(1979) 'From work to text', in Harari 1979a.

(1981) 'Theory of the text', in Young 1981.

Bass, A. (1978) 'Introduction' to Derrida 1967a.

Bayfield, M. A. (1901) 'On some derivatives of τέλος', *CR* 15: 445–7.

Bayley, J. (1974) 'Character and consciousness', *New Literary History* 5.2: 225–35.

Beard, M. (1980) 'The sexual status of Vestal Virgins', *JRS* 70: 12–28.

Beattie, A. J. (1954) 'Aeschylus' *Agamemnon* 281–316', *CR* 4: 77–81.

(1955) 'Aeschulus' Agamemnon 49–59', *CR* 5: 5–7.

Beck, R. H. (1975) *Aeschylus: Playwright, Educator*. The Hague.

Ben-Porat, Z (1976) 'The poetics of literary allusion', *PTL* 1: 105–28.

Benveniste, E. (1966) *Problèmes de linguistique général*. Paris.

(1969) *Le Vocabulaire des institutions indo-européennes*. 2 vols. Paris.

Trans. by E. Palmer, *Indo-European Language and Society*. London, 1973.

Bergren, A. L. T. (1982) 'Sacred apostrophe: re-presentation and imitation in the Homeric Hymns', *Arethusa* 15: 83–108.

(1983) 'Language and the female in early Greek thought', *Arethusa* 16.1, 2: 69–95.

Bergson, L. (1967) 'The hymn to Zeus in Aeschylus' *Agamemnon*', *Eranos* 65: 12–24.

Bertman, S. (1976) ed. *The Conflict of Generation in Ancient Greece and Rome*. Amsterdam.

Betensky, A. (1978) 'Aeschylus' *Oresteia*: the power of Clytemnestra', *Ramus* 7: 11–25.

Beye, C. R. (1974) 'Male and female in the Homeric poem', *Ramus* 3: 87–101.

Billigmeier, J-C and Turner, J. A. (1981) 'The socio-economic roles of women in Mycenean Greece: a brief survey from the evidence of the linear B tablets', *Women's Studies* 8.1, 2: 3–20.

Black, M. (1979) 'More about metaphor', in Ortony 1979a.

Bleeker, C. J. (1965) 'Some introductory remarks on the significance of initiation', in *Initiation: Contributions to the Theme of the Study-Conference of the International Association for the History of Religions: Strasburg September 7–12*. Leiden.

Bloch, M. and Bloch, J. J. (1980) 'Women and the dialectics of nature in eighteenth-century French thought', in MacCormack and Strathern 1980.

Bloom, H. (1979) 'The breaking of form', in Bloom *et al.* 1979.

Bloom, H., de Man, P., Hartman, G. *et al.* (1979) eds *Deconstruction and Criticism*. London.

Booth, N. B. (1957) 'Aeschylus' *Choephoroi* 61–5', *CQ* 7: 143–5.

(1959) 'The run of sense in Aeschylus' *Choephoroi* 22–83', *CP* 54: 111–13.

Booth, W. C. (1977) 'The limits of Pluralism: preserving the exemplar. Or how not to dig our own graves', *Critical Inquiry* 3.3: 407–24.

Borthwick, E. (1976) 'The "Flower of the Argives" and a neglected meaning of ἄνθος', *JHS* 96: 1–7.

Bourdieu, P. (1977) *Outline of a Theory of Practice*. Trans. by R. Nice. Cambridge.

Bowersock, G., Burkert, W. and Putnam, M. C. J. (1979) eds *Arktouros*. Berlin.

Bowra, C. M. (1936a) *Greek Lyric Poetry*. Oxford.

(1936b) 'Pindar Pythian xi', *CQ* 30: 129–41.

Boyd, R. (1979) 'Metaphor and theory change: what is "metaphor" a metaphor for?', in Ortony 1979.

Brelich, A. (1965) 'Initiation et histoire', in *Initiation: Contributions to the Theme of the Study-Conference of the International Association for the History of Religions: Strasburg September 17–22 1964*. Leiden.

(1969) *Paides e Parthenoi*. Rome.

Bremmer, J. (1981) 'Plutarch and the naming of Greek women', *AJP* 102: 425–7.

Brenckman, J. (1976) 'Narcissus in the text', *Georgia Review* 3: 293–329.

Briffault, R. S. (1927) *The Mothers*. London.

Broadhead, H. D. (1959) 'Some passages of the Agamemnon', *CQ* 9: 310–16.

Brooke-Rose, C. (1976) 'Historical genres/theoretical genres: a discussion of Todorov on the fantastic', *New Literary History* 8: 145–58.

Brooks, P. (1980) 'Repetition repression and return: *Great Expectations* and the study of plot', *New Literary History* 11: 503–26.

Brown, A. L. (1982) 'Some problems in the *Eumenides* of Aeschylus', *JHS* 102: 26–32.

Buchler, I. R. and Selby, H. A. (1968) *Kinship and Social Organisation*. London.

Bultmann, R. (1948) 'Zur Geschichte der Lichtsymbolik in Altertum', *Philologus* 97: 1–36.

Bundy, E. L. (1962) *Studia Pindarica*, U.C.P.C.L. 18: 1–2. Berkeley.

Bunker, H. A. (1944) 'Mother murder in myth and legend', *Psychoanalytic Quarterly* 13: 198–207.

Burke, K. (1968) 'Form and persecution in the *Oresteia*', in *Language as Symbolic Action*. Berkeley.

Burkert, W. (1966) 'Greek tragedy and sacrificial ritual', *GRBS* 7: 83–121.

(1970) 'Jason, Hypsipyle and New Fire at Lemnos', *CQ* 20: 1–16.

(1979) *Structure and History in Greek Mythology and Ritual*. London.

Burnett, A. (1973) 'Curse and dream in Aischylos' *Septem*', *GRBS* 14: 343–68.

Butterworth, E. A. S. (1966) *Some Traces of the Pre-Olympian World in Greek Literature and Myth*. Berlin.

Buxton, R. G. A. (1976) 'Peitho: its place in Greek culture and its exploration in some plays of Aeschylus and Sophocles', unpublished dissertation, University of Cambridge.

(1982) *Persuasion in Greek Tragedy*. Cambridge.

Caldwell, R. S. (1970) 'The pattern of Aeschylean tragedy', *TAPA* 101: 77–94.

(1972) 'The psychoanalytic criticism of Greek Tragedy', unpublished dissertation, University of Minnesota.

(1973) 'The misogyny of Eteocles', *Arethusa* 6: 197–231.

(1974) 'The psychology of Aeschylus' *Supplices*', *Arethusa* 7.1: 45–70.

Calogero, G. (1957) 'Gorgias and the Socratic principle nemo sua sponte peccat', *JHS* 77: 12–17.

Cameron, A. (1932) 'The exposure of children and Greek ethics', *CR* 46: 105–14.

Cameron, H. D. (1970) 'The power of words in the *Seven Against Thebes*', *TAPA* 101: 95–118.

Carey, C. (1980) 'ΓΟΝΙΑΣ, Aeschylus *Cho.* 1067', *Glotta* 58: 47.

Cartledge, P. (1981) 'The politics of Spartan pederasty', *PCPS* 27: 17–36.

Cavell, S. (1976) *Must We Mean What We Say?* Cambridge. (First published, New York 1967.)

Chantraine, P. (1968) *Dictionnaire étymologique de la langue grecque*. Paris.

Charlier, M.-T. and Raepsaet, G. (1971) 'Étude d'un comportement social: les relations entre parents et enfants dans la société athénienne à l'époque classique', *L'Antiquité classique* 40: 589–606.

Chase, C. (1979) 'Oedipal textuality: reading Freud's reading of *Oedipus*', *Diacritics* 9.1: 54–68.

Chatman, S. (1981) 'What novels can do that films can't and vice versa', in Mitchell 1981.

Chodkowski, R. R. (1978) 'Organisation du temps dans l'*Agamemnon* d'Éschyle', *Eos* 66: 5–15.

Chodorow, N. (1975) 'Family structure and family personality', in Rosaldo and Lamphere 1975.

Cixoux, H. (1974) 'The character of "character"', *New Literary History* 5: 383–402.

Clay, D. (1969) 'Aeschylus' Trigeron mythos', *Hermes* 97: 1–9.

Clinton, K. (1979) 'The Hymn to Zeus, πάθει μάθος, and the end of the parodos of the *Agamemnon*', *Traditio* 35: 1–21.

    (1973) 'Apollo, Pan and Zeus, avengers of vultures', *AJP* 100: 282–8.

Cohen, J. (1966) *Structure du langage poétique*. Paris.

Cohen, L. J. (1979) 'The semantics of metaphor', in Ortony 1979a.

Cohen, T. (1978) 'Metaphor and the cultivation of intimacy', *Critical Inquiry* 5: 3–12.

Cole, J. R. (1977). 'The *Oresteia* and Cimon', *HSCP* 81: 99–111.

Cole, S. G. (1981) 'Could Greek women read and write?', *Women's Studies* 8.1, 2: 129–56.

Collier, J. F. (1975) 'Women in politics', in Rosaldo and Lamphere 1975.

Collinge, N. E. (1962) 'Medical terms and clinical attitudes in the Tragedians', *BICS* 9: 43–55.

Conacher, D. J. (1974) 'Interaction between chorus and characters in the *Oresteia*', *AJP* 95: 323–43.

Cook, A. (1971) *Enactment: Greek Tragedy*. Chicago.

Costa, C. D. N. (1962) 'Plots and politics in Aeschylus', *GR* 9: 22–34.

Coward, R. (1983) *Patriarchal Precedents*. London.

Coward, R. and Ellis, J. (1977) *Language and Materialism*. London.

Crahay, R. (1974) 'La bouche de la vérité', in Vernant *et al.* 1974.

Crosman, I. (1980) 'Annotated bibliography of audience-oriented criticism', in Suleiman and Crosman 1980.

Crosman, R. (1980) 'Do readers make meaning?', in Suleiman and Crosman 1980.

Culler, J. (1974) 'Commentary', *New Literary History* 6: 219–29.

    (1975) *Structuralist poetics*. Ithaca.

    (1979a) 'Jacques Derrida', in Sturrock 1979.

    (1979b) 'Semiotics and deconstruction', *Poetics Today* 1: 137–41.

    (1980) 'Prolegomena to a theory of reading', in Suleiman and Crosman 1980.

    (1981) *The Pursuit of Signs*. London.

(1983) *On Deconstruction: Theory and Criticism after Structuralism.* London.

Cumming, A. (1973) 'Pauline Christianity and Greek philosophy: a study in the status of women', *JHI* 34: 517–28.

Dale, A. M. (1969a) 'The creation of dramatic characters', in *Collected Papers.* Cambridge.

(1969b) 'Seen and unseen on the Greek stage: a study in scenic conventions', in *Collected Papers.* Cambridge.

Dalzell, J. O. (1970) 'Pleisthenes in the *Agamemnon* of Aeschylus', *Hermathena* 110: 79.

D'Arms, E. F. and Hulley, K. K. (1946) 'The Oresteia story in the *Odyssey*', *TAPA* 77: 207–13.

Davies, M. I. (1969) 'Thoughts on the *Oresteia* before Aeschylus', *Bulletin de Correspondance Hellénique* 93: 214–60.

Dawe, R. D. (1963) 'Inconsistency of plot and character in Aeschylus', *PCPS* 9: 21–62.

(1966) 'The place of the hymn to Zeus in Aeschylus' *Agamemnon*', *Eranos* 64: 1–21.

Dawson, H. S. (1927) 'On *Agamemnon* 108–120', *CR* 41: 213–14.

Delcourt, M. (1961) *Hermaphrodite.* Trans. by J. Nicholson. London. (Paris, 1956.)

Deleuze, G. (1979) 'The schizophrenic and language: surface and depth in Lewis Carroll and Antonin Artaud', in Harari 1979a.

de Man, P. (1971) *Blindness and Insight.* New York.

(1978) 'The epistemology of metaphor', *Critical Inquiry* 5: 13–30.

(1979a) 'Shelley disfigured', in Bloom *et al.* 1979.

(1979b) 'Semiology and rhetoric', in Harari 1979.

(1979c) *Allegories of Reading.* New Haven, Conn.

Derrida, J. (1967a) *Écriture et différence.* Paris. Trans. by A. Bass, *Writing and Difference.* Chicago, 1978.

(1967b) 'La forme et le vouloir-dire: note sur la phénomènologie du langage', *Revue Internationale de Philosophie* 81: 277–99. Trans. in Derrida 1973.

(1968) 'Différance', *Bulletin de la société française de la philosophie* 62.3: 73–101. Trans. in Derrida 1973.

(1970) 'Structure, sign and play in the discourse of the human sciences', in Macksey and Donato 1970.

(1972) *Positions: entretiens avec Henri Ronse, Julia Kristeva, Jean-Louis Houdebine, Guy Scarpetta.* Paris.

(1973) *Speech and Phenomenon.* Evanston. Trans. by D. Allison and N. Garner of *Le Voix et le phénomène.* Paris, 1967.

(1974a) 'White mythology: metaphor in the text of philosophy', *New Literary History* 6: 5–74.

(1974b) *Glas.* Paris.

(1975) 'The purveyor of truth', *YFS* 52: 31–113.

(1976a) *Of Grammatology.* Baltimore. Trans. by G. Spivak of *De la Grammatologie.* Paris, 1967.

(1976b) 'Signature, event, context', *Glyph* 1: 172–97.

(1977) 'Limited inc. abc', *Glyph* 2: 162–254.

(1978) *La vérité en peinture*. Paris.

(1979a) 'Living on – Borderlines', in Bloom *et al.* 1979.

(1979b) 'The supplement of copula: philosophy *before* linguistics', in Harari 1979a.

(1979c) 'Me-psychoanalysis', *Diacritics* 9.1: 4–15.

(1980) 'La loi de genre/the law of genre', *Glyph* 7: 168–232.

(1981) *Dissemination*. Chicago. Trans. by B. Johnson of *Dissemination*. Paris, 1972.

(1982) *Margins of Philosophy*, Chicago. Trans. by A. Bass of *Marges de la Philosophie*. Paris, 1972.

Detienne, M. (1967) *Les Maîtres de vérité dans la grèce archaique*. Paris.

(1971) 'Orphée au Miel', *QUCC* 13: 7–23. Also in le Goff and Nova 1973 and Gordon 1981 (translated).

(1977) *Dionysos mis à mort*. Paris.

(1981) *L'invention de la mythologie*. Paris.

Detienne, M. and Vernant, J.-P. (1978) *Cunning Intelligence in Greek Culture and Society*. Trans. by J. Lloyd. Brighton. (Paris, 1974.)

Deutsch, H. (1944) *Psychology of Women*. New York.

Devereux, G. (1953) 'Why Oedipus killed Laius', *International Journal of Psychoanalysis* 34: 132–41.

(1957) 'Penelope's character', *Psychoanalytic Quarterly* 26: 378–86.

(1967) 'Greek pseudo-homosexuality and the Greek miracle', *Symb. Osl.* 62: 69–72.

(1976) *Dreams in Greek Tragedy*. Oxford.

Dewald, C. (1981) 'Women and culture in Herodotus' Histories', *Women's Studies* 8.1, 2: 65–91.

Diggle, J. (1968) 'Notes on the *Agamemnon* and *Persae* of Aeschylus', *CR* 18: 1–3.

Dimmock, G. E. (1956) 'The name of Odysseus', *Hudson Review* 9.1: 52–70.

Dobson, M. (1978) 'Oracular language: its style and intent in the Delphic oracles and in Aeschylus' *Oresteia*', unpublished dissertation, Harvard University.

Dodds, E. R. (1951) *The Greeks and the Irrational*. Berkeley.

(1953) 'Notes on the *Oresteia*', *CQ* 3: 11–21.

(1960) 'Morals and politics in the *Oresteia*', *PCPS* 6: 19–31.

Donato, E. (1975) 'Lévi-Strauss and the protocols of distance', *Diacritics* 5.3: 2–12.

(1976) 'Here now/always already: incidental remarks on some recent characterisations of the text', *Diacritics* 6.3: 24–9.

Donlan, W. (1978) 'Social vocabulary and its relationship to political vocabulary in fifth-century Athens', *QU* 27: 95–111.

Douglas, M. (1966) *Purity and Danger*. London.

Dover, K. J. (1957) 'The political aspect of Aeschylus' *Eumenides*', *JHS* 77: 230–7.

(1973a) 'Classical Greek attitudes to sexual behaviour', *Arethusa* 6: 59–73.

(1973b) 'Some neglected aspects of Agamemnon's dilemma', *JHS* 93: 58–69.

Doyle, R. E. (1970) 'ΟΛΒΟΣ, ΚΟΡΟΣ, ΥΒΡΙΣ and ΑΤΗ from Hesiod to Aeschylus', *Traditio* 26: 293–303.

(1972) 'The objective concept of ἄτη in Aeschylean Tragedy', *Traditio* 28: 1–26.

Du Bois, P. (1978) 'Sappho and Helen', *Arethusa* 11: 89–99.

(1982) 'On the invention of hierarchy', *Arethusa* 15: 203–20.

Duchemin, J. (1967) 'Le déroulement du temps et son expression théâtrale dans quelques tragédies d'Éschyle', *Dioniso* 41: 197–217.

Dumortier, J. (1935) *Le Vocabulaire médical d'Éschyle et les écrits hippocratiques*. Paris.

Duncan, T. S. (1938) 'Gorgias' theories of Art', *CJ* 33: 402–15.

Dworacki, S. (1979) 'Atossa's absence in the final scene of the *Persae* of Aeschylus', in Bowersock *et al.* 1979.

Dyer, R. R. (1967) 'The iconography of the *Oresteia* after Aeschylus', *AJA* 71: 175–6.

Dyson, M. (1971) 'Aeschylus' Agamemnon 355–8', *CR* 21: 170.

Eagleton, T. (1976) *Criticism and Ideology*. London.

(1982) *The Rape of Clarissa*. Oxford.

(1983) *Literary Theory*. Oxford.

Earp, F. R. (1948) *The Style of Aeschylus*. London.

(1950) 'Studies in character: *Agamemnon*', *GR* 19: 49–61.

Easterling, P. E. (1973) 'Presentation of character in Aeschylus', *GR* 20: 3–18.

Eckert, C. W. (1963) 'Initiatory motifs in the story of Telemachus', *CJ* 59: 49–57. Also in Vickery, J. B. (1966) ed., *Myth and Literature*. Lincoln, Nebr.

Eco, U. (1976) *A Theory of Semiotics*. Bloomington, Ind.

Edwards, M. (1977) 'Agamemnon's decision: freedom and folly in Aeschylus', *California Studies in Classical Antiquity* 10: 17–38.

Edwards, W. M. (1939) 'The eagles and the hare', *CQ* 33: 204–7.

Egan, R. B. (1976) 'The Chalcas quotation and the Hymn to Zeus', *Eranos* 77: 1–9.

Elam, K. (1980) *The Semiotics of Theatre and Drama*. London.

Eliade, M. (1961) *Birth and Rebirth*. Trans. by W. R. Trask. London.

(1963) *Myth and Reality*. New York. Trans. by W. R. Trask of *Aspects du Mythe*. Paris, 1963.

Else, G. F. (1958) '"Imitation" in the fifth century', *CP* 53: 73–90.

Engels, D. (1980) 'The problem of female infanticide', *CP* 75: 112–20.

Engels, F. (1972) *Origins of the Family, Private Property, and the State*. Trans. and introduction by E. B. Leacock. London.

Ewans, M. (1975) 'Agamemnon at Aulis; a study in the *Oresteia*', *Ramus* 4: 17–32.

Farenga, V. (1979) 'Periphrasis on the origin of rhetoric', *MLN* 94: 1033-55.

Farrow, S. (1979) 'The portrayal of women in the *Iliad*', *AC* 22: 15-32.

Fehér, F. (1980) 'The pan-tragic vision: the metaphysics of tragedy', *New Literary History* 11: 245-54.

Felman, S. (1975) 'Madness and philosophy or literature's reason', *YFS* 52: 206-28.

(1977) 'Turning the screw of interpretation', *YFS* 55-6: 94-207.

(1978) *La Folie de la chose littéraire*. Paris.

(1980) 'On reading poetry: reflections on the limits and possibilities of psychoanalytic approaches', *Psychiatry and the Humanities* 4: 119-48.

(1982) ed. *Literature and Psychoanalysis. The Question of Reading Otherwise*. Baltimore.

Fenik, B. (1974) *Studies in the Odyssey*. Wiesbaden.

Finley, J. H. (1955) *Pindar and Aeschylus*. Cambridge, Mass.

(1966) 'Politics and early Attic tragedy', *HSCP* 71: 1-13.

Finley, M. I. (1955) 'Marriage, sale and gift in the Homeric world', *Revue internationale des droits de l'antiquité* 2: 167-94.

(1956) *The World of Odysseus*. London.

(1964a) 'Between slavery and freedom', *Comparative Studies in Society and History* 6: 233-49.

(1964b) 'The Trojan War', *JHS* 84: 1-20.

(1973) *The Ancient Economy*. London.

(1974) 'The world of Odysseus revisited', *Proceedings of the Classical Association*: 13-31.

(1981) *Economy and Society in Ancient Greece*. London.

Fischer, U. (1965) *Der Telosgedanke in den Dramen des Aischylos*. Hildesheim.

Fish, S. (1973) 'How ordinary is ordinary language?', *New Literary History*: 41-54.

(1981) 'Why no-one's afraid of Wolfgang Iser', *Diacritics* 11.1: 2-28.

Fisher, N. R. E. (1976) 'Hubris and dishonour', *GR* 23: 177-93.

Flacelière, R. (1965) 'La femme antique en Crète en Grèce', in Grimal 1965.

Fletcher, A. (1972) 'The perpetual error', *Diacritics* 2.4: 11-15.

Foley, H. P. (1975) 'Sex and state in ancient Greece', *Diacritics* 5.4: 31-6.

(1978) '"Reverse similes" and sex roles in the *Odyssey*', *Arethusa* 11: 7-26.

(1982a) 'The "female intruder" reconsidered: women in Aristophanes' *Lysistrata* and *Ecclesiazusae*', *CP* 77: 1-21.

(1982b) 'Marriage and sacrifice in Euripides' *Iphigeneia in Aulis*', *Arethusa* 15: 159-80.

Fontenrose, J. (1959) *Python*. Berkeley.

(1971) 'Gods and men in the *Oresteia*', *TAPA* 102: 71-109.

Forbes, P. B. R. (1948) 'Law and politics in the *Oresteia*', *CR* 62: 99-104.

Forrest, W. G. (1960) 'Themistokles and Argos', *CQ* 10: 221–42.

(1966) *The Emergence of Greek Democracy*. London.

(1975) 'An Athenian generation gap', *YCS* 24: 37–52.

Fortes, M. (1959) *Oedipus and Job in West African Religion*. Cambridge.

(1962) 'Ritual and office in tribal society', in Gluckman 1962.

Foucault, M. (1967) *Madness and Civilization*. London. Trans. by R. Howard of *Histoire de la folie*. Paris, 1961.

(1972) *The Archaeology of Knowledge*. London. Trans. by A. M. Sheridan Smith of *L'Archéologie de savoir*. Paris, 1969.

(1973) *The Order of Things*. London. Trans. of *Les Mots et les choses*. Paris, 1966.

(1977) *Language, Counter-Memory, Practice*, ed. D. F. Bouchard. Trans. by D. F. Bouchard and S. Simon. Ithaca, N.Y.

(1978) *The History of Sexuality*, Vol. 1. London. Trans. by R. Hurley of *La Volonté de savoir*. Paris, 1976.

(1979) 'What is an author?', in Harari 1979a.

(1981) 'The order of discourse', in Young 1981.

Fowler, B. H. (1967) 'Aeschylus' imagery', *CM* 28: 1–74.

Fraser, B. (1979) 'Interpretation of novel metaphors', in Ortony 1979a.

Freyman, J. M. (1976) 'The generation gap in the *Agamemnon*', in Bertman 1976.

Friedman, J. and Gassel, S. (1951) 'Orestes', *Psychoanalytic Quarterly* 20: 423–33.

Frisk, H. (1960) *Griechisches Etymologisches Wörterbuch*. Heidelberg.

Fromm, E. (1971a) 'The theory of Mother Right and its relevance for social psychology', in *The Crisis of Psychoanalysis*. London.

(1971b) 'The significance of Mother Right today', in *The Crisis of Psychoanalysis*. London.

Fuqua, C. (1972) '*Agamemnon* 1446–7', *CP* 67: 191–2.

Fustel de Coulanges, N. D. (1971) *The Ancient City*. New York. Trans. by W. Small of *La Cité antique*. Paris, 1864.

Gagarin, M. (1975) 'The vote of Athena', *AJP* 96: 121–7.

(1976) *Aeschylean Drama*. Berkeley.

Gallop, J. (1975) 'The ghost of Lacan, the trace of language', *Diacritics* 5.4: 18–24.

(1976) 'The Ladies Man', *Diacritics* 6.4: 28–34.

(1979) 'The seduction of analogy', *Diacritics* 9.1: 46–51.

(1982) *Feminism and Psychoanalysis: the Seduction of the Daughter*. London.

Gantz, T. N. (1977) 'The fires of the *Oresteia*', *JHS* 97: 28–38.

(1978) 'Love and death in the *Suppliants* of Aeschylus', *Phoenix* 32: 279–87.

(1980) 'The Aeschylean tetralogy: attested and conjectured groups', *AJP* 101: 133–64.

(1981) 'Divine guilt in Aeschylus', *CQ* 31: 18–32.

Garton, C. (1957) 'Characterisation in Greek tragedy', *JHS* 77: 247–54.

Garvie, A. F. (1969) *Aeschylus' Supplices: Play and Trilogy*. Cambridge.
  (1970) 'The opening of the *Choephoroi*', *BICS* 17: 79–91.
  (1972) 'Deceit, violence, persuasion in the *Philoctetes*', in *Studi Classici in Onore Cataudella*, eds C. U. Crimi, A. D. B. Zimbone and C. Nicolosi. Catania.
  (1978) 'Aeschylus' simple plots', in *Dionysiaca: Nine Studies in Greek Poetry by Former Pupils Presented to Sir Denys Page on his Seventieth Birthday*, eds R. B. Dawe, J. Diggle and P. E. Easterling. Cambridge.
Gasché, R. (1979) 'Deconstruction as criticism', *Glyph* 6: 179–215.
Gellie, G. H. (1963) 'Character in Greek tragedy', *AUMLA* 20: 241–56.
Genette, G. (1980) *Figures of Literary Discourse*. Columbia. Trans. by A. Sheridan of *Figures* I–II. Paris, 1966–9.
  (1982) *Narrative Discourse*. Oxford. Trans. by J. E. Lewin of *Figures* III. Paris, 1972.
Gernet, L. (1968) *Anthropologie de la Grèce*. Paris.
  (1981) *The Anthropology of Ancient Greece*. Baltimore, Md. Trans. by J. Hamilton and B. Nagy of Gernet 1968.
Ghiron-Bistagne, P. (1978) 'Iconographie et problèmes de mîse en scène: la mort d'Égisthe dans les *Choéphores* d'Éschyle', *RA*: 39–62.
Gigon, O. (1936) 'Gorgias "über das Nichtsein"', *Hermes* 71: 186–213.
Gilleland, M. E. (1980) 'Female speech in Greek and Latin', *AJP* 101: 180–3.
Gillison, G. (1980) 'Images of nature in Gimi thought', in MacCormack and Strathern 1980.
Girard, R. (1977) *Violence and the Sacred*. Baltimore, Md. Trans. by P. Gregory of *La Violence et le sacré*. Paris, 1972.
Gladigow, B. (1974) 'Aischylos und Heraklit', in Hommel 1974.
Gluckman, M. (1962a) ed. *The Ritual of Social Relations*. Manchester.
  (1962b) 'Les rites de passage', in Gluckman 1962a.
Goheen, R. F. (1955) 'Aspects of dramatic symbolism: three studies in the *Oresteia*', *AJP* 76: 113–37.
Golden, L. (1961) 'Zeus whoever he is...', *TAPA* 92: 156–67.
  (1976) 'Fear in the *Agamemnon*', *Rivista di Studi Classici* 24: 324–8.
Goldhill, S. D. (1984) 'τελεσφόρος at *Cho.* 663–4', *JHS* 104 (forthcoming).
Goldman, H. (1910) 'The *Oresteia* of Aeschylus as illustrated by Greek vase painting', *HSCP* 28: 111–59.
Gomme, A. W. (1925) 'The position of women in Athens', *CP* 20: 1–26.
Goodale, J. C. (1980) 'Gender, sexuality, and marriage: a Kaulong model of nature and culture', in MacCormack and Strathern 1980.
Goodman, N. (1981) 'Twisted tales or story, study and symphony', in Mitchell 1981.
Goodson, A. C. (1979) 'Oedipus Anthropologicus', *MLN* 94.4: 688–701.
Goody, J. (1973) ed. *The Character of Kinship*. Cambridge.
Gordon, R. L. (1981) ed. *Myth, Religion and Society*. Cambridge.

Goujon, F. (1976) 'Le nom et le drame: aspects de la function du choeur dans l'*Agamemnon* d'Éschyle', in *Écriture et théorie poétique, lectures d'Homère, Éschyle, Platon, Aristote*. Paris.

Gould, J. (1978) 'Dramatic character and "human intelligibility" in Greek Tragedy', *PCPS* 24: 43–67.

(1980) 'Law, custom, and myth: aspects of the social position of women in Classical Athens', *JHS* 100: 38–59.

Green, A. (1975) *Un Oeil en trop*. Paris. Trans. by A. Sheridan as *The Tragic Effect*. London, 1979.

Greene, W. C. (1951) 'The spoken and the written word', *HSCP* 59: 23–59.

Griffith, M. (1977) *The Authenticity of Prometheus Bound*. Cambridge.

Griffiths, J. G. (1967) 'Aegisthus citharista', *AJA* 71: 176–7.

Grimal, P. (1965) ed. *Histoire Mondiale de la femme*. Paris.

Groten, F. J. (1968) 'Homer's Helen', *GR* 15: 33–40.

Grube, G. M. A. (1965) *The Greek and Roman Critics*. London.

(1970) 'Zeus in Aeschylus', *AJP* 91: 43–51.

Guepin, J.-P. (1968) *The Tragic Paradox*. Amsterdam.

Gundert, H. (1974) 'Die Stichomythie zwischen Agamemnon und Klytaimestra' in Hommel 1974.

Guthrie, W. K. (1957) *In the Beginning*. London.

(1962–81) *A History of Greek Philosophy*, 6 vols. Cambridge.

Hadas, M. (1935) 'Utopian sources in Herodotus', *CP* 30: 113–21.

(1936) 'Observations on Athenian women', *CW* 39: 97–110.

Haldane, J. A. (1965) 'Musical themes and imagery in Aeschylus', *JHS* 85: 33–42.

Halliburton, D. (1981) *Poetic Thinking*. Chicago.

Halliday, W. R. (1913) *Greek Divination*. London.

Hamilton, R. (1978) 'Announced entrance in Greek Tragedy', *HSCP* 82: 63–82.

Hammond, N. G. L. (1965) 'Personal freedom and its limitations in the *Oresteia*', *JHS* 85: 42–55.

Hansen, P. A. (1978) 'The robe episode of the *Choephoroi*', *CQ* 28: 239–40.

Harari, J. V. (1979a) ed. *Textual Strategies: Perspectives in Post-Structuralist Criticism*. Ithaca.

(1979b) 'Critical factions/critical fictions', in Harari 1979a.

Harmon, A. M. (1932) 'The scene of the *Persians* of Aeschylus', *TAPA* 63: 7–19.

Harriot, R. M. (1969) *Poetry and Criticism before Plato*. London.

(1982) 'The Argive elders, the discerning shepherds, and the fawning dog: misleading communication in the *Agamemnon*', *CQ* 32: 9–17.

Harris, G. (1973) 'Furies, witches and mothers', in J. Goody, *Character of Kinship*. Cambridge.

Harris, M. (1968) *The Rise of Anthropological Theory*. New York.

Harris, O. (1980) 'The power of signs: gender, culture, and the wild in the Bolivian Andes', in MacCormack and Strathern 1980.

Harrison, A. R. W. (1968) *The Law of Athens*. Oxford.

Harsh, P. W. (1950) 'Penelope and Odysseus in *Odyssey* XIX', *AJP* 71: 1-21.

Hartman, G. H. (1970) *Beyond Formalism*. New Haven.
  (1973) 'War in Heaven', *Diacritics* 3.1: 26-32.
  (1975a) *The Fate of Reading*. Chicago.
  (1975b) 'Monsieur Texte: On Jacques Derrida: his *Glas*', *Georgia Review* 29.4: 759-97.
  (1976) 'Monsieur Texte II: epiphany in echo-land', *Georgia Review* 30.1: 169-204.
  (1980) *Criticism in the Wilderness*. New Haven, Conn.
  (1981) *Saving the Text: Literature/Derrida/Philosophy*. Baltimore, Md.

Harvey, F. D. (1966) 'Literacy in the Athenian democracy', *REG*: 585-635.

Haslam, M. W. (1979) '"O suitably-attired-in-leathern-boots". Interpolations in Greek tragedy', in Bowersock *et al.* 1979.

Hawkes, T. (1977) *Structuralism and Semiotics*. London.

Heath, S. (1978) 'Sexual difference and representation', *Screen* 19.3: 51-112.

Heidegger, M. (1959) *An Introduction to Metaphysics*. New Haven, Conn. Trans. by R. Manheim of *Einführung in die Metaphysik*. Tübingen, 1953.

Hernadi, P. (1981) 'On the How, What, and Why of narrative', in Mitchell 1981.

Herrington, C. J. (1965) 'Aeschylus: the last phase', *Arion* 4.3: 387-403.

Hertz, N. (1979) 'Freud and the Sandman', in Harari 1979.

Herzfeld, M. (1983) 'The excavation of concepts: commentary on Peradotto and Nagy', *Arethusa* 16.1: 57-68.

Hester, D. (1981) 'The casting vote', *AJP* 102: 265-74.

Hewes, G. W. (1975) *Language Origins: a Bibliography*. The Hague.

Higgins, W. E. (1976) 'Wolf God Apollo in the *Oresteia*', *PP* 31: 201-5.
  (1978) 'Double-dealing Ares in the *Oresteia*', *CP* 73: 24-35.

Hirvonen, K. (1968) *Matriarchal Survivals*, Annales Academicae Scientiarum Fennicae Series B, 152. Helsinki.

Holland, N. N. (1980) 'Re-covering "the Purloined Letter": reading as a personal transaction', in Suleiman and Crosman 1980.

Holwerda, D. (1963) 'ΤΕΛΟΣ', *Mnemosyne* 16: 337-63.

Hommel, H. (1974) *Wege zu Aischylos*, 2 vols. Darmstadt.

Horkheimer, M. (1972) 'Authority and the family', in *Critical Theory: Max Horkheimer*. Trans. by M. J. O'Connell *et al.* New York.

Howe, T. P. (1962) 'Taboo in the Oedipus theme', *TAPA* 93: 124-43.

Hubert, H. and Mauss, M. (1964) *Sacrifice: its Nature and Function*, London. Trans. by W. D. Halls of *Essai sur la nature et la fonction du sacrifice. L'Année sociologique*. Paris, 1898.

Humphrey, S. C. (1978) *Anthropology and the Greeks*. London.

Ireland, S. (1974) 'Stichomythia in Aeschylus', *Hermes* 192: 509-24.

Irwin, J. T. (1975) *Doubling and incest/repetition and revenge*. Baltimore.
  (1980) 'Self-evidence and self-reference: Nietzsche and tragedy, Whitman and opera', *New Literary History* 11: 177–92.
Iser, W. (1974) *The Implied Reader*. Baltimore, Md.
  (1980) 'Interaction between text and reader', in Suleiman and Crosman 1980.
Jakobson, R. and Halle, M. (1956) *The Fundamentals of Language*. The Hague.
Jameson, F. (1971) *Marxism and Form*. Princeton.
  (1972) *The Prison House of Language: a Critical Account of Structuralism and Russian Formalism*. Princeton.
  (1977) 'Imaginary and symbolic in Lacan: Marxism, psychoanalytic criticism, and the problem of the subject', *YFS* 55/6: 338–95.
Janko, R. (1980) 'Aeschylus' *Oresteia* and Archilochus', *CQ* 30: 29–30.
Jeanmaire, H. (1939) *Couroi et couretes*. Lille.
Johnson, A. L. (1977) 'Anagrammatism in poetry: theoretic preliminaries', *PTL* 2: 89–118.
Johnson, B. (1977) 'The frame of reference: Poe, Lacan, Derrida', *YFS* 55/6: 457–505.
  (1981) 'Introduction' to Derrida 1981.
Johnstone, H. (1980) 'Pankoinon as a rhetorical figure in Greek tragedy', *Glotta* 58: 49–62.
Jones, J. (1962) *On Aristotle and Greek Tragedy*. London.
Jordanova, L. J. (1980) 'Natural facts: a historical perspective on science and sexuality', in MacCormack and Strathern 1980.
Josipovici, G (1976) ed. *The Modern English Novel: the Reader, the Writer, the Work*. London.
Jouan, F. (1978) 'Nomen-omen chez Éschyle', in *Problèmes du mythe et de son interprétation*, ed. J. Hani. Paris.
Kahn, L. (1978) *Hermes passe ou les ambiguités de la communication*. Paris.
  (1980) 'Ulysse ou la ruse et la mort', *Critique* 393: 116–34.
Kakridis, J. T. (1978) 'Pleistheniden oder Atriden', *ZPE* 30: 1–4.
Katz, P. B. (1976) 'The Myth of Psyche', *Arethusa* 9.1: 111–18.
Kells, J. H. (1961) 'Aeschylus' *Eumenides* 213–14 and Athenian marriage', *CP* 56: 169–73.
Kennedy, G. (1963) *The Art of Persuasion in Greece*. London.
Kenyon, F. G. (1932) *Books and Readers in Ancient Greece*. Oxford.
Kerferd, G. (1981) *The Sophistic Movement*. Cambridge.
Kermode, F. (1981) 'Secrets and narrative sequence', in Mitchell 1981.
Kitto, H. D. F. (1951) *The Greeks*. London.
  (1955) 'The dance in Greek Tragedy', *JHS* 75: 36–41.
  (1956) *Form and Meaning in Drama*. London.
  (1961) *Greek Tragedy*. London. (First edn 1939).
Klein, R. (1972) 'Prolegomenon to Derrida', *Diacritics* 2.4: 29–34.
  (1973) 'The blindness of hyperboles; the ellipses of insight', *Diacritics* 3.2: 33–44.

Knox, B. M. W. (1952) 'The lion in the house', *CP* 47: 17–25.
  (1966) 'Second thoughts in Greek Tragedy', *GRBS* 7: 213–32.
  (1972) 'Aeschylus and the third actor', *AJP* 93: 104–24.
Kolkey, D. M. (1973) 'Dionysus and women's emancipation', *CB* 50.1: 1–5.
Koniaris, G. L. (1980) 'An obscene word in Aeschylus', *AJP* 101: 42.
Kramer, F. R. (1960) 'The altar of right: reality and power in Aeschylus', *CJ* 56: 33–8.
Kranz, W. (1933) *Stasimon*. Berlin.
Kristeva, J. (1969a) 'Pour une sémiologie des paragrammes', in ΣΗΜΕΙΩΤΙΚΗ. Paris.
  (1969b) 'Le texte clos', in ΣΗΜΕΙΩΤΙΚΗ. Paris.
  (1969c) 'Le mot, le dialogue et le roman', in ΣΗΜΕΙΩΤΙΚΗ. Paris.
  (1969d) 'La productivité dite texte', in ΣΗΜΕΙΩΤΙΚΗ. Paris.
  (1975a) 'La fonction prédicative et le sujet parlant', in Kristeva *et al.* 1975.
  (1975b) 'D'une identité à l'autre', *Tel Quel* 62: 10–28.
  (1976) 'Noms de lieu', *Tel Quel* 68: 40–56.
  (1980) *Desire in Language: a Semiotic Approach to Literature and Art.* Oxford. (Ed. by L. S. Roudiez.)
Kristeva, J., Milner, J.-C. and Ruwet, N. (1975) *Langue, discours, société: hommages à E. Benveniste.* Paris.
Kuhn, T. (1979) 'Metaphor in science', in Ortony 1979a.
Kuhns, R. (1962) *The House, the City, the Judge.* Indianapolis.
La Barbe, J. (1953) 'L'âge correspondant au sacrifice du κουρεῖον et les données historiques du sixième discours d'Isée', *Bulletin de l'Académie Royale de Belgique*, Cl des lettres 39: 358–94.
Lacan, J. (1977a) *Écrits.* London. A selection, trans. by A. Sheridan, from *Écrits.* Paris, 1966.
  (1977b) *The Four Fundamental Concepts of Psycho-analysis.* London. Trans. by A. Sheridan of *Le Séminaire de Jacques Lacan Livre XI. Les quatre concepts fondamentaux de psychanalyse.*
  (1977c) 'Desire and the interpretation of desire in Hamlet', *YFS* 55–6: 11–52.
Lacey, W. K. (1968) *The Family in Classical Greece.* Boston.
  (1980) 'The family of Euxitheus (Demosthenes LVII)', *CQ* 30: 57–61.
Lain Entralgo, P. (1970) *The Therapy of the Word in Classical Antiquity.* New Haven, Conn. Trans. by L. J. Rather and J. M. Sharp of *La curacíon por la palabra en la Antigüedad clásica.* Madrid, 1958.
Lallot, J. (1974) 'Xumbola kranai: réflexions sur la fonction du *symbolon* dans l'*Agamemnon* d'Éschyle', *Cahiers Internationaux de Symbolisme* 26: 39–48.
  (n.d.) 'Retour et renversement dans l'*Agamemnon*', unpublished article.
Lanahan, W. F. (1974) 'Levels of symbolism in the red carpet scene of the *Agamemnon*', *CB* 51: 24–6.

Lane, T. (1976) 'His master's voice? The questioning of authority in literature', in Josipovici 1976.

Laplanche, J. and Pontialis, J.-B. (1973). *The Language of Psychoanalysis*. London. Trans. by D. Nicholson Smith of *Le Vocabulaire de psychanalyse*. Paris, 1967.

Lattimore, R. (1972) 'Introduction to the *Oresteia*', in McCall 1972.

(1979) 'Optatives of consent and refusal', in Bowersock *et al.* 1979.

Lawrence, S. (1976) 'Artemis in the *Agamemnon*', *AJP* 97: 97–110.

Leach, E. (1964) 'Anthropological aspects of language: animal categories and verbal abuse', in Lenneberg 1964.

(1967) ed. *The Structural Study of Myth and Totemism*. London.

Leacock, E. B. (1972) 'Introduction' to Engels (1972).

(1981) *Myths of Male Dominance*. New York.

Leary, D. M. (1969) 'The role of Cassandra in the *Agamemnon* of Aeschylus', *Bulletin of John Rylands Library* 52: 144–77.

(1973) 'The authority of the elders: a note', *CP* 68: 202–3.

(1974) 'The representation of the Trojan War in Aeschylus' *Agamemnon*', *AJP* 95: 1–23.

Lebeck, A. (1964) 'The robe of Iphigeneia in the *Agamemnon*', *GRBS* 5: 35–41.

(1967) 'The first stasimon of Aeschylus' *Choephoroi*: myth and mirror image', *CP* 57: 182–5.

(1971) *The Oresteia*. Washington, D.C.

Leenhardt, J. (1980) *Towards a Sociology of Reading*, in Suleiman and Crosman 1980.

Lefkowitz, M. (1973) 'Critical stereotypes and the poetry of Sappho', *GRBS* 14.2: 113–25.

LeGoff, J. and Nova, P. (1973) *Faire de l'histoire*. Paris.

Le Guin, U. (1981) 'It was a dark and stormy night or Why are we huddling about the campfire?', in Mitchell 1981.

Lenneberg, E. H. (1964) ed. *New Directions in the Study of Language*. Cambridge, Mass.

Lesky, A. (1931) 'Die Orestie des Aischylos', *Hermes* 66: 190–241.

(1943) 'Der Kommos der *Choephoren*', *Sitzungsberichtes Wiener Akademie der Wissenschaft* 221: 1–127.

(1965) *Greek Tragedy*. London. Trans. by H. A. Frankfort. *Die Griechische Tragödie*. First edn Stuttgart, 1938; third edn Stuttgart, 1965.

(1966) 'Decision and responsibility in the tragedy of Aeschylus', *JHS* 86: 78–85.

Lesky, E. (1951) *Die Zeugungs- und Vererbungslehren der Antike und ihr Nachwirken*. Wiesbaden.

Levin, S. (1979) 'Standard approaches to metaphor and a proposal for literary metaphor', in Ortony 1979a.

Lévi-Strauss, C. (1956) 'The family', in H. Shapiro (ed.), *Man, Culture and Society*. New York.

(1963) *Structural Anthropology*. New York. Trans. by C. Jacobson and B. G. Schoepf of *Anthropologie structurale*. Paris, 1958.

(1966) *The Savage Mind*. Chicago. Trans. by *La Pensée sauvage*. Paris, 1962.

(1969) *The Elementary Structures of Kinship*. Boston. Trans. by Bell and Sturmer of *La Structure élémentaire de la parenté*. Paris, 1949.

(1977) *Structural Anthropology Two*. New York. Trans. by M. Leyton of *Anthropologie structurale deux*. Paris, 1973.

Lilja, S. (1976) *Dogs in Ancient Greek Poetry*. Helsinki.

Lipshitz, S. (1978) ed. *Tearing the Veil: Essays on Feminism*. London.

Livingstone, Sir R. W. (1925) 'The problem of the *Eumenides* of Aeschylus', *JHS* 45: 120–31.

Lloyd, G. E. R. (1966) *Polarity and Analogy*. Cambridge.

(1979) *Magic, Reason and Experience*. Cambridge.

(1982) 'Observational error in later Greek science', in Barnes *et al.* 1982.

(1983) *Science, Folklore and Ideology*. Cambridge.

Lloyd-Jones, H. (1952) 'The robes of Iphigeneia', *CR* 66: 132–5.

(1953) 'Aeschylus *Agamemnon* 146ff.', *CQ* 3: 96.

(1956) 'Zeus in Aeschylus', *JHS* 76: 55–67.

(1959) 'The end of the *Seven against Thebes*', *CQ* 9: 80–114.

(1961) 'Some alleged interpolations in Aeschylus' *Choephoroi* and Euripides' *Electra*', *CQ* 11: 171–84.

(1962) 'The guilt of Agamemnon', *CQ* 12: 187–99.

(1971) *The Justice of Zeus*. Berkeley, Calif.

(1978) 'Ten notes on Aeschylus' *Agamemnon*', in *Dionysiaca: Nine Studies in Greek Poetry by Former Pupils Presented to Sir Denys Page on his Seventieth Birthday*, eds R. D. Dawe, J. Diggle and P. E. Easterling. Cambridge.

Longman, G. A. (1954) 'Aeschylus *Choephoroi* 926', *CR* 4: 86–90.

Longo, O. (1978) 'Techniche della communicazione e ideologie sociali', *AQ* 27: 63–92.

Loraux, N. (1978) 'Sur la race des femmes et quelques-unes de ses tribus', *Arethusa* 11: 43–71.

(1981a) *Les Enfants d'Athéna*. Paris.

(1981b) *L'Invention d'Athènes*. Paris.

(1981c) 'Le lit, la guerre', *L'Homme* 21: 37–67.

Lotringer, S. (1973) 'The game of the name', *Diacritics* 3.2: 2–9.

Maccabe, C. (1978) *James Joyce and the Revolution of the Word*. London.

McCall, M. H. (1972) ed. *Aeschylus: a Collection of Critical Essays*. Englewood.

(1974) Review of Lebeck 1971, *AJP* 95: 288–92.

(1979) 'A problem of attribution at Aeschylus' *Supplices* 1055: Stephanus' source', in Bowersock *et al.* 1979.

McCaughey, J. (1972) 'Talking about Greek tragedy', *Ramus* 1: 26–47.

McClees, H. (1920) *Women in Attic Inscriptions*. New York.

(1941) *The Daily Life of the Greeks and Romans*. New York.

McConnell-Ginet, S. (1975) 'Our father-tongue: essays in linguistic politics', *Diacritics* 5.4: 44–50.

MacCormack, C. and Strathern, M. (1980) *Nature, Culture and Gender*. Cambridge.

MacCormack, C. (1980a) 'Proto-social to adult: a Sherbo transformation', in MacCormack and Strathern 1980.

(1980b) 'Nature, culture, gender: a critique', in MacCormack and Strathern 1980.

McCulloch, H. Y. and Cameron, H. D. (1980) '*Septem* 12–13 and Athenian Ephebeia', *Illinois Classical Studies* 5: 1–14.

McDonald, W. A. (1960) 'A dilemma: *Choephoroi* 691–9', *CJ* 55: 366–71.

MacDowell, D. M. (1976a) 'Hybris in Athens'. *GR* 23: 14–31.

(1976b) 'Bastards as Athenian citizens', *CQ* 26: 88–91.

Machery, P. (1970) *Pour une théorie de la production littéraire*. Paris. Trans. by G. Wall, *A Theory of Literary Production*. London, 1978.

Macksey, R. and Donato, E. (1970) eds *The Languages of Criticism and the Sciences of Man*. Baltimore, Md.

Macleod, C. W. (1982) 'Politics and the *Oresteia*', *JHS* 102: 124–44.

Maranda, P. (1980) 'The dialectic of metaphor: an anthropological essay on hermeneutics', in Suleiman and Crosman 1980.

Marin, L. (1977) 'Puss-in-boots: power of signs – signs of power', *Diacritics* 7.2: 54–63.

(1979) 'On the interpretation of Ordinary Language: a parable of Pascal', in Harari 1979a.

Marino, P. A. (1974a) 'The cry of the Hoopoe', *CB* 51: 30–1.

(1974b) 'A lion among the flock', *CB* 51: 77–8.

Mastronarde, D. J. (1979) *Contact and Discontinuity*. Berkeley.

Mauss, M. (1966) *The Gift*. London. Trans. by I. Cussison of *Essai sur le don*. Paris, 1925.

Maxwell-Stuart, P. G. (1970) 'Remarks on the black cloaks of ephebes', *PCPS* 196: 113–16.

(1973a) 'The appearance of Aeschylus' Erinues', *GR* 20: 81–4.

(1973b) 'Clytemnestra's Beacon Speech, *Agamemnon* 281–316', *PP* 28: 445–52.

Mejer, J. (1979) 'Recognising what, when and why? The recognition scene in Aeschylus' *Choephoroi*', in Bowersock *et al.* 1979.

Merck, M. (1978) 'The city's achievement: the patriotic Amazonomachy and ancient Athens', in Lipshitz 1978.

Merrim, S. (1981) 'Cratylus' kingdom', *Diacritics* 11.1: 44–55.

Messing, G. M. (1971) 'Sound symbolism in Greek and some possible reverberations', *Arethusa* 4: 5–25.

Michaels, W. B. (1978) 'Saving the text: reference and belief', *MLN* 93: 771–93.

Michelini, A. (1974) 'ΜΑΚΡΑΝ ΓΑΡ ΕΞΕΤΕΙΝΑΣ', *Hermes* 102: 524–39.

(1978) 'ΥΒΡΙΣ and plants', *HSCP* 82: 35–44.

(1979) 'Characters and character change in Aeschylus: Klytaimestra and the Furies', *Ramus* 8: 153–64.

Mill, J. S. (1970) *The Subjection of Women*, ed. W. Carr. Cambridge.

Miller, D. A. (1977) 'A note on Aegisthus as hero', *Arethusa* 10: 259–65.

Miller, J. H. (1972) 'Tradition and difference', *Diacritics* 2.4: 6–13.

(1975) 'Deconstructing the deconstructors', *Diacritics* 5.2: 24–31.

(1976a) 'Beginning with a text', *Diacritics* 6.3: 2–7.

(1976b) 'Ariadne's thread? repetition and the narrative line', *Critical Inquiry* 3: 57–77.

(1979) 'The critic as host', in Bloom *et al.* 1979.

(1980) 'The figure in the carpet', *Poetics Today* 1.3: 107–18.

(1980–1) 'A guest in the house', *Poetics Today* 2.16: 189–91.

Millet, K. (1971) *Sexual Politics*. New York.

Mitchell, W. (1981) ed. *On Narrative*. Chicago.

Moles, J. L. (1979) 'A neglected aspect of Agamemnon 1389–92', *LCM* 4.9: 179–89.

Morgan, J. L. (1979) 'Observations on the pragmatics of metaphor', in Ortony 1979a.

Moritz, H. E. (1979) 'Refrain in Aeschylus: literary adaptation of traditional form', *CP* 74: 187–213.

Moss, R. (1976) 'Difficult language: the justification of Joyce's syntax in *Ulysses*', in Josipovici 1976.

Most, G. W. (1983) 'Of motifemes and megatexts: comment on Rubin/Sale and Segal', *Arethusa* 16.1, 2: 199–218.

Mourelatos, A. P. D. (1979) '"Nothing" as "not-being": some literary contexts that bear on Plato', in Bowersock *et al.* 1979.

Müller, C. O. (1853) *Dissertations on the Eumenides of Aeschylus*. Second edn, Cambridge. Trans. of *Aischylos, Eumeniden*. Göttingen 1833.

Muller, J. P. (1980) 'Psychosis and mourning in Lacan's Hamlet', *New Literary History* 12: 147–66.

Murray, O. (1980) *Early Greece*. London.

Musurillo, H. (1961) *Symbol and Myth in Ancient Poetry*. New York.

Nagy, G. (1983) '*Sema* and *Noesis*: some illustrations', *Arethusa* 16.1, 2: 35–55.

Nash, L. L. (1978) 'Concepts of existence: Greek origins of generational thought', *Daedalus* 107: 1–21.

Neitzel, H. (1979a) 'ΦΕΡΕΙ ΦΕΡΟΝΤ' – ein aischyleisches Orakel, *Aga.* 1562', *Hermes* 107: 133–46.

(1979b) 'Artemis und Agamemnon in der Parodos des aischyleischen *Agamemnon*', *Hermes* 107: 10–32.

Nelson, R. (1976) 'Ritual reality, tragic limitation, mythic projection', *Diacritics* 6.2: 41–8.

Neumann, E. (1955) *The Great Mother*. Trans. by R. Manheim. New York.

Neustadt, E. (1929) 'Wort und Geschehen in Aischylos' *Agamemnon*', *Hermes* 64: 243–65.

Nietzsche, F. (1956) *The Birth of Tragedy*. New York. Trans. by F. Golffing of *Die Geburt der Tragödie aus dem Geiste der Musik*. Leipzig, 1872.

Norden, E. (1956) *Agnostos Theos*. Stuttgart.

Norris, C. (1982) *Deconstruction, Theory and Practice*. London.

Northrup, M. D. (1980) 'Homer's catalogue of women', *Ramus* 9: 150–9.

Oliver, J. H. (1960) 'On the *Agamemnon* of Aeschylus', *AJP* 81: 311–14.

Ortner, S. (1975) 'Is female to male as nature is to culture?', in Rosaldo and Lamphere 1975.

Ortony, A. (1979a) ed. *Metaphor and Thought*. Cambridge.

(1979b) 'Metaphor: a multidimensional problem', in Ortony 1979a.

(1979c) 'The role of similarity in similes and metaphors', in Ortony 1979a.

Otis, B. (1981) *Cosmos and Tragedy*. Chapel Hill, NC.

Owen, E. (1932) 'An allusion in the *Agamemnon* and the problem of the *Eumenides*', *TAPA* 63: xliii–xliv.

Owen, E. T. (1952) *The Harmony of Aeschylus*. Toronto.

Owtram, T. C. (1978) 'Aeschylus *Choephoroi* 275', *CQ* 28: 475–6.

Papathomopoulos, M. (1980) *Nouveaux fragments d'auteurs anciens*. Ioannina.

Parker, L. (1958) 'Some observations on the incidence of word-end in anapaestic paroimiacs and its application to textual questions', *CQ* 8: 82–9.

Pavlovskis, Z. (1978) 'Aeschylus Mythhistoricus', *Rivista di Studi Classici* 26: 5–23.

Pelekedis, C. (1962) *Histoire de l'éphèbe attique*. Paris.

Pemberton, E. G. (1966) 'A note on the death of Aegisthus', *AJA* 70: 377–8.

Pembroke, S. (1965) 'Last of the matriarchs: a study of the inscriptions of Lycia', *Journal of Economic and Social History of the Orient* 8: 217–47.

(1967) 'Women in charge: the function of alternatives in early Greek tradition and the ancient idea of matriarchy', *Journal of Warburg and Courtauld* 30: 1–35.

(1970) 'Locres et Tarente, le rôle des femmes dans la fondation de deux colonies grecques', *AESC* 25.56: 1240–70.

Peradotto, J. J. (1964) 'Some patterns of nature imagery in the *Oresteia*', *AJP* 85: 378–93.

(1969a) 'The omen of the eagles and the ἦθος of Agamemnon', *Phoenix* 23: 237–63.

(1969b) 'Cledonomancy in the *Oresteia*', *AJP* 90: 1–21.

(1977) 'Oedipus and Erichthonius: some observations on paradigmatic and syntagmatic order', *Arethusa* 10: 85–102.

(1979) 'Originality and intentionality', in Bowersock *et al.* 1979.

(1983) 'Texts and unrefracted facts: philology, hermeneutics and semiotics', *Arethusa* 16.1, 2: 15–33.

Pfeiffer, R. (1968) *The History of Classical Scholarship*. Oxford.

Podlecki, A. J. (1961) 'Guest-gifts and nobodies', *Phoenix* 15: 125–33.
  (1966a) *The Political Background of Aeschylean Tragedy*, Michigan.
  (1966b) 'The power of the word in Sophocles' *Philoctetes*', *GRBS* 7: 233–50.
  (1971) 'Stesichoreia', *Athenaeum* 49: 313–27.
Poliakof, M. (1980) 'The third fall in the *Oresteia*', *AJP* 101: 251–9.
Pomeroy, S. (1973) 'Selected bibliography on women in antiquity', *Arethusa* 6.1: 125–7.
  (1975a) *Goddesses, Whores, Wives and Slaves*. New York.
  (1975b) 'Andromache and the question of matriarchy', *REG* 89: 16–19.
  (1975c) 'A classical scholar's perspective on matriarchy', in *Liberating Women's History*, ed. B. Carroll. Urbana.
  (1977) 'Technikai kai musikai', *AJAH* 2: 51–66.
Pope, M. (1974) 'Merciful heavens', *JHS* 94: 100–13.
Porter, D. (1971) 'Structural parallelism in Greek tragedy', *TAPA* 102: 465–96.
Post, L. A. (1940) 'Woman's place in Menander's Athens', *TAPA* 71: 420–59.
Prier, R. A. (1978) 'Σῆμα and the symbolic nature of pre-Socratic thought', *QU* 29: 91–101.
Prince, G. (1976) 'Narratives with a difference', *Diacritics* 6.2: 49–53.
  (1980) 'Notes on the text as reader', in Suleiman and Crosman 1980.
Pucci, P. (1980) *The Violence of Pity in Euripides' Medea*. Ithaca, NY.
  (1982) 'The proem of the *Odyssey*', *Arethusa* 15: 39–62.
Querbach, C. (1976) 'The conflict between young and old in Homer's *Iliad*', in Bertman 1976.
Quincy, J. H. (1963) 'The beacon sites in the *Agamemnon*', *JHS* 83: 118–32.
Rabel, R. J. (1979a) 'Cledonomancy in the *Eumenides*', *RSC* 27: 16–21.
  (1979b) 'Pathei mathos: a dramatic ambiguity in the *Oresteia*', *RSC* 27: 181–4.
  (1980) 'The meaning of *Choephoroi* 827–30', *Hermes* 108: 252–5.
Rabinowitz, N. S. (1981) 'From force to persuasion: Aischylus' *Oresteia* as cosmogonic myth', *Ramus* 10: 159–91.
Rabinowitz, P. J. (1980) '"What's Hecuba to us?" The audience's experience of literary borrowing', in Suleiman and Crosman 1980.
Ramnoux, C. (1955) *La Nuit et les enfants de la nuit*. Paris.
Reckford, K. J. (1964) 'Helen in the *Iliad*', *GRBS* 5: 5–20.
Reddy, M. J. (1979) 'The conduit metaphor: a case of frame conflict in our language about language', in Ortony 1979a.
Redfield, J. M. (1975) *Nature and Culture in the Iliad: the Tragedy of Hector*. Chicago.
  (1982) 'Notes on the Greek Wedding', *Arethusa* 15: 181–201.
Reed, N. (1975) 'Aeschylus' *Agamemnon* 513–14', *CP* 70: 275–6.
Reeves, C. H. (1960) 'The parodos of the *Agamemnon*', *CJ* 55: 165–71.
Reinhold, M. (1976) 'The generation gap in antiquity', in Bertman 1976.

Reinmuth, O. W. (1971) *The Ephebic Inscriptions of the Fourth Century B.C.* Leiden.

Reis, T. J. (1980) *Tragedy and Truth.* New Haven, Conn.

Richman, M. (1976) 'Eroticism in the patriarchal order', *Diacritics* 6: 46–53.

Richter, D. (1971) 'The position of women in classical Athens', *CJ* 67: 1–8.

Ricoeur, P. (1978) *The Rule of Metaphor.* London. Trans. by R. Czerny with K. McLaughlin and J. Costello of *La Metaphore vive.* Paris, 1975.

(1981) 'Narrative time', in Mitchell 1981.

Riddel, J. N. (1975) 'A Miller's tale', *Diacritics* 5.3: 56–65.

(1976) 'Scriptive fate/scriptive hope', *Diacritics* 6.3: 14–23.

Ridgeway, W. (1907) 'The true scene of the second act of the *Eumenides* of Aeschylus', *CR* 21: 163–8.

Ridley, R. T. (1979) 'The hoplite as citizen' *AC* 48: 508–48.

Rifaterre, M. (1977) 'Semantic overdetermination in poetry', *PTL* 2: 1–19.

Rivier, A. (1968) 'Le "nécessaire" et la "nécessité" chez Éschyle', *REG* 81: 5–39.

Robertson, H. G. (1939) 'Legal expressions and ideas of justice in Aeschylus', *CP* 34: 209–19.

Romilly, J. de (1958) *La Crainte et l'angoisse dans le théâtre d'Éschyle.* Paris.

(1973) 'Gorgias et le pouvoir de la poésie', *JHS* 93: 155–62.

Rorty, R. M. (1980) *Philosophy and the Mirror of Nature.* Oxford.

(1982) *The Consequences of Pragmatism.* Brighton.

Rosaldo, M. (1975) 'Women, culture and society: a theoretical overview', in Rosaldo and Lamphere 1975.

Rosaldo, M. and Lamphere, L. (1975) *Women, Culture and Society.* Stanford.

Rose, G. P. (1979) 'Odysseus' barking heart', *TAPA* 109: 215–30.

Rose, H. J. (1946) 'Theology and mythology in Aeschylus', *HTR* 39: 1–24.

(1950) 'Ghost ritual in Aeschylus', *HTR* 43: 257–80.

Rose, P. W. (1978) 'A dialectical view of Greek tragic form', *Radical History Review* 18: 77–94.

Rosenmeyer, T. (1955) 'Gorgias, Aeschylus and ἀπάτη', *AJP* 76: 225–60.

(1962) '*Seven against Thebes*: the tragedy of war', *Arion* 1.1: 48–78.

(1981) 'The nouvelle critique and the Classicist', *Comparative Literature Studies* 18.3: 215–27.

Roudiez, L. S. (1980) 'Introduction' to Kristeva 1980.

Rougé, J. (1970) 'La colonisation grecque et les femmes', *Cahiers d'histoire* 15: 307–17.

Rousseau, G. S. 'Dream and vision in Aeschylus' *Oresteia*', *Arion* 2: 101–36.

Roussel, P. (1941) 'Les chlamydes noires des éphèbes Athéniens', *REA* 43: 163–6.

(1951) 'Principe d'ancienneté dans le monde Hellénique', *Mémoires de l'institut national de France, Académie des inscriptions et des belles lettres* 43: 123–227.

Rubin, N. F. (1983) 'Why Classics and semiotics?' *Arethusa* 16.1, 2: 5–14.

Rubin, N. F. and Sale, W. M. (1983) 'Meleager and Odysseus: a structural and cultural study of the Greek hunting-maturation myth', *Arethusa* 16.1, 2: 137–71.

Rubino, C. (1972) Review of Girard 1972. *MLN* 87: 986–98.

(1977) 'Contemporary French thought and classical literature', *Arethusa* 10: 63–78.

Ruebel, J. S. (1977) 'Pylades in the Electra plays', *CB* 53: 90–2.

Ruegg, M. (1979) 'Metaphor and metonymy: the logic of structuralist rhetoric', *Glyph* 6: 141–57.

Rumelhart, D. E. (1979) 'Some problems with the notion of literal meanings' in Ortony 1979a.

Russell, D. A. (1981) *Criticism in Antiquity*. London.

Ryan, M. (1976) 'Self (de-)construction', *Diacritics* 6: 34–41.

(1982) *Marxism and Deconstruction*. Baltimore, Md.

Sacks, K. (1974) 'Engels revisited: women, the organization of production and private property', in Rosaldo and Lamphere 1975.

Sadock, J. M. (1979) 'Figurative speech and linguistics', in Ortony 1979a.

Said, E. (1974) 'An ethics of language', *Diacritics* 4.2: 28–37.

(1975) *Beginnings*. New York.

(1978) 'The problem of textuality: two exemplary positions', *Critical Inquiry* 4.4: 673–714.

(1979) 'The text, the world, the critic', in Harari 1979a.

Sainte-Croix, G. E. M. de (1970a) 'Some observations on the property rights of Athenian women', *CR* 20: 273–8.

(1970b) Review of Hanson, *Family Law*, *CR* 20: 387–90.

Sansone, D (1975) *Aeschylean Metaphors for Intellectual Activity*. Wiesbaden.

Saunders, T. J. (1966) 'The stupefied Menelaos, *Aga.* 412–13', *CR* 16: 253–5.

Saussure, F. de (1959) *Course in General Linguistics*. New York. Trans. by W. Baskin of *Cours de linguistique générale*. Paris, 1916.

Schadewaldt, W. (1932) 'Der Kommos in Aeschylos *Choephoren*', *Hermes* 67: 312–34.

Schafer, R. (1981) 'Narration in the psychoanalytic dialogue', in Mitchell 1981.

Schaps, D. (1977) 'The women least mentioned: etiquette and women's names', *CQ* 27: 323–30.

(1982) 'The women of Greece in warfare', *CP* 77: 193–213.

Schein, S. (1982) 'The Cassandra scene in Aeschylus' *Agamemnon*', *GR* 29: 11–16.

Schmiel, R. (1972) 'Telemachus in Sparta', *TAPA* 103: 463–72.

Schneiderman, S. (1971) 'Afloat with Jacques Lacan', *Diacritics* 1.4: 27–34.

Scholes, R. (1974) *Structuralism in Literature*. New Haven, Conn.
  (1981) 'Language, narrative and anti-narrative', in Mitchell 1981.

Schor, N. (1980) 'Fiction as interpretation: interpretation as fiction', in Suleiman and Crosman 1980.

Scott, W. C. (1966) 'Wind imagery in the *Oresteia*', *TAPA* 97: 459–71.
  (1969) 'The confused chorus, *Aga.* 975–1034', *Phoenix* 23: 336–46.
  (1978) 'Lines for Clytemnestra, *Aga.* 489–502', *TAPA* 108: 259–69.

Scully, S. (1981) 'The polis in Homer', *Ramus* 10: 1–34.

Seale, D. (1982) *Vision and Stagecraft in Sophocles*. London.

Searle, J. R. (1976) 'Reiterating the differences: a reply to Derrida', *Glyph* 1: 198–208.
  (1979) 'Metaphor', in Ortony 1979a.

Sebeok, T. A. and Brady, E. (1979) 'The two sons of Croesus: a myth about communication in Herodotus', *QU* 1: 7–20.

Segal, C. (1962a) 'Gorgias and the psychology of the Logos', *HSCP* 66: 99–155.
  (1962b) 'The Phaeacians and the symbolism of Odysseus' return', *Arion* 1: 17–64.
  (1967) 'Transition and ritual in Odysseus' return', *PP* 22: 321–42.
  (1968) 'Circean temptations: Homer, Vergil, Ovid', *TAPA* 99: 419–42.
  (1977a) '*Bacchae*: conflict and mediation', *Ramus* 6: 103–20.
  (1977b) 'Sophocles' "Trachiniae": myth, poetry, heroic values', *YCS* 25: 99–158.
  (1978) 'Menace of Dionysus: sex roles and reversal in the *Bacchae*', *Arethusa* 11: 185–202.
  (1978–9) 'Pentheus and Hippolytus on the couch and on the grid: psychoanalytic and structuralist reading of Greek tragedy', *GW* 72: 129–48.
  (1980–81) 'Visual symbols and visual effects in Sophocles', *CW* 74: 125–42.
  (1981) *Tragedy and Civilization. An Interpretation of Sophocles*. Cambridge.
  (1982) *Dionysiac Poetics and Euripides' 'Bacchae'*. Princeton.
  (1983) 'Greek myth as a semiotic and structural system and the problem of tragedy', *Arethusa* 16.1, 2: 173–98.

Seidensticker, B. (1979) 'Sacrificial ritual in the *Bacchae*' in Bowersock *et al.* 1979.

Seltman, C. (1955) 'The status of women in Athens', *GR* 2: 119–24.
  (1956) *Women in Antiquity*. London.

Serres, M. (1979) 'The algebra of literature: the wolf's game', in Harari 1979a.
  (1982a) *Hermes: Literature, Science, Philosophy*, ed. J. V. Harari and D. F. Bell. Baltimore, Md.
  (1982b) *The Parasite*. Baltimore, Md. Trans. by R. L. Schehr of *Le Parasite*. Paris, 1980.

Shaw, M. (1975) 'The female intruder: women in C5th drama', *CP* 70: 255–66.
Sheridan, A. (1980) *The Will to Truth*. London.
Sider, D. (1978) 'Stagecraft in the *Oresteia*', *AJP* 99: 12–27.
Siewart, P. (1977) 'The ephebic oath in fifth-century Athens', *JHS* 97: 102–11.
Sikes, E. G. (1931) *The Greek View of Poetry*. London.
Silk, M. S. (1974) *Interaction in Poetic Imagery*. London.
Silverman, K. (1982) *The Subject of Semiotics*. New York.
Simon, B. (1978) *Mind and Madness in Ancient Greece*. Ithaca, NY.
Simon, S. T. (1974) 'Euripides' defence of women', *CB* 50: 39–42.
Simpson, M. (1971) 'Why does Agamemnon yield?', *PP* 26: 94–101.
Slater, P. (1968) *The Glory of Hera*. Boston, Mass.
   (1974) 'Greek family in history and myth', *Arethusa* 7: 9–44.
Smertenko, C. M. (1932) 'Political sympathies of Aeschylus', *JHS* 52: 233–5.
Smethurst, M. (1972) 'The authority of the Elders (the *Agamemnon* of Aeschylus)', *CP* 63: 89–93.
Smith, B. H. (1978) *On the Margins of Discourse*. Chicago.
Smith, O. L. (1965) 'Some observations on the structure of imagery in Aeschylus', *CM* 26: 10–72.
   (1973) 'Once again: the guilt of Agamemnon', *Eranos* 71: 1–11.
Smith, P. M. (1980) *On the Hymn to Zeus in Aeschylus' Agamemnon*. Ann Arbor.
Smyth, H. W. (1924) *Aeschylean Tragedy*. Berkeley.
Snodgrass, A. M. (1977) *Archaeology and the Rise of the Greek State*. Inaugural lecture, Cambridge.
Solmsen, F. (1947) 'Strata of Greek religion in Aeschylus', *HTR* 40: 211–26.
   (1949) *Hesiod and Aeschylus*. Ithaca, NY.
   (1981) 'The sacrifice of Agamemnon's daughter in Hesiod's *Ehoeae*', *AJP* 102: 353–8.
Sommerstein, A. (1971) 'Aeschylus' *Agamemnon* 126–130', *CR* 21: 1–3.
   (1980) 'Artemis in the *Agamemnon*: a postscript', *AJP* 101: 165–9.
Sourvinou, C. (1971) Review of Brelich 1969, *JHS* 91: 172–7.
Sperduti, A. (1950) 'The divine nature of poetry in antiquity', *TAPA* 81: 209–40.
Spivak, G. C. (1976) 'Introduction' to Derrida 1976a.
   (1977) 'Glas-pièce: à compte rendu', *Diacritics* 7.3: 22–43.
Stanford, W. B. (1939) *Ambiguity in Greek Literature*. Oxford.
   (1942) *Aeschylus in his Style*. Dublin.
   (1949) 'Studies in characterisation of Ulysses III', *Hermathena* 73: 35–48.
   (1954) 'The looking-glass of society in Aeschylus' *Agamemnon* 838–840', *CR* 4: 82–5.
Stephens, J. C. (1971) 'Odysseus in *Agamemnon* 841–2', *Mnemosyne* 24: 358–61.

Stern, J. P. (1973) 'Occlusions, disclosures, conclusions', *New Literary History* 149–68.

Stierle, K. (1980) 'The reading of fictional texts', in Suleiman and Crosman 1980.

Stigers, E. S. (1981) 'Sappho's private world', *Women's Studies* 8: 47–64.

Stinton, T. (1979 'The first stasimon of Aeschylus' *Choephoroi*', *CQ* 29: 252–62.

Stone, L. (1977) *Family, Sex and Marriage in England 1500–1800*. London.

Strathern, M. (1980) 'No nature; no culture: the Hagen case', in MacCormack and Strathern 1980.

Sturrock, J. (1979) *Structuralism and since: from Lévi-Strauss to Derrida*. Oxford.

Suleiman, S. R. (1980) 'Introduction: varieties of audience-oriented criticism', in Suleiman and Crosman 1980.

Suleiman, S. R. and Crosman, I. (1980) eds *The Reader in the Text*. Princeton.

Sussman, L. S. (1978a) 'The birth of the gods: sexuality, conflict, and cosmic structure in Hesiod's *Theogony*', *Ramus* 7: 61–77.

 (1978b) 'Workers and drones: labour, idleness, and gender definition in Hesiod's beehive', *Arethusa* 11: 27–41.

Svenbro, J. (1976) *La Parole et le marbre. Aux origines de la poétique grecque*. Lund.

Tanner, A. (1980) *Adultery in the Novel*. Baltimore.

Taplin, O. (1972) 'Aeschylean silences and silences in Aeschylus', *HSCP* 76: 57–97.

 (1977) *The Stagecraft of Aeschylus*. Oxford.

 (1978) *Greek Tragedy in Action*. London.

Tarkow, T. A. (1979) 'Electra's role in the opening scene of the *Choephoroi*', *Eranos* 77: 11–21.

Tarrant, D. (1960) 'Greek metaphors of light', *CQ* 10: 181–7.

Tate, J. (1927) 'The beginnings of Greek allegory', *CR* 41: 214–15.

 (1929) 'Plato and allegorical interpretation', *CQ* 23: 142–54.

 (1930) 'Plato and allegorical interpretation' (continued), *CQ* 24: 1–10.

 (1934) 'On the history of allegorism', *CQ* 28: 105–14.

Thomas, C. G. (1973) 'Matriarchy in early Greece: the Bronze and Dark Ages', *Arethusa* 6: 173–95.

Thomson, G. (1934) 'Notes on the *Oresteia*', *CQ* 28: 72–8.

 (1935) 'Mystical allusions in the *Oresteia*', *JHS* 55: 20–34.

 (1936) 'Notes on the *Oresteia*', *CQ* 30: 105–15.

 (1941) *Aeschylus and Athens*. London.

Tierney, M. (1936) 'Three notes on the *Choephoroi*', *CQ* 30: 100–4.

 (1937) 'The mysteries and the *Oresteia*', *JHS* 57: 11–24.

Todorov, T. (1976) 'The origin of genres', 8: 159–70.

 (1977) *The Poetics of Prose*. Ithaca. Trans. by R. Howard of *La Poétique de la prose*. Paris, 1971.

 (1980' 'Reading as construction', in Suleiman and Crosman 1980.

Turner, E. G. (1951) *Athenian Books in the Fifth and Fourth Centuries B.C.*
London.

Turner, T. (1977) 'Narrative structure and mythopoesis: a critique and reformulation of structuralist concepts of myth, narrative and poetics', *Arethusa* 10: 103–63.

Turner, V. W. (1962) 'Three symbols of passage in Ndembu circumcision ritual', in Gluckman 1962a.

(1967) *The Forest of Symbols*. Ithaca, NY.

(1969) *The Ritual Process*. Rochester.

(1981) 'Social dramas and stories about them', in Mitchell 1981.

Tyrrell, W. B. (1980) 'An obscene word in Aeschylus', *AJP* 101: 44.

van Gennep, A. (1960) *The Rites of Passage*. London. Trans. by M. Vizedom and G. Caffee of *Les Rites de passage*. Paris, 1908.

van Nortwick, T. (1979) 'Penelope and Nausikaa', *TAPA* 109: 269–76.

Vellacott, P. (1977) 'Has the good prevailed? A further study of the *Oresteia*', *HSCP* 81: 113–22.

Vermeule, E. (1966) 'The Boston Oresteia krater', *AJA* 70: 1–22.

Vernant, J.-P. (1962) *Les Origins de pensée grecque*. Paris.

(1965) *Mythe et pensée chez les Grecs*. Paris.

(1970) 'Greek Tragedy: problems of interpretation', in Macksey and Donato 1970.

(1973) 'Le marriage en Grèce archaique', *PP* 28: 51–74.

(1974) 'Parole et signes muets', in Vernant *et al.* 1974.

(1977) 'Sacrifice et alimentation humaine à propos du Promethée d'Hesiode', *Annali della Scuola Normale di Pisa* 7: 905–40. Trans. in Gordon 1981.

(1980) *Myth and Society in Ancient Greece*. Brighton. Trans. by J. J. Lloyd of *Mythe et société en Grèce ancienne*. Paris, 1974.

(1982) 'From Oedipus to Periander: lameness, tyranny, incest in legend and history', *Arethusa* 15: 19–38.

Vernant, J.-P. and Vidal-Naquet, P. (1972) *Mythe et tragédie en Grèce ancienne*. Paris.

Vernant, J.-P. Vandermeersch, L. and Gerner, J. *et al.* (1974) *Divination et rationalité*. Paris.

Verrall, A. W. (1907) 'Apollo at the Areopagus', *CR* 21: 6–11.

Vicaire, P. (1963) 'Présentiments, présages, prophéties dans le théâtre d'Éschyle', *REG* 76: 337–57.

Vickers, B. (1973) *Towards Greek Tragedy*. London.

Vidal-Naquet, P. (1964) 'Athènes et l'Atlantide', *REG* 78: 420–44.

(1965) 'Économie et société dans la Grèce ancienne; l'oeuvre de M. I. Finley', *Archives Européennes de Sociologie* 6: 111–48.

(1968) 'The Black Hunter and the origin of the Athenian Ephebia', *PCPS* 194: 49–64.

(1970a) 'Ésclavage et gynéocratie dans la tradition, le mythe, l'utopie', Recherches sur les structures sociales dans l'antiquité classique (Actes de Colloque de Caen 25–6 April 1969), Paris.

(1970b) 'Valeurs religieuses et mythiques de la terre et du sacrifice dans l'*Odyssée*', *AESC* 25.56: 1278–97.

(1974) 'Les jeunes: le cru, l'enfant grec, et le cuit', in *Faire l'histoire*, ed. by J. Le Goff and P. Nova. Paris.

Warr, G. C. W. (1898) 'Clytemnestra's weapon', *CR* 12: 348–50.

Wartelle, A. (1978) *Bibliographie historique et critique d'Éschyle*. Paris.

Webster, T. B. L. (1933) 'Preparation and motivation in Greek tragedy', *CR* 47: 117–23.

(1939) 'Greek theories of art and literature down to 400 B.C.', *CQ* 33: 166–79.

(1957) 'Some psychological terms in Greek tragedy', *JHS* 77: 149–54.

Weinsheimer, J. (1979) 'Theory of character: *Emma*', *Poetics Today* 1: 185–211.

Wender, D. (1974) 'The will of the beast: sexual imagery in the *Trachiniae*', *Ramus* 3: 1–17.

West, M. L. (1979) 'The parodos of the *Agamemnon*', *CQ* 29: 1–6.

West, S. R. (1980) 'Agamemnon's monument', *LCM* 5.2: 41–3.

Whallon, W. (1958) 'The serpent at the breast', *TAPA* 89: 271–5.

(1961) 'Why is Artemis angry?', *AJP* 82: 78–88.

(1964) 'Maenadism in the *Oresteia*', *HSCP* 68: 317–27.

(1980) *Problem and Spectacle: Studies in the Oresteia*. Heidelberg.

Wheelwright, P. (1966) 'Notes on mythopoeia', in *Myth and Literature*, ed. J. B. Vickery. Nebraska.

White, H. (1981) 'The value of narrativity in the representation of reality', in Mitchell 1981.

Whittle, E. W. (1964) 'An ambiguity in Aeschylus' *Supp.* 315', *CM* 25: 1–7.

(1968) Review of Podlecki 1966a, *JHS* 88: 156–7.

Wilden, A. (1968) *The Language of the Self*. Baltimore, Md.

(1972) *System and Structure: Essays in Communication and Exchange*. New York.

Willets, R. F. (1959) 'The servile interregnum at Argos', *Hermes* 87: 495–506.

(1969) 'More on the Black Hunter', *PCPS* 195: 106–7.

Wills, G. (1965) '*Agamemnon* 1346–1371, 1649–1653', *TAPA* 67: 255–67.

Winkler, J. (1981) 'Gardens of nymphs: public and private in Sappho's lyrics', *Women's Studies* 8.1, 2: 65–91.

Winnington-Ingram, R. P. (1933) 'The role of Apollo in the *Oresteia*', *CR* 47: 97–104.

(1949) 'Clytemnestra and the vote of Athena', *JHS* 68: 130–47.

(1954) 'Aeschylus' *Agamemnon* 1343–71', *CQ* 4: 23–30.

(1969) 'Euripides Poietes Sophos', *Arethusa* 2: 127–42.

(1973) 'A word in the *Persae*', *BICS* 20: 37–9.

(1974) 'Notes on the *Agamemnon* of Aeschylus', *BICS* 21: 3–19.

(1983) *Studies in Aeschylus*. Cambridge.

Wittkower, R. (1939) 'The eagle and the serpent: a study in the migration of symbols', *Journal of the Warburg Institute* 2: 293–325.

Wolff, H. J. (1944) 'Marriage law and family organisation in ancient Athens', *Traditio* 2: 43–95.

Wright, F. A. (1923) *Feminism in Greek Literature*. London.

Yorke, E. C. (1936) 'Trisyllabic feet in the dialogue of Aeschylus', *CQ* 30: 116–19.

Young, D. C. C. (1964) 'Gentler medicines in the *Agamemnon*', *CQ* 14: 1–23.

Young, R. (1981) ed. *Untying the Text: a Post-Structuralist Reader.* Boston.

Zeitlin, F. (1965) 'The motif of the corrupted sacrifice in Aeschylus' *Oresteia*', *TAPA* 96: 463–505.

    (1966) 'Postscript to sacrificial imagery in the *Oresteia*', *TAPA* 97: 645–53.

    (1978) 'Dynamics of misogyny in the *Oresteia*', *Arethusa* 11: 149–84.

    (1981) 'Language, structure, and the son of Oedipus, in Aeschylus' *Seven against Thebes*', in *Contemporary Literary Hermeneutics and the Interpretation of Classical Texts*, ed. K. Skresic. Ottawa.

    (1982a) 'Cultic models of the female: rites of Dionysus and Demeter', *Arethusa* 15: 129–57.

    (1982b) *Under the Sign of the Shield: Semiotics and Aeschylus' Seven against Thebes*. Rome.

Zuntz, G. (1981) 'Notes on some passages in Aeschylus' *Septem*', *PCPS* 27: 81–95.

EDITIONS

The tragedies

Dindorf, G.	Berlin 1841
Paley, W.	London 1861
Wecklein, H.	Berlin 1885
Wilamowitz, W.	Berlin 1896

The *Oresteia*

Thomson, G.	Amsterdam 1966

The *Agamemnon*

Campbell, A. Y.	Liverpool 1936
Conington, J.	London 1848
Denniston, D. and Page, D.	Oxford 1957
Fraenkel, E.	Oxford 1950
Headlam, W.	Cambridge 1980
Lawson, J. C.	Cambridge 1932
Lloyd-Jones, H.	Englewood Cliffs 1970
Sidgwick, A.	Oxford 1887
Verrall, A. W.	London 1889

The *Choephoroi*

Lloyd-Jones, H.	Englewood Cliffs 1970
Sidgwick, A.	Oxford 1924
Tucker, T. G.	Cambridge 1901
Verrall, A. W.	London 1893

The *Eumenides*

Davies, J. F.	Dublin 1885
Lloyd-Jones, H.	Englewood Cliffs 1970
Sidgwick, A.	Oxford 1902
Verrall, A. W.	London 1908

Selective Index

Aristotle, 20 n33, 22 n36, 23 n40, 68

Bachofen, J. J., 104, 193–4, 279–81
Barthes, R., 2, 4, 9–10, 167–8, 170
Benveniste, E., 43, 111, 180
Bourdieu, P., 127

character, 42, 63, 69–74, 77–8, 167–8
chorus, role of, 13, 28, 88, 119, 145, 176,
177, 239, 243
cledonomancy, 60, 97–8, 149, 181, 255

Dawe, R. D., 70–2
Derrida, J., 1 n1, 21–3, 26–7, 139–40,
147 n38
Denniston–Page, 40–1, 68–9, 76, 97–8
dogs, 20, 56–7, 86, 179, 204–5, 225

Easterling, P. E., 73
Empedocles, 121 n32
Engels, F., 116, 193, 279–81
etymology, 26, 28, 59–63, 136 n58, 147,
156, 196, 233, 239, 253–4

Felman, S., 140 n76, 164 n117
Foucault, M., 202–3
Fraenkel, E., 1, 9, 11, 16 n20, 41, 43, 53,
69–70, 74–5, 76–7, 82, 94, 97, 128 n45,
129 n48
Freud, S., 35, 174 n144, 191

Gagarin, M., 257–8
Gorgias, 7, 51 n88
Gould, J., 73–4, 150
Green, A., 111 n17
griphos, see riddle

Halliday, W. R., 98
Hartman, G. H., 3, 65, 151 n95
Headlam, W., 34 n67, 41 n78, 74, 77
Hegel, G., 1 n1, 22 n36
Heidegger, M., 22 n36, 121 n32
Hesiod, 8, 95 n146
Homer, 17–18, 54, 56, 74–5, 132, 166,
183–95

Iliad, 18, 56, 165, 184 n155

initiation, 8, 152, 166, 170, 193–4
intertextuality, 132, 193–5

Jones, J., 10 n7, 70, 77, 78

Kitto, H. D. F., 13, 50, 62, 69 n113, 115,
126, 157–8, 180
Knox, B. M. W., 63
kratos, 9–10, 18, 33, 77, 89, 103–4, 133,
151–2, 160, 163, 246, 275
Kristeva, J., 119 n28, 124 n34, 124 n35,
194 n177

Lacan, J., 138–40, 191
Lebeck, A., 2, 20 n31, 24 n42, 117, 129
n48, 136–7, 138, 144, 146–7, 157–8
Lévi-Strauss, C., 14 n11, 45–6, 58
Lloyd-Jones, H., 20 n30, 30 n58, 111
n14, 125–6, 128 n45, 149 n92, 167, 175

Macleod, C. W., 253–5
madness, 202–5, 210, 212, 216, 230
metaphor, 14, 19–24, 60, 68–9, 74, 122,
124–35, 162, 170, 182, 254
metonymy, 122, 124–35

naming, 14, 16–17, 20, 26–7, 35 n70, 39,
45, 47, 55–6, 59–63, 65, 74, 83, 114,
117, 122–3, 132, 141, 190 n169, 209,
247–8, 252, 280–1

Odysseus, 18, 47, 56, 68, 169, 183–95
Odyssey, 18, 47, 56, 68, 169, 183–95
Oedipus, 16, 139, 191

paragram, 118–19, 150, 177–8, 180, 200,
255–6
password, 38–9, 40, 49
Penelope, 74–5, 183–95
Pleisthenes, 95
polis, civic discourse, 127–8, 131, 155,
170, 194–5, 241–3, 245, 253, 261, 262,
263, 266–7, 272–3, 275–6, 277–82
preface, 1 n1
prefix, 109, 240–1
Presocractics, 7, 121 n32, 227 n14, see also
under individuals' names

Printed in the United Kingdom
by Lightning Source UK Ltd.
118041UK00001B/189